Islam in Victorian Britain

THE LIFE AND TIMES OF

ABDULLAH QUILLIAM

Ron Geaves

KUBE
PUBLISHING

First published in England by Kube Publishing Ltd,
Markfield Conference Centre
Ratby Lane, Markfield,
Leicestershire LE67 9SY
United Kingdom
Tel: +44 (0) 1530 249230
Fax: +44 (0) 1530 249656
Website: www.kubepublishing.com
Email: info@kubepublishing.com

Photographic credits: British Library:p. 110; Liverpool Record Office,
Liverpool Libraries: front and back covers, pp.21, 32, 77, 91, 137;
Ron Geaves: pp.272, 285; www.wokingmosque.org: p.252

British Library Cataloguing-in-Publication Data
Geaves, Ron.
    Islam in Victorian Britain : the life and times of Abdullah Quilliam
    1. Quilliam, Abdullah 2. Muslim converts from Christianity
    —Great Britain—Biography 3. Islam—Great Britain—
    History—19th century
    I. Title
    297'.092

ISBN 978-1-84774-003-8 *casebound*
ISBN 978-1-84774-010-6 *paperback*

Cover Design: Nasir Cadir
Typesetting: Naiem Qaddoura

Contents

List of Illustrations

Acknowledgments

A book of this kind involves a considerable debt to a large number of people who have assisted in so many ways. First I have to acknowledge the almost limitless patience of my wife Catherine who put up with the long hours in my study. She accompanied me on the journey to do research at the museum on the Isle of Man with great sacrifice, for she is no sailor! I also thank my son Dominic who at the age of six does not share his mother's forbearance, and demanded that Daddy stopped being boring and came out to play.

There is a very long list of those who have supported the research. My thanks go to Dollin Kelly, the writer of *The New Manx Worthies*, who helped me find my way around the archives on the Isle of Man and who engaged me in many a stimulating conversation about Quilliam. In this regard, I also want to thank the staff at the Isle of Man Museum, who were so helpful in assisting me with requests for documents. I also acknowledge my indebtedness to Martin Moir and his wife who provided the means to access confidential government files and even shared in the expense of this exercise. I thank also the various members of the Abdullah Quilliam Society for their support and access to various documents that they have collected. In particular, I am indebted to them for access to the first registered mosque in Britain on the day that Muslims prayed inside for the first time in over one hundred years. I pray that all their plans come to fruition. There are so many Muslim scholars and academics who have shared with me selflessly their knowledge of Abdullah

Quilliam or the background history of nineteenth-century Islam in Britain. I thank Sophie Gilliat-Ray at Cardiff, Tim Winter at Cambridge, and Muhammad Seddon and Sadek Hamid at Chester, in particular, but there were so many others who approached me at conferences or seminars with nuggets of information.

Abdullah Quilliam has also attracted considerable interest from some British Muslims who have been fascinated by his life. Many have been excited by this venture and have communicated with me. Some have provided invaluable information from their own extensive investigations and others have offered me the support to complete the project by sharing their passion and encouragement with me. In this regard I acknowledge my debt to the kindness of Richard Cain who shared his passion for Quilliam with me and permitted access to the treasure trove of documents that he has collected over the years. I will remember the magical moment of discovering those four large boxes waiting for me on his floor.

Finally, but not least, I thank the undoubted skills of Yahya Birt, a patient and thorough editor and one who is not least amongst the scholars of Quilliam and British Muslims himself, as well as to record my gratitude to Kube Publishing's reader who offered many helpful insights. Liverpool Hope University deserves a mention too for providing the facilities and the support for me to research this book.

There are probably many I have forgotten to acknowledge. I recognise their assistance and apologise for overlooking them.

Look out, for I will be back to you all, for, God willing, I haven't finished with Sheikh Abdullah Quilliam yet nor him with me. There has been a wonderful serendipity at work in this project, so beyond all else I thank the power that has offered me such a wonderful opportunity.

Ron Geaves
January 2010

CHAPTER I

Introduction

On the 28th July 1902, 1,000 Indian troops arrived in the city of Liverpool on a steamship from Bombay. They were en route to London to take part in the Coronation celebrations of Edward VII. The City Corporation took advantage of their presence to organise a parade through the city centre and to host a civic reception that evening at St. George's Hall, the newly-built showpiece declaring Liverpool's status as the second city of the British Empire and displaying the grandeur of the new municipality. The Indian troops took their seats in orderly and disciplined rows dressed in the splendour of their regiments. The hall was packed with civic dignitaries, members of the public who had managed to obtain seats and representatives of the press. An Englishman entered, dressed in the traditional robes and turban of an Ottoman *'alim*. Five hundred of the soldiers stood and shouted, *'Allahu Akbar'*. As the *takbir* resounded around this most English of venues, the man took his seat amongst the official guests. One of the many remarkable things about this incident is that the Indian Muslim sepoys knew exactly who had entered the hall, and were prepared to break ranks to show their respect.[1] An extraordinary life lies behind this one incident, and there are many significant reasons why this should be told, particularly at a time when Muslims in Britain experience considerable challenges concerning their loyalty, identity and citizenship, and when the survival of the British brand of multiculturalism is itself under pressure.

At a time when the British Empire was at its zenith and very few Muslim nations remained free from European domination, one man took it upon himself to promote Islam in the heart of history's greatest colonial enterprise. Fully believing in the truth of the revelation that the Prophet Muhammad received and passionate in his conviction that Islam, a religion that he described as being fully conversant with reason, he succeeded in converting more than 500 British men and women to Islam. For a period of fifteen years, he was rarely out of the media in Liverpool, the Isle of Man, the north-west of England and even nationally and internationally.

On the 29th July 1893, the *Manchester Clarion* reported (in the terminology of the day) that a 'Muhammaden' mission in Liverpool was making converts amongst educated Englishmen. The article described a movement called the Liverpool Muslim Institute, and seemed to be astonished at the idea that a mosque should open every day for prayers in a busy English seaport. The reporter was surprised 'at the turning of the tables', the idea that the East was actually engaged in trying to convert the West. He stated that the honorary secretary distributed explanatory works on Islam and that tracts are scattered about on the premises, 'sowing the seeds of a new religion in the conventional missionary manner, which we, for other use, invented.'[2]

The missionary theme also appeared in an otherwise informative article that was printed in the *Sunday Telegraph* three years later. The article deserves to be set out in full and will be used to introduce readers to the subject of this biography. The article appeared under the headline, 'A Mosque in Liverpool where Britons pray to Allah', and read as follows:

> Here in England there is a Muslim community – British born subjects of the Queen as white as we are, English-speaking yet Mussulmans. They have a Sheikh, a mosque, a college and even a weekly newspaper to advance their interests. Liverpool is the centre of Muhammadenism in England – indeed in the British Isles. It only dates back to the Jubilee year of 1887. In that year

a Liverpool solicitor decided to embrace what he regarded as the true faith. This was Mr W.H. Quilliam, a gentlemen much respected in Liverpool. He is an archaeologist, and a man of learning – the bearer of a well-known name on the Mersey and in the Isle of Man, and as an advocate, one of the most familiar figures in the police and judicial courts of Liverpool ... last year there were 24 converts, making 182 who, since 1887, have renounced Christianity or Judaism. Moreover, Mr Quilliam as a recognition of his devotion to his new religion, was appointed by the Sultan of Turkey, who is the Caliph of the Faithful outside India, as the head of the movement in England. His title in this capacity is the Sheikh al-Islam of the British Isles. It is a peculiar sight to see elderly Englishmen bowing toward Mecca and repeating the well-known formula, the base of Islam, 'la ilah illalah. Muhammad rasul Allah'. They have even begun to send out English Muhammaden missionaries to West Africa to advance the cause of the Crescent against the Cross.[3]

William H. Quilliam (1856-1932) was a well-known Liverpool solicitor who converted to Islam after visiting Morocco in 1887. He formally announced his conversion to Islam in 1888 and changed his name to Abdullah. The Liverpool Muslim Institute and British Muslim Association, which he founded to promote Islam in Britain, opened in September 1887, two years before the Woking Mosque was built outside London; although there may be a dispute about the first building to be used by Muslims in Britain as a place of prayer, there is no doubt that the first attempt to promote Islam publicly from within a mosque and an Islamic centre in Britain took place in Liverpool over the following twenty years.

The British media were not always supportive of Quilliam's efforts, especially in times when patriotic jingoism flared during military campaigns against a Muslim territory or when Muslims rebelled against their colonial masters. *The Porcupine*, a well-known satirical magazine in Liverpool, depicted Abdullah Quilliam with a note of humorous derision, caricaturing him dressed in his Ottoman robes, turban and fez and riding a white stallion through the streets of Liverpool with a monkey on his shoulder, whilst the poverty-stricken women of the city's slums threw flowers at his feet. However, they did remain relatively respectful, as did most of the city's newspapers. After all, Sheikh Abdullah Quilliam, the eccentric Sheikh al-Islam of the British Isles, was also William Quilliam, a Victorian gentlemen, property owner and well-known lawyer who mixed throughout his life with the gentry and with public figures from the city's commercial, legal and political elites.

It is worth taking a closer look at *The Porcupine's* depiction of Abdullah Quilliam, for even today I have met Muslims in the city of Liverpool who take the caricature literally. Behind the attempt to present Quilliam as a harmless but deluded eccentric – a charismatic 'trickster' leading the gullible public astray, quixotically astride his white steed – lay some truths about the man which question the cartoon's representation. The white stallion had been presented to Abdullah Quilliam's eldest son by Abdul Hamid II (r.1876-1909), the ruler of the Ottoman lands and Sultan of the last great Muslim empire (the horse had been shipped to Liverpool from Constantinople). The family had named the horse Abdullah and it was a much-loved family pet. Whether Quilliam ever rode his son's horse through the streets of Liverpool is not recorded. Likewise, the portrayal of the monkey on William Quilliam's shoulder was probably suggested to the cartoonist by the Sheikh's considerable interest in zoology. Like many Victorian gentlemen of independent means, Quilliam was a dilettante; he had a powerful and inquiring mind that sought knowledge of the world around him. He maintained both a private zoo and a museum of oriental artefacts. Muslims from around the globe would send him specimens to enhance both of these collections.

It is unlikely that the women of Liverpool's slums ever threw flowers at his feet, but some of them may have been inclined to do so. Quilliam was a philanthropist with a strong sense of the injustices suffered by the Victorian poor. He often used his considerable financial and legal resources to track down wayward husbands and ensure that their wages went to feed their hungry children.

It is extremely doubtful that Abdullah Quilliam, Sheikh al-Islam of the British Isles, would ever have worn his tarboosh and turban in the streets of Liverpool. Quilliam believed passionately that Islam was a universal religion that required no special dress and had no clerical class. His robes were a marker of his official position, given to him by the Sultan whom he regarded as the spiritual leader of all Muslims, the Caliph of Sunni Islam, and to whom he owed fealty. However, apart from official functions, or when leading *jumu'a* prayers at the mosque and officiating at Muslim funerals or weddings, when he did wear his robes, he usually wore the everyday dress of the Victorian gentleman of his class. He would no more have worn his lawyer's robes in the street as his formal Islamic dress.

However, the depictions of Quilliam in the media beg some serious questions that this book will seek to illuminate. Why would the Caliph of Islam send a valuable stallion to Liverpool as a gift for a Liverpudlian lawyer, even one who had converted to Islam? Why would both the Sultan of the Ottomans and the Amir of Afghanistan confer upon a British convert to Islam the title of Sheikh al-Islam of the British Isles? How did this man's reputation reach Muslims around the globe to such a degree that they not only corresponded regularly with him, but even sent him gifts for his pastimes? And finally, what kind of man took care of the poor, the orphans and the distressed of the wider community in Liverpool, and to what degree did he see these activities as the duty of the faithful Muslim?

This is an appropriate time for a biography of Sheikh Abdullah Quilliam. A study of his small Muslim community in Liverpool not only provides scholars with further knowledge of the Muslim presence in Britain during the nineteenth century, but it is also highly relevant to the issues of Muslims living in non-Muslim western societies in the twenty-first century. In recent years, Quilliam has already begun to attract the attention of many British-born Muslims of migrant descent, who see him as an iconic figure:

a native-born Englishmen who converted to the true faith along with many others, and whose presence in the country was neither as an economic migrant nor as a refugee fleeing persecution or war. Quilliam was a British citizen by birth, and a Muslim by conviction. Consequently he is of interest to contemporary converts to the faith. Some have picked up on Quilliam's Britishness to represent him as the ideal of an integrated and moderate Muslim, able to provide an exemplary bulwark against extremism. The Quilliam Foundation, founded in London in 2008, has adopted his name in just such a manner; whilst in Liverpool, the sterling efforts of the Abdullah Quilliam Society are aimed at purchasing the buildings of his mosque and centre in order to return them to their former glories.

But care needs to be taken with Quilliam. He was not necessarily the friend of British governments, and his faith came first and foremost in his loyalties. When there were conflicts of conscience between loyalty to the laws of men and the law of God, Quilliam had no doubt where his allegiance lay. This study of his life provides insights into the challenges of being both a devout Muslim and a citizen in a non-Muslim nation.

Abdullah Quilliam was a Victorian gentlemen and a native-born Liverpudlian deeply located in his time and place. According to his own estimates, and supported to some degree by the records of conversion that he published each week in *The Crescent*, he successfully converted over 500 British men and women to Islam. He had his own strategies for undertaking *da'wa* (promotion of Islam), and these deserve to be examined in the light of contemporary debates in Muslim communities concerning proselytising non-Muslims. This is of interest both to British Muslims and also to scholars of religion who are interested in conversion. The majority of Quilliam's converts were practising Christians. What does this tell us about the condition of Christianity in the nineteenth century? Were the circumstances of their conversion only applicable locally in Liverpool and its surrounds?

Finally, Quilliam is of contemporary significance because he was an 'alim, a leader of a Muslim community in a large urban environment that was rapidly transforming into a multicultural city. There is a great deal of controversy today about the role of the imam in non-Muslim societies and about Muslim leadership in general. These debates are highly politicised, and the research undertaken by academics in this context will not merely add to scholarly knowledge, but will also help to form government policies. Can anything be learned from this nineteenth century British 'alim that may be useful in helping policy-makers and Muslims improve the quality of Muslim leadership in the diaspora communities of today?

Phillip Waller warns us that anthropomorphizing a city is not an acceptable method of historical writing;[4] but it has to be acknowledged that the city of Liverpool is a central character in the book. The life of Abdullah Quilliam must be viewed in its setting. Although the family originated in the Isle of Man, Quilliam was a Liverpudlian lawyer, and he was born, partly educated and later worked in the city of Liverpool. The mosque could only have flourished in the way that it did in a very small group of British cities, and Liverpool was one of these. John Belchem describes Liverpool as the 'shock city' of post-industrial Britain.[5] The city where Quilliam was born in the mid-nineteenth century was already experiencing massive growth, and during his lifetime this expansion would continue unabated. Even by the last quarter of the eighteenth century, Liverpool was described as 'the first town in the kingdom in point of size and commercial importance, the metropolis excepted'.[6] Although not one of the new Northern industrial centres like nearby Manchester, during the eighteenth and nineteenth centuries Liverpool rapidly became the heart of the Transatlantic trade, the link between Britain and Ireland and, after the invention of the steamship, the fulcrum between industrializing Britain and the rest of the world, especially India and Africa.[7]

From a population of 7000 in 1708, by the time that Quilliam was born in 1856 the population of Liverpool had expanded to 376,000. 80% of this population increase was due to migration. The wealth of the city was in commerce, and the docks were the hub of Liverpool's activity. The tonnage of shipping had grown alongside the population, from 14,600 in 1709 to 4,000,000 in 1855. In order to cope with the burgeoning trade, the docks increased exponentially: seven new docks had been built in the eighteenth and early nineteenth centuries, but this was before the period of Victorian expansion that oversaw the building of the most magnificent dock architecture in Britain.

By the middle of the nineteenth century, the annual value of exports was £55,000,000, accounting for half the exports of the nation. The influx of wealth and human capital resulted in a massive disparity of wealth between the commercial elite and the city's poor, who were mostly dependent on casual dock labour. Consequently, Power is able to say that the city was 'moulded by the powerful forces of international trade, mass migration and appalling public health'.[8]

Migration also brought to the city unique sectarian problems. The majority of Liverpool's migrants were from northern and southern Ireland, Wales and Scotland. They brought with them their own forms of religious life, predominately rival Nonconformist movements and Roman Catholicism. The Irish in particular maintained strong sectarianism, and the presence of Ulstermen in Liverpool brought Orangeism, which would lead to sectarian violence. In addition, the Irish formed the bottom of Liverpool's occupational, social and residential hierarchies and became subject to sectarian abuse. 'No popery' was incorporated into the Tory-Anglican establishment of the city, and some Protestants were prepared to take to the streets to campaign against the perceived empty ritualism of the established Anglican Church. Street rioting was both a symptom of this sectarian strife and a result of temporary breakdowns of social order often caused by abject poverty fuelled by alcohol abuse. The city authorities left the Protestant and Catholic populations to defend their own borders and to discipline themselves, thus forming ghettoized spatial territories demarcated by religious, political and cultural beliefs. Only the city centre was guarded by the authorities in order to prevent riot and disorder. Sectarian rioting remained the characteristic protest in Liverpool until the transport strike of 1911. In 1919, the city experienced its first taste of race riots that moved beyond the Irish to other communities, and skin colour became a factor.[9]

The second city of the Empire was thus marked by severe polarities between wealth and poverty, contained some of the best architecture in the land yet had terrible sanitation problems, and suffered bitter religious conflict, inter-ethnic difficulties and fluctuations of employment caused by the over-dependence on casual labour in the docks. It is not surprising that Charles Dickens visited the city in order to do research for his novels. Migration had brought with it cheap and sweated labour, which was served by a large secondary street economy made up of hawkers and beggars, lodging-house keepers, bookmakers and their touts, pawnbrokers and prostitutes.

This is the scene that would have met the increasing number of recruits to the British merchant fleet from around the world. They were predominantly young men and often Muslim. Kept at a distance from the wealthy middle-class areas in the city, they inhabited areas that the unwary would not enter. The collection of wealth was the main occupation of the city's middle-classes, but the majority of the population received only a minute share of this. It was their fate to live in conditions of brutalising and degrading poverty. As the merchants deserted the old quarter of the town near the docks in favour of the new suburbs, their houses and the cellars that were once used as warehouses formed overcrowded dwellings for a multitude of poor people, many of whom were migrants. The dangerous nature of the area would have been exacerbated by the dingy or even non-existent lighting for, as late as the mid-nineteenth century, fire and lighting were forbidden in the docks for fear of conflagration.

Into this dangerous cauldron was added the fuel of alcohol. Liverpool was infamous for its pubs. According to Abraham Hume in his study undertaken in 1858, there were over 1500 in the city. Even the organisation of labour and sectarian politics, with its link to religion, often took place in pubs. The squalid conditions of this wretched population of transitory labour were not improved by the extraordinary number of licensed houses which the magistrates had permitted. During the eighteenth century it was estimated that every seventh house was open for the sale of liquor and the city boasted thirty-seven large breweries.[10]

All of this was the inheritance of Abdullah Quilliam. Although sheltered from the worst impact of such poverty and drunkenness by his middle-class birth, Abdullah Quilliam was already aware of alcohol abuse during his childhood, when he began to campaign for its abolition. As a young police court lawyer, he would have intimately known the level of crime in the city. As a devout Non-conformist Christian, prior to his conversion to Islam, he would have experienced the dimensions of sectarian conflict and its impact on church unity. In addition, he was very well placed to be at the heart of the major transformations taking place in regard to the balance between the Victorian philosophy of self-help, personal philanthropy and the role of city corporations in providing services to the poor and dispossessed. Figures such as Herbert Spencer took laissez-faire politics very literally, and argued that the natural law of progress and evolution would lead to an improvement in life circumstances. While they argued for a position of non-interference, others like Sidney Webb mocked the typical individualist town councillor's plea of 'Self-help Sir, individual self-help, that's what made our city what it is'.[11]

Victorian urban corporations gradually took responsibility for the general welfare of their citizens, providing parks, art galleries, museums and libraries, universities, sanitation and improved housing.[12] This was also true in Liverpool. All of these changes in the wider society impacted upon Quilliam's adoption of Islam, the way in which he interpreted the religion and how he communicated it to others. Perhaps the most significant element for Quilliam's adoption and promotion of Islam was the rapid improvements in communication, especially the advent of the railways and steamships. Quilliam bridged the periods of Liverpool's history between the development of the city's corporation and the earlier periods of laissez-faire and self-help. He belonged to the local elite who still looked to philanthropic rather than municipal outlets for their displays of public service, although he was a well-known acquaintance and colleague of the city's officials. Quilliam's community of converts and transitory Muslim visitors was intimately rooted in the space provided by the unique and rapid development of Liverpool, even though the city was only a base for Quilliam's national and international activities.

This book is not written as a straightforward description of Quilliam's life. There is a serious attempt to contextualize his conversion to Islam and his subsequent activities. Chapter 2 will locate William Quilliam in the context of his time and place. He was, first and foremost, a Victorian gentleman of his period and a Liverpudlian. Liverpool had unique social and economic features that impacted on its citizens to a degree that they were more influenced by local circumstances than even the national *zeitgeist*. This was particularly true of Liverpool's religious life, where divisions and other problems facing Christians were intensified. The city's alcohol consumption was a horrific addition to the social deprivation and poverty that were faced by large numbers of the population. At the same time, tremendous wealth was generated through transporting the goods of the industrial revolution both within and outside Britain. Above all, this chapter will seek to understand why a devout Protestant Christian decided to convert to Islam.

Victorian England from 1887 to 1907, which includes the key period of Quilliam's conversion and activities in Liverpool, retained a high degree of religious consensus. Most of the population were Protestant Christians who still accepted the Bible as the highest religious authority and who lived their lives believing in and practising the moral principles derived from their Christianity. The majority would have observed the Christian rites of passage: baptisms, marriages and funerals, as well as observing Sunday as a religious holiday and a day of church attendance.[13] Secularism had yet to develop its grip on the nation's civil life and the soul of the people. This had emerged, but it remained as yet in the margins. Even movements of social transformation such as liberalism were not from the secular domain, but arose from Protestant dissenting bodies. As in the Muslim world, religion was accepted by the majority of the population, if only passively and without much considered thought. Another parallel to the Muslim world was that religion could be called upon to reinforce and mobilise tribal identities.

The social historian Hugh McLeod provides a number of key ways in which Victorians expressed and formed their Christian identities. As today's British Christians do, Victorians referred to England as a Christian country. They would provide several examples to support this: that the supreme leader of the established church since Henry VIII had been the reigning monarch; that, during the coronation ceremony, the new sovereign was crowned by the Archbishop of Canterbury; that Anglican bishops sat in the House of Lords; and that Christianity remained legally protected through the blasphemy laws.[14] The most visible sign of Christianity, as today, were the churches whose sacred architecture filled the villages, towns and cities of Victorian England. Indeed, too many had been built towards the end of the Victorian period and they could no longer be effectively used, giving the appearance of declining congregations. None of this has changed greatly in our era, but the ways in which Christian values and practices are taught to the populace has been dramatically reduced.

Most children would have been taught to pray at home before going to sleep, and the main focus of parental upbringing would have been that God expected children to be good, was 'watching' them and would punish any wrongdoing.[15] By the age of five, working-class children were sent to Sunday School for moral and religious education. The overwhelming majority of working-class children went to Sunday School until the age of around thirteen, and many middle-class children also attended in the later nineteenth century. Sunday Schools were so much the norm for respectable people that only the anti-religious or the immoral would keep their children away.[16] The majority of day schools provided religious instruction, and many schools were associated with a specific denomination of Christianity.[17] For very poor children, Christianity meant charity, the place where they could find free meals and perhaps even clothing.[18]

However, Victorian Christianity was not without its problems. The powerful and privileged established church was too often associated with political conservatism, and the many denominations of Protestantism were consequently linked to class divisions and dissent against the status quo. Roman Catholics were still regarded with deep suspicion and were mainly Irish migrants. There were other problems besides church unity. New scientific knowledge and intellectual advances in the study of the Bible challenged Christian doctrines and shook Christian beliefs. McLeod suggests that the clergy were losing their traditional role as the carriers of wisdom and knowledge to secular professionals and scientists. Changing moral sensibilities meant that certain traditional doctrines such as the belief in everlasting punishment were becoming unacceptable.[19]

William Quilliam grew up as a young man in the midst of these new national uncertainties, but he would have viewed them through the lens of the unique religious, social and political life of the north-west of England, and the city of Liverpool in particular. Born into a well-respected Wesleyan family, he started life amongst the largest and most widely spread of the Nonconformist denominations, which was the strongest form of Dissenting Protestantism in northern England. Around him were small but powerful groups of Congregationalists, Baptists, Unitarians and Quakers, which all had their roots in the civil wars of the seventeenth century, but whose members were made up of wealthy business and professional men renowned for their liberal politics who had risen to prominence through their resistance to the slave trade in the city. In addition, while Lancashire contained the historic presence of pre-Reformation English Catholics, Liverpool was being transformed by the massive influx of Irish Roman Catholics. Roman Catholicism thus maintained a strong footing in the city. The Irish influx remains even today the largest migrant population to arrive in England. The dockland areas of the city of Liverpool predominantly housed Roman Catholics surrounded by antagonistic Protestants. Quilliam would have experienced the strains of the Christian lack of unity in a particularly intense form in the city of his birth. He belonged to an age when, although the Christian influence remained pervasive, there were cracks appearing in the edifice. A small but growing group was consciously rejecting all forms of religion, and a much smaller group were joining religions other than Christianity. As McLeod commented, the 'signs of impending crisis had been building up for many years'.[20]

The next two chapters will explore the development of the Liverpool Muslim Institute from the time that Abdullah Quilliam began to proselytize in 1887 until his rapid departure from the city of Liverpool in 1908, precipitating a crisis from which the community did not recover. The focus will largely be on Quilliam as the creator, guiding light, *tour de force* and presiding genius over the Institute; although he had the loyal support of the converts, some of whom were very capable individuals and committed Muslims, it was not unsurprising that the community could not survive his departure from Liverpool, nor the manner in which this happened. However, the converts were important and these chapters will look at some of them in order to provide insights into the kind of person that was converting to Islam in Liverpool during the latter decades of the nineteenth century. The chapters will follow the chronological development of the community, and although there are events which will be picked up because the author considers them significant, they will also acknowledge Sheikh Adbullah Quilliam's account of events that he considered to be formative. These events he conveniently listed in *The Crescent*, his weekly publication, on a number of occasions.

As well as hosting an established Jewish community, the port of Liverpool also provided possibilities for engagement with other religious alternatives. For the spiritually adventurous, there were options which presented themselves outside the fold of Christianity and new sects that offered alternatives to mainstream Christianity. There were small but growing numbers of Buddhists, Hindus and Muslims, together with various new religions of which the largest were Mormonism, Spiritualism and Theosophy. Once again, the role of the city of Liverpool in the late nineteenth century is key to this story. The city was one of the first multi-faith migrant centres in Britain and attracted Muslims from around the globe.

Chapter 5 will focus on the ritual life of the mosque, Quilliam's modus operandi with the various constituencies that made up the Muslim presence in Liverpool and beyond and will argue that he is significant as Britain's first multiculturalist. The chapter will conclude that the mosque and Islamic centre in Liverpool functioned as the fulcrum for all the disparate categories of Muslims that were entering Britain at the time. In dealing with these various groups and with the civic authorities, Quilliam carved out a pattern of operating that became a prototype for twentieth-century multiculturalism with regard to religious minority communities.

Chapter 6 will explore the international dimension of Quilliam's activities. Sheikh Abdullah Quilliam was a keen observer and reporter of events around the world that impacted on the fortunes of Muslims globally. Around 70% of the articles in *The Crescent* deal with foreign affairs. He was intensely aware of the effects of colonialism on Muslim lands and the psychological shock of the loss of *dar al-islam* (the territory of Islam). He commented on a number of occasions on the conflicting loyalties of a Muslim living in a non-Muslim state and walked a very fine line between patriotism and his love of Islam. Although a loyal Englishman, he was not afraid to challenge government policy when he deemed this necessary. This chapter will also examine his fatwas and what they can tell us about his reactions to various political events of the time.

As a Muslim, Abdullah Quilliam was a traditionalist belonging to the Hanafi school,[21] although he was influenced by the modernist thinking of the Egyptian Muhammad Abduh and the Indian Sayyid Ahmad Khan. He drew upon their attempts to rewrite Islam as being fully compatible with reason and able to draw upon the resources of modern knowledge and technical discoveries without any conflict between religion and science. The articles in *The Crescent* are often framed as a counter to the dominant discourse of Victorian England, which presented Islam as an 'enemy of science', a backward civilisation that was inimical to progress, 'warlike', 'fanatical' and 'ill-treating women'. Both Abduh and Khan provided influential voices from within the Muslim world calling for modernisation, but it has to be acknowledged that Quilliam would have had differences with Abduh's Arab nationalism and Khan's refutation of Abdul Hamid II as the legitimate Sunni Caliph.[22] Above all, it was Quilliam's personal conviction that all Sunni Muslims owed their allegiance to the Caliph of Islam, who was also the Sultan of the Ottoman Empire, that marks out his position as a Muslim. He was an Ottomanist by conviction because that is where he was convinced the authority of the Caliphate remained; however, as suggested by Eric Germain, the voices for Islamic modernism were 'of tremendous help' to remote Muslim communities in predominantly Christian nations, and Quilliam's pan-Ottomanism provided the diversity of race and the ideology of a Muslim brotherhood to help achieve unity in a fledgling Muslim community,[23] which was referred to as 'confusion of tongues' by the *Liverpool Review* in 1891.[24] Chapter 7 then examines his relations with the Ottoman state, especially his personal allegiance to Sultan Abdul Hamid II.

Chapter 8 deals with some of the most difficult years of Quilliam's life. In 1908, Abdullah Quilliam suddenly departed for Constantinople with his eldest son. He never returned to live in Liverpool. The remaining years of his life until he died in 1932 are less well documented. It is known that he visited the Isle of Man, where he maintained a property, and spent some time in London where he was active in the group of Muslim converts associated with the Woking Mosque. His beloved Caliphate no longer existed, and neither did the Ottoman Empire, both gone in the aftermath of World War One (1914-18). Turkey had become a secular republic under the leadership of Mustapha Kemal (Ataturk). Quilliam's position as Sheikh al-Islam of the British Isles had gone along with the Caliph. The post was a religious one appointed by the Caliph of Sunni Islam. Once the Ottoman caliphate disappeared, so too did the means to authorise the position of Sheikh al-Islam in the various provinces of the Empire. For various reasons Quilliam believed that he could not return to Liverpool. I have called these years 'the twilight period' of Sheikh Abdullah Quilliam's life. He lived under the pseudonym of his old friend and fellow convert Henri de Léon or Haroun de Leon. However, until his death, he continued to serve Islam as he could in his changed circumstances, and never lost his conviction that Islam was the final and complete revelation from God and the Truth that could 'save' humanity.

The final chapter explores Abdullah Quilliam's legacy and revisits his life in the context of the present-day Muslim presence in Britain. I am certain that the only man to hold the position of Sheikh al-Islam of the British Isles would be thrilled to know that there are around two million Muslims in Britain today, and possibly over a thousand mosques. He would be proud that Muslims in Liverpool have started raising funds to resurrect his old centre at the same premises where he taught for fifteen years in order to make it once again a flourishing focus and symbol of the Muslim presence in Britain. However, the contemporary Muslim communities remain troubled and face crises as they attempt to deal with domestic issues and international problems that haunt the *umma* worldwide. Sadly, the regions of crisis remain the same as in his day: Sudan, Afghanistan, Iran and Iraq still struggle with problems that have their roots in the colonial period. The Balkans remain unstable, and even Turkey has not resolved whether it should reaffirm its Islamic identity or turn to face East or West. The Sheikh's story has much to tell us that can illuminate the burning issues of today.

There is a need for a brief word on the methodology used in researching this book. I am not a historian or a biographer by training. My interest in Abdullah Quilliam is twofold. Firstly, I have been a scholar of the Muslim presence in Britain since I began my academic career back in 1988. My interest is normally in 'lived religions', the horizontal, top-down study of the people who maintain the actual beliefs and practices of the religion at any one time. I am not a textual scholar and I usually undertake the study of living people, rather than the famous or infamous dead. However, for this case it seems almost inevitable that my interest in Islam in Britain would eventually bring me to Abdullah Quilliam and to the history of the Muslim presence in this country. For this study, I have thus borrowed both from the hermeneutical approaches of the humanities and the methods of the social sciences. I am aware that my readers are not only academics; Quilliam arouses the curiosity of many outside that elite club. For these readers I will weave a tale and will try to keep my style one of storytelling. However, at times, it will be hard to avoid the 'rich description' mode of writing familiar to me as a researcher.

Despite the interest in Quilliam amongst British Muslims, there is still little secondary literature to draw upon. Two of the earliest resources are MA dissertations: the first was completed in 1979 at the University of Liverpool by M.A. Khan-Cheema, entitled 'Islam and the Muslims in Liverpool'; while the second was finished two years later in 1981 by M.M. Ally at the University of Birmingham, and was entitled 'History of Muslims in Britain, 1850-1980'. These dissertations demonstrate the growing interest in the earlier history of British Islam among British Muslims after World War II, and this is reflected too in the considerable knowledge of the Liverpool and London Muslim presence in the nineteenth century achieved by 'amateur' researchers. I am indebted to both sources. In more recent years, academic study has discovered Quilliam's role in the development of British religious life in the Victorian and Edwardian periods. In 1997, Gwilliam Beckerlegge wrote a chapter entitled, 'Islam and South Asian Religions in Victorian Britain', in Gerald Parsons and John Wolffe's *Religion in Victorian Britain: Culture and Empire*. The first monograph detailing the history of Islam in Britain was Humuyun Ansari's celebrated *The Infidel Within*, published in 2004. This was followed in 2006 by Diane Robinson-Dunn's monograph, *The harem, slavery and British imperial culture: Anglo-Muslim relations in the late nineteenth century*, which has a chapter on Islam in England. In 2007, Eric Germain published a fascinating article entitled 'Southern Hemisphere Diasporic Communities in the Building of International Muslim Public Opinion at the Turn of the Twentieth Century' in the journal *Comparative Studies of South Asia, Africa and the Middle East*.[25]

There are extensive online resources, including primary materials, concerning Quilliam, while a number of his writings appear in the *Islamic Review*, which was published by the Woking Mosque community in the second and third decades of the twentieth century. Although I have made use of these to a limited degree, the main focus of this book has been Quilliam's Liverpool years rather than his later period in London under the pseudonym of de Léon. I have also drawn upon materials and testimony from Quilliam's surviving grandchildren, but these need to be used with caution as they were very young at the time of his death and were the receivers of family tales that enhanced the reputation of an already charismatic and eccentric personality.

I owe a debt to my colleague Suzanne Schartz, historian of the slave trade in Liverpool, who gave me the phrase 'chasing a dead man'. Quilliam's life was public and controversial, and even at the moment when I was completing the book, information was still coming in from the most unlikely places. On the 9th June 2009, only a few days before I submitted the manuscript to the publisher, I was invited to attend probably the first formal Muslim prayers held in Quilliam's mosque since he left in 1908. I had never entered the building before. It was a building site with prayer rugs on the floor, but I could distinguish the patterns of the Moorish-style arches that Quilliam had commissioned in 1895. In my mind's eye, I could see the rows of Victorian Englishmen and Muslim sailors lined up together in prayers led by their sheikh. The 'feel' of the old sacred space brought home to me the reality of the phrase 'chasing a dead man'. I had discovered that, however hard you chase, it is impossible to catch up with them. They remain elusive and forever beyond one's grasp – the gap between the living and the dead is always in the final analysis unbridgeable. Sometimes I felt that I was getting to know Abdullah Quilliam, and then he would slip away from me. I was immensely intrigued by his life, by the paradoxes and uncertainties that were revealed or concealed. When coming across areas of controversy, I took the route of empathy rather than that of sympathy and drew upon Ninian Smart's injunction to walk 'in the other man's moccasins'.

My second interest in Quilliam is as a scholar of religion. I feel that this gives me insights into Abdullah Quilliam's life that might have been missed by one not trained in this discipline. Sheikh Abdullah Quilliam was above all else 'homo religiosis'. He was a man of faith, a seeker of religious truth and was deeply concerned with the ethical issues of his day. He found his answers in Islam, and they remained true for him until his death in London and burial in the Muslim cemetery in Woking in 1932. Even before he found his solutions in Islam, he was above all else a religious man, and his roots in Christianity need to be understood before assessing why he took the leap to become a Muslim.

My main sources of research have been Abdullah Quilliam's own publications. I have searched through over 800 editions of

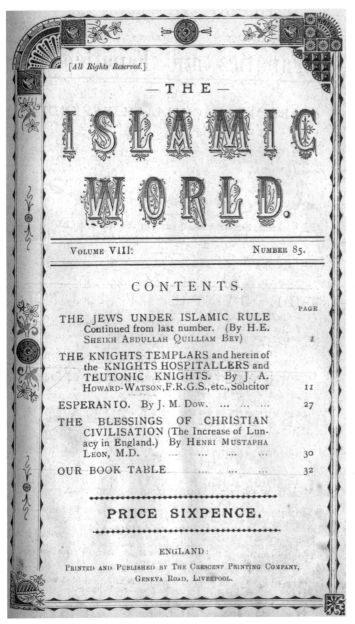

A typical front page of *The Islamic World*, the monthly journal
published by Quilliam that had a worldwide circulation.

his weekly newspaper *The Crescent*, in addition to examining his monthly journal *The Islamic World*. *The Crescent* is an outstanding source of material on nineteenth-century religious life, and I hope that others find their way to it. There is so much more research waiting to be undertaken by scholars of nineteenth-century religious life. Quilliam's books are in the British Library and are another source of his thoughts. Abdullah Quilliam was rarely out of the British newspapers, especially in his home town of Liverpool where he was a celebrity figure and on the Isle of Man where he was proudly claimed as a fellow Manxman of distinguished family background – that is, until the events of the early twentieth century shattered their faith. The newspaper articles have to be treated with care, but they provide a good counterbalance to Quilliam's own undoubted skills as editor and journalist.

There is a danger in drawing extensively upon Quilliam's writings and journalism. Of course, they reflect the world as Quilliam wished to present it to those around him; but they also demonstrate his efforts to promote Islam in an often hostile environment. I will certainly receive criticism from some quarters for spending time on the controversial subject of his family life and his flight to Constantinople. However, these are often used by those who regard Quilliam as a 'fraudster' and 'trickster' to justify their view of him. Although I take the view that charismatic religious leaders are rarely all 'angel', they are also not usually all 'devil' either. Quilliam struggled with his weaknesses, but I believe that his own view of events needs to be respected where there is evidence to support it. In doing this, I risk the accusation of being labelled an apologist for the man, but there will also be those who will not be happy that I covered these controversial elements of his personal life. My final point in this introduction is that there remain enough gaps in the narrative for further research. I hope that others pick up this challenge and take this research further. I have certainly not finished the story yet and will continue to investigate certain incidents in Quilliam's life that shed light on the story of Islam in the West.

CHAPTER 2

William Henry Quilliam:
A Victorian gentleman

Sheikh Abdullah Quilliam began life as William Henry Quilliam, born on the 10th April 1856 at 22 Eliot Street, Liverpool. His parents were Robert Quilliam, a successful watchmaker, and Harriet Quilliam, née Burrows, the daughter of John Burrows, who was a Liverpudlian physician and lay preacher. The 1861 Census records the family as Robert Quilliam, commercial traveller, and wife Harriet living with their four-year-old son William Henry. The 1881 Census mentions the same family, but this time Robert Quilliam's occupation is registered as watch manufacturer. The change in occupation is explained by the death of Samuel Quilliam, Robert's father, in June 1874, and the subsequent acquisition through inheritance of the family business.

Although spending his earliest childhood on the Isle of Man, William Henry was educated at the Liverpool Institute, Mount Street, Liverpool, where he gained renown as a scholar, winning a large number of prizes and certificates during each year of his attendance, including the Queen's Prize for Geology. The latter was awarded by the Science and Art department in South Kensington.[1] In 1872, he left school aged seventeen to work in a lawyer's office, and in October 1873 was articled to William Radcliffe of the firm William Radcliffe and Smith of 12 Sweeting Street, Liverpool.[2] To pay for his studies, he worked for five years with no salary and gained his living writing articles for the press and various magazines. He also joined the staff of the *Liverpool Albion* as an extra reporter. Quilliam demonstrated the famed work ethic of his Protestant heritage. Rising at 5.45am, he would study until 8am and then walk to the office for a prompt start at 9.15am. He would work at the office until 6pm, but three nights a week he also laboured as a junior reporter for a guinea a week. On these nights he would return home at midnight. Three more nights were passed at the meetings of the Good Templars and Band of Hope Temperance Societies, at the latter of which he was a superintendent. By the age of twenty he was editing the *Good Templar* newspaper and editing a Liverpool monthly satirical magazine, *The Porcupine*. He was eventually invited to study law under Alderman William Radcliffe, subsequently a mayor of Liverpool. In November 1878 he passed his final examinations and was admitted as a solicitor in December, immediately working for himself from 16th December at the premises on 28 Church Street in Liverpool but continuing his press activities until 1884. He formed several partnerships, the first in 1882 with Robert Carruthers, which was dissolved in 1883; the next was with Robert Heaton and Arthur Moore in April 1894, forming the legal firm of Quilliam, Heaton and Moore.[3]

The family were part of the small elite of Manx migrants to Liverpool, and were well known on the Isle of Man where they maintained a family home. His father had been born in Drumgold Street in Douglas, the main town of the Isle of Man, and his great-uncle John owned a tanner's yard there. Quilliam himself had been sent to the island as a small child, staying with a relative who owned a farm in Mona, near Crosby. The family residence was at Peel, and until Quilliam purchased the new house at Onchan in 1903, his own children enjoyed the delights of dual residence. Indeed, many Muslim guests of special status found themselves entertained by the family at the house on the Isle of Man. Quilliam was very proud of his Manx descent and as an adult remained an active member and President of the Liverpool Manx Society. The island's principal newspaper, *The Manxman*, published a biography of Quilliam under the banner headline 'Liverpool Manx Worthies', in which it stated that the genealogy of the Quilliams on the island could be traced back over 300 years. According to this article, Sir Robert Quilliam was granted a crest by Elizabeth I in 1571, which remained in Quilliam's possession; while in 1678, it is recorded that John Quilliam was a member of the House of Keys, the governing body of the island. In 1710, no less than seven Quilliams were present at a meeting of the chief parishioners of Kirk Patrick to agree the building of a new church.[4] Quilliam was most proud of his great-uncle, John Quilliam, who had attracted the attention of Lord Nelson at the Battle of Copenhagen and fought alongside him at the Battle of Trafalgar as First Lieutenant of HMS Victory; John was believed to have been steering the ship when Nelson was fatally wounded. There is even evidence that he was one of the pallbearers at Lord Nelson's funeral. John Quilliam had also been a member of the House of Keys, and was buried on the island when he died in 1817. A portrait of the hero of Trafalgar took pride of place in Quilliam's study, and he claimed that he owned his great-uncle's sword and sardonyx ring.

Even in the second half of the nineteenth century, a family link to a hero of Trafalgar would have served to enhance the status of a middle-class family. It was the citizens of ports who most felt the impact of maritime conflicts between nations, and Liverpool had supplied many of its seafaring men to the national fleet in the wars with France between 1756 and 1815. In 1795, the city had provided 1700 sailors to the navy,[5] and these men proved to be heroic defenders of the nation. Liverpool's merchants were undoubtedly concerned about an invasion by Napoleon from the sea and appropriate defences were built, but the victory at Trafalgar removed any fears of this calamity from the wealthy citizens of Liverpool's bourgeoisie;[6] any man of their class, even two or three generations on, would have been fêted for possessing such an illustrious forebear.

William Quilliam's parents were Wesleyan Methodists and long-standing members of the Temperance movement. As a young man, Quilliam attended the Fairfield Wesleyan Chapel where his parents worshipped. He was a devout Nonconformist and taught as a Sunday School teacher at the United Methodist Free Church on Russell Street, which he had attended as a child, but his religious life began earlier than that. William's grandfather, Samuel, had lectured on the virtues of abstaining from alcohol in Liverpool and its surrounds, and the first entry in the small boy's scrapbook of his childhood life was a handbill of a meeting dated 10th May 1864 inviting the public to attend a lecture delivered by his grandfather entitled, 'The advantages of sobriety in both worlds'.

At the age of seven, Quilliam was taken to his first Temperance movement meeting by his grandmother, Mary Quilliam, and it is worth reading the Sheikh's own account of this significant turning point in his young life:

> I was taken to a Band of Hope meeting that was held in the schoolroom underneath the Russell Street Chapel of the United Methodist Free Church body, and there I signed the total abstinence pledge, promising never to take any intoxicating liquor as a beverage, a promise, I thank God, that I have never yet broken.[7]

The Sheikh goes on to recount that he sat on the platform with his grandfather while he delivered his lecture. Indeed, the youthful Quilliam became known as the 'Temperance Child' in Liverpool, and often spoke at meetings where his grandfather lectured. On 6th December 1871, when just sixteen years old, he spoke on the platform alongside well-known orators such as Sir Wilfred Lawson, a lawyer and Member of Parliament, and George Trevelyan, also a Member of Parliament, in the Philharmonic Hall, Liverpool, in support of 'The Permissive Prohibitory Liquor Bill'. By that time he had already been appointed secretary to the Russell Street Temperance Society and Band of Hope, a position he had occupied since the age of fourteen. By 1873, he was also the secretary of the Liverpool Ever Faithful Lodge, another well-known Temperance Society.

In 1874 he was on the committee as 'Worthy Marshall', along with his mother Harriet as District Vice Templar, of the District Vice Lodge for South-West Lancashire.

The youthful Quilliam's activities as a Temperance campaigner are too many to list here. It is certainly true that he was a successor of the mid-1830s, single-minded, Nonconformist crusading zeal against alcohol that was marked by public displays of pledge-signing and testimonies by born-again, redeemed drunkards. On 5th May 1874, Quilliam's name appeared again as the District Assistant Secretary on a window-bill announcing that 'a choir of 1000 juvenile Templars' would appear in a grand concert at the Philharmonic Hall, Liverpool. His activities were not confined to Liverpool. On 21st July 1874, he spoke alongside his mother in Scarborough; while on the 9th September, he lectured alone at Tuebrook as a guest speaker of the Leyfield Lodge of Good Templars. In February 1875, he appears as 'Lodge Deputy' on a handbill for the 'Third Annual Soirée' of the Hope of Kensington Lodge held at the Primitive Methodist Chapel in Gilead Street, Kensington.

His good friend and fellow Muslim convert, the Frenchman Henri de Léon,[8] who stayed regularly with Abdullah Quilliam in the late 1890s and early 1900s, tells us that the young Quilliam's scrapbook for 1875 was filled with tickets, programmes, handbills and circulars relating to monthly entertainments associated with Temperance activities in Kensington, Fairfield, Parliament Fields, Toxteth, Foley Street, Kirkdale and the North Bethel Methodist Church, Bath Street, in which the young Temperance organiser played a prominent part. In the spring of 1875, he was elected as Secretary to the East Liverpool Convention of the Good Templars, and at this time his activities are listed as being Lodge Deputy of the Hope of Kensington Lodge, Secretary of the Kensington Working Men's Concerts, Superintendent of the Fairfield Juvenile Temple and active member of the Liverpool Permissive Bill Association; he was also energetically involved in the Liverpool Temperance and Band of Hope Union. All of this is remarkable when one considers that the young man was articled, studying law and working as a reporter at the same time.[9]

The positioning of Quilliam and his forefathers with regard to the consumption of alcohol was typical of his class and Christian Nonconformist background, especially in the city of Liverpool. From as early as the 1830s, the city authorities had encouraged the newly-created, excise-licensed beerhouses in working-class neighbourhoods of the city. Within a short space of time, there were over 30,000 of these and their numbers moved steadily upwards to peak at around 50,000 in the 1870s, declining slowly thereafter to some 40,000 by the end of the century.[10] The closing of these outlets became the primary target of the Temperance movement, which was supported by much moderate opinion, as it was commonly believed (with some justification) that alchohol consumption was undermining the character, religious life, work ethic and family responsibilities of the poor, finally leading to destitution. A major success was achieved in 1869 when the licensing of all new beer houses was made subject to magistrates' approval. The evidence of the work of Quilliam's family at the heart of the city's Temperance movement in this period shows their involvement in the leadership of this campaign.

It is clear that the family did not share the common hypocrisy of Victorian puritan attitudes, which frowned on the consumption of alcohol amongst the working-class but accepted moderate wine drinking in their own homes or in hotels.[11] It was largely the availability of cheap beer in Liverpool that hardened attitudes towards a strict teetotal position. It could be argued that the total Temperance movement was more a religious movement than a class one, as it was rooted in the Dissenting and Evangelical Nonconformist communities of the city and the surrounding North-West.

From the 1860s onwards, temperance became linked to the cause of Radical Nonconformity, which was often working within the Liberal Party and seeking to put pressure on Liberal national governments. In this period of his life, Quilliam could be marked out as a Liberal in a number of other significant ways. He was a passionate supporter of the campaign against capital punishment and never missed an opportunity to attack the ill-treatment of 'Negroes' in the USA; he had been Secretary of the Good Templar movement when it split over the 'Negro' question after Quilliam had taken up their cause publicly. In 1866 Quilliam independently opened the Mount Vernon Temperance Hall as a result of this division, establishing an annual Temperance Watch Night Vigil and Service, which was held on New Year's Eve in 1886, 1887 and 1888.[12]

He condemned the mainstream churches for their support of slavery in the previous century and observed that all the Anglican bishops in the House of Lords had voted against repeal. In addition, he was a notable advocate of the rights of the working man and was indeed a leader of various trade unions in the city of Liverpool. At various times Quilliam was solicitor to the Lancashire Sea Fishery Board and several trade unions, including the Mersey Railway Quay and Carters Union, the Operative Bakers Union and the Upholsterers and Coppersmiths Societies. In 1897 Quilliam was appointed President of the 8,000 strong Mersey Railway Quay and Carters Union on the resignation of the previous president, Sir John Houlding JP, who had been elected as the first Lord Mayor of Liverpool.[13] He was to hold this post until 1908.[14]

Like Titus Salt, the famed strict teetotaller and campaigner for temperance reform, Quilliam embodied the strict but enlightened values of the Nonconformist conscience. Even during his youth, Quilliam had succeeded in establishing himself as a lively and energetic force in the religious life of the city of Liverpool, and this would continue in later life despite his constant travelling. Like Salt, Quilliam did not believe that anything excused the drunkenness, the violence and the indolence of many of the poorer classes in the city.[15]

However, unlike Titus Salt, William Henry Quilliam was not the archetypal Victorian industrialist. Liverpool, unlike other cities experiencing growth in the north of England, did not possess any large scale manufacturing industry, and the mills and factories usually associated with Victorian industrialisation were notably absent. Liverpool gained its prosperity through commerce, and although the new modern docks had replaced the traditional eighteenth-century waterfront industries, most of Liverpool in the mid-nineteenth century and beyond was comprised of small-scale, largely unmechanised manufacturing.[16]

Belcham informs us that craft workers in luxury trades continued to work in the time-established manner, 'catering to a local market second only to London'.[17] The Quilliam family business of watchmaking would have been typical of this, and the trade was a renowned specialism of the city.[18] At least since 1800, investment was concentrated on trade and the activities of the port, and it is possible that Liverpool produced more millionaires during this period than any other city in the nation.[19] The wealth of the city was displayed in impressive buildings and city planning. It was not the new industrialists of Victorian England that represented the dominant class of the city, but the old and established families with their roots in the eighteenth and early nineteenth centuries who saw themselves as the 'nobility of commerce'.[20]

Alongside these merchants were families who had succeeded through their service to the seafaring activities of the port. Quilliam's naval heritage from early nineteenth century sailors, his family's fame as watchmakers and his ownership of property both in Liverpool and the Isle of Man placed him securely in the Liverpudlian elite. His family, along with others of their class, lived in the 'green' areas of the city's surrounding villages, such as Everton, Walton Hall, Mossley Hill and Woolton, where the wealthiest merchants sought clean air, peace and nature when the old town had been taken over by the docklands.

As commerce expanded and trade with the world brought untold wealth to Liverpool, the family continued its traditional craft of watchmaking, but William Quilliam chose a new career in law, one that would flourish as commercial activity increased. Quilliam became renowned for his legal work. As a solicitor, he built one of the most successful practices of law in the northwest of

England, but he was also known as an advocate, taking on thirty or forty cases per week from the courts. Amongst these were a number of high-profile murder cases. He defended Dr Tomanzes, the black doctor tried at the Chester Assizes, and won the case. He lost the defence of Bhagwan Jassawari, a Hindu sailor who murdered a captain and his wife at sea, but he did manage to argue successfully for a commutation of the death sentence to penal servitude for life. He did the same for Travis, who was charged with murder at Rock Ferry. In this case he not only managed to persuade the court to commute the death sentence, but the defendant was later actually discharged with a free pardon.

Quilliam was proud of his record as a criminal lawyer and a powerful campaigner against capital punishment, often mentioning that he only ever lost one man to the hangman. This was William Miller, the notorious Redcross Street murderer who, on return from a spell at sea, had battered to death his ex-landlord in February 1895, seeking to rob the elderly bookseller of his rumoured stash of money. Miller had also attempted to murder a fifteen-year-old servant boy who lived with the bookseller. It was his failure to finish off the boy with a poker that led to his arrest and prosecution.

He famously defended Yates, a solicitor charged with forgery, who received penal servitude for life when found guilty. Quilliam loved to tell the story of his defence of Henry Burton and James Gilbert Cunningham, tried in London for being involved in a conspiracy to cause simultaneous bomb outrages throughout England and Scotland in 1895. The men in question were supporters of the Irish cause and created panic throughout the nation; public buildings were protected and politicians provided with high-level personal security. After several security scares, an arrest was made. Quilliam told how he was approached late at night by a large man with a muffler covering his mouth and nose and who spoke with a strong North American accent. The man asked him to defend the arrested persons and immediately produced the complete sum of money in cash when Quilliam stated his usual fees.

A rare portrait of William Quilliam, appearing in the
familiar attire of the late Victorian lawyer and gentleman.

During the high profile trial, Quilliam was guarded day and
night by both Fenians and Government officials. One night on his
way to Euston Station, Quilliam and his Fenian bodyguard were
arrested by a detective on suspicion of terrorism. The contents of
Quilliam's small black legal bag aroused deep suspicion and fear
amongst the police. On the way to Bridewell Police Station, a large
angry crowd gathered, throwing cabbage stalks and demanding
that the two men be lynched from a lamppost. Quilliam was held
for nearly six hours, before he was released when recognised by a
detective inspector. He was eventually paid compensation of £20
for the incident. He would tell with amusement the subterfuges
the Fenians undertook to arrange his payment for defending the
two dynamitards and how, on visiting Cunningham's mother in
Ireland, he was received as a hero by the 'boys'of the IRA, despite
the fact that he lost the case.

The *Liverpool Weekly Courier* declared in an article published
on 14th September 1901 that, 'it is his curious distinction to have

defended probably more murderers than any other solicitor', and described him as the 'unofficial Attorney-General of Liverpool'. Quilliam's accounts of his adventures defending the notorious demonstrate the more adventurous side of the Sheikh, and the same article indicates that Quilliam did not look like the stereotypical lawyer. It declares that he had 'none of the over-precise, severe bearing we mentally associate with the learned in law', but rather 'the easy-going aspect of a student'. However, whatever his appearance, he was certainly taken very seriously in his home city, where his portrait and a biographical sketch appeared in B. Guinness Orchard's *Liverpool's Legion of Honour* (1893). Quilliam's inclination to undertake the defence of notorious criminals provides us with some insight into his political position. When we consider these criminal cases alongside Quilliam's other activities with regard to issues of civil liberty and liberal causes, it is fairly safe to surmise that there was more than mere flamboyance and adventurism to Quilliam, and that, in the words of the late John Mortimer, he represented 'the great criminal defender who keeps all our liberties alive' by maintaining the jury system and resisting those forces that would chip away at hard-earned liberties.

His trade union activities were included in his work as a solicitor, as he represented the journeymen bakers, upholsterers, brickmakers, coppersmiths and Lancashire Sea Fisheries, the last a government appointment.

Such enlightened activities were not necessarily part of the worldview of Liverpool's gentry. Equality was not a major feature of the town – as early as 1835 the town was recognised as one of the least democratically governed.[21] The expansion of the docks took the wealthy families away from the city centre to new genteel quarters in the suburbs, including Quilliam's family who lived in Fairfields. However, the separation of the wealthy and the poor did not always lead to complete apathy. According to William Moss, philanthropy was another feature of the town from the eighteenth century.[22] Quilliam was brought up on the values of Nonconformity, and in many cases these led men from the pulpit to strike meetings and eventually to a socialist political platform.

Many of the more liberal of the city's intellectuals and professionals were Unitarians. This sect maintained chapels in Liverpool at Benns Gardens, Rushton Street and Paradise Street. Historically they had been renowned for their resistance to the slave trade and had attracted the more liberal individuals from among the city's elite families. In his teens, Quilliam came under the influence of a Unitarian pastor, Charles Beard, and this may have had a theological impact on his later attraction to Islam. He may well have been drawn towards the Unitarians because they better reflected his liberalism, and he would have found more sympathy for his views in their congregations.

Waller reminds us that the Liberal Party was unsuccessful in cultivating working-class support because their attitude was too patrician.[23] This view is supported by *The Porcupine*, which declared that Liverpool's Liberals were marked by 'restraint, class distinction, and isolation'.[24] Although Quilliam demonstrated remarkable restraint with regard to the use of alcohol, his professional life brought him into contact with the working classes, as did his later activities on behalf of Liverpool's sailors and dockside communities. Although he may have had sympathies with the prevalent Victorian ethos of self-reliance that was promoted so successfully by Samuel Smiles and loved by patrician Liberal reformers, Quilliam found himself drawn towards the City's Conservatives whom he met socially as a Freemason and an Oddfellow. In December 1884, he formed the Conservative Debating Society in West Derby.[25] The Conservatives, although espousing loyalty to the Church, Crown, the landed aristocracy and property ownership, attended trade union balls and were content to mix with the proletariat without any noticeable assumptions of superiority. *The Porcupine* notes that they 'danced cheerfully with the women' and were noted for their allegiance to 'liberty, equality and fraternity'.[26]

If Quilliam did not feel at ease with Liberal social aloofness from the working-class electorate, he was happy with their commitment to social reforms such as public education; Quilliam was however ill at ease with the Conservative allegiance to the established Church. The Church of England did not require its members to be teetotallers, a position that Quilliam would have regarded as hypocritical. However, there was a general loyalty among Conservatives to religious values as represented by the ascendancy of truth over error, or freedom from slavery, which Quilliam as *homo religiosis* and a serious believer in equality and social justice would have been at ease with. The Temperance movement espoused by Conservatives went into issues of serious social reform and advocated free public education, public libraries, museums, sports clubs, friendly societies, savings banks and instruction in sanitation, personal hygiene and domestic science. Although Waller reminds us that this did not reflect a very profound theory of social change,[27] we will see that Quilliam successfully adopted the idea that poor people would cease to frequent public houses or live immoral lives if they were provided with alternative recreational and educational facilities, or if they had contact with well-intentioned middle-class citizens in the Liverpool Muslim Institute.

The stereotypical view of the northern middle classes was one of philistine incompatibility between culture and industry, but it has been argued that this stereotype was a myth.[28] Many northern bankers, industrialists, merchants and manufacturers maintained an extensive involvement in art and culture both in Manchester and Liverpool. They were active in forming new cultural institutions in these cities, such as literary and philosophical societies. By the late nineteenth century, numerous societies were promoting literature and the arts, along with voluntary associations geared to the education and recreation of young clerks who were attempting to recreate themselves on the model of 'Liverpool gentlemen'. We are told by Henri de Léon that, in later life, Quilliam's library contained more than two thousand books on theology, science and legal matters. Like many Victorian gentleman of means, Quilliam maintained a strong interest in the pursuit of knowledge. He was a well-known amateur scholar of the ancient history of the Isle of

Man and a prominent geologist. After his conversion to Islam, he drew upon his contacts around the Muslim world to collect enough artefacts to maintain a museum of Eastern cultures at the Liverpool Muslim Institute in Broughton Terrace. In addition, an interest in natural history resulted in him maintaining a small private zoo at his home.

Similar to Charles Dickens, the great figure of the Victorian literary world, Quilliam was an admired public speaker, an active philanthropist and the founder-editor of newspapers, journals and magazines, albeit locally in Liverpool and the North-West rather than nationally. To a degree, Quilliam was also a critic and a voice of conscience for his age. Like Wilkie Collins, the pioneering thriller writer, he utilised the editorial columns of his publications to condemn the 'national morality' and cant of the Victorian public. We will also see that his sexual life had something in common with these two public figures.

In the 1980s, Prime Minister Margaret Thatcher called for a return to Victorian values; but the Victorian era was never simple, and her call was highly selective. In fact, there were many voices at the time that contested the mores of Victorian society. Quilliam was part of Liverpool's nostalgia for an earlier age of innocence, or even as part of a wider Victorian romanticism. In spite of the gradual victory of the forces of reform over the strident voices of reaction and the progress that was achieved in education, social conditions and the standard of living, there were many who reacted against a perceived decadent society and the modern industrial city, choked with filth, grime, disease and immorality.

Nigel Yates reminds us that, from the 1830s, the conditions in England led to a form of romanticism that looked for a medieval revival, an appeal to a mythical golden age in which free, property-owning peasantry were paternally protected by their feudal masters and where spacious towns were lovingly 'dominated by churches and monasteries'.[29] Christian Europe in the thirteenth and fourteenth centuries was idealised, and societies were established for the study of antiquities. To figures like Pugin, the medieval dream had a political aspect, in that it was necessary to demonstrate how unreal and shallow much of contemporary Victorian society and industrialization was. Quilliam was too much of a rational lawyer to buy into Pugin's mediaeval romanticism, although there are traces of it in his attempts to use archaeology to discover an ideal Celtic past. The romanticism of Quilliam was rather embodied in another Victorian escapism, namely the love of the Orient. Quilliam's Orientalism manifested itself in an overly idealised view of Ottoman culture and society.

However, Quilliam would have agreed with Pugin's view that the Church of England had surrendered its spiritual leadership in favour of becoming a servant of the new secular state. Yates notes that there was a growing body of opinion, even among Church of England clergy, that the bishops had become government spokesmen on religious matters and were no longer spiritual guides for the populace.[30] Quilliam was always keen to point out that, even in the previous century, not one of the Anglican bishops had voted for the Abolition of Slavery Bill. This was perhaps another reason for his flirtation with Unitarianism, a movement with an excellent history of opposition to the slave trade in Liverpool.

Edward Norman has argued that Victorian laymen were far more concerned with religion than many historians have previously appreciated,[31] while David Englander and Rosmary O'Day have called for the restoration of religion to a central position when discussing the history of the period and the motivations of its prime movers.[32] If this line of argument is accepted, then it must be Quilliam's religious journey above all that locates him firmly in his time, place and class.

Quilliam's writings as a Muslim clearly indicate his impatience with the Christian lack of unity, the religion's difficulties with the discoveries of science and the problems caused by modern Biblical scholarship. Although he used all three of these issues in the defence of Islam and as a means of attacking Christianity as a failed and flawed truth when he became a Muslim, these particular difficulties with Christianity were bothering a large number of educated Victorians. While the rise of new technologies and industry created by the new scientific knowledge led the Romantics in the Church of England, like Pugin, to look back to an idealised medieval society where there was harmony between church and state and art existed for the glory of God, other Victorians interpreted the controversies over the *Origin of Species* and its implications for the truth of the scriptural accounts of creation as the death knell of religion and the triumph of science. Englander and O'Day point out that Victorian society craved both 'novelty and innovation, but also took comfort in tradition'.[33] Quilliam resolved this paradox by finding both a new religion and an old tradition when he embraced Islam. Quilliam the geologist was fully aware of the theories of Darwin and the issues surrounding the dating of the world's existence, and we have to surmise that his previous Christian allegiance was deeply challenged by the new knowledge. Indeed, as McLeod reminds us, the first blow in this sphere had come in the 1830s and 1840s from geologists, who had argued even before Quilliam's birth that the earth must be much older than the writers of Genesis had realised.[34]

More fundamental questions were raised by Darwin throughout the 1850s and 1860s, and these spread more widely in the formative years of Quilliam's adulthood. Agnosticism became an acceptable alternative to the prevailing Christian religiosity of Victorian Britain. If atheism remained an unpopular choice, voiced only by the courageous, 'doubt' was to become common parlance in the middle-class Victorian drawing room.[35] If geology and Darwin threatened Biblical accounts of the origins of life and the creation of the world, perhaps of even more significance were the developments in the critical study of the New Testament, which asked questions concerning the accuracy and consistency of the Gospel narratives regarding the teachings and life of Jesus. Although today's Biblical scholars live comfortably with ideas of the polemical purposes of the Gospel authors, such scholarship would have been deeply disturbing to Christian sensitivities in the Victorian period. Although only accessible to the educated minority, they were nonetheless a major contributor to middle-class doubt. In addition, the pride in rational thinking promoted by the discoveries of science led to a deep suspicion of the miraculous events described in the New Testament.

It is not possible to ascertain whether Quilliam was aware of the impact of Comte's philosophy of positivism, but it is hard to imagine that someone so well read and in touch with the currents of thought impacting the educated middle-classes would be ignorant of the social and physical sciences. However, the idea that scientific knowledge from either the human or physical sciences had replaced religion, or even made it much more difficult to believe in any kind of religion, never seemed to appeal to Quilliam. The ardent belief in God that was formed in his childhood and early manhood was never challenged in Quilliam's later writings. Rather he continued to search for a religion that met the intellectual challenges of the period but also kept him in touch with the monotheistic deity that he had previously learned to worship.

Quilliam's later writings and lectures as a Muslim clearly indicate that he found the solutions to these dilemmas of doubt that were affecting so many of his contemporaries within the teachings of Islam. The rationality of Islam is a recurring theme of his activities as a missionary for Islam and he described this as a paramount reason for his conversion. For Quilliam, the teachings of the Qur'an supported the discoveries of science; and, in turn, the discoveries of science and the improved knowledge of the nature of creation increased his awe for the Creator of such complex wonder. In his lectures on geology, he would often recount how his discovery that certain rocks that he had examined on the Isle of Man had been dated to five million years deepened his faith in a Creator-God rather than diminishing it. In addition, he pointed out that Islam did not require a belief in miracles that strained credulity or in supernatural theologies concerning the humanity of the founders of Judaism, Christianity or Islam. He was aware that conventional Muslim doctrines concerning the formation and inviolability of the Qur'an and the critique of Christian and Jewish Scriptures as being tainted by human error were supported by modern Biblical scholarship. Quilliam was something of an amateur theologian and Biblical scholar, and often lectured in Liverpool and the north-west of England on the latest controversies arising from German and British New Testament scholarship.

Quilliam was also reflective about theology and morality. Although his conversion to Islam did not challenge his beliefs in hell, which were strongly emphasised by evangelical revivalist preachers of the period but worried liberal sensitivities, he was more vigorous in his concerns about the doctrines of the Atonement and the Incarnation. The traditional Christian doctrine of Atonement – which Hugh McLeod described in the following way: 'all human beings deserved to suffer in hell for their sins, and God's justice demanded that this should be so. But in his mercy God accepted the death of one sinless man, Jesus Christ, as a substitute for fallen humanity'[36] – worried many educated Victorians.

Rational thinking found the idea that the human race was condemned through inheriting a burden of sin from primal ancestors to be anathema, and many felt that the concept of one person standing in for another was morally offensive. Such ideas are crucial in the Christian doctrines of the Incarnation and the Trinity. Dismissal of these ideas meant the rejection of the central truth of Christianity's message of salvation. Some, like Edward Carpenter in the early 1880s, drew upon the influence of Buddhism and Thoreau to break with materialism and the social conventions of their class, whilst providing a perceived rational solution to Christian doctrines.[37] Buddhism's non-theism would always be a problem for Quilliam, but we can see his flirtation with Unitarianism as a sign of his unease with the Trinitarian solution to salvation proposed by mainstream Christian doctrine. In Islam, he found not only the answers to these dilemmas, but also a vigorous negation of the Christian doctrines of the Incarnation, Original Sin, Atonement and Trinitarianism. He was able to draw upon critiques of these doctrines so effectively in his preaching of the Islamic revelation that he gained converts to Islam from amongst Christians.

In Quilliam's lectures after his conversion we can deduce two other vital concerns that he had with the religion of his youth. These revolve around issues of morality and unity, and both would have been honed by his experience of living in Liverpool in the second half of the nineteenth century. McLeod points out that Christianity in this period had been relativised by a more rational application of moral criteria across the board.[38] In other words, the rapidly expanding knowledge of other religions, gained through the empire, literacy and travel opportunities, provided the possibility of evaluating and comparing diverse belief systems on the basis of moral codes and their application. Many felt that other religious traditions compared favourably with Christian belief and morality.

It is important to clarify how the term 'religion' should be understood in this context. Although in British society today we generally define as Christian those who practise and believe in the religion, this was not so in the Victorian era when there was still a very strong conception of Christian civilisation or Christian peoples, as opposed to 'heathens' or religious communities connected to other world civilisations such as the Muslims or Hindus. Believers would compare the moral behaviour of those who practised Christianity favourably with a nominal mass that adhered to a rival faith only in name. Consequently we need to understand that the daily behaviour that Quilliam observed all around him in the streets of Liverpool seemed to him a sign of the fallen morality of Christians. As a police court lawyer, he had many opportunities to observe the less savoury aspects of Liverpool's urban life.

Described by a contemporary local historian as, the 'first town in the kingdom in point of size and commercial importance, the metropolis excepted',[39] Liverpool had become not only the bridge between England and Ireland, but also one of the key links between rapidly industrialising Britain and the world. Formed by the powerful forces of imperial international trade and mass migration, Liverpool accounted for half of the exports of the nation.[40] From 1835 to 1907, the period in which England became the major industrial, commercial and colonial power of the world, Liverpool became its foremost distributing centre, controlling one-third of the export trade and one-quarter of the import trade; one-third of the nation's shipping passed through her docks, as well as a remarkable one-seventh of the world's shipping. But the expansion of the city and the wealth thus generated did not benefit all of her citizens. Ramsey Muir, writing in 1907, describes the city graphically:

> The port possesses dock space to the extent of 570 acres on both sides of the river. The massive granite walls by which these docks are surrounded give a lineal quayage of over 35 miles, and the creation of new docks still continues.... For seven miles and a quarter, on the Lancashire side of the river alone, the monumental granite, quarried from the Board's own quarries in Scotland, fronts the river in a vast sea wall as solid and enduring as the Pyramids. [...] The population economically dependent upon Liverpool largely exceeds 1,000,000, and has multiplied fivefold in the course of the last 70 years. To accommodate the immense aggregation of human beings, the tide of brick and mortar has spread far afield on both sides of the river. Nothing for eight miles on either shore, but a continuous dense mass of houses, over which there hangs forever a low and broad pall of dun-coloured smoke. [...] Nor can anything be imagined much more depressing than the miles of dull, monotonous and ugly streets in which not only the poor but the middle classes of the town are condemned to live. In Liverpool, as elsewhere, special quarters have developed for the rich, the people of middling fortune and the poor. The people who inhabit these vast congeries of streets are of an extraordinary diversity of races; few towns in the world are more cosmopolitan. And these various races (except in so far as when they belong to the wealthier class) tend to live together in distinct quarters. The most numerous

are the Irish, who have their principal quarter in the Northern part of the old town, and who supply a large proportion of the unskilled labour required at the docks.[41]

The city was renowned for its casual labour force. Since the prosperity was founded on moving goods between ships, warehouses and newly-built railways, a large proportion of the men had no permanent work, but instead lived between the extremes of idleness and sudden heavy labour, when they worked long hours. Muir states that there was probably no city of equivalent size in which so small a proportion of the population was maintained by permanent and stable industrial work.[42] The hard physical work and bouts of idleness in-between resulted in workers resorting to the easily available consolation of alcohol and other vices.

From the late eighteenth century, half of the working-class population lived in narrow closed courts with no sanitary provisions, or worst of all in damp underground cellars. Only the streets where the wealthy lived were served by sewers. Muir reports that the citizens of Liverpool were crammed together 100,000 to the square mile. Such density of population was unknown in any other English town, and as a result Liverpool experienced a mortality rate that was unparalleled, with one in every twenty-five contracting fever every year.[43]

Although the new-found wealth that poured into Liverpool throughout the eighteenth and nineteenth centuries led to an increase in civic pride, resulting in private Acts from 1846 to 1864 concerning slum clearance, the construction of sewers for the whole town, adequate provision of clean water supplies, regular inspection and supervision of lodging houses and enforced control of smoke emission levels for factories, these improvements did not seem to have an impact on public morality. As late as 1874, conditions were so bad that *The Times* commented on the dreadful moral conditions of Liverpool and its death rate.[44]

Prostitution was a major problem in a port where single men came to seek work, recently paid-off sailors waited for ships after their previous voyage and men were often unemployed after bouts of casual labour. The poverty and overcrowding in the slums provided access to juvenile prostitution for those with this preference. The Workhouse and Lock Hospital annually admitted 1000 persons with a venereal disease, and estimates of Liverpool's population of prostitutes in 1885 stood at around 4000; 443 brothels were known to the police in 1889. It was suspected that some of the most respectable citizens controlled the brothel industry.[45] In 1890 Richard Armstrong published *The Deadly Shame of Liverpool* in which he alleged that most respectable citizens cared little for the poverty and squalor as long as it stayed away from their respectable suburbs. He claimed that the wholesale liquor trade, drunkenness and prostitution were present on such an enormous scale that they represented a financial interest that corrupted the governing bodies of the city.[46]

Violent crime was another problem. Certain districts of the city had suffered from gang warfare in the 1860s, and there were around 9000 cases of unpunished violence annually in Liverpool's North-End alone. Fights in slum courts involving men, women and children were commonplace, and Waller argues that the slums bred a 'congenital urge to fight';[47] competition for work was the spur that maintained the proclivity for conflict and violence. However, it was the city's failure to control alcohol consumption which many well-meaning citizens felt to be the main contributory factor to prostitution, violence and other forms of criminality.

As a criminal lawyer and strong advocate of temperance, Quilliam was well placed to observe these moral shortcomings in the working-class population. Although he shared in the common reactions of his class – the call for self-help, the organisation of trade unions and associations, vigilance committees of leading citizens to press for reform and, above all, almost inexhaustible charity and benevolence, especially concerning the rescue of children – Quilliam increasingly saw the problems as the moral failures of the Christian world.

It did not help that much of the violence that Quilliam witnessed in the slums of Liverpool was linked to Christian sectarianism. As a Muslim he would often write on the parlous condition of Christian disunity when compared with the oneness found in the *umma*, even if this rather naively played down the religious heterogeneity of the Muslim world.

Liverpool was Britain's first city of mass immigration in the nineteenth century and, as with later migrations in the second half of the twentieth century, the migrants brought with them the issue of integrating their particular religious traditions. The Irish remained Britain's largest incoming population, and the first port of call for most of them was Liverpool. In the first three months of 1846 over 90,000 entered the town, with a further 300,000 coming in the twelve months following the summer of 1847.[48] These were primarily driven by the Great Famine. Although many were to travel onwards to the USA and other parts of England, around 105,000 remained in Liverpool, enough to have a serious impact on the social, economic and religious life of the town.

However, the Irish had been migrating for work opportunities since the late eighteenth and early nineteenth centuries, and these earlier migrants had already brought with them their particular religious structures and organisations based on Roman Catholic and Protestant hostilities. The first Orange Protestant lodges were organised in 1807-8, brought to Liverpool by Militia regiments and Irish migrations.[49] On 12th July each year, Orangemen paraded with their traditional symbols of the Lamb, the Ark and Bibles on poles, whilst burning counterfeit Catholic insignia. By 1830 the town contained thirteen Orange Lodges and the issue of Catholic Emancipation divided Liverpool. One Tory even pronounced that Catholic Bibles should be locked in iron chests and cast 'into the lowest sinks of the filth of the Corporation'.[50]

The Protestant migrants did not only come from northern and southern Ireland. Liverpool was in many ways the capital of north Wales, and there were almost as many Welsh as Irish in the city.

They would worship together in Welsh-speaking Calvinist chapels and publish their own Welsh-language newspapers. Even as late as 1900, it was estimated that 20,000 Welsh families still spoke Welsh in their homes. In addition, the prosperity of the town attracted Scots, who were also predominantly Protestant. The Welsh and Scottish communities settled in Everton, Toxteth, Walton and West Derby. By the late nineteenth century, Liverpool was a city effectively divided by Roman Catholic and Protestant sectarianism. Great Homer Street was the accepted border between Catholic and Protestant Liverpool, while in places where the boundaries were more fluid there was always the possibility of sectarian violence.

The sectarian hatred was not confined to the migrant communities but spilled over into Liverpool's mainstream political life and the local establishment. The Conservatives drew upon narratives of religious and constitutional freedom, both primary expressions of allegiance for immigrants and natives alike,[51] but as confirmed Anglicans they found it difficult to support Roman Catholicism. The slogan of 'No Popery' was incorporated into the Tory-Anglican establishment, and was also the central theme of militant Dissenters.[52] Protestant Dissenters, however, also took to the streets to protest against the ritualism of the established Anglican Church. Hardline attitudes among Conservatives in turn reinforced the Catholics' desire to remain separate and to build their own schools, even after 1870. Waller argues that it was natural for politicians to take advantage of these active and long-standing sectarian divisions for party political purposes, but it was often to the detriment of the city's public health, education and employment when these issues were viewed through ethnic and sectarian spectacles.[53] The divisions were not merely religious and political: they impacted directly on employment opportunities and public perceptions of worth. It is true that sectarianism offered identity, pride and protection to workers from within a particular community, especially before the advent of trade unions. The Roman Catholic Irish remained at the bottom of the occupational and residential order, whilst the

Ulster Protestants dominated the shipbuilding trades, the Carter's Union was Protestant in its constituency and the Scottish and Welsh Protestants dominated the building trade. In addition, the Roman Catholic Irish were associated with a failure to assimilate, rarely marrying outside their own culture, and some noted that one half of the city's population of paupers and criminals came from their numbers, although they constituted only a quarter of the population.[54] Sunday in the slums was renowned for drunkenness, gluttony and debauchery.

Even among the more industrious Protestants, unity was not a result of their non-conformity. Waller notes that Congregationalists and Baptists were on fairly good terms, but both kept themselves apart from the Wesleyans,[55] the denomination of Quilliam's family where he began his religious journey. Between these orthodox Dissenters and the Unitarians, to whom Quilliam later attached himself before converting to Islam, there was a huge gulf.

If Liverpool demonstrated a high degree of Christian sectarianism and religious factionalism, this only reflected a crisis of unity within the country as a whole. Anglicans and Nonconformists were often at each other's throats concerning the established nature of the Church of England. The Anglicans faced an internal war between those that elevated liturgical ceremony and sacramental worship and those who emphasised the sole inspiration of the Bible and preaching. Meanwhile an Evangelical alliance demanded that all Protestants unite against Catholics. Ironically, Evangelicalism and Anglo-Catholicism, two of the most powerful contributors to Christian revival in Victorian Britain, were major obstacles to the unity of the national Church.

Quilliam's idealism could not tolerate this degree of disunity and the apparent collapse of Christian morality. As someone with his finger on the pulse of the city's *zeitgeist*, he would have been aware of the lack of real religiosity amongst Liverpool's population. Many of the churches in central Liverpool had been constructed for wealthy congregations before their exodus to the suburbs, and when these populations had relocated, the churches were left empty. The Census in Liverpool in both 1881 and 1891 showed that the majority of Catholics were indifferent to attendance at church, a trend that the Protestants echoed.[56] It was noted that Liverpool exhibited fervid sectarianism without any degree of widespread religious observance. Waller argues that the city displayed 'a residual religion linked to patriotic assertion and the clannish camaraderie of slum neighbourhoods'.[57]

By the beginning of the twentieth century, the city was hopelessly divided between its Catholic and Protestant communities. The chaplain of Ireland's Orangemen asserted that Liverpool had reached a religious crisis, and he called upon Protestants to pack the churches and leave no room for either Roman Catholic or 'ritualist' idolaters. The King's visit to the Pope in Rome was watched carefully for any evidence of complicity with Catholicism;[58] priests were accused of living with harlots and 'robbing the poor to feed their bastards'.[59] In June 1903, the militant Protestant George Wise was released from prison and 60,000 people formed a procession to accompany him from the gates of the gaol. Along with visiting American Evangelists, Wise organised street demonstrations where he parodied Catholic rites and encouraged 40,000 Protestants to accompany him as he went to preach in Old Swan, a Roman Catholic quarter of the city. In 1903, Alderman Maxwell warned that Liverpool contained 'certain factions, religious and political, which for their own sakes ought to be kept as far apart as possible'.[60] Quilliam observed the increase in Christian sectarianism and reported it meticulously in *The Crescent* as a 'proof' of Christian depravity and decay.

During the years of his youth, Quilliam had been able to ignore these signs of disunity because his idealistic longing for serious social reform had been diverted towards the Temperance movement, where sectarian opinions were united in favour of promoting a campaign for total abstinence. However, this unity came to an end when the Roman Catholics and the Welsh Chapel goers formed their own Temperance movements. Quilliam's shift to Unitarianism reflected his concerns with mainstream Christian Trinitarianism, but is also partly explained by the fundamentally inspirational role that religion plays in the idea of the ascendancy of truth over error and freedom over tyranny. The Unitarians in Liverpool were a dominant group amongst Liverpool's liberals. Forty-eight Anglicans can be identified among prominent liberals in the city from 1835 to 1885, and the next largest group is the thirty-eight Unitarians.[61] Only three can be identified as Wesleyans, the denomination of Quilliam's birth. In Liverpool, the Unitarians were initially regarded with suspicion for their support of the abolition of slavery, a position that would have not endeared them to most of the city's commercial elites who had made or increased their fortunes from the slave trade. Later in the nineteenth century they were equally frowned upon by their fellow Nonconformists for their support of Roman Catholic toleration, a position that they maintained because of an intellectual concern for human rights along with a renowned commitment to philanthropy. Power states that many Liverpudlian professionals and intellectuals were Unitarians with Whig principles, congregating in chapels at Benns Gardens, Rushton Street and Paradise Street.[62]

Muir feels that this group of friends, often linked by member-ship of elite families and certain of their moral superiority, were 'the glory of Liverpool in this period ... who were not content to cultivate their own minds, but strove to diffuse throughout the money-grubbing community in which they found themselves something of their own delight in the civilising power of the letters and the arts.'[63] It is easy to see how they would have attracted the young Quilliam, with his concern for social justice and his belief in the power of philanthropy, education and the cultivation of the mind. In addition, they attracted him because of his increasing concern with mainstream Christian doctrines. It is tempting to speculate that he learned from their company his indifference to popular opinion and his desire to communicate the truth as he understood it, whether this was acknowledged by the majority or not. These men were Whigs, holding unpopular political opinions and very dubiously regarded by their fellow-citizens, and Quilliam became a greater object of public suspicion once he converted to Islam. It is surprising that Quilliam was not attracted to Christian Social-ism, which was beginning to make itself felt during this period. Quilliam shared much in common with Edward Carpenter and Stuart Headlam. He would have agreed with Carpenter's diagno-sis of late Victorian life as an age when cant dominated religion, science surrendered to materialism, public life was in the sway of commercialism and many of the social conventions of the era appeared futile.[64] It is also likely that Quilliam felt a kinship with Carpenter's critique of hypocrisy in the sexual life: the apparent denial of the body and its needs in the name of respectability, the contempt for human labour amongst the middle-classes, and the barring of women from the natural expression of their emotional lives.[65] In Quilliam, one also senses the kind of cultural rebellion that was manifested in Carpenter and other kindred spirits.

Like Quilliam, the Christian Socialists under the inspiration of Headlam were seriously considering the implications and obliga-tions of being a Christian gentleman with regard to social and political responsibility. Like Headlam, Quilliam could be reckless and mischievous, insensitive to those whose opinions were unlike his own, and he was not afraid to be labelled an eccentric in the face of his contemporaries' conformity.[66] Again, like Headlam, it was the possession of private means that enabled Quilliam to survive, and he was also always at his best when actually working amongst the poor and oppressed. Quilliam believed in the potential of those who were relegated to the periphery of society, and his time in Liverpool gave him firsthand experience of the injustices of the system and its consequences in ruined lives, disease and death. Norman points out that the Christian Socialists retained strong attachments to many of the assumptions of their own class and culture, and this is also true of Quilliam.[67] Both exhibited a benign paternalism and neither really perceived the cause of the problems to be the existence of class conflict. But it is in their solutions to the problems where the two part company.

Headlam's critique of traditional Christianity was based on separating Jesus' call for social justice from the conventional inability to grasp the deepest Christian truths which had been manifested in the history of the Church. For Headlam, Jesus was a man of the people, a social and political emancipator, a preacher of social revolution and personal transformation.[68] Quilliam would have had much sympathy for this stance, but eventually arrived at the position that Christianity had drifted so far from the truths expounded by Jesus that it had become irredeemable fairly early in its existence. The solution was found in the message of Islam, seen by Quilliam as more egalitarian, more concerned with social justice, but which also believed in the humanity of Jesus and possessed a coherent theology to explain the failure of Christianity and Judaism to live up to expectations. In spite of their differences, both men were convinced that the message of revelation offered the solution to the problems of their day, with the age-old warning not to mistake the transient for the permanent in the ordering of human society.

Finally we need to address the controversial aspects of Quilliam's sexual and family life. Although there is no doubt that Quilliam would have defended his rights to live and have children with more than one woman because of Islam's version of polygamy and the problems he saw as inherent within Christian monogamy, it is also true that his own sexual propensities and difficulties with the constraints of monogamy were located within the wider arena of the norms and mores of Victorian family life and the changes that were taking place within this sphere. Philip Collins reminds us that the Victorians placed a very high value on domestic married bliss and the home life that constituted, quoting *The Times* from 1888, 'what may be called the religion of the family throughout England'.[69] But double standards abounded, and extramarital sex was certainly accepted by the upper classes and was tolerated in their stratum of society. In their circles, the sin was not the act itself but the creation of a public scandal through the exposure or humiliation of one of the partners. These double standards were not confined to the upper classes, and the well-known detective fiction writer Wilkie Collins sneered about the public's canting 'national morality' and their blustering 'purity of hearths and homes'.[70]

Quilliam's sex life was convoluted and is difficult to unravel. Clearly any person's sexual activity belongs to the private realm, and this would have been even truer under the rigid codes of Victorian respectability. It is clear that he had at least one partner simultaneously with his legally married first wife. He had been formally engaged to Hannah Johnstone on the 3rd March 1875 at the age of nineteen and they married four years later on the 2nd July 1879 at the Fairfield Wesleyan Chapel on Laurel Road, Liverpool, only three months before their first child was born. The wedding was large and the *Family Annals* records that seven hundred guests attended, with many coming in carriages. The couple were to have four children together: Robert (Ahmed) was born on the 1st September 1879, Elizabeth on the 21st November 1881, Harriet on the 15th August 1883 (whilst Quilliam was travelling in Spain and Morocco) and finally William Henry (Billal) on the 20th April 1885. The first three children were baptised by their maternal grandfather, but there is no record of the last child being formally entered into the Christian religion. Later in Quilliam's life, he lived with and perhaps married the widow of his close friend and fellow convert Henri de Léon after he returned to England from his self-imposed exile, which had begun in 1908. However, this was not until after Hannah had died on the 18th November 1909 at the age of 52.[71]

His grandson, John Deane Potter, described his famous grandfather as possessing views towards women that 'were a mixture of Muhammedanism and Victorianism'. John Potter's grandmother was not Quilliam's legal wife Hannah, the mother of Robert Ahmed, William Billal and the two daughters Harriet and Elizabeth, but in his own words a 'chorus girl', Mary Lyons, at the Liverpool Theatre. Apparently Quilliam had courted her when a young solicitor and had been afraid that she would consider him too 'posh' – he had told her that he was a solicitor's clerk. She had discovered his real identity when she had called one day at his office. By that time, she had already been 'married' to him according to Islamic law for several years. It can only be assumed that the Sheikh had carried out the wedding in the mosque, although he would later honour her wish for a legal marriage after the death of Hannah. From this liaison Quilliam had one son, Muhammad Henry, and four daughters, Fatima, Ayesha, Miriam and Habeebah. The mystery is how he managed to keep his two families out of the media spotlight considering the scrutiny that he was under in Liverpool from 1893 to 1907. He was certainly aware that people speculated on his love life, and commented in a speech on polygamy in 1906 that he was rumoured to have hundreds of wives. He joked that he would like to know their addresses so that he could visit them. It must be assumed that the trusted inner circle of converts at the Liverpool Muslim Institute knew that the Sheikh's children belonged to two different women, even though they appeared in public as the children of his legal wife. It is also clear that Mrs Hannah Quilliam was part of the deception and appeared at some level to be resigned to the arrangement. She may not have been happy with the situation, but since we have no comment from her on the matter we have to assume that she at least agreed to the arrangement, although probably begrudgingly. Apparently Quilliam had spoken to his grandson and claimed that, 'my wives knew their position. They know everything about each other but they refuse to live under the same roof.' He was certainly a staunch defender of polygamy and considered it to be his Islamic right to have more than one wife. He was not a bigamist and broke no British law as far as can be ascertained, and he was careful to observe the Muslim customs of access and equality which Islamic law uses to maintain equity when there are multiple partners. His grandson notes that he was 'always very fair with his wives, children and grandchildren. We were always allotted a holiday in his Manx home.'

The young William Quilliam married at a time when the key elements of Victorian domesticity were already in place. Men of Quilliam's class would still have married for social advantage and wealth, but since the 1830s romantic love had become the principle reason for marriage. The social history of the period clearly tells us that the middle-class image of marriage was one of a union between social equals, which was influenced by the ideal of sensibility that had been prevalent since the eighteenth century that lauded companionship between marriage partners. The reality remained that middle-class and upper-class families maintained vigorous rituals of social control over their offspring, in morning calls, card-leaving, party lists, private receptions, garden parties, dances and balls, and the society press announcing social events, engagements and marriages, all to manage the business of finding the right partner.[72] The arrangements reached their highest stage of development, refinement and rigidity during the Victorian period. This was not confined to the landed gentry, but reached down to the professional classes including Quilliam's chosen profession, the law.[73]

Hannah Johnstone was the daughter of William Johnstone, who came to Liverpool from Cumberland in the 1850s and established himself successfully in the provisions business. He was active in the promotion of building societies and organisations committed to thrift, and he worked as the treasurer of the Guardian Building Society. The family were active members of the Wesleyan Methodist Society, and Hannah's father was a Sunday School teacher at Edge Lane Chapel and a trustee of the Laurel Road Chapel where the Quilliams married. As with Quilliam's family, he was committed to temperance and had abstained from alcohol for over forty years.[74] The *Liverpool Courier* report of his funeral states that, out of respect for such a man, all the private houses and most of the shops en route from the residence of the deceased to the chapel drew their blinds or closed their shutters.[75] Considering the proximity of the families, both being local to Fairfields, as well as their involvement in Wesleyan Methodism and Christian Nonconformist Temperance activities, it would be safe to assume that William and Hannah would have known each other from childhood – she was a year younger than him and only eighteen at their engagement. It seems likely that the two families would have approved of the liaison and the coming together of two much-esteemed Liverpudlian commercial families. Quilliam's choice of a partner would have been further constrained because Nonconformist Christians were expected to select partners from their own sects. Hannah Quilliam was a fellow Methodist.

Thompson points out that love matches that developed through random contact have no place in any historical society or any historical period amongst the elites;[76] however, the arranged marriages that are so typical of the Indian subcontinent, in which parents carry out negotiations between families, had disappeared from British society except amongst royalty since at least the Tudor period.[77] Among the middle and upper classes, property and wealth still did have to be protected, and marriage settlements would generally accompany the betrothal,[78] yet couples were more or less free to discover each other, within the rules of their class.

In principle, all Victorians thus subscribed to the conflicting doctrines that romantic love was one of the important foundations of true marriage, and that mutual affection and devotion could be relied upon to grow naturally as married bliss developed through the post-wedding experiences of married life. However, where marriages were still contracted for social and fiscal benefits, sexual frustration by both partners could be a problem.[79] Tosh suggests that by 1850, in the typical marriage of a man like Quilliam, who commuted daily to the office from his suburban home, the wife who was left at home had little knowledge of her husband's public life. Her domain was the home. There is little to suggest that William Quilliam's life did not conform to this pattern and to the cult of domesticity that had become the ideal of middle-class early Victorian males. Respectability walked alongside domesticity as the principal foundations for Victorian family life and sexual mores, especially amongst the Nonconformist churchgoers of Quilliam's background. This was particularly true of the lower middle-classes; but by the 1880s and 1890s, when Quilliam had already embraced Islam, professional men were beginning to feel the restrictions of the domesticity that they had lived under for two or three generations. According to Tosh, they were beginning to assert their authority, to look for male outlets to diminish their boredom and to remember past pleasures beyond the confines of their marriage.[80] By the end of the century there was a noticeable male revolt against the restraints of domesticity. Quilliam lived at exactly this juncture, when the tensions between masculinity and domesticity were most acutely felt.

Tosh points out that adventure and danger 'exerted their appeal',[81] and Quilliam's travels, his readiness to explore the boundaries of convention in his spiritual life, and his love for criminal law suggest a man to whom the restraints of domesticity would have been irksome. There was no shortage of settings where sexual pleasures outside the confines of marriage could be sought. Victorian double standards, in which men were tolerated for sowing their wild oats whilst women were castigated for similar behaviour, created an environment in which men's attempts to satisfy their sexual proclivities was tolerated in private but resulted in disgrace if made public. Opportunities abounded, as women outnumbered men and the Victorian practice of large age differentials between husbands and wives resulted in relatively young widowhood being common-place. In addition, single women had to be even more scrupulous about public exposure than men, especially since Victorian sexual mores insisted that virtuous women should not enjoy sex. There is no doubt that, in the midst of all this uncertainty amongst the middle and professional classes, the taking of mistresses was commonplace.

In the midst of such hypocrisy and double standards, it is not surprising that some people who were less bound by convention sought for new forms of association between men and women as an alternative to traditional marriage. Quilliam's solution to the challenges posed by the restrictions of marriage to a woman, which may have lost the necessary sexual pleasure that he desired although the marriage was not arranged, was novel. Too bound by the morality of the Bible to pursue satisfaction through paid sex or mistresses, Quilliam pushed the limits of both the moral codes of Victorian society and the license of Islam to permit more than one wife. Divorce remained financially risky and difficult in spite of its legalisation in 1857, and Quilliam was able financially to support more than one family. His lifestyle would have provided him with the freedom to meet the large number of middle-class spinsters that existed as a result of Victorian marriage customs.

In his defence of polygamy, Quilliam followed a strategy that he utilised on several occasions: he sought out allies in the world's media. For example, in May 1905 he reproduced an article from the *Daily Express* in *The Crescent* reporting on a lecture by Ralph Durand to the Ethnological Society which argued that Christian missionaries failed to recognise the true virtues of polygamy and confused the European custom of monogamy with Christian practice.[82] This had been a continuous theme with Quilliam since 1893, when he had published comments made by the Marquis of Queensbury.[83]

Quilliam elaborated on this himself in two articles in *The Crescent*. The first in 1898 defended Islam's advocacy of polygamy by stating that the Old Testament, which is accepted by both Judaism and Christianity, is a pro-polygamy text. He argued that God does not condemn the practice in either the New or Old Testaments, and as these books are regarded as revealed scripture in Judaism and Christianity, it would be inconsistent to pronounce definitive judgements on polygamy.[84] These religious arguments were followed a year later by a contemporary defence of polygamy, which advocated a limited form similar to that in Islam as a solution to various problems experienced in Victorian England. He accuses middle-class and upper-class men of practising 'pseudo-polygamy' through their habit of keeping mistresses and sometimes maintaining two families secretly from each other.

Prostitution was another a massive Victorian urban problem. Quilliam pointed out that Victorian England had a population imbalance, with one million more women than men. He argues that these women are condemned to either being 'old maids', deprived of their natural right to have children or enjoy their sexuality, or they fall prey to predatory males and risk being labelled as immoral or 'scarlet women' if discovered as the mistresses of married men. If they became pregnant and kept the children, these offspring had no legal rights and suffered from the ruined reputations of their mothers. Quilliam suggested that the limited polygamy permitted in Islam would resolve these problems for both men and women.[85]

His solution may have been Muslim, but the dilemma was typical for Victorian gentlemen of his class. This is not to say that Quilliam was insincere in his allegiance to Islam. On the contrary, he displayed a loyalty to the religion and a passionate conviction that its revelation was final to his dying day. However, the route through which Quilliam arrived at Islam traversed through many of the crises of faith, sexuality and moral challenges to Victorian conventions that were felt by many of his class and education. The journey from William Quilliam to Abdullah Quilliam was played out against the backdrop of the Victorian society peculiarly located in the environment of the city of Liverpool, in itself a phenomenon of Victorian life. He began life in a particular class and place; he remained in that location, which was his base for promoting Islam in Britain and abroad; and he never ceased to draw upon his material and cultural resources as a Victorian gentleman in order to make the teachings of Islam relevant to the British public.

CHAPTER 3

Creating the Liverpool Muslim Institute, 1887-1899

It is worth briefly jumping ahead of ourselves to recount a description of the Liverpool Muslim Institute thirty years after Quilliam began to promote Islam in the city. On the 10th November 1906, *The Pall Mall Gazette* wrote the following:

> The mosque at Liverpool is a place of worship for a comparatively large resident membership, as well as for thousands of Mahommedans, merchants, sailors, travellers, who pass through the port in a constantly flowing stream of brown humanity.... The Muslim Institute at Liverpool altogether comprises rooms for members, schoolrooms, a small museum, library and reading room, and also a small lecture hall which is used mainly for club meetings. There is also a large lecture hall for prayers. It seats some 220 people. The Medina Home, not far away, has about a score of children, who are being brought up as Muslims. The whole institution has about 200 members resident in Liverpool, but during the course of the year the mosque is visited for prayer by thousands of Muslim sailors and other travellers who come to the great seaport.[1]

What is the remarkable story behind the existence of this unique mosque in the city of Liverpool and its founder Sheikh Abdullah Quilliam? There are stories that William Quilliam became interested in Islam at the age of 17, when he was sent to Algeria for health reasons. However, I can find little evidence of this and it seems unlikely.[2] The *Family Annals* make no mention of any illness or visit to Algeria or Morocco at this time of his life. On the contrary, it was during this very period of Quilliam's life that he was busy gaining his qualifications in the law. The Sheikh was notoriously reticent about his life story, and I have been able to find only one personal account of his conversion. John Pool, a late nineteenth-century writer, recorded that Quilliam visited Morocco in 1887 and was struck by the lack of depravity that existed in British cities. On his return, he studied the Qur'an and other works on Islam until he was convinced.[3] He did allow Henri de Léon to narrate the story of his childhood in *The Crescent*, and I am sure that his fellow convert to Islam and family physician would have revealed any interest in Islam arising out of medical problems in Quilliam's youth. It is also difficult to believe that Quilliam's family would have permitted a young man of seventeen to visit Algeria alone. Quilliam always claimed that his interest in Islam arose after crossing to Algeria and Tunisia from France in 1882 at the age of twenty-six. The *Family Annals* record that he sailed to Gibraltar on SS *Sidon* of the Cunard Line on 1st July 1883, visiting Spain and Morocco, and returned to Liverpool on 1st March 1884. His interest in Islam seems to have grown gradually. As late as 1886 he opened the Vernon Temperance Hall and engaged in vigils in 1887 and 1888. However, in 1885 he had published an article entitled 'The Mysteries of Muslim Theology'.[4] It would appear that he made several journeys to North Africa between 1882 and 1887 but it was only after visiting Morocco in 1887 that he decided to convert, a decision which was made public in 1888 at the age of thirty-two, when he renounced Christianity in the Liverpool media. He also announced his change of name to Abdullah.

After his conversion, he initially propagated Islam from rented premises in Mount Vernon Street from 1887, but with little success. At the July 1896 Presidential address of the Annual General Meeting of the Liverpool Muslim Institute, Quilliam mentioned that there had been twenty-three deaths amongst the converts since 1888, which he attributed to the fact that most of the people attracted to his message had been elderly. In his first published work in 1890, he described in detail the early failure of his attempts to convince people of the truths of Islam. In the Preface of *Fanatics and Fanaticism*, he explains that his first strategy had been to compare the shortcomings of Christianity with the strengths of Islam, but that he had been treated as a 'species of monomaniac'; and when he tried to persuade people to discuss the 'respective merits of the two religions', he was maligned or ridiculed. Djem Ali Hamilton, who was with the Sheikh during these very early days, describes some of these occasions. He recounts that when Quilliam first began to preach, the halls would fill with 'Christians' who would stamp and shout at him. Quilliam would often wait up to one hour for them to quieten and then say, 'you have had your turn now British fair play states I get mine'. He would then gain their attention and lecture on Islam with total silence from his audience. On one occasion a person blew a blast on a trumpet while Quilliam was speaking and was 'smacked in the face by his companion'. Hamilton also recounts how they would shake hands with him at the end of the lecture and show him the stones that they had brought in their pockets to throw at him.

It was through such events that Quilliam decided to utilise an indirect strategy to introduce the tenets of Islam, one that was to work successfully. This was first applied at a Temperance meeting in the Queen's Hall, Birkenhead, where he had been invited to speak by old acquaintances from the Birkenhead Workingman's Temperance Society, who knew his strong views on the subject of alcohol consumption and total abstinence. It was only at the end of the lecture that Abdullah Quilliam commented on Islam's attitudes to alcohol consumption. At the close of the evening, Quilliam was approached by Djem Ali Hamilton, who came to him privately after the lecture and asked a number of questions concerning the Prophet, according to the Sheikh. Djem Ali Hamilton became his first convert to Islam, followed closely by Elizabeth Cates in the spring of 1887, who took the name Fatima after her conversion. Abdullah Quilliam never again used direct persuasion to bring people to Islam, although there were public occasions when he would defend the religion against its opponents. However, although Quilliam successfully utilised his Sunday lectures on a number of subjects of topical interest to attract attendees indirectly to Islam, his two publications, the weekly *Crescent* and the monthly *Islamic World*, reveal a more direct approach. M.A. Khan shows that Quilliam wrote extensively on a number of topics, including freemasonry and Islam, asceticism and Sufism, Islam and science, the life of Muhammad, the benefits of polygamy and the *dhimmi* system.[5] His writings reveal a much more direct attack on Christianity, for example in the article entitled 'a full exposure of the fraud of Christianity found in the Islamic World'.[6]

Djem Ali Hamilton often told the story of his conversion, providing insights into the opposition that Quilliam would receive in those early days. He explained that he first went to hear Quilliam lecture on temperance because he had followed his court cases in the newspapers and was curious to hear the famous advocate speak. He describes Quilliam at that time as being, 'a mild looking fair headed man of middle height rather than [having] a fierce tall commanding appearance'. Mr Hamilton walked home with Abdullah Quilliam that night oblivious to the Sheikh's conversion to Islam. They talked about their respective concerns over the Christian doctrine of the Trinity and Quilliam explained that Islam was more logical on the subject of monotheism. Hamilton enquired why Quilliam did not become a Muslim if he was so convinced. Quilliam replied, 'I am a Muslim.' Hamilton explained that the Sheikh seemed so normal that he could see no reason why he could not also become a Muslim. Quilliam warned him of people's ridicule if he made this public. That night Hamilton proclaimed the *shahada* before the Sheikh on the walk home. Quilliam explained that there could not be two witnesses to his conversion, as he was the only Muslim in the country to his knowledge.

It was Djem Ali Hamilton who invited Elizabeth Murray, née Cates, to hear Quilliam lecture. He knew her through her membership of the Good Templar Order in Cheshire. Apparently, at the end of the meeting she enquired, 'I would like to know more of their religion.' He took her to meet the Sheikh, who lent her his Qur'an and henceforth maintained a correspondence with her. These letters formed the basis of his book, *The Faith of Islam*. She describes her meeting with Quilliam as taking place at a Temperance meeting when she was only nineteen. Her account of taking the Sheikh's Qur'an home and reading it is informative of attitudes towards Islam that the early converts would have to deal with:

> I accordingly took it home and commenced carefully reading it. My mother who is a most bigoted Christian, on perceiving this asked me what I was reading. I answered, 'The Muhammedan Bible'. She replied, angrily, 'How dare you read such a vile and wicked book? Give it to me this minute and let me burn it. I will not allow such trash into my house'. I answered, 'No, I will not. How can I know whether it is a wicked book or not until I read it?' She tried to take the book from me, but I escaped to my bedroom and locked myself in, and went on reading what I now consider the most precious book that could be bought.[7]

Elizabeth (or Fatima) Murray's account of reading the Qur'an shows not only her spirited and questioning nature, which was necessary for a young woman to convert to Islam in late Victorian society, but also reveals more about the early converts to Islam. Along with this young woman, they were often from devout Christian families, and indeed were normally devout or practising Christians themselves. Elizabeth Murray asked permission of the Sheikh to attend his meetings. There were only three people present, Abdullah Quilliam, Djem Hamilton and herself, and week-by-week they met and discussed readings from the Qur'an. Her family considered her lost to salvation and engineered a number of 'devices' to prevent her from attending meetings.

Fatima Murray, as she became after her conversion, provides valuable evidence of the early history of the Muslim community in Liverpool. She describes the first meetings at Mount Vernon Street as taking place in a little room, the entrance to which was up a flight of stairs in a side street. Under the cover of darkness, the neighbours would pelt them with stones, eggs and garbage, whilst shouting abuse. She informs us that the next converts were a Mr Wardle and Mr Grundy, but for twelve months she was the only woman who came to the meetings.[8] David Grundy was a minister of the Primitive Methodist Communion before his conversion.

By February 1889, the group of English converts consisted of around twenty members, including Fatima Murray's fiancé; but they would increasingly face hostility from the landlady of Mount Vernon Terrace, who vigorously objected to a group of people who met and denied the Crucifixion on her premises. She felt strongly that this was a slight upon a Christian nation and an act of treachery. It is possible that the landlady of Mount Vernon Street may also have been influenced by the degree of animosity and low level harassment experienced by the fledgling movement. Henri de Léon, writing in *The Crescent* at the time of Fatima Cates' untimely death, wrote that not only were the first Muslim converts pelted with eggs and stones, but that the windows of the small mosque were frequently broken and on many occasions 'ruffians' would enter to disturb the meetings. Horse manure was taken from the road and rubbed into the face of Fatima Cates on more than one occasion. However, she remained steadfast, bringing her husband to Islam along with her two sisters, who both married Muslims from India. De Léon stated that, on her deathbed in 1900, she lifted the index finger of her right hand and slowly but clearly pronounced the *kalima* whilst holding the hand of her Sheikh with her left hand.[9]

The fledgling Muslim community continued to experience periodic violence and desecration even after moving from Mount Vernon Street to 8 Brougham Terrace. As the community grew and

Quilliam attracted publicity in both Liverpool and the national press, public derision was bound to increase. Children in Liverpool were brought up from an early age to be aware of the symbols of their own religious denomination, and to regard adherents of even rival Christian denominations in terms of a series of hostile stereotypes. Attitudes to Islam were influenced by political events in the Empire and the missionary branding of all other religions as 'heathen'. Racism was implicit in Victorian society and had been encouraged by the empire builders. This was a period in which not only Christian racism thrived, but early 'scientific' theories of the superiority of the white races were also devised. Although these were primarily aimed at Africans, Islam would have been perceived as non-Christian and associated with the non-white races. However, the position concerning Muslims was complex. Quilliam allied himself with the Ottoman sultan, who was not popular in Britain because of the charges that were made of atrocities against Christian Armenians. Gwilliam Beckerlegge argues that the experiences of the Liverpool Muslims can be compared to Victorian Catholics, whose loyalty was not to be trusted. He states that the 'profession of the faith of Islam was taken by those hostile to it as indicative of a divided political loyalty'.[10] Eric Germain speaks of an 'anti-Asiatic lobby' who 'presented Islam as irreconcilable with Western standards of civilisation'.[11]

From 1895, when the newly refurbished mosque opened with donations from the Amir of Afghanistan, the building immediately attracted Islamophobic vandalism. This began with stones being thrown at the back windows, scattering glass over the carpet upon which prayers were held. *The Crescent* reported this as the 'work of youth' and not evidence of persecution.[12] However, in June of the same year, a crowd gathered outside the mosque and two more windows were broken.[13] The mob had been attracted by a Muslim wedding between Kerim Buksh of Lahore and Miss Ellen Lena Hallemalden of Stamford Hill, London. This was the seventh marriage between mixed couples to be officiated by Sheikh

Abdullah Quilliam in Liverpool, and such occasions were rare in Victorian England. Very often the couples came from London or further afield where such marriages were not possible.

The vandalism was probably not carried out by committed Christians, but by those who resented marriages of white women to Indian men; however, on 5th November, a number of evangelical Christians, identified by the Muslims as Baptists from the Anfield Road congregation because their tracts prohibited infant baptism, interrupted Quilliam's lecture on the death of Muhammad. They shouted, 'no-one can give pardon but Jesus Christ'; 'by no other name can you be saved'; 'the blood of Jesus cleanses us all from shame'. They also cried, 'this is a den of devils and the gateway to hell'. The attack was reported in the *Liverpool Mercury* and the *Liverpool Courier*.[14]

Such attacks were to continue periodically. They would intensify during periods when Muslims were involved in rebellions against or in opposition to British colonial expansion. In October 1895, after Quilliam had begun publicly to defend the rights of the Ottomans to quell unrest in Armenia, police were called to the mosque to investigate a wire that had been stretched across the entrance at a height that would trip worshippers on their way out. The Sheikh had arrived late for prayer and his walking stick had bumped against the wire, which was measured at ten yards long.[15] In September 1897, police were once again at the mosque. This time they were called to restore public order after the Muslims in the mosque had charged into a hostile crowd, shouting, *'Allahu Akbar'*. The Muslims were defending the mosque against a mob which had tried to occupy the premises on the occasion of the Ottoman Sultan's anniversary of succession. This time the crowd were shouting slogans with a more political theme: 'remember Armenia'; 'Down with the Turks'; and 'to hell with the Muhammadans'.[16]

Later in the same month, whilst Quilliam was delivering a public lecture on the demerits of eating pork in the lecture hall of the Liverpool Muslim Institute, a cry went up, 'I love pig! I love pork!' and black puddings were thrown at the Muslims present. The following week, whilst lecturing on the abuse of alcohol, Quilliam showed a model of a pig made from sausage that had been sent to a mosque labelled 'Turkish Delight'. He reported that anonymous hate mail would often arrive with very abusive language.[17] In October, a firework was exploded in the mosque entrance on a Sunday, again during a lecture by Quilliam. The guards appointed to protect the mosque from such incidents reported that the culprits were the same persons who had thrown the black puddings.[18] The *Liverpool Courier* of the 17th September reported that, 'it is fortunate that nearly all the Muslims present were British, for if many foreign followers of the Islamic faith had been present, they probably would have regarded the silly joke as a deadly insult, as swine flesh is abhorrent to the fervent Muslim.'[19] The paper did not seem to comprehend that English Muslim converts would be equally offended.

The attacks continued into the twentieth century, and in March 1902 on the occasion of Eid al-Adha, some 'ruffians' attempted once again to force their way into the mosque only to be repelled by the worshippers. They then pelted the building with mud and stones, breaking windows and a fanlight. Four Muslim women were hurt by the stones and a visiting journalist was pelted with mud. The mob dispersed when rain began to fall late at night.[20] In 1905 the mosque was twice broken into within a space of two months and the donations were stolen.[21]

Activities such as burglary and robbery may be explained as simply criminal, and there was an element of Liverpool's street crime that was directed against Muslim seamen. In 1898, Quilliam had been called to the Assizes to represent local Muslim sailors after an Arab had been stabbed in Portland Street by a gang of nine 'ruffians'.[22] The robbery of the donations from the children's home established by Quilliam for the city's many unwanted children may also have been the work of common criminals, but there is no doubt that the low-level nuisance campaign directed against Britain's first Muslims was also targeted at the Medina Home for Children.

In September 1897, *The Crescent* ran a feature entitled, 'The Latest Christian Trick', which did not doubt that the incident described was another attack on Islam. The story is as follows:

> A woman goes close to midnight to the Society for the Prevention of Cruelty to Children and pretending to be greatly agitated states that the children are screaming in agony, can be heard across the road and it is feared that brutality is taking place. The woman left without leaving a name or address. The Superintendent-Inspector of the Society secured the assistance of two police officers and entered the home by force to discover the Matron awake and alarmed at the intrusion and the children sleeping in their cots. The police withdrew. The incident attracted a large crowd who surmised that 'a child was being sacrificed to an idol called Mahomet'. The police tried to appease the crowd but some women refused to believe that nothing was happening and accused the police of being bribed. Witness testimony was collected by Quilliam – neither taxi drivers or patrolling constables had heard any screaming.[23]

It is important to note that these disturbances and acts of violence against the fledgling Muslim presence tended to flare up when there was conflict between Britain and various parts of the Muslim world. Quilliam on various occasions defended the Afghans who were popularly perceived as 'Muslim fanatical warriors', threatening the stability of British India, and would continuously use his publications to challenge popular stereotypes that Islam was 'the enemy of science', 'backward', 'warlike', 'fanatical' or opposed to Christian values. Germain contends that these writings were a considerable support to remote and small Muslim minorities in Australia, Canada and New Zealand.[24]

It was never going to be easy to convert men and women to Islam in late nineteenth-century England. Quilliam's motives were initially distrusted even in India, and he had to respond to a negative article in *The Madras Times* in 1897. In his defence, Quilliam published his own short history of the progress of Islam in Britain from 1887 to

1897. He claims that on 16th June 1887, there were no native-born Muslims in Britain; but on 17th June 1887, he had publicly declared himself a Muslim whilst delivering a lecture entitled 'Fanatics and Fanaticism' and had gained his first convert. In July 1887, he had formed the Liverpool Muslim Institute with three members. By the end of the year, there were seven converts meeting at Vernon Hall; a year later, the numbers had risen to twelve. In July 1889, the small group had to leave Vernon Hall and, on 20th December 1889, they gained possession of 8 Brougham Terrace.

In 1889 they only gained two more converts, bringing their total number to fourteen, but Quilliam used some of his financial and intellectual resources to publish the pamphlet *Faith of Islam*. The first edition in July 1889 had two thousand copies, and a further three thousand were published in August 1890. By the end of 1890, the number of worshippers had grown to twenty-seven, but the small community had also experienced its first death. On 1st March, David Grundy, who was originally a Bible Reader for the Christian Home Missions before his conversion, died. But significantly, six of the twenty-seven were described as 'foreign-born' Muslims, which shows that the small group of English converts were attracting the attention of Liverpool's Muslim visitors or receiving Muslims from Arab countries who lived outside Liverpool.

Two more significant events occurred in 1890. In October the fledgling Muslim community successfully organised a protest against the opening of the play *Mahomet*, written by Hall Caine. Hall Caine was a well-known Victorian author and playwright. Born in Runcorn, Cheshire, he was a contemporary of Quilliam, even down to sharing his Manx ancestry, and, like Quilliam, he was a passionate lover of the island and its culture. As an owner of a large Manx property, it is highly possible that the two men would have known each other, especially as Quilliam was a friend of Hall Caine's brother. In many ways they were kindred spirits, but any connection would have ended in 1890 when Caine wrote a play called *Mahomet* in honour of Henry Irving, the famous actor-manager. The play was due to be performed at the Lyceum Theatre in London, which was headed by Irving. In the autumn of 1890, a letter appeared in *The Times* stating:

> Within the last few weeks the news has been spread throughout the length and breadth of the Indian Empire that an English theatrical company intends shortly to represent on the stage in this country a play called 'Mahomet', in which the central character is the prophet of Arabia. The Indian Mussulmans are deeply irritated to learn of the proposed mockery of the prophet on the stage of a country which has pledged itself to respect their religious feelings, and the Queen of which has been destined by Providence to reign over a greater number of Moslems than any single ruler, Mahomedan or Christian, on the surface of the globe. Is it right and proper to hurt the religious feelings of so many of your fellow-subjects in the East, to satisfy the whims or fill the coffers of a theatrical company, however influential it may be?[25]

The letter is signed by Rafiuddin Ahmad, who at the time was the Vice-President of the Liverpool Muslim Association, soon to become the Liverpool Muslim Institute. The letter has the hallmark of Abdullah Quilliam, and it is highly unlikely that Rafiuddin Ahmad would have written such a letter to a national newspaper without the close co-operation of his president. Quilliam often employed the fact that Victoria ruled over millions of Muslims on a number of occasions, and especially in his battles with the British Foreign Office. The lawyer would have realised immediately the advantages of having an Indian Muslim write the letter, and it is possible that he did not want to offend his neighbour on the Isle of Man and fellow Manxman directly by adding his own signature to the letter.

In the summer of 1890, details of the theatre production had appeared in both English and Indian newspapers in India, leading to protests that matched those undertaken against Salman Rushdie's publication of *The Satanic Verses* nearly a century later.

Indian Muslims held public meetings and organised protest marches, petitions and letter writing campaigns. It is tempting to speculate that the news of the production was leaked to India from Liverpool. After the letter to *The Times*, the Secretary of State for India warned the Lord Chamberlain of the possible impact on the stability of India, with its millions of Muslims (this occurred before the separation of India and Pakistan). The Lord Chamberlain wrote to Henry Irving and recommended that the production of the play be halted. The intervention of the Lord Chamberlain represented a change in government policy, as previous plays on Muhammad had run in London in the eighteenth and early nineteenth centuries and been very popular.[26]

On 7th December 1890, the Liverpool Muslims received a letter of support from Abdul Hamid Khan II, the Sultan of Turkey, the leader of the Ottoman Empire and the inheritor of the ancient Caliphate of Islam. It is probable that the Hall Caine affair had brought the small community to the Sultan's attention. In the letter, the Caliph recognised the efforts of Quilliam and the British Muslims in promoting Islam to the English nation. It is hard to assess the impact of this official recognition on the small group, but it must have given them inspiration and encouragement to be recognised by such a significant Muslim leader, and there is no doubt that Quilliam would go on to give his complete loyalty and personal service to the Caliph.

1891 saw further growth and recognition of the Liverpool Muslims. In February 1891, Quilliam performed the first public Muslim funeral in Liverpool and he followed this up in April with the first public Muslim marriage ceremony. Although both events attracted some public expressions of anti-Muslim or racist protest, the newspaper publicity, carefully harnessed by Quilliam's own skills as a journalist and the editors' desire not to be seen as overly negative towards a prominent lawyer and a member of Liverpool's upper class, disseminated the activities of the group to a wider audience. In April, Quilliam and his eldest son, Robert Ahmed, were invited to Constantinople at the special invitation of the Sultan. They both stayed at the Yildiz Palace for over a month. Abdullah Quilliam was pressed by the Sultan to accept various Ottoman decorations and honours, but declined; however, his son was given the title Bey and was appointed Bim-Bashi (Lieutenant-Colonel) in the Ertoghroul, the elite regiment of the Turkish army. Quilliam was given a solid gold cigarette case with the imperial monogram set in jewels. On his return to Liverpool, the Muslim boys school was opened at Brougham Terrace. By the end of the year, there were fifty converts and a further eight foreign Muslims had affiliated themselves to the group. Among the fifteen converts made that year, there was an Anglican clergyman, the Rev. H.H. Johnson. Another three of the first converts died.

By January 1892, Quilliam's travels to the Orient had attracted enough attention for him to be invited by the Liverpool Corporation to give a series of lectures on his visits to Morocco and Constantinople. In November, he was invited for the same purpose to speak to the Manchester Geographical Society. He always used these opportunities to praise the virtues of the Ottoman civilisation. By April of the same year, his efforts to promote Islam had become successful enough for him to print twenty thousand copies of *Faith in Islam*. In May, the mosque was visited by Dr. Blyden, the well-known Minister-Plenipotentiary of Liberia, and in October, by His Excellency Hakki Bey, the Imperial Commissioner for the Ottoman Government and their official representative to the Chicago Exhibition, who was en route to the USA. Hakki Bey arrived at Central Station, Liverpool, where he was met by Quilliam and Loutfi Bey, the Ottoman Consul General to Liverpool. A reception was held to introduce Hakki Bey to the Turkish subjects in Liverpool and a visit to the mosque was arranged. This visit by a high profile Ottoman official began a pattern whereby high status or upper-class Muslim visitors to Liverpool were always invited to visit the mosque, received an official reception in the evening and were often invited to Quilliam's home in Fairfields for dinner. The tour would come to include the school, the orphanage and the printing press, and later even the site chosen for the construction of a purpose-built mosque. Visitors would also sometimes be asked to lead prayers, give a lecture or deliver the *khutba* on a Friday.

In August, the British Muslims received the first of their significant donations from abroad. The Muslim community in Rangoon sent them £1000, and the money was used to purchase some of the equity in the properties at 11 and 12 Brougham Terrace. This was followed by a £400 donation from Sierra Leone. In addition, Pir Mahomad Allarakia of India was able to collect enough donations to pay for a printing works, which was housed in 12 Brougham Terrace. 1892 was to be the most successful year so far for the fledgling community, bringing them thirty-three new converts and increasing their numbers to eighty-three, with six more deaths to deal with.

In January 1893, the printing press paid for by the Indian donations was up and running and Abdullah Quilliam was able to expand his activities. He decided to publish a weekly newspaper and a quarterly journal dedicated to articles on Islam. The first edition of *The Crescent* was published at the beginning of the year followed in July by the first edition of *The Islamic World*. In February, Quilliam once again visited Morocco. He was seen off at Lime Street Station by the Turkish Consul and the Stipendiary Magistrate of the city who, although he found it difficult to accept Quilliam's religious convictions, had declared publicly that there was no solicitor 'who stood higher in his court for probity and honesty'.[27] The respect with which Quilliam was held in the legal profession was confirmed around this time by his appointment as Commissioner of Oaths. The newspaper headlines in the city declared, 'An Appointment by the Lord High Chancellor to an English Moslem'.

Quilliam was seen off at the Royal Albert Docks by four prominent London Muslims, including the convert Obeid-Ullah Cunliffe,[28] whose funeral the Sheikh would tragically carry out on his return, and two Indian Muslims, Imam Barakatullah and

Sheikh Fazil ud-deen Ahmed. The first of these would join Quilliam the following year and become the imam of the Liverpool Mosque. Quilliam sailed on the P & O steamship Arcadia at 1pm. By 10pm he had written a letter to the Muslims in Liverpool, conveyed to shore by the pilot. He stated that he was the only Muslim on board and that his fellow passengers were either returning to Australia or were military officers. Missing Muslim company as the time of Maghrib prayer approached, he walked below decks wearing his fez to be discovered by forty Muslim crewmembers. He led them in prayer and they called him Abdullah Sahib. No more news was possible until the ship docked in Gibraltar. In fact, the Liverpool Muslims were to hear very little until their Sheikh returned two months later in April.[29]

His travels to Spain and Morocco further enhanced Quilliam's reputation amongst both Muslims and non-Muslims. Whilst in Morocco he had been appointed an honorary 'alim from a madrasa in Fez by the Sultan and had explored the country. He was to publish a series of articles entitled 'Rambles in Andalucia', which he used to promote the history of Muslim Spain and its tolerant, multicultural society to the British public. The articles would also become a regular feature of his Sunday lectures in the Liverpool Muslim Institute. In addition, he lectured publicly on the Christian missions in Morocco. On the 2nd April, The Crescent reprinted an article from The Levant Herald entitled, 'Morocco and the Moors', focusing on the supposed inaccessibility of entry to remote parts of the country, in which Quilliam described visits to the cities of Zarhoun and Wazan.[30] The Liverpool Mercury, Review and Courier all reported his return to Liverpool.[31] In September, the mosque was visited by prominent Arabs from Makka. By the end of the year, the numbers of converts had expanded to one hundred, with eight deaths.

On 25th February 1894, the body of Obeid-Ullah Cunliffe, the author of The Disintegration of Christianity, was brought to Liverpool for Quilliam to perform the Muslim funeral. However, and more significantly, Quilliam's visits to Constantinople and his contact with the Sultan brought unexpected rewards. In July, the Sultan requested Quilliam to act on his behalf in Lagos, West Africa, at the opening of a new mosque built by the efforts of Mahomad Shitta Bey for the princely sum of £7000. The Caliph of the Muslim world requested Quilliam to take a decoration for the Bey in honour of his efforts on behalf of Islam. Quilliam recounts this journey in an article written in 1898. He writes:

> A pious Muslim named Muhammad Shitta, who had amassed a large fortune in the ivory trade, had at the expense of some 5,000 pounds, erected a handsome mosque at Lagos and was about to present it to the Muslim community there. His Imperial Majesty the Sultan of Turkey having heard of the labours of the pious Muhammad Shitta bestowed upon him the decoration of the Medjidieh, and the title of Bey of the Ottoman Empire, and I was invited to be the bearer of the decoration and the brevet which accompanied it to Lagos and to be present at the formal consecration and opening of the mosque. I consented, and in June, 1894, I embarked upon the *SS Cabenda*, one of the vessels of Elder, Dempster's splendid African fleet, and set sail for Lagos.[32]

Quilliam's visit to West Africa also developed his lifelong friendship and correspondence with Mahomad Sanusi, an interpreter for the Sierra Leone government who presided as chairman at Quilliam's first lecture in Wilberforce Hall, Freetown.

It was unlikely that Quilliam would have underestimated the significance of this journey because it was the first official representation that he undertook on behalf of the Sultan and coincided with the official appointment and confirmation of Abdullah Quilliam as the Sheikh al-Islam of Britain, a position further endorsed by the Amir of Afghanistan. This formal title endorsed by two important Muslim rulers would be recognised by the British establishment, and it provided Quilliam with the legitimacy to claim leadership of all the Muslims in Britain and to represent their interests. The position of Sheikh al-Islam has never been held by anyone else since and Quilliam thus holds a unique status in the annals of Islam in Britain. Quilliam stayed in Africa for several months, visiting the Canaries, Senegambia, the Gambia, Sierra Leone, Liberia, the Gold Coast and Lagos.[33] In honour of his appointment as Sheikh al-Islam, the Muslims of Ceylon sent Quilliam a turban brooch with the letters *as-salam 'alaykum* in Arabic characters picked out with 177 pearls. The awards and gifts were to provide the Sheikh with a platform of credibility, authority and acceptance across the Muslim world.

The Sheikh contracted malaria in West Africa and was seriously ill in September 1894. Malaria troubled him throughout the remainder of his life. In spite of his illness, the year was remarkable despite the fact that there were only six converts and ten deaths, which meant that the overall numbers of the community were slightly down on the previous year. The lack of converts probably reflected Quilliam's absence from Liverpool and the period of his illness. This highlighted a problem for the groving community, in that it depended very heavily on the ability of one man to attract converts.

Quilliam's success at creating a Muslim community in Britain and his rising stock with the Ottoman Sultan and last Caliph of Islam did not pass unnoticed in the Muslim world, especially in those nations where the authority of the Caliph was acknowledged and respected. 1895 was to be a turning point for the small but expanding Muslim community. In July, the Shahzade of Afghanistan, Prince Nasrullah Khan, visited the mosque bringing with him a gift of £2500 from his father Abdur Rahman Khan, the Amir and ruler of the nation. The money was given without conditions and it is said that Quilliam rejected the idea of receiving it as a personal gift and turned it over to the Institute as a donation, stating that it was a 'sacred trust for the establishment of Islam on a permanent footing in this country'.[34] The Liverpool Muslim Institute was able to purchase 8 Brougham Terrace and pay off

The interior of the mosque at the Liverpool Muslim Institute, showing
the Ottoman-style arches designed by the local converts.

the mortgages on 11 and 12 Brougham Terrace. The substantial
donation meant that major alterations could take place, including
redecorating and redesigning the mosque on traditional Ottoman
lines, rebuilding the lecture hall and constructing a large hall for
special occasions such as the celebration of Muslim festivals. In
addition, a playground was provided at the school complete with
swings and latrines, accommodation was created for the Imam and
a khan (hostel) was built for destitute Muslim sailors and other
visitors. Adjacent to the mosque there was a *wudu'* (ritual washing)
area with lavatories and a retiring area for women, also with its
own toilet facilities. The school was equipped with photographic,
chemistry, electrical and metallurgical laboratories.[35]

A plaque in the lecture hall announced that it was reconstructed
in November 1895 at the expense of the Shahzade, but also reveals
that two of the English converts, John H. McGovern (FLAS) and
Abdur-Rahman Holehouse were highly involved in the project
as architect and clerk of the works respectively.[36] John McGovern

also designed the Moorish arches in the mosque. The decoration of the mosque was supervised by Billal Quilliam Bey, T. Abu Bekr Barker, Djem Whitwell, Arabi Whitwell and Hassan Radford. Another inscription in gold letters in both English and Arabic was placed at the front of the mosque with the following dates in the English and Muslim calendars: when Islam was first preached in England; the move to the new premises; the visit of the Shahzade; the munificence of the Amir; and the reconstruction of the lecture hall.[37] Photographs taken at the time show a mosque whose interior was typically Ottoman, and indeed many of the artefacts and objects it contained were given as gifts by the Sultan or other high officials at Yildiz.

By the end of 1895, the number of converts had increased to one hundred and twenty-one, with four more deaths, and Quilliam had been able to announce officially the opening of the mosque and the Liverpool Muslim Institute on the 4th December. Present at the opening were His Excellency M. Kamil Bey (Ottoman Consul-General, Liverpool), R. Ahmed Quilliam Bey (Quilliam's eldest son and Chancellor to the Ottoman Consulate of Liverpool), Professors H. Nasrullah Warren and H. Haschem Wilde, Billal Quilliam Bey, J. Bokhari Jeffery, Djemel-ud-deen Rankin, T. Emin Lawrenson, H. Meyer, John Chapman and many other Muslim converts.

From the very beginning, Quilliam had been keen that the Muslim presence in Liverpool should provide educational facilities. His reasons for this were straightforward. He wanted to demonstrate that Islam was a religion of reason that had always encouraged education and that there was no contradiction between Islam and the developing Western knowledge in science and technology; he also wanted to provide a school for the children of converts that would permit Muslim parents to avoid the 'vices of so-called Western civilisation', and he was pragmatic enough to be aware that there was a demand from Muslim nations and populations abroad to educate their children in the heart of the British Empire. The prospectus for the school advertised a high-class English education to the children of Muslim parents, in which the activities of Christian missionaries could be avoided. The prospectus went on to list some of the advantages for Muslim parents, including boarding with fellow Muslims, specially prepared food and a mosque for prayers, all of which remain concerns for Muslims in Britain today. The curriculum included French, German, Latin, the Classics, Mathematics, Arabic, Turkish and Persian. Quilliam points out that Liverpool possessed a fine university college at which degrees in Natural Science, Logic, Law and Medicine could be obtained for successful students from the school.[38]

In 1896 Abdullah Quilliam made a major decision to open a Muslim home for unwanted children. In December 1895, the idea of the Medina Home had been established at the Annual General Meeting. The home for young children had been discussed by the Committee of the Liverpool Muslim Institute as another means to promote Islamic principles in Britain. The Sheikh had recounted an incident at the Annual General Meeting in 1895 in his annual President's report of a Jewish woman who had offered him her child in the street. The mother had asked him if it was true that a Muslim would be prepared to adopt a child as long as it was brought up in the faith, and had apparently offered him a sum of money. Quilliam had reflected on this incident in the light of a number of infamous cases where such homes had been established by unscrupulous women for profit and where children had been severely abused. He had decided to adopt the child and had renamed him Ishmael. However, personally rescuing one child in distress led him to consider the overall problem of unwanted infants. He was aware that mothers often wished to keep their children, but could not find work while caring for them. He proposed a place of reception, maintenance and education for such children and suggested initially a small farm on the Isle of Man so that they could be kept away from the corrupting influences of the city.

Quilliam blamed the laws of monogamy for the daily occurrence of the seduction of women and the birth of illegitimate children.

He cited two hundred cases that had come to the Liverpool courts for orders of affiliation and estimated that around two thousand such children were born in Liverpool each year. He argued persuasively that a Muslim children's home would provide a check against infanticide and that mothers would have an opportunity to retrieve their good character, something they could not do under the existing requirements of Christian establishments, which insisted that fathers had to be deceased to permit entry.

Opened at the new premises on 12 Brougham Terrace, the Medina Home was the fulfilment of these earlier plans. The conditions were that the children would receive Muslim names and the parents would remove all claims to the child and give their consent for the child to be brought up as a Muslim. Quilliam proposed that the children would not wear a uniform, but that the boys would wear fez caps. In his annual address he referred to such children as the vanguard of Janissaries in the Western world.[39] The home opened with three children in January 1896. The first child brought to the home was a boy aged four months, followed by Walter (aged 3) and Joseph (aged 4), whose mother had died and whose father had not been able to secure lodgings because landladies objected to small children remaining in the house whilst he worked. The parents agreed to pay five shillings per week and were permitted to visit on Sundays. By the end of the year, seven children had been admitted, including a newborn baby girl. In addition to the children, who were never counted as Muslims because of their age, that year there were twenty new converts and a further five deaths.[40]

By the end of 1896, Quilliam had found and perfected the method through which he would promote Islam in Liverpool and beyond. The mosque provided the centre for worship and was renowned across the Muslim world as a centre for the spread of Islam in one of the most important locations of the British Empire. Quilliam was able to draw upon his official status as Sheikh al-Islam to promote his activities, and was able to reach out to the Muslim world through the weekly *Crescent* and the monthly *Islamic World*. The first was a newspaper that carried any news from across the globe that might be of interest to a Muslim reader, while the latter was produced in the style of an academic journal. Quilliam's previous experience as a journalist and editor was drawn upon heavily. In addition, he continued to lecture both in Liverpool and nationally on a number of diverse topics through which he was able to develop his profile as an erudite Muslim public speaker. The end of year report on the activities of the Liverpool Muslim Institute shows that fifty-six lectures were delivered by the society, of which thirty-one were given by Quilliam as Sunday lectures. He also gave regular lectures to the Liverpool Manx Society, to various Temperance Societies in Birkenhead and Liverpool and to the Liverpool Geographical Society.[41]

The printing press provided the means to publish his various writings and lectures on Islam, but he avoided direct proselytising after his early experiences of confrontation and negative labelling. He chose a more indirect route that arose from his experience of reaching his first two converts through temperance lectures, which were fully part and parcel of urban Victorian social and cultural life. I have already mentioned that the school was equipped with photography and science laboratories. In addition to the latest science and technology being taught at the Muslim schools (to boys and girls), evening educational classes taught photography and photometry, chemistry and electricity, astronomy and geology, drawing (freehand and architectural), construction, shorthand, French and Oriental languages. The subjects that were taught say something about the expertise of the converts and the social class from which many of them were drawn, but by teaching these subjects in the evenings they were able to attract to the Institute members of the lower middle-classes, both male and female, who wished to improve themselves after working hours.[42] There was also a Young Men's Literary and Debating Society, which catered to another popular pastime amongst Victorian young men who wanted to develop themselves by learning the skills of the classes above them. None of these activities made direct attempts to convert the students to Islam, but each created an environment in which Muslims and non-Muslims freely mixed with each other, which helped to diminish the popular prejudices against Islam that it was an exotic religion with a bad press.

However, the users of these facilities knew where they were. The flags that flew from the windows and the roof displayed the symbols of Islam and their teachers wore the Turkish-style fez. An advertisement placed in *The Crescent* each week for the Liverpool Muslim Institute and its schools reveals the way that Quilliam presented the group's activities. It stated that:

> All Moslems are eligible to membership and to the privileges of the Institution. The Mosque is open every day for prayers. Jumma and Namaz every Friday. Reading Room, Library and Museum open daily.
>
> Public lectures, which strangers are invited to attend, every Sunday evening at 7pm. Explanatory works on Islam can be found at the Mosque.

This information made it clear that the central activity was Muslim worship, and Muslims would have been in no doubt that they had found Liverpool's world-renowned Islamic centre. However, the second paragraph confirmed that the Sunday lecture was open to all. If anyone wanted to find out more about Islam, they were referred back to the mosque. The celebrated Sunday lectures were usually delivered by Quilliam, although if he were away, another prominent convert or one of Quilliam's two eldest sons would stand in. Sometimes visiting lecturers were invited. More often than not, these represented other religious convictions of interest to Victor-ians, such as spiritualists, Mormons or Theosophists. Quilliam's lectures were usually scientific or cultural in nature. He would speak on Geology, History and Comparative Religion, or would deliver travelogues based on his journeys to exotic locations. Islam was introduced indirectly. Yet it was here at these lectures that the conversions took place. *The Crescent* keeps an account of those who formerly embraced Islam and the Liverpool Muslim Institute maintained a new members' list. The typical pattern for conversion was regular attendance for some weeks at the Sunday lecture, followed by a request to convert. A formal ceremony of witnessing (*shahada*) was then held at the mosque, in which the Sheikh would bestow a Muslim name and provide basic instructions on the daily life of a Muslim.

The Sheikh's subtle method of introducing Islam, by drawing upon the Victorian thirst for knowledge, was consciously acknowledged in the aims of the evening classes:

1. To do good to all, irrespective of gender, creed, race or nationality (Cardinal principle of Islam).
2. To demonstrate that Islam is the partner not the enemy of science, literature and art.
3. To widen the sphere of influence and remove prejudice.
4. To induce those who join the classes to take an interest in the Institution – to see what kind of people we are, to cultivate the spirit of enquiry.
5. From the study of science, natural history and languages, they might be brought to think of the All-Powerful One.

In a discussion with the Young Men's Literary Society at the mosque, Quilliam spoke about promoting Islam in the West and argued that there needed to be three emphases: firstly, the Unitarian doctrines of Islam; secondly, that Islam was a religion of reason compared with Christianity; and thirdly, there should be a focus on the ethical principles contained in the teaching of Muhammad.[43] This approach to the promotion of Islam was to remain the central strategy for the successful London group of converts who gathered at the Woking Mosque in the first decades of the twentieth century.

In addition to the Sunday lecture that was open to all, there was a form of congregational worship that was described in an article published by the *Christian Monthly* entitled, 'A Sunday with the Muslims', as part of the series 'The Sunday at Home'. The article states that, at Brougham Terrace, 'visitors will find a house bearing conspicuously on its front the Mohammadan symbols – the golden star and crescent. Here daily at noon, and at other hours, the muezzin of the Mosque calls the followers of the Prophet to prayers, using the balcony instead of a minaret to deliver the summons.' The article also goes on describe the gatherings that took place on Sunday evenings at 7pm, in which 'the proceedings are of a more congregational character' with the delivery of an address and the singing of hymns. The hymns were collected in a book compiled by Quilliam and entitled *Hymns suitable for English-Speaking Muslim Congregations*. The journalist notes that many were traditional hymns written by Wesley, Watts, Doddridge, Cowper and Bonar, but these had been adapted to bring them theologically in line with the Muslim understanding of the unity of God (*tawhid*). He quotes, for example, the famous chorus of the well-known hymn, 'Abide with me. In life, in death, Allah abides with me!'[44] He noted that the English Muslims appear to be in the hands of 'leaders remarkably susceptible to Western and Christian culture', but this innovation did not compromise the fact that Friday rather than Sunday is significant to Muslims, and on that day the service is entirely in Arabic and the attendance is confined to Muslims.

The article finished by noting that the mosque was frequently visited by distinguished 'Asiatics' during their temporary stays in England. Not all of these culturally influenced Muslims were at ease with Quilliam's Sunday innovations, and in his address to the 1896 Annual Meeting he answered the criticism made in some Muslim quarters that there was an organ kept in the mosque. He began by denying categorically that there was any such musical instrument in the mosque and that nothing happened in the place of worship that would offend an orthodox Hanafi Muslim. He referred to the Sunday meetings as a means of propagation devised by him in 1887, and not considered by him to be a Muslim religious service or substitution for regular prayers. He described these occasions as Muslim missionary meetings that were held in the lecture hall rather than the mosque. In his words, they are explanatory lectures on some aspects of Islam and, as most of the people attending were Christians and accustomed to a certain form of service, 'consequently in order to make them feel at home at our missionary meetings we held a service something like the ones they had been accustomed to in the "days of their ignorance"'.

The order of the Sunday meeting was described as a rendering of the *fatiha* (the opening chapter of the Qur'an), another recitation of a portion of the Qur'an, hymn singing from the songs adapted by Quilliam and a lecture on Islamic doctrine or history. He justified their existence by the fact that there were 150 new converts to the faith, most of whom had attended the Sunday events, and that Islam in Liverpool was now respected and honoured by many who had previously considered it a bloodthirsty, heathen faith.

In addition to the Sunday lectures and the evening classes, the converts also enjoyed a social life with each other that would have been typical of the period. For example, every summer they had a picnic at Raby Mere near Bromborough in Cheshire. They travelled together by the newly-opened Mersey metro railway, which took them under the Mersey. Together they walked, boated, fished and mused on nature. They played games and competed in sports together. The children went pony riding and, when hungry, they all enjoyed a picnic next to the mill house consisting of cold beef and tongue, pickles and tomatoes, cucumber, preserved pineapples, peaches, pears, strawberries and cakes of various kinds. The young people took the opportunity to court each other, 'standing around as couples and watching the scenery'. Quilliam notes that, 'we forgive them, we have been young ourselves'.[45] They then returned to Liverpool laden with flowers and fruit that they had picked. The picnic was to become a treasured annual event along with the Muslim festivals of Eid, the *mawlid* and the high-profile celebration of Christmas when the Muslim community fed the city's poor.

The content of the 1896 Presidential address also revealed something about the processes and the constituency of conversion. Quilliam commented on the high death rate of the converts and noted that a number of elderly people had embraced the faith in the early days at Mount Vernon Street, but he observed that there were now younger people, married couples and children of the converts who attended the Muslim schools.[46] He also mentioned that there were a number of motivations for conversion, some of which he considered to be suspect. He defined these as the curious, the lovers of novelty, the faddist, those who seek personal gain thinking that there is money to be made out of it, and those who see conversion as a stepladder to fame. However, he wryly commented that the difficulties of adverse publicity and social ridicule have sorted out the genuine converts from the above categories and praised the converts for their courage in adversity. He wrote that, 'English Muslims have adopted the faith not for personal advantage but because they believe it to be true, and the world will then know how to appreciate these courageous men and women who have boldly made a stand for truth.'

The Crescent maintained a record of the converts on a weekly basis. From this, the social constituency of the converts can be ascertained. A number of them were professional men, such as Hasan Arculli, Professor Nasrullah Warren and Professor Haschem Wilde, who taught at the schools; then there was Yehya-en-Nasr Parkinson, a well-known Victorian poet, Walid F. Preston, a well-known artist with a national reputation, and Resched P. Stanley, a magistrate who had been the Mayor of Staleybridge. There were also representatives of Liverpool's famed crafts and trades, but many were young male clerks. The most common superior status employment in Liverpool was clerical, with an estimated 17,400 clerks employed on Merseyside in 1870. Their status was, however, uncertain, and Muir notes that profound fears burdened their lives at home and at work.[47] They were suffocated by conventions of 'respectability'. As a class they were downtrodden, often working in cold, cramped,

ill-lit and unsanitary offices.[48] Waller notes that the conditions of
a clerk's life usually rendered him conventional, respectable, timid
and unadventurous. He states that their 'work does not encourage,
but rather represses, individuality and openness of mind'.[49] This
would hardly seem a promising group from which to gain converts,
but these young men desired above all to ape their social super-
iors, and societies had sprung up to promote literature and the
arts alongside voluntary associations geared to the education and
recreation of young clerks attempting to become 'Liverpool gentlemen'. Quilliam's lectures and other cultural activities would have
attracted some of these, but above all there was the social equality
of the converts that allowed the clerks to rub shoulders with men
such as Quilliam and others from Liverpool's social elite.

In July 1897, contact between Sheikh Abdullah Quilliam and the
Ottoman court was strengthened by the official visit to the mosque
of His Excellency General Mahomed Feridoun Bey of the Imperial Ministry of Foreign Affairs and Minister Plenipotentiary of the
Sultan. As was customary, the VIP guest attended Zuhr prayers. He
was visiting England on the occasion of Queen Victoria's Jubilee. By
now, Quilliam was established enough in the city of Liverpool that
he was nearly always chosen to receive such visitors and introduce
them to local dignitaries. The evening visit from the Sheikh's home
to the mosque took place in an open carriage with Quilliam and his
wife. These regular high status visits brought the mosque and its
community into the civic life of the city, and with this came official
acceptance.[50] Mr and Mrs Quilliam were invited to most civic
engagements in the city and each year were guests at the Mayor's
annual banquet. In addition, the appointment of Quilliam as an
official at the city's Turkish Consulate and the acceptance of his
title by Queen Victoria would have assisted in him gaining respectability.[51] He had even won over the media. At the Annual General
Meeting in 1897, he referred to media criticism and complimented
the secular press for their fair coverage, except for the 'convenient
bogey – the Armenian Question'.[52] On the other hand, he accused

the Christian press of being 'intolerant, mendacious and unfair'.[53] The *Christian Soldier* had, for example, declared that all the converts were bound for hell. By 1897, Quilliam's influence in the city was certainly sufficient to apply pressure on the owners of the Liverpool local satirical paper, *The Porcupine*, for printing a series of articles that Quilliam described as a 'tirade of low vulgar abuse'.[54] As a consequence of his complaints, a new editor and editorial staff were appointed and the paper changed its tone towards him.[55] Quilliam's standard response to negative press was to go on the attack, usually through the medium of his publications or through letters to the papers concerned.

By 1896, the circulation of *The Crescent* was large enough to bring the Liverpool Muslims into contact with communities around the world, especially those where the religion existed as a minority and where devout individuals were struggling to propagate the faith. Requests for copies of the weekly paper were received, along with letters from Muslims from around the globe. Quilliam received information regarding the promotion of Islam to non-Muslims from Europe, Australia, Canada and the USA. For example, Quilliam received a letter from a Musa Khan in Australia, one of a number of Afghan Muslims struggling to make an impression on the European settlers, who had succeeded in securing a few converts in Melbourne. The letter from Musa Khan claimed that there were 300 Muslims in Victoria, and he sought back issues of *The Crescent* and *Islamic World*.[56]

By the end of 1897, eleven new converts had brought the membership of the Liverpool Muslim Institute to 152. Quilliam had performed the funerals of seventeen deceased members and had carried out twelve Muslim marriages. The Muslim community boasted 53 children, including ten in the Medina Home. The community was also expanding beyond the confines of Liverpool. *The Crescent* published a letter from Forfar in Scotland, in which the writer asked how he should convert to Islam after reading Quilliam's *The Faith of Islam* and Sale's translation of the Qur'an.[57] The same edition reports a Scottish convert from Lanarkshire, who was a fitter by trade and was formerly stationed in the Manchester Regiment in India. He had spoken to many Muslims in Awadh and later in Egypt, and was struck by their absence of drunkenness and their sincerity. He travelled from Glasgow to be formally admitted into the faith by the Sheikh.[58] In December, two new Muslims, a journalist and a machinist from Forfar, formally became members of the Liverpool Muslim Institute after conversion.[59] In addition, twenty-four members of the Liverpool Muslim Institute had moved abroad and were active in promoting Islam in their new places of residence. Several others had moved to other parts of Britain and were active in bringing Islam to those around them.

The Crescent of 13th October carried a lecture delivered by Quilliam to the Cambridge Literary Society on the Life and Teachings of Mahomed. A contingent of English Muslims had attended the lecture dressed in Turkish Fez caps and carrying Islamic banners. Quilliam stated that, 'Islam has no sympathy with idleness or begging; it is essentially a faith which inculcates the doctrine of the dignity of labour and the necessity of self-reliance and industry.'[60] He quotes the Prophet as saying, 'God is gracious to him who earns his living by his own labour and not by begging. He who is able and fit and does not work for himself or for others, God is not gracious to him.' This is a very good example of how Quilliam was able to communicate the teachings of Islam in line with the key values of the day. The lecture drew criticism from Christian journals and papers, and Quilliam's response was typical of his aggressive approach to Christian critics: 'The fruits of Christianity are public-houses at the corners of every street, drunkenness, gambling, and prostitution rampant throughout the land, and gambling in the form of raffles being part of every church bazaar. The whole bench of Bishops in the House of Lords voted against the abolition of slavery, opposed the introduction of railways, and at one time denounced teetotal-ism as being a form of atheism.'[61]

One curious feature of 1897 was the creation of the Osmanli Regiment: a number of boys and youths of the Liverpool Muslim

Institute were organised into a band of Muslim soldiers. A few adult members formed an organising committee under the leadership of Quilliam. The first drill was conducted by Ali Hasan McPherson, formerly a sergeant instructor in the British Army. *The Crescent* reported a second drill carried out by the new convert Cassim Loader. The officers of the regiment included Quilliam as Colonel, Billal Wilkins (Lieutenant Colonel) and Ahmed Quilliam as Captain. Billal Quilliam was a non-commissioned officer.[62] They drilled regularly on Monday evenings. There is no mention of the purpose of the regiment and the Liverpool media make strangely little of it, reporting it only as a form of Muslim Boys Brigade. It is safe to hazard a guess that Quilliam had created the regiment to protect against the continuous low-level harassment at the mosque, although he would also have been aware of the militarization of Britain's youth, the founding of boy's regiments and the justification of character building.

The year 1898 began with the promise of success. On the 9th of January, eight people chose to convert to Islam on the same evening. Quilliam had been lecturing on the topic of 'heroes', in which he recounted the deeds and qualities of great men and women. He had included a eulogy to Muhammad, and at the end of the lecture five women and three men, all from Liverpool except one from Seacombe, Cheshire, requested to embrace Islam. This was the largest number of people to accept Islam on one occasion. The recognition and acceptance of Quilliam's activities amongst the official bodies of the city was confirmed by the Lord Mayor's formal civic visit to the mosque as part of the celebration of Eid al-Fitr. Quilliam felt confident enough to form the Osmanli Regiment, described by him as the 'Janissaries of Britain, to protect the fledgling community against racism and anti-Islam activities'. On this occasion, they formed an official escort for the Mayor and performed a grand parade and march past consisting of thirty members. *The Crescent* reported that they formed squares and drilled with swords.[63]

The architect's plans for the unrealized Jami'a Masjid that Quilliam
planned to build near West Derby Road in Liverpool.

Perhaps the most significant sign that confidence was high
can be found in Quilliam's plans to erect a 'Cathedral Mosque' in
Liverpool. The plans for the mosque, as described by the Sheikh,
revealed a 'Saracenic' style of architecture. The costs were estimated
at £6000, and it was agreed that Quilliam would show the plans to
the Sultan and seek his financial assistance during his forthcoming
visit to Constantinople. The Liverpool media described the mosque
as having room for 1,500 worshippers, while the building included
minarets. It was to be located in Marsden Street and Baker Street
on the site of 11 and 12 Brougham Terrace, would contain a gallery
for the exclusive use of women and would provide space for a
khan and a printing works. The flat roof was to be crowned by an
oriental dome. The paper also reported that a domed tomb would
be reserved in the courtyard for the Sheikh and his family, but this
was vigorously denied by Quilliam.[64]

1899 arrived with new challenges for the Liverpool Muslim community. The first would concern the burial of the Muslim dead. The city authorities had closed the Necropolis for sanitary reasons due to the immense growth of Liverpool's population. For a period of forty years, Muslims had been buried in the cemetery and the Liverpool Muslim Institute had used the site for burials since 1888. Although actively seeking a new site, the new land would have to be purchased and this would need to be outside the city because of the rising costs of inner city real estate. Most of the burials were of Indian sailors, and Quilliam considered that Indian Muslims should bear the brunt of the costs of burying their compatriots. However, Indian Muslims had been less generous to Quilliam than the Ottomans, possibly because of Quilliam's criticisms of their overall lack of loyalty to the Ottoman caliph and suspicions concerning the use of donations that were collected by various people claiming to be Quilliam's agents in India. The problems of financing the activities of the Liverpool Muslim Institute, especially printing costs, were growing. The members had long been concerned that it was deeply unsatisfactory for the Sheikh to pay so much out of his own pocket towards the costs of promoting Islam in Britain.[65] However, the propagation of Islam continued to go well, and the century closed with thirty-two new Muslims becoming members of the Liverpool Muslim Institute.

Quilliams' reputation was soaring in other domains, and at the beginning of the year he had been chosen as one of the four representatives of 'exiled' Manxmen to address an audience of two thousand Isle of Man migrants in Liverpool and Merseyside, held at St. George's Hall and with Mayor William Oalton presiding.[66] However, in spite of these moments of respectability, the twentieth century ended with Quilliam finding himself increasingly distressed with British foreign policy and the number of conflicts occurring in the Muslim world involving British occupying forces.

In the final years of the nineteenth century, his response became notably more aggressive towards the non-Muslim world's relationships with Islam and towards Christianity in particular. It could be argued that the Sheikh was on the offensive. He had not only issued a number of fatwas or religious rulings condemning various actions by British military forces, but the Muslim Liverpool Institute had also petitioned Parliament. On the 3rd of May, Quilliam launched a ferocious attack on Christianity after the Reverend Parker had insulted the Caliph by referring to him as 'the great assassin'. Parker's article had been written on the anniversary of Cromwell's death, and Quilliam reminded the clergyman that Christians had exhumed Cromwell. He went on to mention the sectarian deaths at Tyburn, the Christian support of the slave trade and the continuing mistreatment of 'Negroes' in the USA. He declared that, at the end of the nineteenth century, Christianity was in a decadent and debased condition, and its demise was imminent. He refuted the condemnation of Muslim law as backward and declared that the punishments inflicted in England upon members of Christian sects and petty criminals compared very unfavourably with Islamic law through the ages.[67]

The struggles with the British media and the energy he expended on challenging British foreign policy took their toll on the Sheikh's health. In March he came down with quinsy, an infection arising from acute tonsillitis, and two weeks later he had developed rheumatic gout and could only walk with the aid of a stick. He went to Italy and France with the family to convalesce.[68] By June he had returned to Britain fully recovered, and he continued to urge Muslims to seek closer union with each other in order to resolve problems around the world. Not all agreed with his stance in this. In August, the *Madras Mail* complained that *The Muhammadan* had reprinted articles from a disreputable paper named *The Crescent*, which had contained vile abuse of Englishmen and English soldiers. The Indian newspaper declared that the weekly newspaper published by a band of English Muslims may do no harm to Liverpudlians, but its seditious utterances should be prevented from reaching Muslim subjects in India and elsewhere.[69]

In June, the Liverpool Muslim Institute held its Annual General Meeting, the last one of the century. It was reported in *The Crescent* that 182 Jews and Christians had converted since 1887. The expansion of the community had led to the sale of 11 and 12 Brougham Terrace and the purchase of a large property at 4 Shiel Road in Elm Park, Fairfield, near the Sheikh's home. Some land and outhouses near the property had also been acquired. The new property was intended to house the expanding Medina orphanage.[70] The same issue reported that Robert Ahmed Quilliam had departed to Constantinople, where he would study Turkish and Arabic at the Mekteb Sultanieh.

The loss of the Sheikh's eldest son from the Liverpool community was only temporary, but other significant founding members would depart permanently from this life before the end of the year. Rosa Warren, the wife of Professor Henry Warren, the Principal of the school, who had converted soon after her husband in 1890, died in December at the age of 59. J. Ali Hamilton, who had converted in 1887, died soon after.[71] There is no doubt that Quilliam felt the loss of these early companions grievously.

Some of the activities recorded over the autumn of 1899 provide insights into the typical activities of the Institute. In September the mosque was used to celebrate the 33rd anniversary of the Sultan's accession to the throne, and the Sheikh addressed a large number of Indian Muslim sailors whose ships were docked in the city.[72] On the 29th of October, *The Sunday Telegraph* printed a full feature article on the activities of the Muslim converts and thus increased their national profile. In November Quilliam attended the Jewish Synagogue in Princes Road with the Lord Mayor, who was on an official visit. Quilliam was invited to speak at a meeting in aid of the Hebrew Philanthropic Fund. In the same month, there was a classical music concert at the Liverpool Muslim Institute in aid of victims of an earthquake in Asia Minor.[73]

By the end of the century, Quilliam had consolidated the community in Liverpool. The number of converts was steady and the mosque was known throughout the Muslim world. Although finances remained a problem and a drain on the Sheikh's personal income, he had succeeded in his wish to hold the price of *The Crescent* at one penny since its launch in 1893, and it would remain at the same low price until its demise in 1908. Quilliam was confident that some of the Liverpool converts were competent enough to maintain activities in the city without his continual presence, and he began to reach out to the rest of the country to ensure that his position as Sheikh al-Islam of the British Isles was recognised nationally.

CHAPTER 4

The Rise and Fall of the Liverpool Muslim Institute, 1900-1908

The previous chapter showed that, by the end of the nineteenth century, Quilliam had consolidated the Muslim presence in Liverpool and was beginning to look to further horizons. A large number of converts had adopted Islam under the Sheikh's inspiration who lived further afield in North-West England, Scotland and even in southern England. Some had travelled abroad and were trying to follow in the Sheikh's footsteps by establishing Islam in other non-Muslim territories. Famous among these was Alexander Webb, who lived in New York. Yet others were working with Indian and Arab Muslims in London and would be among the pioneering group in Woking. The demand from around the country for the Sheikh to visit and lecture was becoming greater and Quilliam was spending less and less time in Liverpool. By 1906, in addition to lectures on Islam given at Alexandra Hall and the Ethical Society's Hall in Liverpool, he spoke twice in Sheffield, once in Glasgow and in London on a number of occasions. In Sheffield he had indicated that he was personally responsible for five hundred and thirty-two conversions in Britain, only slightly over two hundred of which were in Liverpool. When Henri de Léon wrote of Quilliam's success he claimed that the Sheikh had personally been involved with the conversion of over six hundred people to Islam in the UK. He declared that barely ten people had been converted by other means and insisted that all Muslims in the country should accept the Sheikh as their leader.[1]

Quilliam's focus was now on the British Muslim Association and its activities nationwide. In 1902 *The Crescent* announced that the second annual meeting had been held at the Liverpool Muslim Institute. The new organisation was probably formed by Quilliam to represent his interests nationally, as opposed to the Liverpool Muslim Institute's more local remit. De Léon had accepted the post of secretary in 1905 and appeared to be staying in the city for prolonged periods of time. The Association continued until after 1908, when it formed an organisational home for the remnants of the Liverpool community who moved to London. It was eventually supplanted by Lord Headley's British Muslim Society.

In the following issue of *The Crescent*, congratulations were sent to Khalid Sheldrake for establishing the Young England Islamic Society in London and becoming the official correspondent for *The Crescent* in the city.[2] In February, Quilliam visited London and spoke with representatives of Islam in the city. He met with Abdullah al-Mamun Shurawardy and Muhammad Kahia of the London Pan-Islamic Society, and with S.G. Bullen and Khalid Sheldrake of the Young England Islamic Society. These meetings give some indication of the groups that Quilliam considered like-minded and sympathetic towards him in the capital.[3] At the Annual General Meeting of the British Muslim Association in 1905, the Sheikh pointed out that a new organisation had been formed in London and that he realised that there might be competition with an already existing group. He hoped that there would be a degree of collaboration. The move into London clearly showed the Sheikh's ambitions and his antipathy towards the Woking Mosque.[4] He also complained that certain people were trying to confine his work to Liverpool despite the evidence of converts scattered throughout the country. The statement would indicate some rivalry and was probably aimed at the Woking group. An article by Djaffer Mortimore praised the mosque in Woking and decried the fact that, although so many people in Britain were desirous to see a real mosque, visitors to Woking were discouraged because the Mosque was virtually unused and owned by a 'Jewish gentleman'. The article states that British Muslims or Muslim travellers in Britain had to apply for a permit to pray in the mosque and that no attempts were made to promote Islam from its premises. Djaffer expressed his surprise that money from India was not invested in a mosque in Liverpool or London, where real work was going on to bring the message of Islam to the British people.[5]

January 1906 marked the nineteenth anniversary of Quilliam's efforts to promote Islam in Liverpool and beyond. Twenty-seven volumes of *The Crescent* had been successfully published. The pattern he had established for the Liverpool Muslim Institute was largely unchanged. The schools, the evening classes, the Medina Home and to a lesser extent the museum provided the thrust through which Quilliam counteracted the propaganda that stated Islam was backward and not concerned with education or protecting the poor and vulnerable. Quilliam's public lectures on numerous topics provided a means to attract audiences that would not respond to invitations to discover more about Islam per se. While these were the main vehicle through which Quilliam and others introduced Islamic principles and gained converts, his many books and pamphlets provided a more direct introduction to Islam.

The Crescent and the *Islamic World* provided outreach to all corners of the globe, and the mosque and its Sheikh were becoming well known in the Muslim world. 1903 opened with the news that *The Crescent* was playing a significant role in bringing Muslims together from around the world. It had become one of the widest and most circulated Muslim publications, and the paper had been recommended in the *Sierra Leone Weekly News* for its international reach. The West African newspaper declared that *The Crescent* was the only Muslim media outlet where correspondence could be found from Muslims as far apart as Bhopal and Fourah Bay.[6] The success of the paper in West Africa resulted in Quilliam employing a local agent in the region to take care of distribution. By 1905, there was international media coverage of the activities of the Liverpool Muslims. The *Lahore Observer* published an account of the Prophet's birthday celebrations in the city;[7] and in September, *The Porcupine* ran a feature article in which it proclaimed that Liverpool was the most important Mahommedan centre in the British Isles, and was visited by people of the Muslim faith from all parts of the world who came to see and participate in the activities at the mosque.[8] The main vehicle used to reach the world's press remained *The Crescent*, but its success was attracting the attention of some governments who did not take kindly to the pro-Ottoman line on the Balkans. In July, the Government of Bulgaria banned the newspaper in its territory.[9] This global reach was vital because, as the nineteenth century ended and the twentieth began, Quilliam would be increasingly concerned with foreign affairs and would need an international network of support. The newspaper also played a vital role in linking the increasing number of minority Muslim diasporic communities that were forming in the far-flung places of the Empire. Several of these communities were active in the proselytising of Islam and sometimes contained a small contingent of active converts. The letters to *The Crescent* tell the tale of Quilliam's influence and inspiration to the converts and the way in which his writings on Islam were used to support these small communities and their efforts to promote their faith. In addition to the circulation of *The Crescent*, Quilliam drew upon individuals in these communities, especially South Africa and Australia, to create a pioneering 'transnational network'. Eric Germain calls these individuals, such as Hassan Musa Khan in Perth and Joosub Moulvi Hamid Gool in Cape Town, 'translocal agents' and argues that they 'were staunch advocates of the mobilization of an international Muslim brotherhood'.[10]

Quilliam was also linked to the wider Muslim world through the number of prominent international visitors who found their way to his door. In 1900 alone, the mosque was officially visited in May by Saleem Mahmood Hadjiar and Hadji Muhammad from Ceylon, and a week later by Ibrahim Fohmy, a Turkish army captain.[11] Agha Adem Mesic of Bosnia, the owner of the Journal *Behar* which was published in Sarajevo, visited in July, followed by A.M. Huk, a medical student from Hyderabad, who was studying at Edinburgh University, and the prominent Ottoman citizens Abboud Zedah Muhammad Teflik Bey of Constance, Hadji Abdul Hak of Beirut, Zekki Bey Karsa of Smyrna, as well as Mustapha Karsi, the Consul in Manchester, in August.[12] In September, an unnamed Muslim from Beirut visiting Manchester paid a flying visit to Liverpool to meet with Quilliam, followed by Captain Mumtaz Yar Jung, an officer in the Nizam of Hyderabad's household guard, who came with his wife.[13] Two Muslim gentlemen on a world tour, Mohammad Khan of Bombay and Mahomad Ibrahim of Cape Town, were guests in October.[14] In November, S.A. Rahman from Burma visited the mosque when staying in Edinburgh. He explained that he had heard his elders in Rangoon speak of the famous English Sheikh who was introducing Islam to England and had decided to meet him.[15] In addition to these visits from foreign Muslims, Quilliam received audiences from the Shah of Iran and the Khedive of Egypt on their respective state visits. In November 1901, the Prince of Siam (Thailand) attended a Town Hall reception in Liverpool and asked where he could meet the English Sheikh.

In 1902, the coronation of Edward VII brought to Britain even more prominent Muslim rulers and dignitaries, many of whom would visit Quilliam in Liverpool. In May the mosque was visited by Shareef Abdul Karim Murad, the guardian of the sacred mosque in Medina and one of the most respected leaders in the Muslim world. On the 31st May, the Shareef gave a lecture in the mosque, after which Quilliam also spoke of the Mussulman chiefs attending the Coronation to witness the crowning of the 'greatest Muslim monarch on earth who ruled over 90 million Muslim subjects', declaring that many of the leaders of the Muslim world were arriving by steamship in Liverpool, including the Aga Khan.

The small community would soon feel the impact of this gathering of temporal and religious leaders. The Sultan of Perak sent his congratulations to the Liverpool Muslims,[16] and in June, Alimanni Mahomed Gheirawani of Sierra Leone arrived in Liverpool, where he led the prayers and gave the *khutba* at *jumu'a* prayers, attending a reception at the mosque on Sunday evening when he lectured on Islam in West Africa.[17]

Prominent visitors from the Muslim world would continue to visit Quilliam throughout the first decade of the twentieth century, including high officials from the Ottoman court. In June the Sheikh entertained Ahmed Pasha, Chief of the Designing Department of the Imperial Navy Arsenal in Constantinople, who was en route to the USA.[18] Some visitors were more concerned with learning how to promote Islam nationally or internationally. In January 1901, Quilliam had been instrumental in establishing the Cambridge Muslim Association, the first university Islamic society in Britain, after meeting with and advising the first Chairman, Fazlur Rahman, in Liverpool.[19] In March, Quilliam addressed the newly-formed Cambridge Muslim Association and was made an honorary life-time member in token of his services to Islam. At the end of July 1902, Quilliam was visited by a Muslim convert from Dublin who sought advice on how to establish a Muslim centre to promote Islam in Ireland.[20] In April 1904, two Muslims from the Middle East, Sheriff Dia and Abdur Rahman, arrived in Liverpool en route to Canada. They were intent on setting themselves up in business in Halifax as merchants. They met with the Sheikh at the mosque, where discussions took place on establishing *da'wa* activities in Canada. The next day they departed on board the *SS Parisian*.[21] This incident shows how travelling Muslims who were intent upon establishing themselves in the various nations of the West utilised Quilliam's knowledge in their attempts to promote Islam in new locations. These brief contacts in Liverpool were useful and were maintained by Quilliam through the use of the mail, telegraph and telephone. Again in April, Quilliam was joined in Liverpool by John

Le Mesurier, the renowned Ceylon civil servant and convert, who was embarking on a new life in Australia having completed his law examinations.[22] Quilliam used *The Crescent* to request the Muslims of Freemantle and Perth to assist Le Mesurier in his endeavours to re-establish himself after persecution in England and Ceylon.[23]

Quilliam had been a guest of the Sultan in Constantinople early in the century and would visit again in 1905 when the Sultan requested his presence on official business. He passed some time in hospital in the city due to ill health. Returning to England with awards and gifts that were bestowed upon him by a grateful Caliph, Quilliam represented the Sultan at the presentation of an award to Dr Blyden at the mosque in Liverpool.[24] However, Quilliam's high profile in the Muslim world did have its downside. As international tensions rose, such visits would create an environment of distrust of the Sheikh in Britain, along with the unwanted attention of a suspicious media and the intelligence community. Quilliam had to decide who his friends were, and it is revealing that when he entertained the champion Turkish wrestler who had been ill in America, and had been deserted by his Greek companion, Quilliam quoted the Qur'an's verse which declared that Muslims should not take Jews or Christians as friends.[25]

1901 had begun against the backdrop of war between Turkey and Bulgaria while 1903 presented Quilliam with a major challenge that would result in international media coverage. The European powers including Britain became embroiled in the various rebellions taking place in the Balkans against the authority of the Ottoman Empire, and Quilliam would use all of his resources to defend the Caliph and pleaded with the British government to support the ailing Ottoman Empire. However, the campaign to defend the Ottomans would be viewed as treason by many in Britain, and, even as early as January 1903, Quilliam was becoming aware of the tensions between his dual loyalties to Islam and to his nation of birth. On the 25th January he lectured on the subject of high treason and declared controversially that a man or woman who denied the existence of

God was in his opinion guilty of a far greater crime than the person who committed an act of treason. He used the lecture to justify the punishments for apostasy revealed in the Qur'an and compared these to the savage laws that dealt out terrible punishments to traitors in Britain throughout its history.[26]

Throughout the year, the activities of the Liverpool Muslim Institute continued unabated against the backdrop of Quilliam's frustrations with the changing public mood on Britain's growing imperial excursions. In April he asserted that Christian missionary activities in the Muslim world took place with the 'support of British bayonets' and with, at least, the moral approval of the Government. The Sheikh was incensed that this policy went against the pledge made in the time of Queen Victoria, after the uprising of 1857 against the British in India, that indigenous religions would not be interfered with.[27] Shortly after expressing his frustrations in *The Crescent*, his speech defending Islam and the Ottoman position in Macedonia was published as *The Trouble in the Balkans*.[28] The international situation forced the Sheikh away from the views of the Muslim modernists to express a more polarised position, and in doing this he rejected the language of toleration and pluralism and rigorously defended the more controversial elements of the Qur'anic message on apostasy and the rejection of other communities.

The attention on foreign policy and the worsening international situation would not improve. By 1905, most of Quilliam's energy was occupied with the worsening situation in the Balkans. In *The Crescent* he made one of his rare interventions into politics by using his right to issue fatwas (which is discussed in greater detail in Chapter 6). This time the proclamation was addressed to British Muslims and concerned the pressure that was being placed on the Ottoman Sultan by various European powers, including Britain, to rein in his responses to the uprisings in the Balkans. The fatwa referred to the British sending warships to participate in naval manoeuvres against the Ottomans. This order had been given by Arthur Balfour, the Prime Minister, and Lord Lansdowne, the

Foreign Secretary. Quilliam stated that the Government in Britain had 'fallen' and declared that Allah had taken his vengeance on the two men for their ill judgement. He requested British Muslims not to vote for them to be re-elected. The fatwa ends:

> O true believers, rise ye equal to this occasion, and let your voices be heard loud and clear. And in no uncertain voice sound in protest against and condemnation of the vile and wicked act and disgraceful insult offered to the True Religion of God and His Holy Prophet, and the Caliph of the True Believers.[29]

This is surely the first recorded fatwa in Britain that requested Muslims to withhold their suffrage from a political party whose policies were seen to be disadvantageous to the wider Muslim world. There were probably not enough voting Muslims to make a major difference, but it is the historic precedent set by Quilliam that is so significant.

In May 1906, the mosque celebrated the birthday of the Prophet and Quilliam used the occasion to deliver a significant lecture on the relationship between Britain and Turkey. He accused the British Government of abandoning their traditional friendship with the Sultan and argued that this constituted a betrayal of trust. He went on to state that, although Muslims in Britain numbered only around one thousand individuals, the Empire contained millions. In a veiled threat, he declared, 'Islam is not like Christianity. It is a fraternity. He who strikes one Muslim injures every Mussulman. The True-Believers are brethren, and the power which strikes at the Caliph of the Faithful at once places itself in antagonism with the whole of the Muslim world.'[30] The full text of this speech was sent to the Prime Minister, the Foreign Secretary and the King. The Liverpool media reported and reprinted extracts of the speech extensively. The national press were disparaging, accusing Quilliam of being a one-man band in support of the 'great assassin'.[31] The latest crisis concerned the exact location of Ottoman territory in the Sinai and the demarcation line between this and the British protectorate in Egypt. Henri de Léon reported within a month that a strange coincidence had taken place. The Sheikh had prophesised that the British Empire would begin to unravel if British guns fired a shot on the Ottomans in Egypt. Two weeks later, on the 18th May, the British torpedo boat No.56 sank with the loss of the lives of all crew members. The same day, the British steamer *Morocco* ran aground in the Suez. De Léon made much of the numbers, noting that 18 and 56 made up the numbers of the Sheikh's birth and that Morocco was where he had converted to Islam. The Sheikh's prophetic speech was delivered on the seventh day of May and seven crewmen lost their lives.[32] Henri de Léon continued to track every disaster recorded in the news in which British interests were represented and attributed them to the power of the Sheikh's prophetic utterances.

In August, Quilliam returned to the issue of Egypt. A letter written in response to a White Paper on the Anglo-Turkish Question, published by Lord Cromer, was sent to *The Times* and other British newspapers. The Sheikh was furious that Cromer had spoken of a highly-educated Egyptian who had written to him complaining that the imams preached in the mosque, 'the curse of God to be upon the Christians, may hell be upon the unbeliever, his household and his possessions'. Quilliam stated firmly that no true believer could make such a pronouncement, as it was contrary to the teachings of Islam. However, he went on to explain why Muslims were angered by the foreign policy of the British in Egypt and re-emphasised that the British were forcing 102 million Muslims to choose between 'loyalty to an earthly ruler and loyalty to their religion'.[33]

In February 1907, *The Crescent* published an article on pan-Islamism written by S.M. Kidwai of the Anjuman-i Islamia in London. The speech, which had been made on the occasion of Eid al-Fitr, stated that the movement supported the British Protectorate in Egypt and 'would never interfere in any direct political question or affair of any country whatsoever'. Rather, it seeks to better the 'moral, educational, social and even political condition of Mussulmans of different countries under their respective governments'. Quilliam's more confrontational version of pan-Islamism was revealed in a rejoinder inserted at the end of the article, added by the editor, which stated unequivocally that the British should evacuate Egypt because they were trespassers and interlopers in Muslim territory. Quilliam went on to state that his intentions had always been to work for Islam as the dominant creed and for Muslims as the dominant race throughout the world.'[34]

It proved difficult to keep these international dilemmas away from the daily affairs of the mosque in Liverpool. On the 28th September 1903, another of Quilliam's early converts and his close confidante, John Yehya Chapman, died at home aged 84. At the mosque, the sadness was reflected in special prayers and a memorial service (*janaza namaz*) that were also held for the death of the Sultan's youngest son. Quilliam had been invited as a special guest to the opening of the University of Liverpool's medical faculty and had given public lectures defending the position of women in Islam after the Bishop of Liverpool delivered a sermon defending the rights of Christians in Macedonia to break free of the Muslim yoke that had been placed around them by Ottoman rule.[35] In late October, Quilliam publicly refuted the Bishop at a meeting in the Town Hall and defended the religion of Islam and its cultural and political manifestations in the Ottoman Empire.[36] His defence of Islam was picked up and reported worldwide, with many newspapers printing extracts of Quilliam's speech. The next three editions of *The Crescent* carried the full text of what became an almost legendary event amongst Muslims in Britain over the next three decades. In contrast, Muslim migrants to Britain after 1945 had no knowledge of its historical aignificance.

The success of the Liverpool Muslim Institute during the early years of the twentieth century did not pass unnoticed by the official representatives of Christianity in the city. On the last week of 1902, immediately after the Christmas festivities at a special service held at the Anglican cathedral, the Bishop of Liverpool offered a prayer of supplication in which he requested God to assist in the re-conversion of the city's Muslims who had been led astray into the path of a 'false prophet'. Quilliam responded by announcing that, within seven days of the divine appeal, three more individuals had embraced Islam in the city.[37]

Quilliam's activities were also beginning to conflict with the social mores of middle-class England, and in February 1903 the *Daily Mail* complained about the number of foreign men who were marrying English women; it ran a report of a wedding carried out in Liverpool between a Muslim Indian national and an English bride who had converted. The newspaper was outraged, and called for a halt to such liaisons and a clampdown on those who facilitated or encouraged such relationships.[38] Quilliam's response was to perform several more weddings at the mosque during the course of the year.

Neither the speech in Liverpool Town Hall nor the negative media coverage appear to have impacted significantly on Quilliam's official standing in the city. On the 29th October, he was invited along with Ahmed and his granddaughter to attend a dinner at the same Town Hall that was organised by Lord Mayor William Rutherford, to which 120 members of the consular corps and officials or businessmen representing foreign powers in the city were invited.[39] The media coverage appeared to have no detrimental impact on the family. Billal had been selected to play rugby football for Lancashire and was playing regularly for the University of Liverpool first fifteen. The mosque celebrated the Sultan's sixty-third birthday and, in December, Quilliam presided over the Annual General Meeting of the Mersey Quay and Carter's Union as its honorary president and legal advisor. He was congratulated by the 4000 members present for the £11,000 he had recovered in compensation for injuries since the union's inception.[40]

1904 began with continued press coverage of Quilliam's Macedonian defence,[41] as well as an invitation for the Sheikh to meet with Arthur Balfour, the Prime Minister, at a special reception at the Philharmonic Hall in Liverpool. This reception had been organised by Lord Stanley as the president of the Liverpool Constitutional Association prior to his death in December.[42] It is clear that neither conversion to Islam nor his strong critique of British foreign policy in the Balkans had any significant impact on Quilliam's continuing respectability and the value of high-status converts in providing connections to the highest echelons of British society. This would be demonstrated to a great extent by the Woking Mosque group a decade later. The invitations continued to arrive throughout the year. In July, Quilliam was invited as one of three hundred and sixty-five leading citizens of Liverpool to be present at the Council Chamber to witness the Lord Mayor of Liverpool being knighted by the King.[43] In November, he addressed the annual dinner of the Directors of the London and Manchester Insurance Company at Cobhams Restaurant in Lord Street.[44] Finally, at the end of the year, Quilliam was once again re-elected as President of the Mersey Quay and Carter's Union after presiding over the Annual General Meeting.[45]

To some degree, these invitations were a result of Quilliam's reputation in other walks of life rather than his role in promoting Islam in Britain; but this was not true of his invitation to the London African Society in June to meet the Alake of Abeokouta, which was a direct result of his growing recognition in Africa and the many articles that had been printed in *The Crescent* that vigorously decried white racism and the colonisation of Africa by various European powers.[46] His contacts as a prominent Mason also helped him to make connections in the business and political worlds. In October, he was elected as Vice-President of the Liverpool Geological Association, an organisation he had joined in 1878. The Association was highly respected as Liverpool's oldest scientific society and had extensive library holdings at the Derby Museum.[47] Quilliam was a long-standing member of various Masonic lodges.[48] Germain notes that, on his return from Morocco shortly before his public announcement of conversion to Islam, he had been initiated into the Masonic Royal Oriental Order of the Sat Bhai.[49] He had been a Freemason in one of the Liverpool Lodges for twenty-five years, and was re-elected as its Presiding Officer in June 1904. Both his father and grandfather had been distinguished Masons, and in August Quilliam was elected as Worshipful Master. This was the first time that a Muslim had been placed in the Chair of a Masonic lodge in Britain.[50] National recognition came in November, when he was appointed Grand Deacon of the Grand Council of the Allied Masonic Degrees of Great Britain and its Dependencies Beyond the Seas, and was duly invested by the Earl of Euston.[51] Quilliam was fully aware that Freemasonry owed its roots to Christian contacts with the Muslim world at the time of the Crusades, and had delivered several lectures on this topic.[52]

To a certain extent, the success of the Muslim converts owed much to their integration into mainstream British civil society, often in positions of prominence or through demonstrating sporting or intellectual prowess that was admired by the wider society. Quilliam, for example, was the legal advisor and solicitor for the Liverpool Society for the Abolition of Capital Punishment, an organisation under the Presidency of Annie Burrows, a Muslim convert. This organisation was active and benefited from Quilliam's successful legal career. His efforts to reform the law on capital punishment were complimented by one of the city's magistrates later in the year.[53] In fact, 1904 was the year that brought a number of Liverpool Muslims to the attention of the wider public. Yusef Nunan, the famed explorer, had been made a Fellow of the Royal Geographical Society in March,[54] and later in the same month had received national media coverage for his expedition to northern Brazil.[55] Ahsan al-Haq, a member of the Institute, was playing cricket for Middlesex; and later in the summer, Jaffer Ramjhan won the 880 yards and the 440 yards Handicap at Salford Athletic Festival.[56] In August, this seventeen-year-old Asian Muslim was second in the 100 yards final in Glasgow after giving a 28-yard handicap to the winner; the *Scottish Referee* reported that the boy was running the 100 yards sprint in eleven seconds.[57]

The ethnically-diverse members of the Liverpool Muslim Institute at the Eid al-Fitr celebrations of 1905, wearing traditional Ottoman-style fezzes.

Back in Liverpool, a brilliant young scholar called Hassan al-Arculli, who was sent by his Chinese father to study at the Muslim College, had passed the senior examination of the British College of Preceptors[58] and came to the attention of the Liverpool media for his translation activities at the trial of a Chinese murderer. At the age of eighteen, he became the first person to translate the death sentence to a convicted murderer in a British court.[59] Prominent Edwardian professional men continued to convert in the city. On the 21st September 1906, Joseph Evans, the Curator of Birmingham University, embraced Islam at the Liverpool Mosque and took the name of Youssef.[60]

Even the Sheikh's children seemed to be aware of the need to transform the profile of Muslims in Britain. In early 1905, Billal observed a man drowning off a landing stage in Liverpool and dived in to rescue him. The man struggled and almost drowned, but Billal managed to bring him to shore after fifteen minutes fighting the currents of the Mersey.[61] The local newspapers praised his bravery, and the following week the Royal Humane Society announced that they were awarding him a silver medal for courage.[62] More mundanely, Ethel Mariam Quilliam, the daughter of the Sheikh's Muslim marriage to Mary Lyon, had passed her entrance examination to the Royal Victoria College of Music, whilst the Sheikh celebrated the silver anniversary of his marriage to Hannah.

In 1903, all appeared to be normal in the world of the Liverpool Muslim Institute and the personal life of its leader. The only significant change was that Quilliam sold the family home in Peel on the Isle of Man and purchased a new home in Onchan. Henceforth, Quilliam declared his official address to be Woodland Towers, Onchan, rather than the family residence in Liverpool.[63] It can only be speculated that, underneath the respectable facade that was presented to the British public, all was not well within the domestic realm of the Sheikh's life and that the tensions of his multiple relationships with women were beginning to be felt.

However, the Sheikh was skilful in managing his personal and public lives, and in most ways the family presented a successful middle-class image of their private life. Quilliam's two families must have co-operated to ensure that no scandal occurred to disturb the Sheikh's public activities, and the success of this strategy is measured by the difficulties of the contemporary researcher to discover the means through which they covered their tracks in the midst of intense media scrutiny. Quilliam would involve all the family members in his public engagements. Typical examples of such activities covered by the press took place in the summer of 1902; for instance, in June, Quilliam and his eldest son participated in a Liverpool peace procession by invitation from the Mayor, which had been organised as part of the Coronation festivities. The media reported that the most picturesque feature of the procession was undoubtedly Sheikh Abdullah Quilliam dressed in the robes of a 'Muslim amir' and his son in the full uniform of Turkish cavalry officer.[64]

Later in the month, Quilliam, Robert Ahmed and Hanifa were invited to attend the official reception of the US envoy to the Coronation, the Hon. Whitelaw Read and his wife.[65] This official recognition of Quilliam as the representative of British Muslims would culminate in a formal invitation to carry out the funeral of a Muslim soldier who had died whilst taking part in the Coronation parade in London. In July, Billal passed the preliminary examinations of the Incorporated Law Society of England and Wales, and was entered into gaining his Articles to qualify as a solicitor under his father at the family's law firm. In addition he was becoming a successful rugby player of international standard. Quilliam's daughters and his youngest son Henry Mahomet achieved prizes at the Liverpool Institute.[66] In July, Quilliam and his two eldest sons were guests at a Town Hall reception held by the Mayor for the Commander and officers of a French frigate, *Duguay Trouin*, which was visiting British waters.[67] In December 1906, young Habeebah May Quilliam passed the entry examination to the Royal Victoria College of Music. Only nine years old, the Sheikh's youngest daughter was the youngest candidate in Britain,[68] but tragically would never attend the school because she died two years later of diphtheria.

In September 1905, Quilliam lost another child to migration. His youngest son, Henry Mahomed, also the offspring of his relationship with Mary Lyon, left for Canada on board the *SS Parisian*. In November it was announced in *The Crescent* that he had arrived safely in Quebec. The newspaper reported that he hoped to join up with Canadian Muslims, where by 'precept and example' he would help to introduce Islam to the far West.[69] On the whole, 1905 was a quiet year by the Sheikh's standards. Quilliam had begun the year hospitalised in Constantinople and ill health dogged his footsteps throughout the year. In November, special prayers were conducted for the Sheikh when it was announced that he had been taken seriously ill. Henri de Léon, in his position as the family physician, wrote regular reports of the Sheikh's condition for all that were concerned. By mid-November he had not recovered, and even the Sultan had enquired about his chances of recovery. By the end of November, to the relief of all the Liverpool Muslims, their Sheikh attended a few public meetings, albeit against medical advice. Shortly afterwards he left for the Isle of Man in the company of one of the converts, Youssef Chipchase, where he would stay to convalesce.[70] These activities of the family reveal both the degree to which they were in most ways integrated into the normal conventions of British social life, but also how the Sheikh's public life was lived out in the glare of media coverage.

At the end of August 1904, the national media spotlight on the Liverpool Muslims continued with an article in the *Daily Express*.[71] As the end of the year approached, Quilliam must have looked around him and thought all would be well in his world. The only clouds upon the horizon were in his personal life, as he continued to manage his various households and the more mundane challenge of seeking finances for extensive repairs required at the Mosque. At the end of October, the lecture hall floor was re-laid, a new stage was erected and ventilators and heating were installed. The total cost was over £100, and Quilliam hoped that Muslims from around the world would support their 'English brothers'.[72] If not, the brunt of the costs were going to come out of his pockets.

Finances were a constant challenge to Quilliam. At the very beginning of the century, the Annual General Meeting for 1900 reported that Quilliam had once more subsidised the donations to the tune of £200. Indian Muslims had donated £30 towards the cost of a Muslim cemetery plot, but there was now a new challenge to the already meagre finances of the Institute. More and more destitute Indian Muslims were arriving in the city, either directly by ships that docked in Liverpool or from other British seaports in Tyneside, Cardiff or London. The police had started to direct all these destitute lascars to the mosque. The Liverpool Muslim Institute found that it was not only looking after their accommodation, but also organising their passage home. In June 1900, the Institute was looking after the interests of over thirty such men. Some needed clothing and medical treatment, and the resources of the converts were being stretched to breaking point. Quilliam advised the members that a proper hostel needed to be established by Indian Muslims to meet the needs of their compatriots.[73]

In 1902, the accounts revealed a deficit of £313, which was divided between £100 owed by the Medina Home and £213 by the Mosque. On the plus side, the commercialisation of the printing press had generated an annual income of £80. Disappointingly, Quilliam announced that the lack of funds meant that many children were being turned away from the Medina Home. The Christmas festivities of 1905 had only just been completed when Quilliam again faced an old problem in Liverpool. Shortly before the New Year celebrations, the police telephoned to tell him that an Indian Muslim sailor had been attacked and robbed by two men demanding money to buy alcohol. That the police notified the Sheikh shows that the Mosque was becoming increasingly involved in working with the various agencies that were responsible for dealing with the city's social problems. On New Year's Day, Quilliam appeared as the prosecution lawyer in the case and called upon the magistrate to set an example because such incidents were far too common on Liverpool's streets. The magistrate agreed with the Sheikh and sentenced the attacker to one month's hard labour.[74] At the end of June, the Sheikh penned an article detailing how immigrants were being fleeced at the Liverpool docks while in transit to America. He accused private hostel keepers of being unscrupulous, whilst praising the Jewish organisations for looking after their own people, adding that the Liverpool Muslim Institute was working to protect Muslim migrants. However, at the time of writing, there were over sixty penniless Muslims in the city who were being sheltered and fed at the Institute.[75]

Meanwhile, twenty-eight Indian Muslims en route to Nigeria to seek work were accommodated in the Medina Home.[76] In April, *The Crescent* carried an article expressing its view on immigration, clearly stating that no land had any right to prohibit or expel migrants. The moral position was that, although all lands maintained borders, the earth was the grand heritage of humanity.[77] However, these types of activities were costly and a drain on the Institute's resources. The issue of finances always remained a major concern, and in May 1901 Quilliam had created a sub-committee to address specifically the issue of making the Liverpool Muslim Institute financially secure without reliance on the Sheikh's personal wealth. Ironically this was the very same year in which an article appeared in *The Truth* magazine accusing Quilliam of the misuse of funds collected in India.[78] The information appears to have come from anonymous sources in Constantinople, and the Liverpool Muslim Institute issued a very strong rebuttal; many Indian and Ceylonese Muslims wrote letters to the journal defending Quilliam's integrity. It should he noted that several of these letters expressed initial distrust of the Sheikh's motives when he began in the 1890s, but all were now convinced of his sincerity.

In addition to the problem of money, the Sheikh would also have felt the impact of the deaths of a number of his first converts. He reported to the Annual General Meeting at the end of the nineteenth century that a number of the early converts had been elderly and therefore the death rate was high. Although the age profile had lowered by the opening of the twentieth century, and the convert community consisted of many younger families and single people, Quilliam would have felt the loss of old friends who had been with him from the beginning. Yehya Chapman had died in 1900, Thomas Omar Byrne in 1901 and, tragically for Quilliam, the same year saw the death of two of his first converts, Elizabeth Cates and the Sheikh's mother. Her funeral was reported in the Liverpool media, where it was noted that Henri de Léon was the chief mourner.[79] The loss devastated Quilliam, but he had the presence of mind and the compassion to accept the guardianship of Elizabeth Cates' son and ensured his continued Muslim upbringing. Another of the original converts, Djemel ud-din Lawrenson was also seriously ill and died in May. Captain Olson, the well-known Victorian explorer who had converted in 1894, died later in the year.

Another death was of great significance for all in Britain as the new century began. In 1901 Queen Victoria, who had ruled over the nation and its Empire, finally died. The previous century had begun with Britain making its mark around the world as one of several European nations competing for trade. Her reign ended with Britain in possession of the largest empire in history and the undisputed dominant world power. Amongst Britain's possessions overseas were many Muslim regions, and the Queen had always been genuinely interested in the religion of Islam, Quilliam had certainly drawn upon her empathy with her Muslim subjects to argue for citizenship to be acknowledged as 'British by birth and Muslim by religion'. Her loss would mean a new era for Britain and a period of uncertainty for British Muslims.

Supplications were made at the Mosque at Eid al-Fitr that year on the Queen's behalf, and Quilliam delivered a eulogy on her death. In January, Quilliam officially represented His Majesty's loyal Muslim subjects in England when Edward VII was officially proclaimed King and Emperor from the balcony of Liverpool Town Hall. In February, *The Crescent* reported that Quilliam had represented Liverpool Muslims at the cathedral dressed in fez and full regalia. A memorial service was held at the Mosque, in which Quilliam read a letter from the Home Office, thanking the Liverpool Muslim Institute on behalf of the King for their loyalty. The Sheikh also revealed that Queen Victoria had shown a personal interest in the spread of Islam in her kingdom, personally requesting a copy of *Faith of Islam* shortly after its publication and ordering a further six copies for her children a month later. One of these had been presented to the new King, then Prince of Wales.[80] In a strange way, the official representation at the various state functions associated with the death of the Queen and the succession of Edward VII helped the Liverpool Muslim Institute to demonstrate its loyalty and to relieve the pressure created by divided loyalties. *The Crescent* reported that conversion to Islam continued in Liverpool, including some high-profile citizens who declined to be named because of their official status in the city.[81] Quilliam was also invited to be the guest of honour at a special banquet with Sir Alfred L. Jones, the Lord Mayor, the Principal of Liverpool University College along with Professors Boyce and Carter, the Chief Constable of Liverpool and Miles Burton, the Secretary of the Mersey Docks and the Harbour Board.[82] It is clear that, in spite of all the publicity, he remained a highly respected figure amongst the civic leaders of Liverpool and mixed with them freely both socially and professionally.

December 1903 brought with it a very high profile Muslim convert death. Abdur Rahman or Henry Edward John Stanley, the third Baron of Alderley, was given full Muslim funeral rites at his stately home at Alderley Park, with Hamid Bey, First Secretary at the Ottoman Embassy in London, among the chief mourners. Quilliam officiated at the funeral and held a *janaza* service in his memory at the Liverpool Mosque.[83] On the 23rd December, Quilliam defended

the Earl's conversion to Islam and defended his own stance on
Macedonia.[84] The publicity surrounding the death of Lord Stanley
provided the opportunity for the *Daily Dispatch* to report on
conversion to Islam in Liverpool. The paper noted that the converts
included a clergyman, three Wesleyan preachers, two medical men
and a barrister. These men had formerly been affiliated to various
Christian denominations, including Catholicism, Nonconformism,
the Salvationists, Unitarianism and spiritualism.[85]

In creating this unique community, which remains unparalleled
to the present day, Quilliam was assisted by some remarkable men
and women whom he had convinced that Islam was the true and
final revelation of God, replacing for many their previous loyalty
to Christianity. It is worth looking at the profiles of some of these
prominent converts, who together created the life of Britain's
first Muslim community based on faith conviction. Many of
these profiles are taken from Quilliam's obituaries, for he was
to officiate at many of their funerals during the first years of
the twentieth century. Others provided their stories of how they
came to Islam in *The Crescent*, that invaluable source of Victorian
and early Edwardian Muslim life in Britain. This is the age when
Britain remained predominantly Christian in belief and practice
and atheism remained a rare choice. Most of the converts were
Christian before embracing Islam and they generally provided
their reasons for losing faith in their religion of birth. To many,
it involved a journey to Unitarianism and disenchantment with
contemporary sectarianism. Elizabeth Lehlah Warren, the wife of
the early convert Professor Henry Nasrullah Warren, a chemist and
the first headmaster of the Muslim school, declared herself to be a
Unitarian. A mother of two children, a musician and music teacher,
she had taught in the Muslim girl's school. She had converted along
with her husband after attending a lecture on Constantinople given
by Quilliam in 1890. They had found out about the lecture from
a newspaper advertisement. Her daughter also became a Muslim.
Rosa Warren was much loved and was known as the 'mother of

Muslims' by the children of the community. She was renowned for her charity work and always assisted when free meals were distributed at the mosque.[86]

John Yehya Chapman was more explicit concerning his previous allegiance to Christianity. A devout Wesleyan, he left the church after it failed to condemn war at the time of the Crimean War. A lay preacher and a staunch member of the Temperance movement, he began to have doubts concerning the central tenets of Christian dogma after considerable reading and consequently joined the Spiritualists in 1868. He attended a lecture by Quilliam in 1895 and first enrolled as a member of the Debating Society at the Liverpool Muslim Institute.[87] John Ali Hamilton also declared himself a Christian and an Anglican until 1887, when he met Quilliam. John was a lithographic writer and illuminator who regularly attended church at St. Augustines, Church Street in Liverpool. For a time he ran his own business, until his premises were destroyed by fire. He afterwards worked as a sales manager in Nobletts Confectionary Business.[88]

J. Bokhary Jeffery was one of the first converts who had listened to Quilliam in 1887, and he worked for many years as the librarian of the Liverpool Muslim Institute. He was a master plumber and decorator, employing between twelve and twenty men. A freemason and founder member of the Liverpool Workingmen's Conservative Association, he was a staunch Protestant and a member of the Orange Loyal Protestant Order of which he was appointed Grand Lodge Officer in 1854. He was an old friend of the Sheikh and was initiated by him into the Ancient Order of the Zuzeimites in 1876. He had originally only attended the meetings out of friendship, but had been disturbed at the level of violence directed towards the first Muslims in the city. After becoming involved in a fracas at the mosque, in which he personally evicted several violent protestors, the Sheikh had thanked him for his assistance. Brother Jeffery had replied, 'Such conduct as was exhibited by those scoundrels I have just helped to eject proves to me that the religion they hold to cannot be correct. From this day forth I am a Muslim.'[89]

Another prominent convert was Professor H. Haschem Wilde. A former teacher and scholar of literature and theology, educated at Cambridge and London Universities, Professor Wilde's parents had been devout evangelical Anglicans who hoped their son would enter the priesthood. He had been trained at the Theological College of St. Bees, but never entered the clergy due to the death of his father. After holding various teaching posts and suffering a gradual disillusionment with mainstream Christian doctrines caused by his reading of the New Testament and comparing this with contemporary Church practice, he applied for the post of assistant master at the Muslim school. He had personally researched several Christian denominations and had even been dismissed from one school post for teaching 'blatant Unitarianism'. It was only after teaching at the Muslim College and engaging in many intellectual conversations with the Sheikh that he accepted Islam. He would go on to become one of the most active Muslims in Liverpool, functioning as Secretary, Treasurer and Vice-President of the Institute and President of the Debating Society, as well as headmaster of the school. He undertook the post of auditor for several years.[90]

Thomas Omar Byrne, who was praised for his kindness by a new convert in 1900, died in 1901. His family were Irish immigrants who had come to Liverpool from County Wexford around 1850. Devout Roman Catholics, their son was born in Liverpool in 1856 and had desired to become a priest, to which end he had been educated by the Jesuits at St. Xavier's College, Liverpool. After the death of his father had plunged the family into debt, he had taken up a post as a solicitor's clerk and had met William Quilliam when he joined the firm as junior solicitor aged seventeen. They were neighbours and walked home together every night from the office where they shared a room with each other. The two boys had studied shorthand and Hebrew together. When Quilliam started his own law firm, Thomas had joined him. They worked together until Thomas was invited to London to work with the Irish Home

Rule offices. He was then selected to be a candidate for Parliament for an Irish constituency, campaigning for Home Rule. He went into journalism, writing for an Irish newspaper, and returned to Liverpool to pursue his career as a reporter. For one of his first assignments in July 1887, he was sent to Vernon Hall to cover a lecture by Quilliam on 'Fanatics and Fanaticism', the very first speech that the Sheikh employed to interest people in Islam. He continued to listen to the lectures of his old friend and embraced Islam in 1889. He was also active and fulfilled the roles of librarian and Secretary. He also taught shorthand to the children in the Muslim College.[91]

Some converts would join the community after coming into contact with Muslims during military service. Typical of these is Ahmed Branne, who converted after reading *The Crescent* in London. He wrote to Quilliam after accepting Islam formally at the Regents Park Mosque in London,[92] and later joined him in Liverpool. In Branne's letter to Quilliam, he describes himself as a former member of the Church of England who had enlisted for the Devonshire Regiment at the age of eighteen and been sent to India. After two years in Rawalpindi, he was transferred to Burma and had received the Indian Medal and Clasp for active service. He became aware of Islam on his return to Rawalpindi in 1892. Muslims had impressed him in their devotion to religion and their lack of blasphemous language, even amongst the lower classes. He began to enquire about Muslim literature and was directed by an Indian Muslim to write to the Liverpool Muslim Institute and request a copy of *Faith of Islam*. Another Muslim had recited and explained the Qur'an to him in Urdu and he lost faith in Christian doctrines. On his return to Britain in 1896, he began to read *The Crescent* regularly and saw the address of the Regent Park Mosque in one edition. At the time he had no opportunity to visit Liverpool.[93]

Other members of the Liverpool Muslim Institute were less conventional, living creative or unusual lives that brought them to the attention of the media and kept them in the public eye. Walid

F. Preston was a well-known artist in both Hull and Liverpool, who remains represented in the Merseyside Maritime Museum and other Liverpool galleries. Preston was known for painting the activities on both coasts of the United Kingdom. He was a resident of Argyle Street, Birkenhead, Liverpool, in 1895. It is not known when he became a member of the Liverpool Muslim Institute, but Quilliam brought him back a decoration from the Sultan after he delivered a commissioned painting of the Hoylake seafront to decorate the walls of the Yildiz palace. His painting 'Danse' was exhibited throughout Britain. T. Olson Edwards was a renowned arctic explorer and sea captain. As the Commodore of the Papayannia Line, which specialised in sailing ships from Liverpool to the Levant, he converted to Islam in 1894 after meeting with Quilliam when he was a passenger on route to Constantinople.[94] He was a colourful character who led expeditions to the northern Klondike and was decorated by the Sultan for saving Muslim sailors when their ship sank in the Bosphorus.[95]

Some insights into the process of conversion can be gleaned from an article published in *The Crescent* under the title, 'two more converts to Islam in Liverpool'. After a lecture by the Sheikh on the subject of 'The Islamic Path', two men had jumped up and announced their intention to convert. They had both been attending the evening lectures for some time. On being invited to speak to the attendees after repeating the *kalima* in the mosque, John Pugh described himself as a student of theology for forty years who had not been able to come to terms with 'the insurmountable difficulties of the popular forms of Christianity', and who had first learned of the growth of Islam in Britain in *The Tablet*, the Roman Catholic newspaper. As a result he sought out an interview with the Sheikh, but instead met with Omar Byrne, a convert who gave him a copy of *Faith of Islam*. He was attracted to Islam by the welcoming kindness that he received from Omar Byrne. The other convert, James Rankin, described himself as a Sunday School teacher who had been invited to train for the clergy. An engineer by profession, he had also slowly become disenchanted with the current condition of the churches.[96]

Throughout all the events of the first decade of the twentieth century, the Mosque continued to provide the ritual life of Islam and to act as the focal point where various Muslim constituencies could visit and gather on public occasions. Quilliam continued to carry out the Muslim rites of passage and officially represented Muslims in the region to the various civic authorities. In January 1900, he made one minor addition to the activities of the community. He introduced a social event on Thursday nights at the lecture hall, where the gathered Muslims would play board and card games with each other and cement their social relationships through the popular pastimes of the period.[97] In the same year, he also instituted a weekly Qur'an reading and exposition of the verses delivered by him at Friday prayers.[98] The Sheikh had become concerned that Muslim converts in Britain should be able to practise the Islamic ritual life properly. In 1906, Quilliam published the precise details of the *janaza* (funeral prayers) in English for British Muslims who could speak no Arabic. The following issues of *The Crescent* contained similar instructions for *wudu'* (ritual ablution), *salat* (prayer), *du'a* (supplication), *dhikr* (litanies) and various types of Muslim creedal formulae.[99] Conversion continued as a small but regular event, and various Muslim newspapers from around the world published articles on the activities of the Liverpool mosque. In addition, Quilliam was becoming a feature item in the national media. On the negative side, the international situation was making it more difficult to promote Islam in Britain without provoking jingoistic sentiments and historic stereotypes of Muslim backwardness and enmity towards Christianity.

The competitive relationship between Islam and Christianity was also being played out less dramatically, but no less significantly, in Liverpool. Quilliam, as always astute in recognising an opportunity, drew upon Christian rivalries in the city to promote Islam as being more in harmony with the city's growing multiculturalism.

In 1904, the city of Liverpool experienced terrible religious riots throughout the summer, almost on a daily basis. These riots had been stirred up by the activities of the Reverend George Wise, who was leading Protestant processions through the Catholic areas of the city and inciting the storming of Catholic households in Toxteth.[100] Quilliam used *The Crescent* to preach on the lack of unity amongst Christians and to ask rhetorically, 'whatever happened to turning the other cheek?'[101] His involvement in the Christian sectarian violence brought the Sheikh to the attention of the firebrand Protestant minister, and in October Quilliam allowed Wise to publish a letter in *The Crescent* in which he explained his actions against the Catholics.[102] In contrast to this Christian division in the city, the Mosque in Brougham Terrace reflected the growing multiculturalism of early twentieth-century Liverpool. At the feast of Eid al-Adha, which was held at the Mosque in March, over seventeen languages were spoken and the festivities included juggling, fire-swallowing, music recitals, a slide show about Islam in West Africa and a wrestling match between Billal ibn Abdullah, the Turkish Lightweight champion, and Jaffer ibn Yussef, billed as the 'Chinese Marvel'.[103] Although surely seen as an exotic occasion in the life of the city, such celebrations of Muslim culture would become the prototype for present-day cultural events in the city, such as the annual Arabic Festival. The increasing multiculturalism of the city was further demonstrated by the conversion of a Hindu to Islam on the 8th April. Later in the year, he would deliver a lecture on Brahmanism at the regular Sunday evening event at the Islamic Institute. The lecture would compare the inequality of the Hindu caste system with the egalitarian spirit of Islam.[104]

In 1906, Sheikh Abdullah Quilliam celebrated his fiftieth birthday. He was entertained by Yehya Parkinson, who lectured at the Mosque and read his latest poem in praise of the Sultan. In October, further good news arrived with the award of an honorary Doctorate of Law from Barrett College, North Carolina. The letter from the College stated that the award was for services to literature through his contribution to Oriental and Islamic subjects.[105] In 1907, he entered his thirtieth year of unremitting efforts to promote Islam in Britain. The year opened quietly for the Sheikh and permitted him to pursue his normal routine of public engagements and religious activities peacefully without distraction from crises in the Muslim world. The month of January was typical of the Sheikh's public engagements throughout the year, and provides a guide to what was now his routine way of life. On the 3rd January, he presided over the meeting of the Ancient Order of Zuzeimites and, on the 6th, the special committee meeting of the Mersey Quay and Railway Carter's Union. The next week saw him giving a lecture on geological theory to the Liverpool Geological Society (7th January), addressing the Liverpool Board of Legal Studies (8th January), attending the installation of a new freemason lodge in Liverpool (9th January) and a reception at Milton Hall, Liverpool (12th January) and giving a lecture in Manchester on 'Morocco and the Moors' (13th January). The next week began with a lecture on a 'Trip up the Mediterranean' in Liverpool at the Phythian Hall (14th January), a mass meeting of the Liverpool Coal Owners Association (16th January) and another meeting of the Zuzeimites. On the 23rd January, he addressed the Birkenhead Temperance Lodge. The month was actually lighter than his schedule later in the year, but it provides some insight into Quilliam's interests other than Islam and his punishing schedule of public lecture engagements.[106]

In February came news of another honorary law doctorate being conferred on the Sheikh, this time by the University of Liberia. Quilliam had always supported the efforts to promote Islam in the African nation and often provided them with tracts and pamphlets. Officially, the degree had been awarded for the same reason as that he received from Barrett College.[107] On the 10th March 1907, the Sheikh lectured at the Manchester Sunday Society, accompanied by his daughter Hanifa. This was a routine engagement on the topic of 'Constantinople', a standard lecture delivered by him throughout the years. But this time there was a different mode of transport. Instead of the train, Quilliam drove by car and the journey was reported as taking just under two hours. Ever aware of the effectiveness of new technologies, the railways, steamships, wireless, telephone and now the automobile, Quilliam utilised them all to facilitate his activities. On the 4th December 1907, Quilliam received another acknowledgement of his scholarship. This time the Geological Society of London, the oldest geological association in the world, made Quilliam a Fellow in honour of his lifetime commitment to the subject.[108] The year finished in the way that it had begun, with Quilliam carrying out a daily schedule of lectures throughout December.

These first two chapters have provided an in-depth and detailed account of the activities of the Liverpool Muslim Institute and its founder. Uppermost amongst the achievements has to be the creation of a community of Muslims consisting of over two hundred and fifty converts, the majority drawn to Islam through contact with the Sheikh's lectures. To a degree still not matched in twenty-first century Britain, he was able to show that Islam was a religious system compatible with the lifestyle of Europeans. Quilliam's converts came from all walks of life. In this, the Liverpool community differed from Woking, as the latter was formed predominantly of upper-class Englishmen and women and their South Asian equivalents. To join the Friday or *jumu'a* prayer in Liverpool meant to participate in worship with working-class, middle-class and upper-class Englishmen, poets, writers, athletes, artists, explorers, schoolteachers, lawyers, doctors, clerks, artisans, tradesmen, soldiers and even the occasional peer of the realm. Alongside the English Muslims at prayer were penniless sailors from India, Yemen and Somalia, upper-class Muslims passing through Liverpool on world tours, Ottoman diplomats and military officers, visiting Muslim students, performers such as the occasional wrestler, juggler and acrobat, even a dervish or two, and perhaps a Muslim potentate or prince accompanied by a newly-married English bride. In the social life of the community, the children of the wealthy joined with the orphans of the Medina Home, and the families of converts and foreign Muslims joined with each other in various activities.

The stories of the English converts reveal a considerable disenchantment among some devout Christians in the final decades of the Victorian era. The converts represented a sector of respectable society imbedded in the business, professional and shipping establishments of the city. They were often deeply religious men and women of conservative morality, but committed to a search for the truth. That Quilliam was able to inspire such figures to embrace Islam and involve themselves in the activities of the Liverpool Muslim Institute, when such a course of action would bring upon them the often acerbic criticisms of their peers, speaks volumes for the ability of the Sheikh to represent Islam in a way that appealed to their reason and religious sensitivities. The acrimonious way in which the community was often treated inspired the Sheikh to claim that there were parallels with the first converts to Islam in Makka. He was right in many respects, with one exception: neither the Makkan nor the Medinan communities had been required to weld such social and ethnic diversity into a body of people united by faith.

Quilliam was successful in this endeavour through a combination of applying the ideals of Muslim modernists, such as the Egyptian thinker Muhammad Abduh, along with a determined conviction that certain principles of Islam were non-negotiable. The conflict between the two views, as will be seen in later chapters, reached a crisis point when British foreign policy was seen to be incompatible with the Sheikh's loyalties to the Ottoman Caliphate. Le Mesurier provided the appropriate epitaph for the Liverpool Muslim community when he declared, 'England leads the way in all that tends to freedom and independence, and in like manner the Liverpool band of Muslims is looked upon as leading the way in liberal Mohammedan thought.'[109] However, it is apparent that Quilliam found it difficult to balance the demands of Britain's cultural emphasis on freedom and tolerance at home and its imperial incursions into the Muslim world abroad. In the day-to-day running of the Liverpool Muslim Institute, Quilliam demonstrated a liberal approach to Islam that was based on an understanding that it was necessary to adapt the religion to suit the unique requirements of Britain's cultural life. He believed that only British Muslims could achieve this, as all Muslims originating from abroad would bring with them their own cultural baggage. Throughout his life he tried to show that Islam was a religion that was moderate; yet his responses to British foreign policy and their relations with the wider Muslim world pushed him into making statements or issuing proclamations that would not be tolerated in the contemporary British context and would be regarded as 'extremist' if made by any Muslim *'alim* in Britain today. As 1908 approached, any informed observer who asked the question, 'where does danger lurk?' would probably have answered that, sooner or later, Quilliam's public demonstrations of righteous anger with British foreign policy would lead him into trouble.

There was nothing to suggest that 1908 would be any different to the years that had preceded it. The Sheikh was looking forward to attending the Hajj and visiting India in August. By now, the Liverpool Muslim Institute operated on a pattern that had been established over a quarter of a century earlier and then perfected in the early years of the twentieth century. During December 1907, visitors had come from Teheran, the Persian Gulf, Arabistan, Cairo, Mount Lebanon, Turkey, Batoum and even some Cossacks from Russia.[110] At the beginning of January, he had lectured at the Mosque on the subject of the Arab kings of Hira; in the audience were three Persians, two Indians, a Caucassian, two Turks, an Egyptian and a visitor from Sierra Leone.[111] In February, he addressed a packed audience at the Palace Theatre in Manchester, where he reiterated his usual themes that there should be better relations between Britain and Turkey, complete with eulogies to the Sultan. Again he emphasised that there were eighty million Muslims under

British rule and that the Government should avoid interfering with their belief or practice. He declared that loyalties had already been severely tested both in Egypt and through the expulsion of Indian Muslims from the Transvaal. He condemned the Lord's Day Observance Act that was about to be introduced in Britain, in which it was proposed to compel Muslims and Jews to avoid employment on the Sabbath.[112] On the 9th February, he delivered a lecture in the Liverpool Alexandra Hall on Genesis and Geology and two days later left for Paris in order to assist the Imam of the Ottoman Embassy with the funeral of Selim Faris Effendi, who was buried in the Muslim quarter of the Pere La Chaise cemetery in the city.[113]

In April he performed another funeral, but this time in tragic circumstances. At the family burial ground in St. James Cemetery, Quilliam performed *janaza* prayers in Arabic and Hassan al-Arculli recited the Qur'an over the remains of Jaffer Ramjhan, the brilliant young Muslim athlete. He was twenty-one years old. No mention is made of the cause of death.[114] The funeral followed on from another that would have brought bitter grief to the Sheikh and deep sadness for his Muslim community. In March, Henri de Léon had reported the illness of the Sheikh's two daughters.[115] Zuleika and Habeebah had contracted diphtheria. On the 8th April, the Sheikh buried Habeebah, aged eleven. She had died of complications after catching scarlet fever along with diphtheria.[116] Quilliam was grief-stricken at the death of the young girl and many years later would declare that his hope after death was to be reunited with her in Paradise.

The month of May began normally with a lead editorial in *The Crescent* commenting on the heterogeneous nature of the gatherings in the Mosque, declaring that the international diversity of the Muslim community at *jumu'a* prayer could only be bettered in London.[117] On the 13th May, *The Crescent* suddenly announced without prior warning that Quilliam and his eldest son had been summoned to Constantinople by the Sultan. Apparently,

Ahmed was to become the Caliph's First Secretary at Yildiz for a period of time. At *jumu'a* prayers, the Sheikh spoke of the short notice of the visit and hinted at foul play by Christian opponents.[118] It is announced in *The Crescent* that a farewell party would take place on the 31st May and that the Sheikh would return after six weeks. Everything seemed normal. The Sheikh and his son had both been on extended trips to Constantinople many times before. Oddly, on the 27th May, *The Crescent* does not mention Quilliam's departure. Instead the focus is on a profile of Yehya en-Nasr Parkinson, described as a 'gifted poet' and 'sweet singer of Islam', who was a regular contributor to *The Crescent*. The article states that his poems had been published by Keegan Paul and Tranch, entitled *Lays of Love and War*. The article goes on to say that he was born in Scotland in 1874 and had accepted an invitation by Abdul Karim Jamal of Rangoon to visit Burma.[119] There is no mention that this was to be the last edition of the newspaper, that the mosque would close and that the various properties that formed the Liverpool Muslim Institute would be disposed of by the Sheikh's sons. At the beginning of June 1908, the Sheikh departed for Constantinople, never to return as Sheikh al-Islam of the British Isles or again to live in the city of Liverpool, where he had spent the last thirty-two years committed to promoting Islam in the city. In spite of the efforts of some of the converts, the Mosque closed and, until the arrival of further migrants from Yemen, Somalia and South Asia in the 1950s, there was no official Muslim place of worship in the city.

CHAPTER 5

Quilliam in Liverpool: The first multiculturalist

Quilliam's multiculturalism[1] developed in response to the changing demography of Liverpool. As the city's population transformed in the latter half of the nineteenth century to include more ethnic and religious minorities arriving through migration, the leaders of these communities learned to represent them effectively to the civic authorities of the city. This was not always easy, and certainly Roman Catholics, Jews and Muslims had to struggle with various forms of racism that included stereotyping and religious discrimination. Quilliam, as the leader of Liverpool's Muslims, represented both religious and ethnic constituencies of the Muslim presence, but he was also in a very strong position to represent their interests. He was not a new migrant struggling to overcome economic and class disadvantages, but was a highly respected and successful lawyer belonging to the city's elite class. He knew how the system worked and possessed the wherewithal to manipulate it to the advantage of the Muslims in the city.

The Sheikh's multicultural perspective did not only arise from the micro-politics of representing the interests of a minority community to the civic representatives of the city. He was heavily influenced and impressed by the multi-faith nature of the Ottoman Empire and their historic institutions, which accommodated Jewish and Christian communities and provided them with a legal framework based upon the Qur'an's injunctions to protect and live side-by-side with the 'People of the Book'. In Quilliam's understanding, Islam was a religion with a multicultural view of the world that was based on its own ethnic plurality and the concept of *umma*, which perceived the world's populations as being distinct religious communities formed by previous revelations.

Quilliam regarded Islam as being far more tolerant than Christianity of other religious beliefs and was amazed when Christians showed their ignorance of the inclusivity of the religion. At the end of December 1903, after the death of Lord Stanley of Alderley Edge, a number of Christians, including clergy, expressed their strong disapproval of Quilliam and other prominent British Muslims performing a Muslim funeral for the well-known Cheshire peer of the realm.[2] Quilliam was furious, as he had been present when the Earl had recited the *kalima* at the mosque in Liverpool and possessed Lord Stanley's written request for a Muslim funeral. The churchmen's arguments were based on their knowledge that Lord Stanley had personally donated large sums of money both to the upkeep of existing Christian places of worship and to the building of new churches on his ancestral lands. The financial commitment to maintaining Christian sacred spaces was proof to the clergymen that Stanley was a committed member of their congregations.

Quilliam responded by stating that the Christians knew nothing of either Islam or the patronage exhibited by the Ottomans towards Christian places of worship. He argued that Lord Stanley's duty as a Muslim landowner whose tenants were Christian was to ensure that the worship of God took place in a manner appropriate for the majority religious community, for whom he had responsibility. He went on to declare provocatively that this was a fundamental difference between the two religions. Christians sent out missionaries to their Empire to convert the people of other faiths, whereas Muslim empires had always permitted Christians and Jews on their territory to continue in their practices and beliefs as long as they did not engage in the conversion of Muslims.

In this incident, we can observe Quilliam's understanding of Islam as a model for multi-faith living, which he applied in his approach to social work in Liverpool. One of the distinct and most well-publicised works of the Liverpool Muslim Institute was the feeding of the city's poor. As reported by the Liverpool press, he had initiated this practice in 1888, when he began providing breakfast for poor children at Mount Vernon Street. The practice was to continue every year until 1908. The lecture hall was decorated for this, and songs and musical recitations were performed by the women amongst the Muslim converts. The event became so popular that two feedings took place each year on Christmas Day. Between 200 and 400 children would be fed in the morning and a further 400 to 600 in the evening. Each year the media would be invited to attend the event, and Quilliam would never miss the opportunity to ensure that the gathered reporters heard about the universality and beneficence of Islam. He would ask the representatives of the city's press the question, 'who is more close to the teachings of the merciful and compassionate Jesus (Isa)? Is it the Christians who eat and drink all day or the Muslims who perform acts of charity for the hungry?' The food was wholesome and consisted of beef sandwiches and fruit buns served up with mugs of tea to keep the children warm. The media responded favourably and every year wrote about Christmas amongst the Muslims who celebrated Christmas in the spirit of Christ and who revered him as a Prophet of God.[3]

In 1895, Quilliam wrote that the occasion was an opportunity to show Christians that Muslims 'revere, honour and respect the memory of Christ as a prophet and apostle of the One only true and Undividable Deity' and that the religion of Islam inculcated almsgiving to the deserving poor and needy as one of the pillars of the faith. This edition of *The Crescent* reports that free meals were given to the destitute and distressed without any distinction of religion or nationality. The mosque opened at 9am, offering plates of meat sandwiches, bread and butter, seed and bun loaf and gallons of tea and coffee. It describes 210 'ill-clad Christians neglected by their own community' accepting the 'hospitality of the followers of the last Prophet'. As was customary, the event was repeated at 6pm, when 368 children were fed. At 8pm, the Muslims and the children were entertained by magic lantern entertainment, including images of Quilliam's travels, which was followed by comic slide shows and Chinese fireworks.[4] By 1897, crowd control had to be introduced to deal with the numbers that gathered to be fed. The formula of the event remained the same. The flags of the Muslim world, including the green banner of Islam, the crimson ensign of the Ottoman Empire, the red flag of Morocco, the Standard of Afghanistan, the Lion and the Sun of Persia, and the striped banner of the Sudanese dervishes hung from the walls of the dining hall, where beef, bread, bun-loaf, seed-loaf and milk, tea and coffee were supplied after the 'Basmallah' (saying *bismillah* – 'in the name of God') had been pronounced over the food by the Sheikh. The poor of the city were fed 200 at a time. Over 400 were fed in the evening session, when delegations from Liverpool's Jewish community attended. On the following Sunday, the lecture by Quilliam, never one to miss an opportunity, was on the position of Jesus in Islam.[5]

Quilliam's position on Christianity did not differentiate between the religion and Christian civilisations and cultures. He considered the many civic engagements that he carried out in Liverpool or elsewhere, where he represented the Muslim community and often shared a platform with the official leaders of the Christian churches, as multi-faith engagement with 'Christian' society. Yet his presence at such events was not always welcomed by the representatives of Christianity in the city. Quilliam had often criticised the sectarian conflicts in Liverpool and other perceived inadequacies in the dominant religion of the nation. In addition, historic Christian attitudes towards Islam and the current political crises in Armenia and the Balkans kept Quilliam and most Christian leaders at odds with each other.

Thus interfaith dialogue and multiculturalism would not be achieved without a struggle. One event is worthy of consideration because it demonstrated not only the growing consciousness of the significance of a mosque in Liverpool, but also an increased awareness of multiculturalism on the part of the city's officialdom. In February 1898, *The Crescent* reported that the Lord Mayor of Liverpool had promised to attend the Eid al-Adha (or Bayrami) festivities at the mosque.[6] Sir John Houghton was the Lord Mayor of Liverpool to be appointed when the town first became a city. He was a famous figure and a controversial mayor. Indeed, his visit to the mosque indicated his propensity to take risks. It is unlikely that the visit would have taken place without Quilliam's influence in the highest circles of the city's elite and his personal friendship with the Mayor. Abdullah Quilliam was aware of the political significance of a formal civic visit from the Lord Mayor and First Magistrate of the city, and the occasion was a personal triumph for the Sheikh. As reported by *The Crescent*, the formal civic recognition of the Muslim community by the first citizen of the second city of the Empire on the occasion of Eid was at least symbolically significant. John Houghton was not unaware of his role in a multicultural, multi-faith city either. In his speech, he stated that, as Lord Mayor, he had attended functions at the Protestant cathedral, Catholic and Nonconformist churches, the Jewish synagogue and now after some years he had visited the Muslim mosque.[7]

The accounts of the Mayor's visit provide historical evidence of the very first celebrations of Eid to take place formally in a British mosque. As the community consisted predominantly of British Muslims, or at least they dominated the Committee, there was no dispute concerning the rising of the moon. The muezzin had looked for it to rise over the mosque in Liverpool to signify the end of the fast, and the following day was observed as a holiday following traditional Turkish customs. The children of the Medina Home were given cakes, sweets, nuts, figs and oranges. That evening, there was a meeting and a reception. Muslims gathered from Liverpool and around the north-west of England. There were representatives from Manchester, Beirut, Jaffa in Palestine and Morocco. Mustafa Karsa, the Turkish Vice-Consul in Manchester, led a grand parade that consisted of the newly-formed Osmanli regiment, a form of Muslim Boy's Brigade, numbering thirty as a guard of honour, forming squares and drilling with swords, to receive the Lord Mayor.

So many gathered outside the Mosque that uniformed police under the command of Superintendent Churchill and Chief Inspector Bryson were there to keep the peace. John Houlding was met by the Sheikh al-Islam at the door of the Mosque. At 7.30pm, the Lord Mayor and Abdullah Quilliam appeared on stage in the lecture hall, whose walls had been embellished with the names of Allah, His Prophet, the first Caliphs and early Islamic martyrs, the *kalima* and certain verses from the Qur'an, all splendidly mixed with flags and banners. These proudly flew from the roof of the building. Gas jets cast various lights over the gathering. Quilliam thanked the Lord Mayor for attending and declared the occasion 'a red letter day' for the Liverpool Muslim Institute and an historic event in the annals of Liverpool.

The Sheikh was sufficiently aware of the significance of the occasion to state that he hoped future Lord Mayors would possess the courage to make it an annual fixture to join the Muslim festivities in the city. This was something of a prophetic statement when one considers the frequency with which mayors visit mosques in today's multicultural environment. Sir John Houlding responded that he did not know under which title to address Quilliam, and so used 'my old and esteemed friend, Mr Quilliam'. The Mayor expressed his surprise to see the size of the Muslim gathering. He mentioned that he had known Quilliam for the last twenty-five years and acknowledged his surprise that the well-known lawyer was now dressed in the robes of the foremost Muslim in the country. He went on to acknowledge the Muslims to be reputable citizens, well

An illustrated portrait of Quilliam published in *The Porcupine*,
a satirical newspaper in Liverpool.

ordered and obedient to the government and the state, and admired
for their devotion to their faith. In addition, he spoke of his own
travels in Muslim nations, to Algeria, Tunisia, Syria, Palestine and
Turkey, and mentioned the magnificent hospitality and kindness
that he had always received. He stated that he found Muslims to
be honest, industrious and God-fearing. He finished his speech
by declaring that he was aware that his attendance at the mosque
would be criticised by bigots, but that he was 'clear in his own
conscience'. Mustapha Karsa thanked the Lord Mayor and stated
that the eyes of the Muslim world were on Liverpool because of
Quilliam's activities, and it would be noted with pleasure that the
Lord Mayor of the city had attended the festival of the Eid. Then
night fireworks were released over the city and the celebrations
continued until midnight.

The Mayor's visit received considerable coverage in Liverpool's
media. It was reported in *The Liverpool Mercury* and *The Evening
Express* on the 23rd February. Both articles adopted a factual
tone. *The Liverpool Mercury* provided further coverage on the 24th
February and estimated the number of Muslims in attendance
at around one hundred. *The Daily Post* and *The Liverpool Courier*
on the 24th February, along with *The Liverpool Review* on the 26th
February, began to adopt a more sensational tone. *The Porcupine* of
the 26th February, ironically a magazine that Quilliam had once
edited, declared, 'The Lord Mayor will have a score of *houris* at least
apportioned him in the Muslim paradise. Muslims across the world
will rejoice.'

The Lord Mayor's comments that his visit would prove controversial for certain elements amongst the citizens of Liverpool were
proven to be accurate. In letters written to *The Daily Post*, some Christians expressed their outrage that the Lord Mayor, who was after all
a Christian himself, should visit and celebrate with Muslims on Ash
Wednesday. The Lord Mayor issued a statement that was carried
by *The Liverpool Echo* on the 25th February, which was essentially
repeated by the President of the Liverpool Hairdressers Society at

their annual dinner where the Mayor was the guest of honour. The President stated, 'Muslims of Liverpool pay their taxes like all other citizens and were entitled to the same official patronage as has been given to the Church of England and other religious bodies.' The Lord Mayor declared in his after-dinner speech that jealousy and controversy always followed a man 'who had made his mark'. He also commented that it was his job to respect creeds other than his own. Muslim responses were more robust. Omar Byrne, the Secretary of the Liverpool Muslim Institute, wrote in *The Crescent* that at least the Muslims were at prayer, which is more than could be said for most of the 'Christians' on Ash Wednesday.

The incident and reaction demonstrate that the city was waking up to its multicultural reality at the end of the nineteenth century, but that the dominant religion of the city was not yet prepared to accept other faiths as equals. Many Christian evangelists remained convinced that their religion was the only path to salvation and that the followers of all other faiths were doomed to eternal damnation. They expected a Lord Mayor of the city of Liverpool to believe likewise.

But the city also hosted other religious communities both new and ancient. If Quilliam had difficulties with the official representatives of orthodox Christian churches, he welcomed members of sects whose views on matters of doctrine were unorthodox. The records of the Sunday guest lecturers at the Liverpool Muslim Institute reveal spiritualists, Mormons, Unitarians and Jewish speakers. Quilliam's relations with the Jews in Britain were formed by his understanding of them as a companion monotheistic religious minority, authenticated by the Qur'an and living precariously in the country as migrants. They were allies in the struggle with the dominant culture, and his attitudes towards them were also formed by his view that the millet system practised in the Ottoman territories was the best model for genuine multicultural relations.

The city was rapidly becoming home to an expanding Jewish community in the closing decades of the nineteenth century and

Quilliam maintained strong links with the synagogue, being invited along with the Rabbi and their respective families to civic functions in the city. For example, on the 19th November 1899, Quilliam, one of his sons, and Professor Nasrullah Warren, the Secretary of the Liverpool Muslim Institute, accompanied the Lord Mayor of the city to the Jewish Synagogue in Princes Road as part of an official visit in aid of the Hebrew Philanthropic Society.[8] However, the relationship must have been more cordial than the simple performing of civic functions for, even as early as 1898, Bernard Kaufman, the President of the Fountains Road Synagogue, had presented a bouquet of flowers to the Sheikh's wife at Lime Street Station on the departure of the family to Constantinople.[9]

Quilliam was a powerful advocate of the Jewish community and a strong opponent of racism directed towards Jews in various parts of Europe. On a number of occasions he published articles in *The Crescent* that commented on anti-Jewish incidents in East Europe or Russia and would compare the attitudes in these places with the tolerant acceptance of Jews as 'People of the Book' in the Ottoman Empire. In addition, he noted that Jews were entering Britain in larger numbers as a result of these incidents and defended the increased immigration against those who were disturbed by the trend. He never missed an opportunity to defend Islamic attitudes towards Jews as being superior to the record of Christians. He commented upon an article in the *Jewish Chronicle* dated the 10th June 1898 on the riots between Sephardic Jews and Bulgarians. He noted that the Turkish authorities quelled the riots and took the side of the Jews. Quilliam quoted the *Jewish Chronicle* as saying, 'there is probably not a single country in Europe where the Jews enjoy more complete tolerance than Turkey, and greater goodwill on the part of the authorities.'[10]

The Sheikh was invited on a number of occasions to speak at Jewish functions in Liverpool, Manchester and other parts of Britain. Often on these occasions he delivered a lecture entitled, 'The Treatment of Jews under Islamic Rule'. On the 25th February

1903, Quilliam delivered this lecture in Manchester at Derby Hall, Cheatham. He commented on the shelter given to Jewish communities by the Ottomans and the Fatimids after the Christians expelled them from Spain in 1492. His conclusion was that there had been traditionally close relations between Muslims and Jews. The meeting was chaired by Chief Rabbi Dr J.L. Landau of the Manchester Synagogue. The audience consisted of over 1000 people, and at the conclusion Quilliam was given a standing ovation and requested to repeat the lecture in London. In December 1905, he continued his lectures on Jews and Islam, this time entitled 'Jews under Ottoman Rule', and delivered in West Derby Street, Liverpool. The hall was full and many could not gain entry. Both *The Jewish Chronicle* and *The Jewish World* covered the speech in full.

On the 6th January 1908, Quilliam was invited to speak at Cardiff University College. The title of the lecture was 'Islamic and Christian Conceptions of the Jew'. He was met by Dr Hirchowitz and visited by Dr Zalkin, Professor of Hebrew and Oriental Languages. His condemnation of Christian attitudes towards the Jews and his defence of the Muslim position was unequivocal. He said, 'the Jew must expect no mercy or consideration from the Christian who regarded him in a very different light from that in which he was regarded by the Muslim.'[11]

Most of these meetings took place at the behest of local Zionist groups. Amongst the fledgling Zionists, who were still castigated by most of their fellow religionists, Sheikh Abdullah Quilliam was a hero. It is hard to imagine a Muslim supporting Zionism today but, at the end of the nineteenth century, Palestine was a territory of the Ottoman Empire. In 1902, Quilliam had declared:

> It is back into Turkish territory, under the rule of Sultan Ghazi Hamid Khan that he (the Jew) flies in order to find that security for life and limb, and that religious freedom which is being denied him elsewhere. Where can you find a more prosperous Jewish community than Salonica, a city I had the pleasure of visiting just twelve months ago. Out of a population of about

120,000 souls about half profess the Jewish faith, and enjoy the
fullest liberty of conscience. Therefore surely it is no chimera
to look forward to the establishment of a successful Jewish
community in Palestine under the benign rule of the Sultan.[12]

The Sheikh had been advocating this position for a number
of years and had even lobbied the Sultan to make land available.
In requesting the Jews to place their trust in the Ottoman Sultan,
Quilliam was not only demonstrating his faith in Jewish-Muslim
relations, but also revealing his conviction that the millet system
through which the Sultan ruled over large Christian and Jewish
communities was the epitome of the multi-faith ideal.

At a lecture given at the Sheffield Jewish Men's Working Club
entitled 'Treatment of Jews under Islamic Rule', which was reported
in *The Independent* of Sheffield on 24th February 1908, Quilliam put
forward his position that the Jews should not attempt to settle in
the towns of Palestine, but he advised them for their own benefit
to settle in the country districts. He argued against the common
stereotype that the Jew was not agricultural. He suggested that they
had not been given an opportunity for farming for several centuries
and therefore had no choice but to become traders. Controversially,
he advised the Jews not to press for treaties and agreements, but to
go directly and settle on the land. He stated that, 'trust begot trust;
trust the Turks and they would trust them.'[13]

Quilliam's position brought him a number of plaudits from
the Jewish community in Britain. He received a letter from the
Manchester Zionist Association after his lecture in the city
thanking him for the support that he rendered to Zionism both
locally and generally through his speeches. In September 1902,
the Liverpool Central Zionist Committee passed a resolution to
express its thanks to Quilliam for so ably seconding a resolution at
a demonstration in Liverpool on 10th September. The Committee
stated that, 'His words have given all Zionists new hope and
enthusiasm, and inspired greater confidence in his most gracious
Majesty the Sultan of Turkey.'[14] This accolade came after Quilliam

had seconded a resolution for a return to Palestine at a national meeting that was held at Hope Hall in Hope Street – one of the most significant events organised by Zionists in England to interest the general public in the movement.[15]

Mr Joseph Cowan had moved that, 'this meeting is of the opinion that the only practical solution to the Jewish question lies in securing for the Jewish people a publicly legally assured home in Palestine.' When seconding the resolution, Quilliam stated that, 'he represented in this country a people who had always recognised that the Jews were a people neither to be persecuted or assimilated. Hence he was glad by his presence to demonstrate the sympathetic feeling which the members of the Islamic faith held towards the ancient "People of the Book".'[16]

Quilliam's brand of multiculturalism went beyond his relations with other faith communities or the way in which he engaged with civic authorities. Both are aspects of contemporary British multi-faith community relations; but when Quilliam spoke of the Jews as a people who should not be 'persecuted or assimilated', he suggested a model of inter-faith living and the treatment of minorities that became the unique model of British multicultural policy in the second half of the twentieth century. Quilliam pre-empted the idea of a migrant faith community living side by side with the dominant culture, yet maintaining the unique features of its social and religious life. It is, above all, in the celebration of Muslim rites of passage that we find this exemplified.

The Muslim community in Britain was formed of converts, students, foreign travellers, entertainers, embassy staff, businessmen and sailors in the merchant fleet. Although some of these were not resident or only temporary residents, the converts, along with small but significant port communities made up of sailors who had decided to settle and Manchester's business communities from the Levant, managed to weld the disparate groups into a whole. The converts may have taken responsibility for the promotion of Islam, but Quilliam served the other constituencies through Muslim worship and ensuring that rites of passage were available. The mosque at Liverpool became a national and international hub for both residents and non-residents alike.

In May 1898, at the Feast of the Greater Eid (Eid al-Adha, or Kurban Bayrami as it is known in Turkish) held at the mosque in Liverpool, there was a circus procession in which several Arabian and Egyptian Muslims participated riding on camels and dressed in native costume. The Muslim performers were part of Barnum and Bailey's Circus and they were almost as surprised and delighted to see the mosque in Liverpool as the crowds of bystanders were to see them. They spotted the banner 'There is only one God and Muhammad is His Prophet' hanging from the building, and passed the news to all the Muslims in the parade. Abdullah Quilliam said to his small but growing British Muslims, 'Doubtless some of these circus performers will find their way to prayers in the coming weeks!'[17] He was right and the following week's *Crescent* was able to report that two Muslims from the circus had attended prayers and expressed their delight at being able to pray at a mosque in the UK.[18] The exotic circus performers represented one small strand of Muslims drawn to Britain to seek employment; other entertainers who arrived at the mosque consisted of musicians, dancers, fire-eaters, a wonder-working dervish, magicians and two champion wrestlers. Muslim celebrations at the lecture hall in the evenings after worship would often include exotic entertainment, including a wrestling bout between the Turkish and Chinese champions.

Entertainers may have formed a small part of the diverse groups and individuals that constituted the Muslim presence in the nineteenth century, but each group was the result of the expanding British Empire. Lascars, the term used to describe Indian, Yemeni and other Arab sailors, were growing in numbers throughout the period and formed a significant proportion of the British merchant navy's crews. Servicing the Empire, many came to Britain from the colonies or protected territories, such as the Aden hinterland, British Somaliland, Malaya and the Yemen. Small but growing numbers were found in British seaports, especially in London, Cardiff, Tyneside and Liverpool. The coal-burning steamships also made Britain accessible to high profile Muslim visitors, especially those from India, who increasingly embarked on world tours or escorted their sons who were beginning their education at British public schools or universities. In addition, Humayun Ansari reminds us of the pressure that was placed on educated and upper-class Muslims in the Empire to obtain a 'modern' outlook and bring themselves in line with the 'modern' world. Some Muslims were genuinely impressed by Western ideas.[19]

Very often these wealthy, upper-class visitors would arrive first in Liverpool before dispersing to London, Oxford and Cambridge, or to travel onwards to other parts of the Empire; some visiting Europe or crossing the Atlantic to North America. Their sons formed the third group of resident Muslims, which consisted of students at Cambridge, Oxford, Edinburgh and Dublin universities.

Some of the lascars, especially those from Yemen, created a small settled presence in Britain's seaports. There were opportunities for more settled employment and lifestyle through the provision of service industries to their fellows. The remainder utilised these various services, such as restaurants and hostels established by their countrymen in the docklands of Liverpool, Cardiff, Tyneside and London. In Manchester there was a more established community of Syrian and other Levantine merchants in the textile industries. They were generally wealthy businessmen who travelled between their places of origin, Manchester and other locations in the Muslim world. Beginning in the early 1830s, these migrants arrived to work as traders and had formed a community of a few dozen families in Manchester. A further group were the converts to Islam, most of whom resided in Liverpool, as a result of Abdullah Quilliam's efforts. London also hosted a number of upper-class English Muslims.

Generally speaking, most historical analysis of the various groups of Muslims in Britain has suggested that there was little contact between them; but a close study of Quilliam's weekly newspaper suggests that the Liverpool Mosque and Islamic centre operated as a religious hub where many came to visit and attend *jumu'a* prayers or to be guests at the Sheikh's home in Liverpool. The Liverpool Muslim Institute maintained a visitor's book and carefully recorded visits by Muslims from across the globe or from inside Britain. High profile visitors from overseas would, more often than not, disembark in Liverpool and Quilliam's fame was spreading throughout the Muslim world. Not only did *The Crescent* reach over one hundred nations in the Muslim world, but the Sheikh also maintained correspondence with Muslims around the globe. For many Muslims, there was both curiosity and pride in the fact that Britain itself had a Sheikh al-Islam undertaking *da'wa* (Islamic mission) amongst Christian Englishmen and women.[20] In addition, Muslim sailors staying in Liverpool between ships would attend the mosque for prayer and, as already noted, Muslim entertainers passed through Liverpool as part of their circuit.

Fred Halliday suggests that the communities of Muslims at the end of nineteenth century consisted of a few hundred Lebanese, Syrians, Palestinians and a few thousand Yemenis and North Africans; but migration in this period extended beyond small populations of isolated Muslims.[21] Liverpool was a special case and could be described as Britain's first multicultural, multi-faith city. Although London also contained a strong presence of communities from around the globe, their impact would not have been felt in the same way due to the comparative size of the two cities. The central areas of Liverpool contained Britain's first Chinatown, a historic Jewish community and, of course, the politically and religiously problematic Irish presence; all of this was in addition to the polyglot global villages formed by sailors, many of whom jumped ship to live in the city. The Irish had been arriving in large numbers since the potato famine in the 1840s, but had been present in the city since the eighteenth century. Although many used Liverpool as a place of transit to the USA, many others found their home in the city. The city also hosted a substantial Jewish presence consisting of those who had fled Eastern European pogroms from the 1880s onwards. Even before World War I, there was a large Chinese presence. In addition, the city contained a small but settled Yemeni and Somali presence; and many more, including Indians, maintained a temporary presence in the city whilst they searched for a ship to take them home again. It is estimated that, by the time of World War I, 10% of the city's population were migrants.[22] During the lifespan of Abdullah Quilliam, Liverpool became the busiest port in the British Empire and owed its prosperity and diversity to the docks. It was this source of labour which attracted migrants from all over the British Isles and the Empire. The compact size of Liverpool meant that these international visitors and migrant settlers made their presence felt on local government policies, local economies, the religious and cultural diversity and intermarriage in a way that was unprecedented in any other British city of the time, including the capital.

Fred Halliday draws upon a combination of police returns and census data to estimate the number of Muslims in the city during the fifty years of its greatest prosperity. The term 'Turk' generally indicates a citizen of the Ottoman Empire, and in Quilliam's time this would have referred to Syrians, Palestinians, Lebanese and Iraqis. In 1881, only seven years before Quilliam's conversion, Liverpool contained eight Egyptians and 44 Turks and Lebanese. The figures peaked in 1911 when 110 Egyptians and 239 Turks were calculated to live in the city. After World War I the numbers declined, probably as a result of the defeat and demise of the Ottoman Empire.[23]

In this multicultural environment, Abdullah Quilliam practised law whilst actively and publicly promoting Islam from the premises of the Liverpool Muslim Institute. As the official Sheikh al-Islam of the nation appointed by the Sultan, and with a claimed endorsement from Queen Victoria, he had a public face in the city and the Liverpool media rarely left him alone for long. Throughout the world, Muslims began to hear of the English Sheikh in Liverpool.

The city was not only accessible by steamships that came from all over the Empire and connected to the transatlantic trade, but it was also opened up to the rest of Britain through the expanding Victorian rail network. Late nineteenth-century Britain experienced a communication revolution that was no less significant with regard to globalisation than that of the second half of the twentieth century. People across the nation and throughout the world were being put in touch with each other in ways unforeseen a century earlier. Quilliam was the first Muslim in Britain to realise the implications of the communication revolution that could bring Muslims together from across the world and put them in touch with each other.

The growing Muslim presence created a demand for Islamic rites of passage, but it took considerable courage to initiate and declare them publicly as part of the civic life of the nation. Mixed marriages in particular were taboo. Quilliam was not afraid of public acrimony, bad publicity or negative attention from public officials. He believed that the first Muslims had to be prepared to sacrifice reputation, friendship, professions and even family connections in their witness to Islam. His inspiration was the Makkan community in the first years of Islam.

It is recorded in *The Crescent*, which frequently chronicled significant events in the life of the Liverpool Muslim community, that the first public Muslim marriage ceremony (*nikah*) took place in April 1891. However, this occurred before the first edition of the newspaper appeared in 1893. Thus it is not until the 3rd December 1893, when Abdullah Quilliam performed a Muslim marriage ceremony at the mosque, that any details emerge of the ceremony. The marriage that was performed in 1891 was the first of many at which he personally officiated. In spite of attempts to keep the event private in 1893, the British media discovered the occasion and covered it widely. This was the first of the many weddings performed by Abdullah Quilliam in which the couples consisted of Asian or Arab Muslim men marrying English brides. It was inevitable that such unions would take place as more and more Muslims arrived in the country from overseas. The Yemeni and Indian sailors would frequently marry English girls that they met at the docks whilst searching for a passage back home. Such liaisons would generally result in the couple settling in the dock areas, where they would run hostels or cafes for fellow seamen. Other marriages were more high profile and came about from meetings of Muslim professional or upper-class men with English women. These marriages were highly taboo in India, where they were perceived to undermine the relationship between ruler and the ruled, but were seen as less scandalous in England. Even so, they raised the hackles of the British media, not only because of chauvinism towards mixed race marital partnerships, but also because such marriages would involve the conversion of the woman to Islam. By the first decades of the twentieth century, the number of such marriages performed by Quilliam had attracted the attention of the Foreign and Home Offices. The Law Society was approached to try and prevent the ceremonies, but their response was that such liaisons might be immoral but were not illegal.[24]

Abdullah Quilliam would normally arrange to perform both legal and religious ceremonies on the same day. In 1893, the legal marriage took place in London at the registry office, but Muslim law required a ceremony in the mosque. The couple travelled to Liverpool by train. The groom was an Indian doctor and had put up a £1000 dowry before the ceremony was performed. In the marriage contract he had promised not to take a second wife. The bride was described as a wealthy English woman, who was heiress to a title.[25] Quilliam performed the ceremony in Arabic, translated into English for the sake of the bride and into Hindi for the groom, who could speak very little English. That the woman stayed in Liverpool for one month to learn the rudiments of Islam from the Sheikh indicates the seriousness with which he considered conversion. After this experience, Quilliam arranged for the legal marriages to take place in Liverpool.

This was not the only high profile society wedding performed by Abdullah Quilliam. In July 1898, His Highness the Nawab Mahmood Ali Khan, the son of the independent ruler of Rampur in northern India, married Emily Florence Blanche Rony, the youngest daughter of Count Emilie Rony, who was of French nationality but resided in Bayswater, London. Once again the same format was followed. The *Liverpool Mercury* reported that the couple had a civil wedding in London before coming to Liverpool, but the paper is more interested in the age difference of the couple – the groom was forty and his bride sixteen – and the dowry of £20,000 settled on the bride.[26] The young woman renounced Christianity prior to the Muslim wedding and accepted Islam by affirming the *kalima* in English and Arabic, whereupon she was immediately surrounded and congratulated by her Muslim sisters of the Liverpool Muslim Institute. We are told by local newspaper reports that the marriage took place in the lecture hall, and the ceremony was recited by Abdullah Quilliam in Arabic and English drawing upon extracts from the Qur'an. These descriptions tally with the previous account and indicate that Quilliam's ceremony was based on an established format. The bride then signed the membership list of the Liverpool Muslim Institute, whilst Quilliam and the witnesses signed the Marriage Register. The Nawab donated £5 to the Medina Home for Orphans. The Sheikh entertained his high profile visitors for dinner at his home. The next morning, the newly-weds left Liverpool on the mail steamer *Prince of Wales* bound for the Isle of Man where they were guests of the Quilliams for twelve days at their house in Peel.

Such an occasion would have attracted attention in the city of Liverpool. Indeed, the *Evening Express* describes the groom as wearing a frock coat and a turban of cloth of gold surrounding an Afghan *koola* of rich gold; whilst the presiding Sheikh wore the full robes of his office as Sheikh al-Islam. The paper reports that over one thousand 'Jews and Christians' waited outside the mosque for a glimpse of the couple.[27] Nor did such marriages escape the anger of the Liverpool citizenry. The seventh marriage performed at the mosque between Kerim Buksh of Lahore and Ellen Lena Hallema Ilden of Ravenswing House, Stamford Hill, London, an English convert to Islam, also attracted a considerable crowd who watched the festivities, but on this occasion two windows were broken.[28]

In the case of the Nawab's wedding, the respective ages of the groom and his bride and the size of the dowry provided were bound to provoke the suspicion of the media, especially as the bride's sister had also been married to a wealthy Sikh. Yet such weddings would have been deemed an exotic social occasion, and they certainly provided Quilliam with considerable publicity. His reputation was established as someone who would perform controversial marriage ceremonies between 'native' Muslims and Englishwomen. Indeed, *The Liverpool Review* picked up the issue of Muslim marriages and stated, in a tone of outraged disapproval, 'if any Moslem in England desires to be married, he should make a pilgrimage to the Liverpool mosque, to have the ceremony performed there.'[29]

The exotic nature of the occasion and Abdullah Quilliam's enthusiasm to court media publicity as part of his strategy to promote Islam in Britain ensured newspaper coverage of the marriages, and consequently it is possible to discover something of the details of the wedding ceremonies. The outside of the mosque premises were hung with the green flag decorated with the crescent moon and star, and the corridors leading to the mosque itself were decorated with Indian rugs. The public were permitted into the lecture hall, avidly curious to see how an Eastern marriage was performed. The organist entertained with Oriental music predominantly of Turkish origin, including such pieces as *The Sultan's March* and *The Turkish Patrol March*, both rousing and triumphant Ottoman military marches. Around 8pm, the wedding procession approached the *minbar* headed by the Sheikh and the mosque's imam, followed by the groom and his sponsors, and then by the bride and her attendants. Shoes were removed as the party reached the carpets in the corridors. Upon reaching the *minbar*, they would all begin to slowly chant the *fatiha*, the opening chapter of the Qur'an, and then the principal parties were requested three times whether they accepted each other as man and wife and whether they 'undertook to do all that they as married Muslims should do'. A short address was delivered by the Sheikh, and then the newly married couple were wished the same happiness as that enjoyed by Adam with Eve, the Prophet with Khadija and Ali with Fatima. A short prayer recommending the married couple to the blessing of God concluded the ceremony. The bride and bridegroom left the mosque to be showered with rice outside by friends. Generally, the ceremony was conducted in Arabic and English and was translated into the vernacular language of the groom.

Twenty-three marriages took place from 1887 until 1903 in which one of the partners was a convert, but one more is worth attention. In February 1902, one Selim Hanowye, described as a merchant and shipper of 'Beyrout and Manchester', was wedded to Emilie Bostock in Liverpool. The bride was under twenty-one, a Liverpudlian convert and the congregation was requested to witness the vows. Abdullah Quilliam gave a patriarchal blessing to the young bride himself. The wedding is significant because it underlines the connections between the Liverpool English convert community and the earliest settled Muslim presence of wealthy Middle-Eastern merchants and traders in Manchester.

Most of the weddings carried out by the Sheikh were between partners who had met each other as converts in Liverpool. Obviously it took some time for the fledgling Liverpool community to generate enough converts to develop its own social life, including marriages and births; but on 22nd June 1897, Quilliam announced in *The Crescent* that the first wedding had taken place with full Muslim rites between two English converts. It is not recorded whether Abdullah Quilliam performed any marriages for the less high-profile relationships between Lascars and working-class British women. However, it should not be assumed that the Sheikh was only interested in upper-class rites of passage that would generate publicity. The descriptions of Muslim funerals tell another tale and reveal an altogether different side to Abdullah Quilliam's personality.

England in the nineteenth century was a dangerous place for the Asian and African seamen who arrived in its seaports. *The Crescent* reports the death of two sailors who died from the infectious illness, beriberi, in the Royal Southern Infirmary, Liverpool, who were buried by Quilliam at the Toxteth Smithdown Road Cemetery;[30] it also tells of a Berber from Morocco who had landed in Cardiff, but travelled to Liverpool by train to search for a ship to take him to Egypt. Only 21 years old, he died of kidney failure through overexposure to the cold. Quilliam had visited him in hospital and read passages from the Qur'an to him. He was buried in Fazakerley Cemetery by the Sheikh.

The Sheikh had carried out the first public Muslim funeral in Liverpool in February 1891. This was by no means the first burial of Muslims in the city, as Salter reports visiting the graves of thirty Ottoman sailors buried in a Liverpool cemetery in the mid-nineteenth century.[31] However, the first report of a Muslim death and funeral is that of Michael Hall, a forty-four year old Primitive Methodist preacher from Garston who had converted in 1890. This event was covered in the first edition of *The Crescent* and prompted Quilliam to deliver a public lecture on the theme of immortality the Sunday evening following the death.[32] On the 15th January, the funeral took place in Garston with formal prayers in English and Arabic recited over the grave by Said Adam, an imam from Makka, who was officiating at the mosque in Liverpool. Several of the early converts were present, including the Sheikh and his two sons, Ahmed and Billal. The Muslim mourners wore their tarbooshes and, although there was no attempt to molest or harangue them by a quickly-gathered crowd, the event was not without controversy. *The Daily Post* reported with some dismay and even outrage that some Liverpool Muslims had 'marched boldly into the churchyard at Garston, without so much as asking leave or permission', and had 'performed their peculiar burial service over the grave' of Michael Hall, who had been buried a fortnight earlier by the Garston branch of the Buffalo Lodge in accordance with Church of England rites. The writer of the piece demands that, 'such a piece of cool impudence should not pass unchallenged'.[33] Quilliam was to reply in *The Crescent* on the 28th January that consent had been received from Michael Hall's wife.[34] Further prayers were recited at the mosque and described as identical to those used by Muhammad at the death of his son Ibrahim. There were to be several other funerals of converts over the following few years because, as observed by Quilliam in the 1896 Annual General Meeting, a number of the first converts were elderly.

In November 1893, another significant funeral took place which demonstrates the communication that was beginning to take place between the various elements that made up the Muslim presence in Britain at the time. This time the deceased was a Muslim student aged 23 studying medicine in Edinburgh, who had died from an enlargement of the spleen in London. The body was brought to Liverpool by train in order for proper observance of Muslim funeral rites to take place. The dead student was named as Mahomad Abdus Salem, the eldest son of Habitut Taukhid of Patna. Accompanied by six Muslims, who were representatives of the Anjuman-i Islamia and Ikhwanna Safa Society in London, the body was met by a hearse at Liverpool Lime Street Station. The remains were covered with a green pall and were taken in procession by Indian Muslim sailors to the Necropolis Cemetery. Over one hundred and twenty Muslims participated in the funeral, which was led by two imams, Barakatullah, the muezzin of the Liverpool mosque, and Hafiz Mohammad Dollie, the South African leader of the Anjuman-i Islamia in London. The service was led at the graveside by Quilliam, who conducted it in English. The event also attracted over six hundred bystanders who followed the remains to the cemetery.[35] *The Liverpool Courier* reported that this was the ninth Muslim funeral to take place in the city and that eighty-eight Muslims were buried at the Necropolis. The newspaper also noted that, on this occasion, the funeral was conducted without incident, unlike the previous one in the city where 'rowdies' had attempted to push the mourners into the grave.[36]

The presence of Indian Muslim sailors in large numbers at the funeral indicates that, even as early as 1893, the lascars of Liverpool were aware of the Liverpool Muslim Institute and participated in its activities along with the converts. Ansari calculates that the number of lascars in Britain had increased rapidly, from 470 in 1804 to 1,336 in 1813. Around 3000 arrived in 1842 and, according to an estimate, between 10,000 and 12,000 in 1855. Salter calculated that 3271 Lascars arrived from 40 ships in 1873, of which 1653 were Muslims from India, Egypt, Malaya and Turkey. Of the 7814 Lascars surveyed in 1874, 4685 came from India while 1440 were Arabs, 225 Turks and 85 Malays.[37]

Not all of these arrived in Liverpool; but this is the period when the city was becoming one of the busiest ports in Britain. Shipping grew from the mid-nineteenth century onwards at an impressive annual rate of 2.6%.[38] As trade and shipping with the Middle East, India and Africa grew, people arrived from every corner of the Empire in search of opportunities. As the steamships increased, the numbers of lascars being employed by the British merchant fleet grew and, by the early twentieth century, Muslim seamen formed a significant part of the migrant population in Britain and the dock areas of Liverpool.

Ansari reminds us that the lascars were employed not only as cheap labour, but also because it was believed that, with the coming of steam, Oriental sailors used to the climate of the tropics and desert were better suited to the heat generated by the furnace-like engine-rooms below decks.[39] Although the pay may have appeared attractive to many young men and their families, there is compelling evidence that life was cheap and dangerous on board the steamships. It was not long before Abdullah Quilliam was made aware of their plight and he made them an integral part of the Liverpool Muslim community. In turn, the stories of the mosque in Liverpool and its English Sheikh spread through the Muslim sailor communities.

During the first week of November 1893, Abdullah Quilliam received a letter from Birkenhead Union Hospital explaining that they had an Indian Muslim sailor as a patient. The Sheikh visited the sick 29-year-old at the hospital. The report in *The Crescent* of that week is instructive, as it provides the details of the information that was ascertained by the Sheikh at the sick man's bedside. The sailor was from Calcutta, where his wife still lived; we are told that he prayed in the Ghowbara Masjid near Delhi Khan. He had departed on the *SS Daman* three months previously. As with all the sick sailors met by Quilliam, their main concern seems to have been a fear that they would not receive Muslim funeral rites, rather than any fear of death itself. An article in *The Liverpool Review* in February of 1898 commenting on a Muslim funeral performed by the Sheikh states, 'it is amazing that the man was not afraid of dying but only that he would not receive a Muslim funeral.'[40] The Sheikh relieved these hospital bed anxieties immediately, guaranteeing the sailors that full Muslim funeral rites and burial practices would be observed. In this case, the invalid was visited again on the following Sunday by both Quilliam and a party of Liverpool Muslims, but fortunately he seemed to have recovered.[41]

There was a very good reason for Abdullah Quilliam finding out the precise details of the sailors' backgrounds. On the 2nd November 1903, a young Indian sailor named Rahim Buksh lay dying at Borough Hospital, Birkenhead. He was only 22 and in the last stages of tuberculosis. He had been in the hospital since June. The Sheikh discovered that eight months salary were due to him at a rate of 16 rupees per month. He took the details of the charterers in Liverpool and the address of the young sailor's relatives in Calcutta.[42] We are informed that the Sheikh visited the shipping agents and ensured that the back wages which were owed to the sailor were sent to his relatives in India. The Sheikh was hard to refuse, as his legal reputation in Liverpool went before him. On the 14th November, Quilliam and some British Muslims went to

Bebington Cemetery to bury the young man. On another occasion, when a sailor aged 51 named Munto Abbas of the *SS Rangoon* died without being able to inform Quilliam of his address in Calcutta, the Liverpool Muslim Institute took out advertisements in Indian newspapers to trace the family so that the wages could be sent to the appropriate next of kin.

Almost a decade earlier, it is already possible to discern Abdullah Quilliam combining his role as Sheikh al-Islam with his undoubted legal skills in the defence of Muslim sailors' rights. In October 1894, a Turkish Muslim sailor named Mahomet Ali suffered a horrible accident aboard the *SS Dartmoor* when he was badly scalded by a steam pipe explosion in a boiler. A city police superintendent informed Abdullah Quilliam in his capacity as Turkish Vice-Consul and Quilliam, along with the Consul-General, visited the badly burned man in hospital where they found him in a critical state. By the next morning he was dead.[43] The sailor was only thirty-seven years old and was married. Abdullah Quilliam attended the coroner's inquest into the death on behalf of both the Ottoman Consul and the local Muslim community in Liverpool, claiming the man was not only a Turkish citizen but also a temporary Muslim resident under his jurisdiction and care as the Sheikh al-Islam of the British Isles. As a skilled advocate, he was more than capable of cross-examining witnesses and was primarily instrumental in bringing the court to the decision of gross negligence on the part of the steamship company. Quilliam had hoped to persuade the coroner to bring a verdict of criminal negligence.

In the meantime, the Sheikh's eldest son was able to ensure that a grave was dug at the Necropolis in the Muslim plot. Abdullah Quilliam began to work on the funeral rites with Omar Byrne, the Honorary Secretary of the Liverpool Muslim Institute. The body was draped in a green pall with the crescent moon and star and was carried to the hearse by Liverpool Muslim converts wearing their fezzes. In honour of the dead man, the Sheikh wore his *koola-izzat*, which had been given to him by the Amir of Afghanistan.

They proceeded to the mosque where prayers were led by the imam
in English and Arabic in front of the Muslim congregation. The
funeral at the graveside was conducted by the Sheikh al-Islam
himself.[44]

The above incidents set the pattern for the fifteen years of the
Sheikh's activities in Liverpool and further afield. Very quickly,
hospital, police and workhouse authorities learned that Abdullah
Quilliam was the person to contact when very sick or deceased
Muslim sailors arrived on their premises anywhere in the north-
west of England. Some of these incidents deserve recounting since
they tell us something more about the nineteenth-century Muslim
presence in Britain and the role of Abdullah Quilliam as a Muslim
religious leader. The above accounts indicate the degree of pastoral
care that became the pattern for the Sheikh's treatment of the sick
and dying amongst the lascars. He was to perform funerals for
sailors from India, Yemen, Somalia, Zanzibar and Morocco, and he
later ensured that not only British Muslim converts attended the
funeral, but in addition he contacted any Muslim sailors present
in the port and invited them to participate as mourners. He was
particularly keen that their shipmates from the same line or vessel
should attend.

The Sheikh also conducted funerals and marriages for the
Arab communities in Manchester. In 1897, a Syrian Muslim, one
Selim Muhamad Idielbe, described as a merchant of Beirut and
Manchester, was buried in Liverpool. He had arrived in Manchester
in 1892 and had become a member of Liverpool Muslim Institute.
Many Muslims from Manchester attended, but on this occasion,
because they were dealing with one of their own members, Quilliam
and other Muslims from Liverpool carried out the necessary
washing of the body after bringing the deceased from Sale by train.
As usual, large numbers of non-Muslims described as 'Christians'
gathered outside the mosque and followed the entourage to the
cemetery. We are informed that they behaved with decorum, which
was not always the case at Muslim funerals in Liverpool. By 1902,

the Sheikh had worked out a strategy for dealing with the large numbers of bystanders drawn to the exotic nature of the Arabic rites. He had quickly seen the opportunity of promoting Islam, and at the funeral of one Sheikh Ram-Jan, formerly a steward on the *SS Rhine*, who died in Liverpool on the 16th January and was buried in Toxteth Cemetery, the children of the Medina Home distributed two hundred copies of *The Crescent* to the curious.

It is from a funeral of another Syrian merchant of the Manchester community that details of the funeral rites followed by the Sheikh al-Islam are recorded. Mahomed Hollarby died in the city aged 75 in 1902. He had come to Manchester in the early 1870s and still maintained a house in Beirut, but had lived alone in the city without relatives. The Ottoman Consul of Manchester, Mustapha Karna Bey, a very good friend and colleague of Quilliam, had invited the Sheikh to perform the funeral at Manchester Southern Cemetery. The account of the event supplies the details of the funeral prayers or *janaza* that were provided by Quilliam. The Sheikh al-Islam recited the prayers, the *adhan* was given by Said Asha and the Invocation was recited by Sadik Hanowya, both Manchester Muslims. The Invocation recited in both Arabic and English was proclaimed at the graveside:

> God is Great, God is Great, God is Great! I bear witness that there is no other deity but God, and I bear witness that Muhammad is the Prophet of God.

The Sheikh al-Islam was dressed in a chocolate-coloured robe striped with green and gold, complete with fez and turban, while the mourners were dressed in customary British black suits but with scarlet fezzes on their heads. The Invocation was followed by a final prayer delivered by the Sheikh.

> In the Name of Allah, Merciful and Compassionate
> Know then, that this present life is only a toy and a vain
>   amusement;

A world of pomp and affection of glory anyhow,
And this multiplying of riches and children are as the plants
    sustained by the rain,
And the springing up whereof delighteth the husbandman;
Afterwards they wither, so that thou seest the same turn yellow
    and dwindle like dry stubble.
Have you not seen land which is barren, having been parched
    by the sun?
Yet from heaven the rain descends upon it, and from that dead
    earth
Springs up flowers and plants and fruits of diverse kinds.
Is not He who does this marvel able to raise the dead?
Have you considered how there is seed which is lost,
And then comes up as the green blade, fructifies, and after the
    flower again prepares the seed?
God permits man to come from an insignificant thing not
    greater than a drop of water.
It is placed in a sure receptacle for a certain time
And then brought forth to enjoy life for a while.
Man passes away and returns to his elements.
But in like manner the eternal part of him is placed in a sure
    receptacle until the Day of Judgement.
Death like birth is but a milestone of life. *Amin!*

After these verses, the Sheikh cast a small mound of earth upon the grave, followed by others from the mourners. This was done after the recitation of the Qur'anic verse, 'From earth thou camest, and unto earth shalt thou return.' When the last clod of earth was thrown upon the grave, the following prayer was recited: 'O thou soul which art at rest, return unto thy Lord, well pleasing with thy works upon this earth, and well pleased with thy reward.' After this, the following words were delivered in Arabic and English as final instructions to the dead individual:

O you whose body is now laid in the tomb, who are the servant of God, and the son of His man-servant and His maid-servant, let it be known unto you that God is truth, and that death is truth, and that the lowering into the grave is truth, and that the last hour is undoubtedly truth, and the resurrection is truth. When the two angels of kindness, upon whom is the mercy and pleasure of God, come to catechise you, they will set you to stand erect, and they will ask you about God who accepted the Faithful, and they will say unto you, 'Who is your God? What is your creed? And in what faith did you die?' Then do thou reply unto them, without fear and without quivering, 'The Lord is my God, the Lord is my God, the Lord is my God. Islam is my religion, the Muslims are my brothers and my sisters, the Koran is my Book, and Muhammad is my Prophet. Fasting, prayers, the pilgrimage to Mecca and charity are my rites.' And in a word you are to bear witness that there is no other deity but God and that Muhammad is His Apostle. Out of the earth God created you, and to the earth art thou returned again, but of the earth shall God raise you again. Thou wert created by God to receive the reward of this life, and to it, and to the worms art thou returned, and out from the soil of the earth shalt thou be raised to give an account of thy doings in the flesh. May God, the One, the True, bestow mercy and peace upon you as you lie in your grave, for He is the Merciful and the Compassionate and the Forgiving God. *Amin!*[45]

The funeral was completed with a final benediction by all present. The coffin was made of thin wood to enable rapid dissolution and the body was faced towards Mecca in the appropriate manner.

We know that the format of the funerals was standardised because the *Daily Dispatch* article in the same issue of *The Crescent* reports that the ceremony followed exactly the same set of ritual prayers at the nationally publicised funeral which took place in London only a few weeks before that of the Manchester merchant.[46]

There is one other funeral of interest in Manchester that took place in 1897, after the opening of the Manchester Ship Canal had permitted access to the city for sailors employed on the Clan Line and other companies trading with the Orient. An Indian sailor named Sheikh Hassan, who was employed on the *SS Imperialist*, had met with a fatal accident and been admitted to Salford Royal Infirmary. Ibrahim Saleh, a member of the Liverpool Muslim Institute who resided in Salford, had been asked to visit the man in order to translate. The sailor, only 21 years of age and from Bombay, admitted that he was a Muslim and personally asked for the Sheikh al-Islam of the British Isles as he feared that he was dying. Quilliam was sent for and arrived in time to carry out the funeral in Manchester. The Sheikh was annoyed that the officers of the steamship company had not notified the sixty Indian Muslim sailors employed on their vessels who were present in Salford Docks. This incident not only illustrates the networking that took place amongst British Muslims, but also that the Sheikh's reputation was known among Indian sailors.

The funeral in London mentioned above is significant because it demonstrates that, by 1902, Sheikh Abdullah Quilliam was officially recognised as the chief representative of Islam in Britain. Thirteen members of the Cyprus Regiment had been selected to represent the military of their nation at the Coronation of Edward VII. The British climate was too much for Sergeant-Major Mehmet Hassan, who succumbed to first bronchitis, then diabetes and finally Bright's disease, before he died. The British commanding officer went to the trouble of ensuring that the soldier received the full rites of a Muslim funeral and contacted the Turkish Embassy for assistance. A telegram was dispatched to the Sheikh al-Islam officially requesting him to come to London and officiate at the funeral. Under his guidance, the body was washed and on Friday, the 15th August, the body was taken out from the Military Hospital on route to Woking Cemetery.

Borne only by Muslim hands, it was placed in a hearse and then escorted by his comrades-in-arms, with the Sheikh at their head in his official robes. It passed through the streets of London at a slow walking pace. For two miles, from Rochester Row to Blackfriars Station, passing such London landmarks as the Houses of Parliament, Westminster Bridge and Westminster Abbey, the Sheikh melodiously recited passages of consolation from the Qur'an. As

London policemen stopped the traffic, the cortège arrived at the doors of Westminster Abbey, where for over a thousand years Christian funerals had been performed for the great of the land. The Sheikh al-Islam of the British Isles loudly chanted in Arabic outside the Abbey doors, 'Say, God is One, He begetteth not, neither is He begotten, and there is none like unto Him.' Quilliam was not one to miss an opportunity to promote the superiority of monotheism (*tawhid*) over Christian Trinitarianism and the symbolism of the moment was certainly not lost on him.

Both the procession and the funeral performed at Woking by the Sheikh were fully covered by the national press, including *The Daily Mail* on the 16th August. An interesting postscript to the story is that the troops returned to Cyprus from Liverpool. They attended *jumu'a* prayers at the mosque, where they personally thanked the Sheikh for his services to their dead companion.

One last word needs to be mentioned concerning funerals. The most emotionally difficult services performed by the Sheikh were those of infants and small children who tragically died of illnesses at the Medina home. There were at least three of these. Younous, a small child of fourteen months, died from murasmus, a form of severe protein-energy malnutrition characterized by energy deficiency, and was buried in the Necropolis adjacent to the Muslim plot. Another ten-month-old child who was admitted to the Home soon after birth, but who was already delicate on admittance, went into sudden convulsions and died. One other child's funeral is of interest. Gholam George Percival Price, aged five months, was buried in the Muslim plot at the Necropolis as a Muslim at the request of his parents. His mother was not a Muslim but she had been attending lectures at the Mosque and desired her child to receive Muslim rites. Since Islamic teaching states that all children are born Muslim, Quilliam agreed, arguing that in this case the child had 'never received the heathenish practice of baptism'.[47]

Later in 1898, a small child died of whooping cough at the Medina Home. There was no longer a burial site at the Necropolis, which had been closed by the Corporation, and the funeral took place at a non-Muslim plot at the cemetery in Fazakerley. After that, Quilliam and the officers of the Liverpool Muslim Institute began to campaign for the City Corporation to put aside a plot that could be purchased for Muslims who died in Liverpool. Donations were requested from Muslims in India because so many of the sailors who met tragic deaths were from the subcontinent. These were never forthcoming in sufficient amounts for the plot to be purchased.

The rites of passage performed by Abdullah Quilliam show the degree of communication among the various constituencies that comprised the Muslim presence in Britain during the last decades of the nineteenth century. They provide overwhelming evidence of the increasing multiculturalism of Liverpool, as the steamships brought in both sailors and passengers from many parts of the Muslim world.

It is in Quilliam's many references to the Ottoman millet system that we can discover a spirit of multiculturalism that chimes with the development of Liverpool as a truly nineteenth-century, multi-faith city. Here is a case of 'cometh the hour, cometh the man'. Quilliam's spirit of the times went beyond merely performing Muslim rites of passage or participating in multicultural events on behalf of the Muslim community, and was rooted in his humanist liberal values. Indeed, it can be argued that he converted to Islam because he believed that it was the religion in which he could find the justice that he felt the world deserved. Victorian Christianity was too harsh in many respects for the Sheikh's idealism. We have already seen his liberal views on capital punishment and his determination to side with the plight of the American 'Negro' in Chapter 2. Quilliam's multiculturalism was part and parcel of his liberalism, a humanist set of values which believed that the world belonged to all races and individuals, whose rights included the choice to settle in the country of their choice; and, once they settled, they deserved legal protection from bigots and racists and the right to preserve their own religious practices.

Quilliam was ahead of his time. In organising a community of Muslims in an increasingly multicultural Liverpool, by trial and error he stumbled across the main constituents of British multi-faith and multi-ethnic society that have become a hallmark of twenty-first century life. The way in which he conducted the rites of passage and religious worship of Muslim life, engaged in discourse with other religions and discovered ways to participate in civic life and the micro-politics of local governance were all familiar terrain to the Muslim immigrants of the later twentieth century. Quilliam was already pre-empting questions that concern British policymakers today. Does multiculturalism mean the dissolution of separate identities into one national 'British way of life', or does it involve the existence of separate identities that come together under some form of shared citizenship that acknowledges and respects difference? When should various religions and cultures come together and when should they remain apart in order to protect cherished beliefs, values and customs that are stamped as inviolable by religion? Who has the authority to decide when accommodation can take place and when a stance has to be made against assimilation? Quilliam's answer to the question of the enrichment of British life through plurality would have been a resounding affirmative, but he knew there were challenges. As with today, the crisis of multiculturalism would occur primarily through the inability to resolve Britain's foreign policy decisions in the context of the wider Muslim world. British Muslims in the nineteenth century would also face the conflict of loyalty that arose when Muslim lands were invaded and fellow Muslims were killed by British forces because they rebelled against colonial occupation. Quilliam could not resolve this issue then, and it remains equally thorny today.

CHAPTER 6

Quilliam and British Colonial Foreign Policy

Abdullah Quilliam was passionate about the direction of British foreign policy. He had always been interested in politics, but his conversion to Islam determined his views on British expansion overseas, and particularly where Muslim territory was involved in the colonial enterprise. His patriotic loyalty to the nation of his birth and the intense feelings for the religion he had adopted by choice of conviction were never easy to resolve.

Quilliam lived through a period of British history when the expansion of empire on a dramatic scale created extraordinary challenges to the national identity. Not everyone was at ease with the way that empire was sold to the British people. The blatant hero-worship, the sensationalising of glory and adventure, the magazines and books lauding romantic exploration of 'untamed' nature, the 'civilising' of 'native' peoples by missionaries and accounts of brave military exploits created unease for some individuals who tried to distinguish patriotism (a wholesome love of country) and jingoism (unhealthy xenophobia).[1] Quilliam was one who struggled with these dilemmas. His pan-Islamism was idealistically drawn from an instinctive sense of the oneness of humanity and he would never be at ease with xenophobic or racist attitudes towards other peoples. But more than this, his confirmed view that Islam was the final truth of God led him to the certainty that his new religion would ultimately triumph and that a future view of history would show a political and spiritual struggle in which Islam would be revealed as mankind's correct choice. With this view of the world, he regarded Christianity not simply as another possible monotheistic choice, but as irredeemably locked in the political struggle that was Europe's and especially Britain's colonial enterprise. Like many Muslims of his time, he remained at some level in a deep state of shock at the misfortunes of the Muslim world, yet convinced of its innate moral superiority over the decayed civilisation that Christendom had become. The solution in his eyes was for the British government to recognise that its self-interest lay in an alliance with the last Muslim empire, the Ottoman. Although an apparent political solution, this also resolved his personal dilemma of a conflict of loyalty. As the nineteenth century came to an end, he used *The Crescent* as his platform for representing his political view of the world to both the British media and his Muslim readership around the globe.

The period was marked by the Government's imperialistic 'little wars' that took place nearly every year of Victoria's reign after 1870. These provided a backdrop of military campaigns and the creation of British heroic figures who were involved in recurrent and forcible suppression of native resistance, some of it Muslim rebellions, that parallelled Quilliam's sense of the political injustices inherent in the colonial venture, with Quilliam finding a meaning and purpose in Islam. Just when military values were becoming almost mandatory for British young men, and the cultural and intellectual world of the 1880s and 1890s was popularised by the war correspondent and the war artist,[2] Quilliam was at the peak of his activities on behalf of Islam in Liverpool.

Emergent Victorian nationalism did not flourish in the colonial wars of Africa or Asia; that was to come later. Quilliam was born in the period of the Crimean War, a clash between the great powers, which involved Britain, Russia, France and the Turkish Ottomans. The Sultan and nominal Caliph of Sunni Islam declared war upon

Russia in October 1853, only to have his wooden fleet destroyed in Sinope by a Russian Black Sea squadron that was equipped with new shell-firing guns. Britain and France were drawn together in spite of their historic rivalries to take common action in order to forestall Russian domination of the Ottoman Empire. The following January, British and French warships entered the Black Sea.[3]

Nicholas I's conviction that the collapse of the Ottoman Empire was imminent aroused suspicions that Russian intentions towards the Empire were hostile. British foreign policy looked forward to the maintenance of the Empire as a bulwark against Russian expansion, whereas the latter looked to its disintegration.[4] During this period of British foreign policy, it was the fear of Russia above all that gave urgency to relations with the Muslim world. Since 1774, Russian foreign policy had been aggressive towards what it regarded as a decadent Ottoman Empire. The focus of attention was the Crimea, which had been a vassal state of the Sultan, but which Russia perceived as the key to increasing her influence in the Near East. The immediate issue at stake was the free use of the Straits that gave access to the Black Sea, which since the sixteenth century had been closed to non-Turkish shipping. Russia's aim was to make herself the dominant power in the Black Sea and to force the Turks to grant freedom of passage through the Dardenelles and the Bosphorus to Russian warships and merchantmen. Such Russian expansion alarmed the major European powers. France was the traditional ally of the Ottomans and was heavily involved in trade with the Levant; Austria feared Russian advances towards the Hapsburg Empire and saw Ottoman territory as a buffer zone; Britain was concerned that changes in the European balance of power would affect trade.[5]

Marcham argues that, since the Prime Ministership of Pitt the Younger (1759-1806), British foreign policy was the instrument of British trade and that no nineteenth-century Foreign Secretary had disagreed with this notion. George Canning (1780-1827), a long-serving Foreign Secretary, had never ceased to proclaim this strategy to his Liverpool constituents. Free trade and self-help were the dominant doctrines and were heralded as the guarantors of prosperity both at home and abroad; in addition, free trade was perceived as being the main instrument to the maintenance of peace between the great nations.[6] Consequently, Russia's attempts to dominate the Near East were problematic as they involved increased foreign competition. Certainly, whatever the arguments that were made for British imperial expansion, throughout the eighteenth century and into the nineteenth, respective British governments became aware that Russia was not only an Asiatic power, but an Empire whose influence was being felt as a major player in Eastern and Central Europe.[7]

Complications arose in 1820. Alexander Hypsilantes, a Russophile Greek, became the leader of the Phelike Hetairia, a Greek revolutionary society founded in 1814, whose aim was to liberate Greece from Ottoman rule by looking to Russia for support and invoking a common Christian Orthodox heritage. In 1821 the Greeks rose up in the Peloponnesus and this rebellion rumbled on for year after year. The main worry for British interests and other European powers was that the rebellion would become a catalyst for a full-scale assault on the Ottoman Empire by the Russians.[8] As Foreign Secretaries, both George Canning and Lord Castlereagh (1769-1822) were concerned to protect Britain's trade in the Mediterranean and declared the Greeks to be the belligerents in 1823. British foreign policy would remain neutral in the struggle between Greek and Turk, yet sought to avoid at all costs a war between Russia and the Ottomans.[9]

The balance of power shifted in 1824, when the Sultan appointed the son of Mohammad Ali (1769-1849), his powerful vassal in Egypt, as Pasha of the Peloponnese. The increased naval and military support led to defeats for the Greek insurgents, who appealed to Britain for assistance. Canning had begun to wonder whether working with Russia over Greece might be useful to British interests, and in 1826 signed a protocol for Anglo-Russian co-operation to resolve the

Greek problem. In the 1827 Treaty of London, which was signed by Britain, Russia and France, the three Powers agreed to work towards securing the Greeks some form of limited sovereignty.[10] In 1827, ten weeks after Canning's death, a joint Anglo-French fleet destroyed a combined Turkish and Egyptian fleet at Naverino Bay; and in 1829, the Turks were forced to agree to Greek independence and, to grant Russia a protectorate over the Danubian Principalities. These joint concessions brought an end to the threat of a Russian-Turkish war.[11]

The problems created by the movement for Greek independence brought a major player in the Middle East into the sphere of European interests. Ever since the Napoleonic Wars, when Bonaparte had invaded Egypt in 1798 and Syria in 1799, the Middle East had become part of the struggle for domination between the various European powers. The British had followed Napoleon's precedent and, in the years after 1805, when Mohammad Ali made himself master of Egypt, both nations sought to be his friend. However, following Greek independence in 1830, Mohammad Ali, the Pasha of Egypt who was nominally under the sovereignty of Sultan Mahmood II, attempted to gain control of the Arab provinces of the Ottoman Empire in Palestine, Syria and Arabia. The powerful Egyptian armies under Mohammad Ali proved to be unstoppable, and the Sultan appealed to both Britain and Russia for support against a major threat to his Empire. In 1833 he signed a treaty with Russia, which appeared to give them a privileged position as protectors of the Ottoman Empire; in turn, the Turks agreed to close the Straits to all foreign warships. Britain was faced with the political dilemma of ensuring that Russian inroads into the Ottoman Empire did not encroach any further and thus destroy the fragile balance of power in Europe.[12]

In January 1834, Vice-Admiral Rowley was told that, if the Sultan requested aid, he might sail up the Straits to defend Constantinople against the Russians. In 1839, after the Sultan unsuccessfully renewed war, Lord Palmerston (1830-65) discovered (as Canning had in the 1820s) that it was easier to restrain Russia by co-operating with her, this time through the Quadruple Alliance. A settlement was forced on Mohammad Ali and the new Sultan, Abdul Medjid (r.1839-61), agreed that henceforth the Straits would be closed in peacetime to all foreign warships. Queen Victoria announced that, once again, the special protection of the Porte was confined to the tender mercies of Russia.[13]

In the early 1850s, encouraged by the British ambassador, the Sultan refused to accept the Russian insistence that they had the right to protect all Orthodox subjects in the Ottoman Empire. The Russians occupied Moldavia and Wallachia, the Sultan declared war and he gained British and French support in what was to become the Crimean War. Britain entered the war in 1854, arguing that the preservation of the Ottoman Empire within its existing borders was essential to the maintenance of the balance of power among the states of Europe. In March 1856, the Peace of Paris imposed upon Russia an acknowledgement of the integrity of the Ottoman Empire, and reaffirmed the Straits Convention of 1841. Russia suffered the indignation of having her warships excluded once again from the Black Sea.[14]

It has been important to dwell at some length on the events leading up to the Crimean War because it is not possible without this background to understand Abdullah Quilliam's position on British foreign policy and the Ottoman Empire. Although these events took place in the half century before his birth, or whilst he was a very young child, Quilliam was well-informed about the recent history of Britain. He was a journalist and a lawyer with a keen interest in international affairs. As Abdullah Quilliam, the leader of British Muslims and the Sheikh al-Islam with a duty to report to the Sultan, he insisted that Britain's interests lay in supporting and encouraging a strong Ottoman Empire as a bulwark against the threat of Russia. He maintained this position until the outbreak of the World War I. In analysing and critiquing British foreign policy in the last two decades of the nineteenth century, he looked back to those Foreign Secretaries and Prime Ministers who had pursued the policy of maintaining British interests through seeking alliance with the Ottomans, and declared that they were right. He condemned British politicians who tried to change this strategy. But Quilliam would not simply support all Muslim efforts to re-establish their ancient hegemony in the Middle East. For instance, he never sympathised with Muhammad Ali of Egypt, whom he perceived as a traitor to the Sultan and Caliph.

With regard to issues that might affect Britain's relationships with Muslims outside the Ottoman Empire, especially those under British colonial rule in India or elsewhere in Asia, Quilliam's position was more ambiguous. His dual loyalty to the British monarch and the Muslim caliph involved a juggling act in which he differentiated between British intervention into independent Muslim nations under Ottoman rule or influence, and those Muslims who owed a loyalty to the Empress as citizens of the British Empire. In order to achieve this double position successfully, Quilliam argued that Queen Victoria was a ruler whose Empire contained more followers of Islam amongst her subjects than the Sultan's did. Although critical of British incursions into Afghanistan and Sudan, French activities in North Africa and Russian influence in the Ottoman domains, he never challenged the rule of Britain in India or other parts of the Empire. Indeed, he considered the British form of 'benign' paternalistic colonialism to be the pinnacle of world civilization. However, he did argue that British politicians should be careful not to embarrass the monarch by their heavy-handed treatment of the Empire's Muslim populations. His consistent plea and political strategy was to remind the respective governments of his time that Queen Victoria ruled over more Muslims than even the Sultan.

However, the overall situation had changed dramatically by the time Quilliam converted to Islam and was appointed the official representative of Muslims in the British Isles by the Ottoman Sultan. Platt suggests that, by the 1880s, there had been a change of attitude with regard to the motives behind imperial expansion and the series of colonial campaigns from 1877 to 1888 against the Zulus, the Afghans, the Boers and the Egyptians. He suggests that these campaigns were more concerned with territorial expansion than the necessary defence of Britain's trade and economic interests abroad. Imperialism was no longer reluctant or benign. Although Quilliam vigorously defended Britain's struggles against the Boer, he was deeply distressed by the events in Afghanistan, Sudan and Egypt.

In 1893, Quilliam had returned from North Africa with an acclaimed honorary title of 'alim, awarded to him by the Sultan of Morocco. He interpreted the award of 'alim and his status of Sheikh al-Islam as conferring on him the right to issue fatwas, which were not only binding on British Muslims but on Muslims around the globe. There was no indication that he would use this privilege to influence the minds of his fellow Muslims or to express himself on matters of religious law until the situation in Egypt and Sudan enraged him. *The Crescent* and the *Islamic World* provided the means for him to promote this first fatwa to the Muslim world, whilst the Annual General Meeting of the Liverpool Muslim Institute gave him a public platform on which to pronounce it.

The fatwa (*fetva*) reads as follows:

> In the name of Allah, the most merciful and compassionate! Peace to all True Believers to whom this shall come!
>
> Know ye, O Muslims, that the British government has decided to commence military and warlike operations against the Muslims of the Soudan, who have taken up arms to defend their country and their faith. And it is in contemplation to employ Muslim soldiers to fight against these Muslims of the Soudan.
>
> For any true believer to take up arms and fight against another Muslim who is not in revolt against the Khalif is contrary to the Shariat, and against the law of God and His Holy Prophet. I warn every true believer that if he gives the slightest assistance

in this projected expedition against the Muslims of the Soudan, even to the extent of carrying a parcel, or giving a bite of bread or a drink of water to any person taking part in this expedition against these Muslims, that he thereby helps the Giaour (infidels) against the Muslim, and his name will be unworthy to be continued on the roll of the faithful.

Signed in the Mosque of Liverpool, England, the 10th Day of Shawal 1313. W.H. Abdullah Quilliam Sheikh al-Islam of the British Isles.[15]

Not all Muslims were happy with the proclamation, and Quilliam himself mentions the controversy in Muslim circles and a letter that he received from India which pleaded with him to confine himself to religion and leave politics alone.[16] Some Muslims in India, recognising the sensitive and delicate position that they held in India since the failed uprising in 1857, accused him of high treason, while the *Muslim Chronicle of India* stated that there was no support for such views amongst Indian Muslims.[17] Quilliam's response was controversial, but also revealed that he understood the complexities of separating religion and politics in the Islamic context. He quoted the Prophet on the subject of Muslim unity and stated that, if Muslims were being set against each other to the detriment of the unity of the *umma* (universal Muslim brotherhood) by the politics of Giaour (infidel) nations, then this became a matter of religion. He declared that the aim of all Muslims should be to work actively for the union of Muslim people and Islam.[18] Controversially, he announced that the ultimate religious goal for all Muslim endeavours was the 'world for Islam'.[19]

The situation which had aroused Quilliam's ire in 1896 was the British Expeditionary Force's entry into Sudan under the command of Major-General Sir Horatio Herbert Kitchener and his utilisation of native Egyptian Muslim troops. General Kitchener had been a Major with the ill-fated Gordon relief column in the 1884-5 campaign in the Sudan,[20] and there were those who suspected that one of the motives behind the incursion into Sudan was revenge for Gordon's death at the hands of the Mahdi.

Egypt had come under British control when the Suez Canal had opened in 1869, and Britain had quickly realised its significance in regard to imperial strategy in the Eastern Mediterranean and the route to India. The route to India and the East was considered vital for reasons of trade, but political and strategic concerns also arose from the expansion of Russian influence that could threaten both the Eastern Mediterranean and British interests in the subcontinent. Egypt was still at least nominally part of the Ottoman Empire, and the Khedive ruled as a viceroy of the Sultan.[21] As a result of the American Civil War, Egypt had experienced a cotton boom in the earlier 1860s, which had brought vast profits to her ruler, Khedive Ishmael; but in 1866, all of this collapsed. In 1876, Benjamin Disraeli (1804-1881) seized the opportunity of Egypt's decline to forestall France and acquire 44% of the Suez Canal shares belonging to the Khedive.[22]

Egypt was pressured to repay her foreign creditors over a period of sixty-three years, and the Khedive was forced to accept a Prime Minister from America, a Finance Minister from Britain and a Minister of Public Works from France as guarantees of financial solvency. When the Khedive drew upon nationalist sentiments in Egypt to remove these officials, the European powers persuaded the Ottoman Sultan to replace him with his more pliable son, Tewfik. In 1879, Colonel Ahmed Arabi (Arabi Pasha) became the focus for various nationalist organisations and obtained the position of War Minister under Tewfik in 1882. Both Britain and France were concerned about the security of the Canal and warships were sent to Alexandria, effectively beginning a British occupation of Egypt. Although another long-serving Foreign Secretary, Earl Granville (1815-1891), assured the European powers that the British occupation was a temporary measure, it was not easy to withdraw from Egypt. This was highlighted when the security of the Canal was threatened once more by a revolt in the Sudan led by Muhammad Ahmad, the Mahdi, who raised the Sudanese tribes and the dervishes in a jihad against the disliked Khedive of Egypt.[23]

The campaigns in the Sudan provided the opportunity for intense media interest. Springhall notes that, from 1882 to 1888 and once again in 1898, Egypt and the Sudan attracted dozens of war correspondents and war artists, as clashes between natives and British forces supplied continuous incidents for 'the chroniclers and portrayers of patriotic adventure', in which the heroism of the troops could feed articles for the new mood of jingoism.[24] However, others only saw the misery of ill-armed natives or foreigners at the wrong end of the maxim gun. Whatever the political opinions regarding the war amongst the British public, there is no doubt that this was one of the first occasions when magazines and papers kept the British middle-classes informed and up-to-date and were able to influence the public mood. In February 1884, the Liberal Government had sent a former Governor-General of the Sudan, Charles 'Chinese' Gordon, to Khartoum to report back on the situation and to rescue Egyptian troops hard pressed by the Mahdi's revolt. Just before his arrival, an Egyptian army under General Valentine Baker had been destroyed in the Eastern Sudan at the wells of El Teb on the Red Sea coast by the Mahdist leader Osman Digna, who commanded a force consisting of dervish warriors of the Hadendowah tribe. In March 1884, General Sir Gerald Graham came up against Osman Digna in the same place.

The raw courage of the dervishes, labelled as fanaticism by the British press, and the tactic of feigning death when fired upon by the murderous maxim guns – only to jump up and kill soldiers searching for the wounded – made the Black Watch and Royal Welsh Fusiliers at El Teb less fastidious about the rules of war. A sketch by a war artist in March 1884 created intense protest from anti-government factions in Britain against the apparent brutality exhibited by troops shooting wounded rebels en masse. British military leaders responded by stating that British troops had no alternative but to bayonet and shoot the wounded dervishes.[25]

In spite of these protests, the 1884-5 campaign in which an expeditionary force led by Sir George Wolseley marched to the rescue of the besieged Gordon in Khartoum was largely presented by the media in a crusade-like manner, with a 'sea of heathens' threatening the lives of brave and patriotic Christians. The march to liberate Khartoum was not without incident, and when a maxim gun seized up in January 1885 at the Battle of Abu Klea, murderous hand-to-hand fighting broke out resulting in the spearing to death of Colonel Frederick Burnaby. Eventually the British forces broke through to Khartoum, only to find that they were too late. Two days earlier the Mahdi had stormed the town and General Gordon had been killed.[26]

For a while after the death of the Mahdi in 1885, events in the Sudan were fairly quiet; but, in the late 1890s, conflict was renewed by one of his successors. The campaigns from 1882-8 occurred before Quilliam converted to Islam, and certainly before he had the vehicle of *The Crescent* to publicise his opinions of the war. However, the situation was different in the 1890s. Quilliam's early reporting of the war was not completely condemnatory. He found himself under the weight of a confusing clash of loyalties. In a speech celebrating the Ottoman Sultan's birthday in 1898, Quilliam announced that British troops were once again fighting dervish movements, but also that there was a 'need to crush Mahdism and free the people of Sudan from their tyranny'.[27] *The Crescent* of the 12th January reproduced a number of articles from both French and British newspapers to represent a variety of views on the situation in the Sudan. Quilliam's equivocal position arose from his admiration for the Ottoman Empire and his undying loyalty to the Sultan. The Khedive in Egypt was the official representative of the Sultan, and therefore in Quilliam's opinion the Mahdi's forces were rebels against both the religious and political authority of the Caliph of Sunni Islam and the Sultan, the rightful ruler of all Muslims under the dominion of the Ottoman Empire. In addition, French excursions into the Sudan provoked Quilliam's sense of patriotism and he could not abide the thought of the old enemy of the British gaining an upper hand in Africa. In April, he published an article in

The Crescent in which he argued that British forces needed to strike at Khartoum before the French Expeditionary Force marched up from the south.[28]

The Battle of Omdurman on the 2nd September 1898 would severely test Quilliam's already stretched loyalties whilst providing the newspapers with a new arena for war reporting. However, the media found itself faced with the same conundrum as the Sheikh. Sir Horatio Herbert Kitchener's methodical conquest of the dervishes did not fulfil the romantic expectations of heroism that fed the British popular imagination. With machine-like precision typical of the organisation of the campaign, the British artillery pounded the tribesmen from gunboats moored on the Nile, whilst the army rained down rifle and machine gunfire from the heights onto charging ranks of Sudanese tribesmen.[29] With the loss of very few British lives, over 11,000 dervishes were slaughtered, breaking the back of Sudanese resistance. In spite of the imposition of strict censorship, the news was carried by the British media and the victory was celebrated with special parades and church services. However, some members of the British public were outraged, and even the *Daily Mail*'s George Stevens departed from the celebration of patriotic jingoism that was more typical of the war's media coverage when he wrote, 'It was an appalling slaughter. The Dervish army was killed out as hardly an army has been killed out in the history of war.'[30]

The first reports of the defeat of the Sudanese dervishes by an Anglo-Egyptian force indicated that the dead and prisoners amounted to 7000, and that the leader of the dervishes had been captured. Quilliam noted that even French newspapers were writing that the Nile valley was now open to the British.[31] A week later, Quilliam announced that Omdurman had fallen and that the 10,000 dervishes who had stormed the Anglo-Egyptian troops had been repulsed with great loss of life from maxim fire. Quilliam's tone is somewhat ambiguous, but he notes that, 'though they were not well-equipped, their meritorious conduct, bravery and dauntlessness leave an ineffaceable memory in the annals of recent chronicles of Muslim bravery'. He goes on to report British losses of only 500 men and praises the 'patriotism' of the dervishes. He compared their foolhardy attack on the British positions with the Charge of the Light Brigade and notes that, contrary to the previous week's report, the Khalifa had escaped with his harem. Quilliam's view on the rebellious and treasonous Mahdi forces had now transformed so that he viewed them as men fighting to protect their legitimate territory from colonial invaders. He described them as men 'in whose veins runs the blood of freedom and patriotism, and who preferred manfully to be slain on the battlefield rather than to yield in subjection and humiliation, and to enjoy martyrdom in defending their dear and beloved native country'.[32]

By the following week, Quilliam had consolidated his position sufficiently to write an article on Omdurman entitled, 'War or Murder, Which?' He claimed that 20,000 Muslims had lost their lives in the campaign, murdered by machine guns, who had never done any harm to anyone in England. He argued that these 'simple sons of the desert' were merely protecting their families, homes, country and religion against Englishmen who had no right to be in their land. He blamed industrialisation and capitalism for the slaughter, asking, 'Is the desire to supply the simple child of the sandy waste with shoddy cloth, Manchester prints, Sheffield cutlery, Belfast whiskey and Birmingham jewellery a sufficient justification for the invasion of another person's land?' He went on to challenge the media perception of the heroism of the British forces and condemn Christian clergy for their religious services thanking God for victory:

> Where does the much-vaunted bravery of the British troops come in? Possessed with murderous weapons dealing death and destruction all around, the British troops at a safe distance poured showers of bullets upon a brave but ill-armed concourse of noble patriots. Place them man to man, with equal chance and equal weapons, and who can doubt what the result would

be? The shout of victory would be with the Dervish ... it is the victory of the pirate and the robber, the pillager and the land-grabber. Victory may be with the English, but the honour of the day rests with the 20,000 men whose murdered bodies lie bleaching on the desert sands. 'War in the Soudan' forsooth! 'Twas murder and nothing else.[33]

The same edition of *The Crescent* contained letters in praise of the dervishes' bravery reprinted from the British and international media. A week later, Quilliam had resolved the various ambiguities he was feeling by regarding the conflict in the region as a colonial attempt to deprive the Sultan of his legitimate territory in order to further British interests by building a railway from Cairo to Capetown. In a letter to *The Liverpool Courier*, he declared that 119,000 Muslims had been killed in total in Egypt and Sudan by Christian forces intent upon stealing the Valley of the Nile from its rightful owners.[34] Even so, he remained adamant that the British government had to remove the French force stationed at Fashoda at all costs.[35]

In March 1899, Quilliam noted that the forces of resistance in the Sudan were far from destroyed and that the dervishes had defeated Arabs loyal to the British. Furthermore, he wrote that a force of 10,000 was marching back to Omdurdan to recapture the town. Quilliam observed that if the 'kalifa' attacked frontally, he would be destroyed once again, but that if he played cat and mouse, he could remain a major irritant to the British occupiers.[36] The renewal of conflict with the revitalised forces of the 'Mahdi' would bring with it a severer test of loyalty than even the slaughter at Omdurman. Some of Kitchener's troops desecrated the shrine and grave of the 'Mahdi', digging up his corpse and removing the head. Rumours stated that the head was in the possession of Kitchener himself, something that the General never denied. It was even said that the head would go on exhibition in a museum in Cairo. At a meeting of the Liverpool Muslim Institute, it was decided to send a letter to the British Parliament on behalf of British Muslims to complain formally. The Sheikh clarified his position to a gathering of British Muslims at the Liverpool mosque. He explained that no political party was represented by his views, but only Muslims and friends who were outraged by such desecration. In detail he explained the various meanings of 'Mahdi' in both Sunni and Shi'ite Islam, and stated that he did not personally feel that the fallen hero of the Sudan fitted any of them, nor indeed could his successors claim the title of the Caliph as this belonged to the Ottoman sultan alone. However, they were devout Muslims and no Muslim grave should be desecrated. He declared that, as an Englishman and a true-born Briton, he felt that the reputation of the nation had been sullied and that he was personally ashamed and degraded. He demanded that the perpetrators be brought to justice and the remains of the 'Mahdi' be returned.[37] It was agreed to petition Parliament, and the Petition was presented to the House on the 27th March 1899 by Charles McArthur, the Member for the Exchange Division of Liverpool. Entitled 'The Muslim Petition to the Imperial Parliament of Great Britain and Ireland', the document read:

> To the Honourable the House of Commons of the United Kingdom of Great Britain and Ireland in Parliament assembled.
>
> The humble petition of the Undersigned showeth; that at a meeting of persons professing the Muslim faith and residing in England, held in the lecture hall of the Liverpool Muslim Institute, West Derby Road, in the City of Liverpool, on the 21st day of March, 1899, it was unanimously resolved:- that this meeting hereby records its earnest protest against the outrage that was committed in the Soudan, in the rifling of the tomb of him who was called the Mahdi at Omdurman, and the mutilation of his corpse, and respectfully requests the Imperial Parliament of Great Britain to hold an enquiry with reference to the same, so that the perpetrators of this scandalous outrage can be reprimanded and punished, and that the copies of this resolution shall be forwarded to her Majesty the Queen, Lord Salisbury and Sir Henry Campbell-Bannerman.

Your petitioners therefore humbly pray that your Honourable
House will cause an enquiry to be granted into the above matter
in accordance with the sentiments of the said resolution.
And your petitioners will ever pray,

Signed on behalf of the persons assembled at such meeting as
aforesaid

W.H. Abdullah Quilliam
Sheikh al-Islam of the British Isles and Chairman of the said
meeting.

The document was stamped with the Ottoman seal given to
Quilliam by the Sultan to show that he officially represented the
Caliph in the British Isles and to announce his authority. The
next few editions of *The Crescent* reprinted articles from various
newspapers that were opposed to the desecration, including the
Irish Weekly Independent, and noted that journalists were forbidden
to report from Sudan and were confined to Cairo. Quilliam thanked
the Irish newspaper and a number of Members of Parliament for
their 'spirited protest', and noted that Kitchener had responded to
charges of cruelty and that Lord Cromer has defended his actions
as justified and necessary on the grounds that the tomb functioned
as a focal point for the 'Mahdi' rebellion to continue.[38] Quilliam
responded to this statement by noting that the desecration would
only increase the fervour of the Muslims in Sudan and, adopting an
ironic note, he added that Christians should be the last people on
earth to believe that an empty tomb would put an end to religious
fervour.

The Sheikh picked up the religious theme once more by noting
that Kitchener had at least forbidden missionary activity in Sudan
for fear that it might further inflame the populace. However, he
was angered by an article in the *American Sentinel* published on
the 9th March, which argued that the combination of church and
state in Great Britain was hindering the spread of Christianity in
Sudan by interfering in the freedom of Christians to carry out
missionary activity. The US article sent Quilliam into an aggressive

stance towards such Christian sentiments and he reprinted an 'unauthored' article in which a 'journalist' wrote: 'The religious world is at war. The religious world has always been at war, and the battle with its ten thousand attendant horrors, will go on until the true religion – the religion of love, of brotherhood, of humanity and righteousness – arises in its might and sweeps the hypocritical smug faced combatants from the field.'[39]

The 'journalist' condemned Christianity for raising the flag of Christ and, in doing so, making people 'fight against him and make mockery of his words; they fight for wealth, luxury and self; instead of truth they love falsehood; instead of charity they are full of greed, and instead of love, they nourish feelings of enmity and hate, the principles of the Lord have been distorted by the narrow-minded bigots of a thousand sects, and brotherly love is forgotten in this mad wars of the creeds. It is in the Christian camp where hatred, uncharitableness and treachery most prevail.'[40]

The use of the third party, anonymous journalist is a device that Quilliam often used to publish his views. He had certainly expressed his position towards contemporary Western Christianity on numerous occasions, and this article encapsulated his position succinctly and accurately. In it we see the reasons why Quilliam had abandoned the religion of his birth. The Muslim Quilliam had become convinced that Christianity had sunk to this position of decay even before the birth of Muhammad, and this was the reason for God to send again a prophet and a book. Quilliam took the orthodox Muslim position that Jesus remained a true messenger and prophet and that the religion of love, brotherhood, humanity and righteousness that he preached was Islam. The wars in Sudan and elsewhere between the colonial (Christian) powers and the oppressed and resistant (Muslim) forces were part of a titanic struggle in which Islam would be ultimately victorious. The events in Omdurman focused Quilliam's loyalties in ways that other incidents could not, and his second proclamation as an *'alim* expressed his anger. Significantly, the target was no longer Muslims in Egypt who fought against fellow Muslims in Sudan as part of the British forces, but against the British forces themselves who were linked to a wider cosmic religious struggle between Allah and Shaytan (Satan). The battle lines were drawn and no true Muslim could side with the British excursions into Muslim territory. It is notable that, for the first time, the Sheikh al-Islam uses the term 'fatwa' as opposed to the English adaptation of 'proclamation' that he had used formerly:

> In the name of Allah, the most merciful and compassionate! Peace to all True Believers to whom this shall come!
>
> To all true believers in Allah and in his Holy Prophet in whatever land they may dwell: this message is from Abdullah Quilliam, the humble instrument whom Allah hath appointed to preach Islam to all English speaking people.
>
> Brethren peace be unto you!
>
> Brethren, it is written in the Koran that the true believers are brethren. Each Muslim, is therefore, my brother, your brother. It is the bounden and sacred duty of every Muslim to assist his brother while alive, and to respect and protect his mortal remains when it hath pleased Allah to call him to rest. It matters not whether the true believer be Hanifee, Malekee, Hanballee or Shafee; if he believe in Allah and His Prophet, he is our brother.
>
> Brethren, a few years ago a certain Mussulman, Mahommad Ahmed ibn Abdullah by name, gained great victories in the Soudan; the giaours and kaffirs opposed him in vain; Allah in His divine wisdom brought their devices to naught, and gave the victory to this son of Islam. Allah Akbar. This man was a Muslim; as such he lived, as such he died, as such he was buried. Years after this true believer had died and entered into rest, the giaours came to the place where his corpse was buried. Nothing is sacred to these men, who follow a vain delusion, and who deny that Allah is one, and refuse to follow the true path revealed by the blessed Mustapha al-Amin. They are blind and deaf, and take the rebellious Shaitan for their patron, and the truth is not in them. These Nasuranee came like loathsome swine, filthy dogs, cowardly jackals and offal eating hyenas to defile the grave of

this great Mussulman, Mahommad Ahmed ibn Abdullah, the Soudanee. With sacrilegious hands they dragged his corpse from the grave and hacked off his head, and hath borne it off to exhibit in their own lands to their women and children as a proof how the Nasuranee hates the Mussulman. Then they took the body of this great Mussulman and dragged it with every mark of dishonour to the riverside and flung it therein, that it might become the food for the voracious crocodile.

Brethren, this is what the Nasuranee have done to the mouldering corpse of a dead Mussulman. By this shameful outrage upon the dead every Muslim in the world has been insulted, has been outraged in his feelings, and wounded in his self-respect.

Brethren let the remembrance of this outrage be engraved deeply upon each Muslim's heart. Until every one of the perpetrators or assistants in this diabolical outrage are adequately punished for their participation therein, there can be no friendship, no communion, between any true believer and those of the same religious creed as these despoilers of dead men's graves. Shun the presence of these wicked men – these human ghouls – as ye would flee from the presence of a leper! Shun them as ye would one who Shaitan has infected with a touch! Brethren, Allah will support you against those who are in manifest error, for he is the Hearer, the Wise!

The fatwa goes on to quote the Chapter *Al 'Imran* from the Qur'an, which commands the Muslim, 'contract not a friendship with any besides those of the true faith; they will not fail to corrupt you.'

The message of the fatwa is uncompromising and expresses the anger and indignation of Quilliam; but he was in no doubt that the Muslims around the world would feel the same way. He appealed to a Muslim unity that would override lesser loyalties to schools of law or sectarian divides, but significantly names the enemy as 'Nasuranee', or Christians and Christianity, as a 'vain delusion' rather than the British powers. He declared that Christians have always hated Muslims right from the time when they refused to hear the message of the Prophet, and thus they fall on the side of

Shaytan and not God in the struggle between God and the Devil. However, he falls short of demanding rebellion or insurrection, but requests Muslims to isolate themselves from communication with the Christian world until the perpetrators have been identified and tried and the remains of the 'Mahdi' returned. However, Quilliam's condemnation of British actions would not go unnoticed by the colonial rivals. The press of both France and Russia published the fatwa. In his outrage at this tactic, Quilliam reported the heroism of a Muslim soldier in the Uganda Rifles who had fought with a crocodile to save a comrade and had been awarded a medal from the Royal Humane Society. The message is twofold: firstly, to note the corresponding honourable behaviour of Muslims; and secondly, to make a statement of the loyalty of Muslim troops to the British cause and ask the implicit question whether such true-hearted people deserve to be treated with such treachery by the non-Muslim allies.

The Crescent continued to report the situation in Sudan sporadically, noting that the nation would be opened up to trade and that Europeans were now free to acquire land, effectively colonising more Muslim lands.[41] As a note of caution, Quilliam noted that the 'Kalifa' was still wandering the Sudan with a force of 3000 dervishes. In this issue, he also criticised the award of £30,000 granted by Parliament to Kitchener as the 'Butcher's Bill' and satirically published an invoice from the nation:

> John Bull Esq.
> To Kitchener of Khartoum
> To killing and slaying 10,000 dervishes; also digging up the mouldering corpse of a dead Mussulman, chopping his head off and throwing his body in the Nile ...
> £30,000 settled with thanks.[42]

At the end of November 1899, he reported that the Khalifa's forces had been defeated by Wingate at Abu Asdil and both the 'Kalifa' and his army were destroyed.[43] In December, Quilliam wrote a biography of the 'Kalifa' and commented that, although guided by mistaken fanaticism, his courage and heroism had to be acknowledged and that his death demonstrated the difference between someone who was certain of his faith in Allah and that of unbelievers who feared death more than anything. The article finished with a description of the 'Kalifa's' last words addressed to his warriors: 'O noble Emirs! "Tis great Allah's Will we die, then let us meet our deaths as Muslims". He then sat down upon a Sheepskin rug and gathered around him his bodyguard.'[44]

Quilliam's final comments on the Sudan have a contemporary resonance. In January 1900, the Sheikh noted that Omdurman was being Westernised under Kitchener, who had introduced European-style shops, cafes run by Greeks, a music warehouse and a concert hall, a postal and telegraph system and a regular ferry linking it to Khartoum.[45] In case there were those who were not clear that he disapproved of the introduction of European culture to the Sudan, the following week he commented that, 'Omdurman only needs a brewery and a bishop and its Christianisation will be complete'.[46]

There are two more important articles in *The Crescent* that indicated Quilliam's difficulties with these colonial incursions into Muslim territory, local rebellions and final absorption into empire. In the spring of the first year of the twentieth century, Quilliam published an article by Henri de Léon attacking the French occupation of Inghar Oasis in present-day Algeria, in which 2000 tribesmen lose their lives. De Léon echoed Quilliam's position very precisely stating:

> O Muslims throughout the world, why stand so calmly by while these Christian land-robbers dye their hands red in the blood of your brother true-believers. Arise brethren, place yourself under the leadership of the Caliph of the Faithful, and resist to the death the encroachments of each and every one of these hypocritical lying thieving murderous Christian nations. See in them only Giaours, eaters of swine flesh, and enemies of the true faith. May dogs defile their graves.[47]

The de Léon article makes a stronger statement because this time the colonial intruders are French, and Quilliam does not have to fear British sensitivities and knows that the public will support criticism of France. Quilliam commented that the situation in Algeria simply demonstrated that 'Christian Europe in its wild and insatiable land-hunger has brutally slain over 600 Muslims, and cruelly wounded 1000 more.' He stated that 'the only crime that these poor tribesmen had committed was to stand up for their rights, for their liberty and for the possession of the country in which their ancestors were born and bred. For this, they were murdered by a band of infidels armed with machine guns and other terrible weapons of destruction. Such an action compels us to regard the French as a gang of murderers and assassins.'[48]

However, the situation in Algeria directly parallels the crisis in Sudan, and the editorial is therefore an implicit criticism of the British colonial presence in Muslim territory. Yet it is more difficult for Quilliam to be so forthright in his views when Muslim land became part of the British Empire and began to receive the benefits that Quilliam, as a loyal citizen and patriot, believed accrued to those who found themselves under the rule of the Empress, as the following report in *The Crescent* indicated clearly. Quilliam reproduced a speech by Lord Cromer to the Sheikhs in Khartoum which proudly noted that they were now ruled by Queen Victoria and the Khedive, and as a consequence their religion would be respected, taxes fairly collected and the railways extended. He noted that the Queen had millions of Muslim subjects and would be fair in her treatment of all the population, which had not been the case with the dervishes who had defended the interests of their tribes.[49]

Fortunately for Quilliam, the focus of the British government, people and media was now on the Boer War, which had no Muslim involvement, at least as regards the combatants. On the contrary, the Ottoman Sultan made things easy for Quilliam by announcing his regret at the British defeat in the Transvaal in 1899 and offered his support. The Sheikh noted that, if the Caliph was supporting

Britain, then so should all Sunni Muslims in Britain. He argued that there was a far greater likelihood of Muslim freedom of worship in South Africa under British rule than under the dominion of the fanatical Dutch Protestants. He speculated that a British victory would open up South Africa to Islam as in the rest of the continent of Africa and commented that Muslims in Capetown had pledged their loyalty to the British crown, noting that the Government had requested them to provide hospitality to Muslim refugees displaced by the war in the Transvaal.[50] In February, the Sultan offered Britain mules from Syria to help supply the troops in Transvaal, and Quilliam noted that the 'Noble Caliph is ever on the side of truth and justice'.[51] Quilliam had recently visited Constantinople and, although this is only speculation, it is possible that he may have advised the Sultan accordingly.

During the course of the Boer War, he proudly noted that several members of the Liverpool Muslim Institute were fighting in the Transvaal, including Halem Churchill, Ahmed Brann, Ismail Smith and his own cousin, Frederick George Quilliam, and that a Muslim sister was a nurse with the ambulance corps. On the cessation of conflict and the announcement of British victory in 1902, Quilliam issued a proclamation in which he celebrated an honourable peace and effulgently praised the British nation for their military prowess. In this official proclamation, which was signed by the 'Sheikh of all the true believers in the British Isles', Abdullah Quilliam showed that it was possible to be a Muslim who was highly critical of some aspects of British foreign policy, yet still remain intensely patriotic to one's country of birth. He wrote, 'no other nation but the British has ever in the history of the world attempted to launch a force of more than a quarter of a million of men upon the shores of a hostile nation 6,000 miles away overseas from the main base of the expedition'.[52] But it was in the last paragraph of the Proclamation that we most clearly hear Quilliam's delight and pride in British achievements:

> Let Britons everywhere throughout the mighty British Empire
> rejoice today; and let the result and conclusion of this lengthy
> and tedious contest find expression in silent, dignified patriot-
> ism and the returning of thanks to the Eternal Ruler of all for
> the sweet blessings of peace now vouchsafed to the nation.[53]

However, his call for celebration distinguished between patriotism and 'jingoism' and called for the remembrance of God. This is
consistent with Quilliam's position on overt expressions of jingo-
sim and reflected the discomfort of a growing number of the British
middle-class. During the Boer conflict, Quilliam only expressed one
criticism of British policy with regard to the conduct of the war. He
was dismayed and ashamed that 'coloured' subjects of the Queen
were not allowed to fight the Boer. He is amazed that those who
have benefited from the rights that accrue the Queen's subjects,
regardless of religion, race or colour, are forbidden to participate
in a just cause on her behalf. He stated that it was 'morally wrong
to accept assistance in time of war based on colour of skin as it
results in a conception of empire whereby fifty million whites rule
over three hundred and fifty non-whites rather than four hundred
million fellow-subjects of the Queen'.[54]

Quilliam always felt himself to be on safer ground when British
intervention in Muslim territory coincided with the interests of the
Ottoman Empire or with other Muslims who acknowledged the
authority of the Caliph as, for example, in Afghanistan. Consequently he wrote frequently on events in Persia and Afghanistan, both
regions where Russian domination threatened both Muslim
sovereignty and British interests. His attitudes towards the Indian
Muslims were more complicated. As citizens of the British Empire,
he demanded their loyalty to the Queen Empress and took the
view that the British Empire was, by virtue of the number of
Muslims citizens that lived within its borders, a Muslim as much
as it was a Christian state. The Balkans or the Near East were more
problematic. Most European powers, including Britain, supported
the attempts of Macedonia, Bulgaria, Armenia and Greece to free

themselves from the Ottomans and upheld the various rebellions. This enraged Quilliam, and he spent a lot of his energy as a writer defending his beloved Ottoman civilisation and trying to explain the hypocrisy inherent in the Western European position, pointing out that in no circumstances would they have allowed breakaway movements from their respective empires.

Quilliam's attitudes towards Persia and Afghanistan were always coloured by the relations that he had with their respective rulers. It was important to the Sheikh that the rulers of Muslim lands had conferred upon him awards, prizes and titles that offered him authority and legitimacy. The Amir of Afghanistan had not only donated the large sum of money that made it possible for the Sheikh to open the Mosque and Islamic Centre in Liverpool, but he had also made him a Sheikh in Afghanistan with awards of land. In addition, he had been presented with a *koola-izzat*, or hat of honour, and a gold medal. The Shah of Persia had made Quilliam the Persian Consul for Liverpool in October 1899 in honour of his work to promote Islam in Britain. This was after Quilliam and his eldest son had been granted a private audience at the Palais de Souverains in Paris, where the Shah was recovering from an attempted assassination, after the Shah had cancelled a visit to Liverpool because of concerns for his safety.[55]

We can only speculate on what Quilliam thought of Shi'ite Islam as a Hanafi Sunni, but his instincts were always towards Muslim unity and he acknowledged that it was a great source of pride for him that he had been recognised by the Qajars of Persia and the Sultans of the Ottoman Empire. The situation in Afghanistan presented Quilliam with some of the same difficulties as that in Sudan had. The tribal rebellion against the British in the North-West Frontier and the declaration of jihad by the 'Fakir' once again took Quilliam into the realm of loyalty and identity conflict.

On the 12th November 1893, the Foreign Secretary of the Government of India had made an agreement with Abdur Rahman Khan, the Amir of Afghanistan, who had supported the Mosque in Liverpool and honoured Quilliam, that drew up a line which confirmed the borders of India and Afghanistan.[56] Known as the Durand Line, the Amir accepted this as the north-eastern limit of his authority. However, problems arose for thousands of ethnic Pushtun tribesmen who saddled both sides of the border and now found themselves ostensible subjects of the British Empire. Pushtuns and Afghans were synonymous in the minds of the local people, and the Amirs of Afghanistan considered themselves to be the 'de facto' rulers of all the tribes. As a result of the Durand Line, the Amir found himself in a quandary, ruling over subjects who were also under the sovereignty of the Queen of England and her government in India.[57]

The unrest caused by the division of traditionally Pushtun and Afghan territory led to various tribal rebellions against both the British and the Amir. When Quilliam uses the term 'Fakir', he is referring to the uprising led by Saidullah, a Pushtun Sufi leader who was also known as the Mullah of Mastun, who led an army of 10,000 against the British garrison in Malakand. The British troops, although heavily outnumbered, were able to hold out for six days until they were relieved. Depending on who represented him, the perceptions of Saitullah were markedly different. The British media named him the 'Mad Mullah' or the 'Mad Fakir', whilst Pushtuns called him 'lewanai faqir', meaning 'God-intoxicated'. Quilliam initially commented that, 'a few mountain tribesmen fired with religious zeal and breathing the pure air of their native mountains, had set the whole power of Britain at defiance, captured their forts and driven in their advance guard.'

He went on to describe Afghanistan as, 'the country where a few tribes of brave Muslims are fighting for freedom and the right of retaining in their own possession the land enjoyed by their fathers for many generations. We cannot break down a tribal system which is everything to these people and put nothing in its place.'[58] Although these two statements reflected the reality of the local situation, Quilliam's further comments showed his brand of pan-Islamism that was based on loyalty to the Caliphate and his particular view of the clash of civilisations that was founded upon the differences between Islam's basis in the revealed laws of God and the man-made laws of the European Christian powers. He asserted that the tribesmen 'want no man-made laws of the British Parliament. They have the divine law as revealed to Muhammad and contained in the Koran, and they want neither Britain, her laws, her troops nor her money.'[59] Additionally, Quilliam was furious at this time at the perceived insults that were directed at the Ottoman Sultan over the situation in Armenia, and he less realistically declared that the Afghans have 'heard how Britain have insulted the Sultan of Turkey, the Caliph of Islam'.[60] He rhetorically finished the speech with a statement that, 'the Muslim world was not to be despised'.

The situation became more complicated when some of the tribesmen used the opportunity presented by the Durand Line to rebel against the authority of the Amir. In the summer of 1896, the Amir sent a force of militia to occupy the Mittai Valley in Bajaur, where the clans had previously received his demand for taxes. The Khan of Nawagai complained to the government of India that this territory was now British – a strategy intended to avoid paying dues to the overlord. The Amir was forced by the situation to acknowledge his obligations under the Durand Treaty and not meet with the Khan; but the Afghan outpost still remained at Mittai at the end of year.

At the end of 1896, a small skirmish took place with the forces of the Khan of Nawagai, who deemed that his territory was threatened by the presence of Afghan forces loyal to the Amir at Mittai. The Afghan forces moved down the Kunar River to protect their communications with Jalalabad, but nothing more serious developed and the frontier question lay dormant. In 1897, although Afghanistan was peaceful, the new Amir, Abdul Rahman, struggled to balance his commitments and loyalty to Britain with placating the tribes on the North-West Frontier. He was accused by the

British of harbouring Afridi refugees, but he replied that these were fugitive Muslims and he could not send them away without prearrangement if they sought refuge. After investigation, the Amir was not implicated in the supply of arms and ammunition to the tribesmen. Although there were suspicions that Abdul Rahman was not always completely faithful towards the British, these were dispelled by his refusal to provide aid to the rebel tribesmen engaged in jihad at the frontier, or even to sympathize with them. As early as 1895, Quilliam had defended the Amir. He printed a proclamation drawn up by the Amir denouncing the activities of the tribesmen and affirming his treaty with the British. Quilliam condemned their declaration of jihad and support for the 'Fakir'.[61] Once more, Quilliam was forced into a contradiction between his previous defence of the tribesmen and his later statement opposing their activities.

The real international concern was Russia. In October 1896, it was suspected that Russia was making movements in the direction of Herat and intended not only to extend the railway from Merv into the Kushk Valley, but also to build a line from Charjui along the Oxus to Karki, close to the Afghan frontier. The British Press reported that Russian troops were ready to advance on Herat and that the Russians had mobilised their forces in Tiflis, moving them to only sixty miles away from Herat. Quilliam reported that the Russians had taken over Khorasan when they had sent Cossacks to Herat, ostensibly to prevent the movement of people from India and back during the plague outbreak in Bombay. Quilliam insisted that Russia was in complete control of northern Afghanistan and wished to disrupt British trade.[62] He also interpreted the massing of troops on the border of Afghanistan as Russia taking advantage of Britain's problems in the Transvaal to consolidate their influence in Central Asia.

He noted that Russian and Armenian forces had crossed into Ottoman territory close to the border with Persia.[63] Quilliam's anxieties about Russian intentions echoed those of successive

British governments of the period. The rivalry between the Russian and British Empires in Asia was named 'The Great Game' by Arthur Connolly.[64] The British feared that Russia had designs on India and perceived that the Tsar's defeats of the Central Asian Khans were a means of subduing Afghanistan in order to use it as a launching pad for an invasion of India. It was against this background that Britain launched its first invasion of Afghanistan in 1838.

Quilliam's view remained consistent until the events of the World War that began in 1914 rendered his position impossible. He argued that Britain's interests were best maintained by a strong alliance with the Ottomans and other Muslim powers that were threatened by Russian expansion. He was furious with various foreign ministers who did not take advantage of opportunities to strengthen alliances with the ailing Ottoman Empire and the reformist Sultan Abdul Hamid II. He perceived Britain's policy of siding with rebellions in the Balkans and Armenia as a Christian conspiracy against Islam aimed at breaking up the Ottoman Empire. He accurately foresaw that such a policy would eventually send the Ottomans into the arms of Germany in search of a powerful European ally. For Quilliam, the ultimate beneficiary of such a policy would be Russia.

In 1902, Quilliam was able to express his views fully through writing a review of the book *Muhammedanism and the British Empire*.[65] Quilliam endorsed the view of the author that Britain was the most important Muslim power in the world, directly or indirectly ruling over the destinies of over 107 million Muslims – only a little less than half the total Islamic population of the world. He noted that these Muslims enjoyed religious freedom combined with opportunities to benefit from the fruits of science and education unparalleled elsewhere in the Muslim world. Consequently, they had enormous possibilities to 'exert an influence for good' both within and outside the borders of the Empire and to claim their place in the political deliberations of the Muslim world. This was especially true in the way they influenced events in the struggle between

Russia and Britain. However, he also noted that British concerns in Africa were best represented by persuading Muslims that the best interests of Islam and Britain were identical. Quilliam noted that this challenge was not easy because the majority of Europeans harboured prejudices against Islam, 'which they imbibed with their mother's milk' and which were derived from secondhand sources rather than 'Arabic documents'. He also noted that this prejudice was primarily sustained by Christian missionaries and theologians, with 'despicable insinuations and the assignment of the basest motives in everything, and their unremitting assumptions of superiority'.[66]

In 1904, Quilliam's sense of righteous indignation exploded again after the victory of British troops at the battle of Jidballi in Somaliland. In a passionate yet ironic piece of writing, he lambasted Christians for their hypocrisy, arguing his usual case that military colonial thrusts into Muslim territory were masking a Christian war on Islam.

> Shout Hurrah, ye blatant followers of the Prince of Peace!
>
> Shout Hurrah, ye Britons, whose thirst for blood and slaughter is so great that many of us use your favourite adjective the word 'Bloody'!
>
> Shout Hurrah, shout Hurrah and dance for joy ye Christians who see in Islam the veritable Antichrist predicted in your often revised scriptures.
>
> Shout Hurrah, ye devils and imps from Hell, to whom blood, rapine, and slaughter is congenial sport.
>
> Shout Hurrah and dance for very joy, for on the 11th day of January, 1904 of the Christian era, one thousand two hundred Muslims in Somililand, 'fighting for home and country dear' were brutally slaughtered by three thousand two hundred Christians dressed in khaki.[67]

Quilliam lived through a period of rapid expansion of Britain's influence abroad, changing attitudes towards patriotism and a new professionalism at the Foreign Office. Many of the changes impacted on the Muslim world either through the direct expansion of British colonial influence in Muslim territory or in changing alliances between the Muslim world and various European powers. Britain increased its domination of the Persian Gulf, especially after the completion and opening of the Suez Canal in 1869. Always competing with other European powers, the nation gained vast Muslim territories in the Middle East and Africa. Egypt had been occupied in 1882, and an Anglo-Egyptian influence had been extended to the Sudan in 1898 as we have seen. In East Africa, Zanzibar and Somaliland were shared with other European powers, and Aden was acquired as a key port in the Arabian Peninsula. Persia was divided between two spheres of influence, with Russia annexing Muslim Central Asia. Britain also absorbed the Muslim Sultanate of Sokoto into its Nigerian colony in Africa, while in the Far East, after the Dutch took Indonesia, Britain established authority over the Sultans of the Malay states. Whilst these expansions of Britain's colonial influence were taking place, the Ottoman Empire, the only significant centre of Muslim power, lost ground to Europe. In spite of the efforts of the reformist Sultan Abdul Hamid II, the final dissolution of the Empire took place after its defeat at the end of World War I, which resulted in the Turks losing control over the Balkans and the division of their Arab territories between Britain and France. By 1919, only Afghanistan, the Yemen (excluding Aden) and Hejaz and Nedj on the Arabian Peninsula retained any semblance of independence.[68]

Quilliam's significance in the Muslim world and his nuisance value in opposition to various British Foreign Secretaries took place in the context of Muslims worldwide coming to terms with the threat of European imperial states. The material and human resources of the Muslim powers that had formerly dominated large areas of the world were exploited for the needs of the European empires. Whilst this took place, European ideas began to shape Muslim institutions and to alter the existing systems of the Muslim world to represent Western interests. British laws and policies transformed Muslim societies that came under British control, threatening Islamic education, governance and legal systems.[69] It is not surprising that many Muslims were psychologically fascinated to learn of the Sheikh's activities and overjoyed to discover that a middle-class Muslim convert was promoting Islam in Britain itself.

Quilliam did not understand why various Foreign and Colonial Office officials in the final decades of the nineteenth century, such as Percy Anderson, Julien Pauncefote and Philip Currie, could not understand the significance of alliance with the Muslim world, especially the Ottomans, to maintain strategic dominance over the old enemies of Russia and France. However, it was Lord Salisbury (1830-1903), the Prime Minister, who in 1895 was considered the most influential diplomat in Europe, who really ran the Foreign Office. Yet things would change under Joseph Chamberlain's (1836-1914) spell as Colonial Secretary. More than any other Colonial Secretary, Chamberlain worked from the principle that imperial concerns and foreign relations were inextricably interconnected and he pushed the Prime Minister to take a firmer line with rebellion or insurrection.

The Prime Minister rarely interfered with Chamberlain's decisions, probably due to ill health and a desire to preserve the unity of the Cabinet during the difficult days of the Boer War. Britain's crisis had led both the French and the Germans to consider invading the country, and there were not only the inherited problems of the Straits and Turkey to consider but also new challenges in the Far East, the Middle East and Africa.[70] Lord Salisbury's other trusted aid was Charles Sanderson. His advice was followed completely during the Cretan Crisis between the Ottomans and Greece in 1897, and also during the Persian negotiations of 1898 and 1899. However, Sanderson headed the African and Asiatic Departments during Salisbury's final years, where his touch was less sure.[71]

Two portraits of Professor Henri Mustapha Léon, the one on the right
showing some of the medals and honours conferred on him
(as Quilliam) by Sultan Abdul Hamid II.

Quilliam railed against the policies of all these figures. His
views had been formed earlier, at a time when Britain worked for
the maintenance of the Ottoman Empire and Russia towards its
disintegration. But by the beginning of the twentieth century,
everything had changed. Lord Lansdowne succeeded Salisbury
in 1900 and began to change the direction of foreign policy.[72]
Lansdowne had experienced that repeated attempts to come to an
agreement with Russia had not succeeded. The government tended
to overestimate Russian strength and feared Russian advances in
Central Asia and in the Far East. Central Asia remained a thorn in
the side of the India Office, and there was a sense of hopelessness
generated by the Russian advance into Persia amongst some
high-ranking Raj administrators.[73] All of this was gist to Quilliam's
mill, and he continued at every opportunity to use this line as a
reason for Britain to cultivate the Muslim world. The arrival of Lord

Percy (1871-1909) at the Foreign Office brought some optimism to Quilliam, since Percy, who had travelled extensively in Asiatic Turkey, was one of the leading Turcophiles amongst the Conservatives. His speeches and writing indicated that he was extremely suspicious of Russian influence in Constantinople and Teheran. His solution was to develop a partnership with Germany in the Middle East to offset the Russian advance, but Quilliam remained opposed to developing such an alliance, preferring the cultivation and strengthening of the Ottoman state.[74]

In Quilliam's eyes, the problem with Percy's solution was that it still cast the Ottomans as villains in need of interference by various European powers, rather than as respected allies. This was to become even more marked under Hardinge, who was Foreign Secretary from 1906 and 1910 and who looked for ways to strengthen ties with the Russians. One such attempt at co-operation was over Macedonia, where the two powers of Britain and Russia joined together to put pressure on the resistant Porte to introduce reform programs in the region. It was hoped by Hardinge that closing ranks against the unwilling Ottomans would help to cement agreements with Russia, but co-operation with them was difficult. The Ottomans balked at Macedonian reform, and there was a conflict between England's new alliance with Russia and her historic support for an independent Turkey, which was anathema for Quilliam. While Hardinge did not want the break up of the weak Ottoman Empire, the Russians did not share this view and actively supported Balkan attempts at independence.[75] Britain was caught between conflicting loyalties, but Hardinge considered the maintenance of the new friendship with Russia to be the primary goal of foreign policy in the region and went ahead with attempts to strengthen this position.

In 1908, Quilliam left Liverpool to live with his eldest son in Constantinople, and would have been even more concerned to ensure that relations with the Porte did not disintegrate. From 1909, the Foreign Office became increasingly involved in extremely technical diplomatic problems connected with Turkey, the Balkans and Persia.[76] Britain maintained its alliance with Russia as German ambitions in the area increased. From 1912, when Balkan questions again came to the fore in European diplomacy, the major British concern was the preservation of the collapsing Ottoman Empire; but, by this time, Britain's involvement with Russia had led to a loss of influence at the Sultan's court. Seeking to maintain links between the Ottomans and their Balkan territories proved to be impossible and one by one the Balkan states secured their independence, leaving Turkey vulnerable. Attempts were made after the Balkan War to preserve what was left of the Ottoman Empire and not to conciliate the Russians any further; but it was too late. It is hard to know what Quilliam felt as he endured his exile from Britain in 1908 and 1909, but one can only imagine his uneasiness and despair. It is safe to assume that he would have done whatever was possible to advise the Porte to engage with Britain.

In June 1913, the Turks again approached Britain for an alliance, but the situation by this time was complex. Under no circumstances did British interests permit a division of Asiatic Turkey from its European territory, which might even have brought about a European war.[77] An alliance with Turkey would have been viewed by the Germans as a direct threat to their growing interests in the region, whilst a negative position towards Turkey's dissatisfactions would throw the Ottomans into the arms of the German Alliance. The British solution was a joint declaration by all the powers to respect the independence and integrity of the present Turkish dominion, whilst seeking greater financial control and pressure for reform from the Porte. Quilliam considered the Caliph to be one of the most enlightened rulers in the world who was already seriously committed to reform and feared that the British position of non-alliance would eventually drive the Ottomans into alliance with Germany. In 1914 his worst fears were realised and his position towards the Government in Constantinople became untenable; yet he continued in various guises to transform British views on Ottoman civilization and culture.

During the closing decades of the nineteenth century, when Quilliam was desperately trying to convince successive British governments that their best interests lay in drawing upon the resources of the Muslim world through friendship and mutual interest, the attitudes towards empire were changing dramatically. The supporters of imperialism were intensely aware of the problem of bringing Britain's youth on board.[78] British public schools were turned into centres for promoting 'heroic self-sacrifice', 'pride of patriotism' and 'fortitude and self-reliance' required to form generations of young people who would be ready to serve in far-flung parts of the globe. Fiction became one of the primary tools for reaching the nation's youth. Boy's magazines became filled with masthead Prince of Wales' feathers and Union Jacks above cover pictures of big game in combat with white hunters. Inside they contained full-colour pullouts of the ships of the Navy, badges of the regiments, insignia of chivalric orders and the flags of the dependent world. A new jingoistic patriotism proclaimed racial pride, militaristic values and an enthusiasm for conquest.[79] This was very different to an earlier period of a quieter patriotism, which had regarded British direct rule with some reluctance and only justified it in protecting trade interests. Quilliam's own patriotism had been forged in the earlier Victorian period, and he viewed the new mood with considerable distaste. It took considerable courage to resist the new mood of the times with very public statements in the newspapers and through *The Crescent*. In Liverpool, he publicly offset the waving of flags of the dependent nations controlled by the British Empire with a very public display of the banners of the independent Muslim nations on the roof of the mosque. In 1903, his public defence of Islam in Liverpool's Town Hall brought to a head his frustrations and was reported by both British and European newspapers.

However, Quilliam would find, as would other British Muslims a century later, that the position of defending Islam, when the country was intent on invading territory where Islam was the dominant faith, was not tolerated by the government in power, the dominant media or the majority of the population. Although liberal by inclination and passionate in his belief that Muslims needed to embrace modernity, the Sheikh found himself forced by circumstances to express his anger at what he considered inadvisable foreign policies through recourse to statements from the harsher side of Islam. Such statements would draw the ire of the media and would reinforce the very prejudices against Islam that he had spent his life trying to dispel. The dominant view is always hard to argue against, especially when the country is at war, but there are always minority views of dissent. Such voices may in the long term be shown to be right in their views, and may sometimes even change government policy through the means of legitimate protest. Quilliam's continuous struggle against a foreign policy that he believed to be misplaced and headed in the wrong direction provides an example of engaged citizenship to British Muslims today and shows the pitfalls of divided loyalties when allegiance to state and the dictates of conscience and religious revelation point in opposite directions.

CHAPTER 7

The Ottomanist: Abdullah Quilliam's Pan-Islamism

Abdullah Quilliam's understanding of Islam was fairly typical of many educated Muslims and European converts in Britain. Above all, he understood Islam to be a rational religion, and on several occasions he praised the modern outlook of India's great reformist, Sayyid Ahmad Khan.[1] Whereas Khan was impressed by the scientific knowledge and educational methods of Europe and wanted Muslims to learn from the British presence in India, Quilliam looked the other way and wanted Britain to learn from Islamic civilisation. He would have been in sympathy with the sentiments of Vivekananda, the nineteenth-century reformer of Hinduism and traveller to the West, who declared that the West had a long material leg whilst the East had a long spiritual one. Vivekananda believed that each limped because of either a spiritual or a material imbalance, and each therefore needed to learn from the other so that the world could progress in both domains of life.

Quilliam asserted that Muslims had to come to an understanding that the interests of Britain and Islam were identical, but that in order to realise this both the British and the Muslims needed to understand the real teachings of Islam. He believed that millions of Muslims practised a religion that was not found in the Qur'an and that they had lost the ability to exercise private judgment over matters of faith and politics. As such, he was not always sympathetic to the ulema and accused them of being stuck in a ninth-century mindset with no concept of the needs of the nineteenth century. He would cite the Hadith in which the Muslim governor of the Yemen was asked by the Prophet about the rule that would guide him in governing the province; he first replied, 'By the law of the Qur'an'. When further challenged that there might be areas where there was no direction, the governor replied that he would 'act according to the example of the Prophet'. On the final challenge, that even the Qur'an and Prophet's guidance might not serve to resolve all situations, the governor responded that he would rely on his own judgment. Quilliam noted that the Prophet liked the answer and approved it to all who were present. He would request contemporary Muslims, 'many of whom are superstitiously careful to imitate Muhammad in the minutest particulars', to take the lesson to heart.[2] He preached that a return to the 'well of Islam undefiled' was the greatest challenge for the Muslim world, and argued that the British psyche was best positioned to appreciate the 'genius of Islam', which was 'pre-eminently the religion of practical common-sense'.[3] Quilliam believed that the British presence on the global stage could be utilised to help Muslims to recognise the true spirit of Islam and apply this to the demands of the modern age. But before this could be achieved, the Western man had to learn the real teachings and history of Islam. For Quilliam, Islam was an enlightened religion that was the natural ally of knowledge and human progress, and he would often remind people that it was the Arabs who had maintained the torch of learning in the dark ages of European history. He would cite the examples of the translation of the works of Aristotle into Arabic, the geometry of Apollonius, Arab contributions to algebra and chemistry, and the adornment of the great Umayyad and Abbasid cities with libraries and colleges, as well as mosques and palaces. In particular, he would point out that it had been Muslims in Spain who had supplied Europe with philosophy and medicine.[4]

Quilliam was deeply critical of contemporary European Christianity for its difficulties with the discoveries of modern science, but also blamed Christians for their historic attempts to blacken the name of Islam by denouncing the life of the Prophet and claiming that Islam had no theological conception of the true nature of God. Most of all, he reserved his anger for the Christian missionaries who continually solicited subscriptions from the public to 'propagate the Gospel in heathen and Muhammedan lands'.[5] From time to time, he would discuss polygamy, divorce and attitudes to slavery and religious warfare from an Islamic point of view and would argue that on each position Muslims were more humane and concerned with social justice than Christian history indicated. However, it was Muslim fraternity that most particularly appealed to Quilliam and he claimed that, whilst others such as Socialists and Christians spoke the language of universal brotherhood, only Muslims actually practised it. He argued that Muslims had truly overcome the differences of caste and race and that their history demonstrated a virtual monopoly of such social action.[6]

Quilliam's call for independent judgment and a return to the teachings of 'real' Islam may have led some to a belief that he sympathised with the teachings of the Wahhabi reformers from Saudi Arabia or their kindred spirits elsewhere in the Muslim world. He did know about them, but he condemned them as being a new sect who had deserted the four schools of law. Quilliam saw himself as a traditional Hanafi, but above all he called for Muslim unity. He stated that:

> United under a trusted leader we could bid defiance to any combination of Christian sects or countries. The union of Islam might easily become an established fact. The differences between our schools of thought are so slight that they soon could be smoothed over and adjusted. I call upon our brethren throughout the world to promote such a union.[7]

For Abdullah Quilliam, there was only one way to achieve this unity, which was for all Sunni Muslims to come together and profess loyalty to the successors of the historic Caliphate that had been established after the death of the Prophet. In Quilliam's reading of Muslim history, the only legitimate successors of the Caliphate were the Ottoman Sultans and all true Sunni Muslims owed allegiance to the Sultan as the current Caliph of Islam. To represent and serve the Caliph was not only an honour, but a duty beholden upon all Sunni Muslims. He was always clear that his personal loyalty to the Sultan had nothing to do with fealty to the Turkish Empire, but was an aspect of being a true Muslim. In 1903 he declared, 'I do not officially represent Turkey in Liverpool, but I do represent the Muslim faith, and I am the Sheikh of the Mussulmans in the British Isles. I do not receive one penny from the Turkish government.'[8]

Yet Quilliam's personal loyalty to the Caliph and his conviction that Muslim orthodoxy was expressed through allegiance to the Caliphate were bound to run into difficulties when the spiritual leader of the Muslim world was also the sovereign lord and potentate of the Ottoman Empire. Just as Quilliam had to negotiate his conflicting loyalties to his nation and his religion, so also he had to resolve his dual allegiance to the Queen Empress and to the Sultan. The real difficulty with Ottoman allegiance was that it remained a power in Europe and a historic rival of the various European empires. The last of the Muslim empires had secured territories in the Balkans, but also officially ruled over lands such as Egypt, the Middle East and Africa, where European powers were extending their rivalries in the nineteenth century.

The history of Muslim incursions into Europe had resumed with the Ottoman victory over the Byzantine Empire in 1453. They subsequently swept through the Balkans, even besieging Vienna in 1529. These conquests ensured that the Muslims became an acknowledged power in Europe, and formal recognition of Ottoman strength was confirmed when Elizabeth I made an offer in 1588 to enter into an alliance with Murad III (1546-95), whom she described as a 'fellow monotheist'.[9] Elizabeth wanted help in bringing down the papist and 'idolatrous' King of Spain. Quilliam commented that the Protestant queen regarded Muslims as closer to her brand of Christian monotheism than the Roman Catholics. During this time, the Ottomans and the British successfully collaborated in various ways, as trading partners and as military allies to outwit their European rivals. The main rival of both was Russia, and they were equally concerned to prevent Russian expansionism. Travel and commerce between the two countries led to even more substantial interactions.

By the end of the eighteenth century, Turkey and Britain had forged close commercial, political and military relationships and were engaged in a wide range of interactions, with many visits by Ottoman subjects to Britain. Ottoman sailors and traders arrived in British ports more often and for longer periods during the nineteenth century, with some taking up permanent residence. The 1881 Census recorded eight Egyptians and 44 Turks living in Merseyside, and Salter's *Sketches of Sixteen Years among Orientals*, published in 1868, provided an imaginative account of the transient Muslim population in the ports and urban centres of Britain. He noted that trading vessels and warships belonging to the Ottoman navy were frequent visitors to many British ports, including Liverpool.

Relationships with the West were influenced by the Porte's position directly facing both Europe and Asia and the desires of various Sultans to modernize Turkey on European lines in order to revitalize their Empire and compete with Europe's power. The Sultans attempted to secure themselves against any threat from the West by introducing into their society many of the secular systems of thought which they believed had rendered the Europeans powerful. Although they brought in reforms in the law, education, military know-how and other major institutions of the state, they were not able to make any fundamental changes to the absolutist tendencies of the political regime that they ruled over and they did not want to relinquish their personal power. Foremost amongst such reformers was Sultan Abdul Hamid II (r.1876-1909), who was perceived by many liberal republican intellectuals in Europe and Turkey as being politically repressive, but to Quilliam he could do no wrong. He epitomised the enlightened Muslim ruler who represented the rational outlook and concern for social justice that formed Islam. The Ottoman Empire consisted of many Muslim nationalities, races and colours, and included populations of Jews and Christians who lived as citizens with special privileges. As was shown in Chapter 5, the Ottoman Empire manifested everything that Quilliam regarded highly in the teachings of Islam, and most especially its universality. The significance that Quilliam gave to the concept of universal brotherhood inclined him towards pan-Islamism and Islamic unity. Quilliam's version of pan-Islamism was, however, unique in that it did not include, or at least certainly did not sympathise with, Muslims who rejected the authority of the Ottoman Caliph. He was selective in his dealings with Muslims around the globe and in Britain, favouring those who supported the Caliph and ignoring or rejecting those who did not. It was for this reason that he did not acknowledge the Muslims at the Woking Mosque, at least not until the first decade of the twentieth century after his return from exile in Turkey. In London he preferred to work with the South African Muslim, Muhammad Hadji Dollie of the Anjuman-i Islamia, who was a strong supporter of the Sultan and an opponent of the Indian Muslims who rejected the Caliph's authority. Quilliam had first reported the opening of a Muslim place of prayer in London by the Anjuman-i Islamia on the 7th December 1895, noting that it was a temporary mosque near Regents Park; the Muslims who attended believed that the propagation of Islam in Britain should conserve the spirit of the religion and avoid the customs and rituals peculiar to Asian culture. In this view of Islam we can hear the voices of the Islamic modernists of India and Egypt, the later lifestyles of the London convert community, the Woking group of South Asian students and echoes of Quilliam's strategies in Liverpool. Quilliam quoted from the opening speech, in which it was declared that, 'as Christianity has adapted itself to the modern era so should Islam. The Islam of Asiatic countries can never be the Islam of modern Europe.' As far as Quilliam was concerned, the Anjuman was the official representative of Islam in London because of their loyalty to the Caliph and their acceptance of the authority that the Caliph had conferred on Quilliam as the Sheikh al-Islam of the British Isles.

The Sheikh was never at ease with Indian Muslims because he knew that the Mughals had never historically paid more than lip service to the Caliph and that, in the present time, with the exception of India's Khilafat movement,[10] India's vast population of Sunni Muslims had little real regard for the Turkish Caliph. His suspicions of Indian Muslims' attitudes towards the Sultan can be discerned in an incident that took place on the thirty-third anniversary of the Sultan's accession to the throne, which was celebrated in Liverpool on the 31st August 1896. The Liverpool Muslim Institute was joined by a large number of Indian Muslim sailors whose ships were in port. The Sheikh met with them personally and spoke to them, thanking them for attending the occasion. His conversation with them consisted of praise for the Caliphate and he asked them to go back to India and inspire Muslims to love their Caliph.[11]

Quilliam gave a forthright statement of his position, announcing in 1895 that pan-Islamism consisted of a 'duty of all Mussulmans on earth to rally around the throne of the Caliph, which represents Islamism. Of all the Muslim empires the only surviving one is the Ottoman, which fills the world alternately with terror and admiration. The Koran itself commands every believer to be faithful to the Caliph.'[12] In 1899, Quilliam explained that the problems of the Muslim world could only be solved by a closer union between all Muslims around the world and that this could only be achieved through allegiance to the Sultan.[13]

Quilliam's version of pan-Islamism differed radically from that expressed by the rising tide of Arab nationalists, who were seeking separation from the Ottoman yoke. Quilliam lived through a period in the Middle East which saw the liberal patriotism of the nineteenth century begin to give way to a more radical nationalism that sought independence, which in turn came to see liberal politics as incapable of carving out nation-states on a European model.[14] This resulted in a twentieth-century version of pan-Arabism, which argued that the fortunes of the Arab world would be better served by an Arab alliance that modified the ultra-nationalist creed of loyalty to the *watan* (nation-state) and sought closer ties and even unions. However, the development of Arab nationalism and the subsequent creation of Middle Eastern nation-states arose alongside the Ottoman decline and British political and military intervention during the First World War.

Quilliam's version of pan-Islamism was much closer to the pan-Arabism that had first been encouraged in the nineteenth century amidst a plethora of reform and modernisation programmes, which were introduced in reaction to colonisation and the superior technology of various dominant European powers. As a result of European sovereignty, there was a 'broad commitment to the idea of reviving Arab culture in its positive and glorious aspects'.[15] This was achieved by highlighting past episodes of Arab civilisation and trying to understand the reasons for the decline of Muslim greatness and the way to achieve renewal. Along with the rediscovery of some past Arab greatness that was perceived as a glorious golden age came a desire to learn the knowledge of the modern European world. Choueiri declares that the combination of these two intellectual thrusts was the hallmark of nineteenth-century pan-Arabism.[16] Throughout the Muslim world, religious reformers and politicians began to see the need to reform Islam and Muslim culture under the pressure of European ascendancy, and although this was initiated in the Middle East by the Ottoman Sultans and debated by conservatives and modernist reformers in their Arab territories, it was also keenly felt beyond their domains in Persia and India. Quilliam was knowledgeable enough of the contemporary Muslim situation to recognise the struggle that was taking place across the Muslim world, as modernists tried to grapple with 'superstition' and hidebound traditions; moreover, he was aware of the role of the reforming Sultans. For him, the solution was to follow the Caliph's lead not only in Ottoman territory, the obvious place for revival since it was the last Sunni empire, but also across the Muslim world. Quilliam's version of pro-Ottoman pan-Islamism was increasingly divorced from the move towards nationalism in pan-Arabism. In this respect, Quilliam would have parted company with Muhammad Abduh, even though he respected many of his views on Islam and modernity.

A number of Ottoman Sultans had attempted to halt the decline in the Empire by introducing reforms. Sultan Selim III (1789-1804) had begun this process by giving the Arab subjects of the Empire the chance to participate in the modernisation programme. It was as a result of this newfound embracing of the Arab populations and their historical heritage that cultural Arabism came into existence, with its 'imagined models of Arab achievements' that were believed to have taken place during a past golden age. These Arab achievements were synonymous with Islam to pan-Islamists of Quilliams' ilk. However, he extended the great cultural achievements of the Arabs outwards to the hinterlands of Islam. The content of Quilliam's lectures in Liverpool was often on the various golden ages of Islam in Spain, Baghdad, Timbuktu and Central Asia.[17]

An unexpected product of the inclusive policies of the reforming Sultans and their drawing upon the glories of the Arab past was an awakening of various Arab nationalisms that called upon the ideal of a fatherland (*watan*) in order to promote a new concept of citizenship that was based on loyalty to a smaller territorial space than the Ottoman Empire or the wider Muslim *umma*. Egypt, Syria, Iraq, Jordan, Tunisia and Algeria all began to emerge as entities within the Ottoman unity, and the ideal of the *watan* began to dominate political discourse in the Arab world.[18]

The centre of the Ottoman Empire was not immune from these new nationalist tendencies, and Quilliam's vision of a Muslim world that brought together the best of the religious teachings of Islam combined with the progress made by Western Europe was threatened by these newfound nationalist sentiments. Quilliam, like many in the nineteenth-century Ottoman world, did not separate Islam from Turkish identity, nor did he perceive this identity as being incompatible with some elements of Westernisation. But Quilliam was proud above all of the multi-ethnic, multicultural Muslim empires that had come into being in the early centuries of Islam, the only survivor of which was the Ottoman Empire. He acknowledged the sentiments that were attached to localities, but it was religion that remained the determining factor of identity in his romanticised vision of the Ottoman state.

Quilliam would often refer to the millet system in the Ottoman Empire as being the prime example of Muslim universalism and tolerance carried out in state policy and organisation. As a deeply religious man, the millet system embodied for him the significance of religious identity that made religion paramount in defining who people were; but at the same time, it also gave them supposedly equal opportunities to participate in a Muslim state. The institutionalisation of religious identities provided a powerful sense of religious communal identity, which included Christians, Jews and the dominant Sunni Muslims. To Quilliam, nationalist sentiments would transform these religious identities into various loyalties to a nation-state.[19]

The rapid rise of various Arab nationalisms combined with similar tendencies in the predominantly Christian European territories of the Ottomans in the Balkans to destroy the ideal of the millet system that had underpinned the Ottoman multi-ethnic and multi-religious Empire. Eventually the idea of loyalty to territorial spaces based on a common language, a shared history and local identities spread to Turkey and completely undermined the identification of the Turkish nation with Islam. Three crisis points placed the Ottoman Empire under serious threat and eventually led to its disintegration and destruction.

Not all Arab movements wished for independence from the Ottoman Empire. Al-Kawakibi (1849-1902) had tried to redefine Ottomanism as an equal partnership between Turks and Arabs, and called for the creation of new national entities based on religious freedom and equality that could exist within the framework of the Empire. However, his vision could not compete with the powerful currents of loyalty to a fatherland that many felt had provided so much success to European nations and that had the advantage of providing their inhabitants with a clear reference point.[20]

Although Turkish nationalism was one of the last to appear in the troubled Ottoman Empire of the late nineteenth century, its impact on the survival of the last Muslim empire and the Sunni Caliphate was emphatic. In the same year that Quilliam and his eldest son left Liverpool to take up residence in Constantinople as guests of the Sultan, the Young Turks took part in a revolution that was intended to overthrow the Ottoman Caliphate. In July 1908, Sultan Abdul Hamid II, who was destined to become the last Caliph with any real power, was forced to restore a constitutional form of government that had first been adopted in 1876 and then suspended in 1878. In 1909, one year after Quilliam's arrival, his beloved Sultan was forced to abdicate, and between 1908 and 1913 the Ottoman state lost most of its European territories. The decision to side with Germany in World War I was disastrous for the Turks, and Britain took advantage of Arab national sentiments to aid and fund various movements to fight against the Turks with the promise of securing independent Arab nations upon victory. On 17th November 1922, the last Ottoman Sultan was sent into exile and, on 3rd March 1924, the caliphate was officially abolished by the new Turkish state under Mustapha Kemal Ataturk.

These events would determine to some extent the actions that Abdullah Quilliam would take as an English Muslim. His authority as Sheikh al-Islam was vested in the fortunes of Sultan Andul

Hamid II, and as much as Quilliam would perceive his loyalty to the Caliph to be religious, he could not avoid the political implications of the collapse of the Ottoman Empire. Quilliam's loyalty to the Ottomans was encouraged by their leading role in the Islamic world. As much as he loved the ideal of religious multiculturalism, he was also proud of the Ottoman presence in Anatolia and in central and south-eastern Europe. Quilliam passionately believed that the presence of Islam in Europe permitted a freedom of religion and a Muslim sense of social justice to the Christians and Jews under Ottoman dominion that was unparalleled elsewhere in the world. Nothing would ever convince him that Ottoman claims to these territories were illegitimate and, as will be seen, he campaigned extensively in Britain to change political and public opinion on the various East European rebellions against Ottoman rule.

Abdullah Quilliam found out very painfully that conversion to Islam was not simply an act of personal belief, but also a significant shift of identity that involved voluntary participation in the Islamic community of believers; and, in his case, the identification with Ottoman political ideology and culture was unavoidable. Although the power of an Islamic identity and the privileged position of Sunni Muslims that was enjoyed in the Ottoman Empire had at first acted as a deterrent to the rise of nationalist ideas, rebellions or acts of disobedience would break out in various Arab territories in the last decade of the nineteenth century. In 1896, the Sheikh had been outraged by the discovery that Egyptian nationalist tracts calling for independence from the Ottoman Empire were being distributed in Cairo, London and Paris. Quilliam's anger led to the issuing of a fatwa on the 20th April 1896, in which he makes his position on loyalty to the Caliph very clear.

> In the name of God, Most Compassionate, Most Merciful!
> Peace be to all the faithful everywhere!
>
> 'O True-Believers, fear God with His true fear; and die not unless ye also be True-Believers. And cleave all of you unto the

covenant of God, and depart not from it; and remember the favour of God towards you.' Sura 3, 'The Family of Imran', Ayat, 103

All praise be to God Who, in His unlimited goodness, has favoured us with the gift of the True religion of Islam, and Who has ordered the brethren to be united, and declared this to be His law in the before-quoted Ayat of the Holy and Imperishable Koran!

Among Muslims none should be known as Turks, Arabs, Kurds, Ajem, Afghans, Indians or English. They are all Muslims, and verily the True-Believers are brethren. Islam is erected on the Unity of God, the unity of His religion, and the unity of the Muslims. History demonstrates that the True-Believers were never defeated while they remained united, but only when disunion crept into their ranks.

At the present time, union is more than ever necessary among Muslims. The Christian powers are preparing a new crusade in order to shatter the Muslim powers, under the pretext that they desire to civilise the world.

This is nothing but hypocrisy, but armed as they are with the resources of Western civilisation it will be impossible to resist them unless the Muslims stand united in one solid phalanx.

O Muslims, do not be deceived by this hypocrisy. Unite your-selves as one man. Let us no longer be separated. The rendezvous of Islam is under the shadow of the Khalifate. The Khebla of the True-Believer who desires happiness for himself and prosperity to Islam is the holy seat of the Khalifate.

It is with the deepest regret that we see some persons seeking to disseminate disunion among Muslims by publications issued in Egypt, Paris and London. 'Verily, they are in a manifest error.'

If their object – as they allege it – be the welfare of Islam, then let them reconsider. We fraternally invite these brethren to return their allegiance, and call them to the sacred name of Islam to re-unite with the Faithful.

Muslims all! Arsh is under the standard of the Khalifate. Let us unite there, one and all, and at once!

Given at the Mosque at Liverpool, this 5th day of Dhulkada, 1313, which Christians in their error call the 20th day of April, 1896

W.H. ABDULLAH QUILLIAM, Sheikh-ul-Islam of the British Isles.[21]

Quilliam's fatwa was unequivocal in its support for the Caliph. The final line, in which he declared that ''*arsh* is under the standard of the Khalifate', revealed his position. The Arabic term *'arsh* was used to describe the Throne of Allah. It is unlikely that the Sheikh regarded the literal throne of God as being under the Ottoman banner, but *'arsh* was often metaphorically seen to represent the power and authority of God. This is more likely to have been Quilliam's interpretation and this thereby reveals the religious significance that he invested in the Ottoman Caliphate. He regarded those Muslims who opposed Ottoman rule in favour of a nationalist worldview as being 'in manifest error' and called upon them to return to the true path.

His view of colonialism is also of interest, in that he regards direct control of Muslim lands as a plot by Christians to destroy the true religion of God under the pretext of bringing European civilisation, drawing upon the material resources of the European powers. This is consistent with Quilliam's position that it is Christianity and its missionary impulse that Muslims need to fear. As long as Western technology, education, systems of governance and military prowess were kept in the secular domain, Quilliam encouraged Muslim nations to adopt them. However, he argued that unity under the Caliph was the only way for Muslims to prevent the onslaught of Christian missionaries operating within the orbit of colonial expansion. It is also worthy of notice that Quilliam endorsed the modern view of many devout Muslims that all ethnic and national identities should be subsumed under an Islamic identity. Whereas contemporary Muslims look to an imagined *umma* to fulfil this call to unity, Quilliam's pan-Islamism could only be fulfilled in loyalty to the Caliphate.

The fatwa reveals the depth of Quilliam's loyalty to the Caliph, and it is important to realise that this is more than theoretical or merely doctrinal. Quilliam's relationship with the Porte remained close and he continued to serve its political interests in Britain and elsewhere in a number of practical ways. His brand of Islamic practice also demonstrated his allegiance to Ottoman Hanafi traditionalism. Quilliam had no time for Wahhabism, especially since the Wahhabis were in opposition to traditional Ottoman practices. At the time of festivals, the mosque in Liverpool would be decorated inside and out with flags and banners, Chinese lanterns and fairy lamps; and on the annual celebration of the Prophet's birthday, Quilliam would follow the Turkish custom of handing out sweets and pastries to the children.[22] While in Constantinople in 1900, Quilliam participated in the ceremony of the veneration of the Prophet's mantle which took place during Ramadan. He described how the Caliph opened the casket of the holy relic and kissed the mantle whilst verses from the Qur'an were recited and songs were sung in the Prophet's honour.[23] There is also a highly romanticised account of the 'Doves Mosque' or Masjid Sultan Bayazid in Istanbul, which describes the rosaries and perfumes that were sold and the Muslim loungers who popped in from dawn to dusk to see the countless doves of Bayazid and often remained to sleep at the Mosque.[24] Yet he did not endorse all traditional practices and openly criticised the carrying of miniature coffins on the tenth day of Muharram, describing this as, 'the acme of superstition to the disgrace of Islam'. He noted that it was practised by Shi'ite Muslims at London's East India Docks and at the Valileh Sultan Khana in Istanbul. He claimed that the origins of the practice lay in India and that it was 'born of stupidity amongst Lascars and among the outcasts of Muslim people', whom he accused of ignorance and fanaticism.[25]

It was far easier to imitate Ottoman Muslim traditionalism at the mosque in Liverpool and to offer up supplications for the Caliph's health at *jumu'a* prayer on Friday than it was to balance

Ottoman interests with those of Britain's, especially when foreign policy, the media and public opinion opposed events in the Ottoman territories. Quilliam discovered that the distinction that he tried to make between the religious institution of the Caliphate and the personage who also happened to rule the last Muslim empire as its Sultan and Potentate was not so clear cut in the daily working out of policy and governance that was required of such a figure. It was unlikely that British government ministers were ever able to comprehend, let alone sympathise with, Quilliam's distinction between Sultan and Caliph, nor was the British public likely to understand the Sheikh's declared dual loyalty to Queen Empress and Caliph. The only parallel that they would have been familiar with was the Roman Catholic allegiance to both Pope and Nation, and there was very little sympathy for that position in British Protestant mainstream life in the Victorian period, and even less in the religiously divided city of Liverpool. However, English Catholics tended to be more sympathetic and when the Reverend Parker, a Liverpool Protestant Minister, accused Quilliam of treason and hurled abuse at the Sultan, the *Lancaster Standard*, popular with a Catholic readership, responded by stating that Quilliam's anger directed towards the minister was justified because he rightly felt that his religious leader, the spiritual leader of Muslims across the world, had been insulted and abused.[26]

At this point, it may be useful to remember that Abdullah Quilliam was a native-born Briton, proud of his lineage in the Isle of Man and his ancestors' patriotic heritage. He regarded himself as a loyal citizen of the British Empire and would frequently point out that this Empire had more Muslim citizens than even the Ottomans; as such, they were as loyal to the Queen-Empress as he was. However, he did not consider that loyalty to the Empress was the same as loyalty to her Governments and their attempts to represent her interests. Policy makers could be (and often were) misguided, and Muslim citizens of the Empire had a duty to maintain a circumspect eye on policy towards the Muslim world and to protest when necessary. The main error of successive British Governments, as far as Quilliam was concerned, was their failure to ally closely with the Ottoman Empire as a bulwark against Russian expansion. The Sheikh's preferred solution was personal loyalty to the Queen Empress as a citizen of the Empire and also to Sultan Abdul Hamid II as a Sunni Muslim, since he was simultaneously the legitimate Caliph of Islam.

The Sheikh's position of dual loyalties in the realms of religion and nation are presented clearly in an article reprinted in *The Crescent* in the summer of 1898. The original appeared in a South African newspaper entitled, 'South African Muslims and the Jubilee – An Object lesson in Loyalty'. The article began by presenting the case that Muslims in the Empire always had a sense of pride and pleasure that the Queen and her Government had, in spite of antagonistic feelings that existed in some quarters, remained friendly with the Caliphate and maintained a 'thoroughly cordial understanding with our Father of the Faith – the Sultan of Turkey'. The article goes on to praise Allah, who had conferred extraordinary benefits upon the citizens of the Empire by permitting such a monarch as Queen Victoria to rule. The final paragraph concludes, 'while therefore we do not forget our religious ties with the Khalif, we should never forget how much we owe to the just rule of our great queen.'[27]

In June 1898, Quilliam printed a letter from the Regents Park Mosque sent to him on the occasion of the Queen's birthday. The letter observed that the Queen Empress was toasted on her birthday and that complete loyalty was expressed by the gathering of Muslims; but it also informed Quilliam that the Chairman of the Mosque confined himself to toasting the Queen 'of whom he spoke most highly', and spoke only about actions which had benefited Muslims under British rule. A comment was added by Mullah Abdullah, the imam of the mosque, that he had 'keenly observed the good things done by the Royal family, especially the Queen, but would not venture to speak on British foreign policy because the present situation was not the occasion for it'. Another Indian

Muslim, Muhammad Omar, thought that it 'looked extraordinary that Muslims should celebrate the birthday of a Christian sovereign, but since they were all in England they were therefore British subjects, or at least subject to British rule, and he considered one of the duties of the Faithful to be obedient to their sovereigns'.[28]

Even in this one letter, there were nuanced positions declared with regard to accepting the sovereignty of a non-Muslim ruling the state. Quilliam's political position was clearly enunciated at the anniversary of the Sultan's accession that was celebrated by the Liverpool Muslim Institute at its mosque. In his praise of the Sultan, Quilliam comprehensively blamed the troubles experienced by the Porte on Christian insurgents who were ungrateful for the tolerance extended to them through the millet system.

> Our excellent Caliph ascended the throne during turbulent times when the Christians of Bosnia and Herzegovina, forgetting the tolerance extended to them by their magnanimous rulers, openly rebelled and murdered many innocent, law-abiding Muslims. In 1876 Serbia declared war against the Porte, Prince Nikita declared holy war on the Turks in front of an assembled Montenegrin army.[29]

Quilliam did however acknowledge that there were internal problems caused by the incompetence of various officials and the mental illness of the previous Sultan:

> Abdul-Aziz had ruined the finances and administration of the Porte and Sultan Murad was mentally ill. Russia was supplying war materials to the insurgents; the Montenegrins and the Serbs. Murad was removed from the throne with the issuing of a fetwa by the Sheikh al-Islam and his brother (Sultan Abdul Hamid II) ascended the throne on 31st August 1876.[30]

After describing the ensuing victories over the Serbian and Montenegrin insurgents, which took place on the same day that the Sultan acceded to the throne, and the vicious war between Russia and Turkey that followed, Quilliam quotes the Sultan as saying: 'I should re-establish the reputation for honesty and the credit of my country, which has been so unhappily shaken by measures for which I am not responsible and which I greatly deplore.'[31] With this sentence, Quilliam marked out Sultan Ahmed Hamid II as a serious reformer and peacemaker, and a welcome break with events in the past for which the ruler could not be held responsible. In the remainder of the speech, Quilliam continued to reinforce the Sultan's credentials as a social reformer, noting that 'the last 23 years have seen improvements in railways, the progress of education, and reconstruction of the army which was now one of the most perfect military organisations in the world.'[32]

The remainder of the speech comprised a criticism of the failures of the British government to ally with the Sultan against Russia. He criticised the withdrawal of Lords Derby and Carnarvon from the Conservative government when Lord Beaconsfield sent the British Fleet to Besika Bay and noted that Britain should be proud of such a statesman. He cited Lord Beaconsfield as saying, 'Russia would never be permitted to take Constantinople while England had a ship at her command or a soldier she could send'. He went on to assert that, if England had assisted Turkey against Russia, the latter would have been crippled for fifty years and Britain would not have its present troubles in the Far East; an alliance between Turkey, Great Britain and Germany would have secured the peace of the world. He finished the speech by sending a note of warning to Lord Salisbury that he should take heed of these words. Quilliam reasserted that the true policy of England was to stand by Turkey, and that the government should remember that Turkey was now led by a Caliph of Islam who, throughout his distinguished reign, had never failed to live up to his promise to reform his country and empire.[33]

However, such sentiments were not likely to receive much support at the end of the nineteenth century, when colonial attitudes had been revitalised with a new moral purpose and the general view of the Turkish Sultan can be summarised by expressions such as 'the Turkish tyrant', 'the Great Assassin', 'brutal, barbarous, perfidious' and 'an enemy of domestic happiness, of Christianity and civilisation'.[34] Quilliam had to assert his loyalty continuously to the Queen, whilst simultaneously trying to alter public perceptions of Sultan Abdul Hamid II. In the mosque, supplications were made each week at *jumu'a* for both Monarch and Caliph.

Quilliam's relationship with the Caliph began when Sultan Ahmed Hamid II sent a telegram to Liverpool on 7th December 1890 congratulating the new convert on his attempts to establish Islam in Britain. In 1891, both Quilliam and his eldest son Ahmed were invited to Constantinople as guests of the Sultan and stayed at the Yildiz Palace. On this visit, Quilliam claimed that he turned down offers of decorations from the Sultan and requested that the title of 'Bey', which had been offered by the Caliph for his services to Islam, should instead be conferred on his eldest son. Quilliam recounted the occasion of this first visit to Constantinople to *Tit-Bits* magazine in 1897, and described being invited to a banquet at the Yildiz Palace and being granted a two-hour audience with the Sultan. Quilliam's son was asked if he wanted to serve the Sultan and he replied in the affirmative, stating that he desired to be a soldier. The Sultan made him a lieutenant-colonel in the Ertoghrosi regiment and ordered that his horse and uniform be prepared. Quilliam reported that a white stallion Arab horse was sent to Liverpool by the Sultan along with a gold cigarette case.[35] During this first trip, they both stayed for several days as guests of the Sultan at the Yildiz Palace and met with court officials.[36]

In July 1894, Quilliam was honoured by the Caliph of Islam with the official title of Sheikh al-Islam for the British Isles and was sent on an official mission to Lagos, West Africa, in which he represented the Sultan at the opening of a mosque donated by Mahomet Shitta Bey. He decorated the donor on behalf of the Caliph. Although returning seriously ill with malaria, an illness which bothered him throughout his life, the trip had been a resounding success. In 1899,

The *Liverpool Mercury* carried an article by Henri de Léon describing the trip to Lagos, which claimed that around 10,000 Muslims gathered to hear the Sheikh speak. A Christian missionary from West Africa had claimed in an article written for a local West African newspaper that Quilliam had been a very successful missionary for Islam during his visit and had made it very difficult for Christian missionaries to work in the area. Apparently this was because local people remembered that an English gentleman came to Lagos who had practised Christianity devoutly, but had abandoned it in favour of Islam. The article recounted that Quilliam had preached the message that Islam was more suited to the African temperament, since it was not racist, had major 'Negro' figures in its midst and abhorred the use of alcohol introduced by Christians to Africa. Quilliam had declared that the only reason for the British to concern themselves with Africa was for material gain through the sale of their goods. The missionaries claimed that Quilliam had made it very hard to spread Christianity in the area, and many were still converting to Islam in Lagos as a result of his preaching and statements.[37]

Quilliam's successful mission to Lagos on behalf of the Sultan cemented the relationship between the two men, and also drew Quilliam into the political machinations of the Ottomans as they struggled for survival. It was useful for the Ottoman ruling classes to have an English lawyer based in Liverpool as an agent provocateur and a voice to defend their position to a hostile British media and people. Certainly a number of high-profile Ottoman officials visited the Sheikh in Liverpool and were entertained at his home. In December 1897 he received Ismail Bey, the departing consul-general to New York, and Obeid-Ullah Effendi at his villa in Fairfields and both attended his lecture on 'The Triumph of Islam' at the Liverpool Muslim Institute.[38] Earlier that year, in August, Quilliam had received from the Sultan the official seal cut in silver affirming his position as Sheikh al-Islam.[39] In the same year, Kamil Bey, the private secretary of the Sultan, attended the Mayor of

Liverpool's reception for distinguished guests at the International Geographical Congress and sought out Quilliam, whom he had met in 1894 at Yildiz. He attended the mosque along with Sheikh Abdul-Fatteh of Aleppo at *jumu'a* prayers and gave the *takbir*.

In early April 1899, in anticipation of another visit to Constantinople, the Osmanli Regiment formed by Quilliam paraded publicly through the streets of Liverpool and was inspected by the Sheikh. The public were provided with bread and beef, bun loaves, seed loaves and tea. Turkish marches were played in front of guests from Damascus, Beirut, Smyrna, Aleppo and India, as well as the British converts. A blue silk robe was presented to Quilliam by Mustapha Karsa, the Ottoman Vice-Consul in Manchester, as a gift from the Manchester Muslims for the Sheikh to wear in Constantinople. Karsa also invited Quilliam to visit Beirut and Damascus whilst in Turkey.[40] A special meeting was held at the mosque where the British Muslims swore their loyalty to the Caliph and agreed to send statements of loyalty along with Quilliam.[41]

The Sheikh left Liverpool on the 26th April, travelling overland to Constantinople by train. His departure was reported in the *Liverpool Courier*. Within a few days a telegram was received from Budapest, where Quilliam had been met by the Ottoman Consul General and a number of Turks residing in the city. He had left for Constantinople the same evening. Before the Sheikh arrived in Constantinople, the train stopped at the Turkish border for passport control. Local Muslim dignitaries received Quilliam and his son with a guard of honour and joined him with food on the platform, delaying the train for fifteen minutes. Fraternal greetings were sent to the Muslims in Britain.[42]

On arrival in the city, he and Ahmed were met by high-ranking Ottoman officials including Woods Pasha, Vice Admiral of the Turkish Fleet, Hakki Bey, Principal Legal Councillor to the Sublime Porte, and Ahmed Pasha, Chief of the Imperial Arsenal. Two carriages from the imperial stables were used to collect the travellers. An invitation to attend the Yildiz Palace arrived for the day after their arrival, but even before that event, several significant figures visited the Quilliams at the hotel, including Fatima Hanoum, the former Mrs Robinson of Liverpool, who had renounced Christianity after marrying her husband Ahmed Bari, an officer in the Turkish army, who had already been highly decorated by the Sultan.[43] Quilliam observed with approval that Mrs Robinson and her daughters were veiled.

The next day he attended *jumu'a* prayer with the Sultan at the Hamidah Mosque in the city. After prayers, Quilliam was informed that the Sultan would soon grant him a private audience; he spent the afternoon with the Vizier at the palace. A few days later, *The Crescent* reported that a Turkish decoration of the Grand Cordon of the Order of Medjidieh had been awarded to Walid F. Preston, the convert Liverpool artist, in recognition of his talent and that the Sultan had commissioned a painting of Hoylake seafront for the palace in Yildiz. At the time Preston was famous throughout Britain for the painting 'Danse', which had been exhibited across the country.[44]

The next day, Quilliam and his son attended Eid festivities in the mosque and formed part of the royal procession from the mosque to the palace at Dolma-Batche. They were given places of honour in the throne room during the customary hand-kissing ceremony with the Sultan, and at the end of the ceremony Quilliam and his son were given a private audience which lasted over thirty minutes and were invited to stay as guests at the home of the Sheikh al-Islam of the Muslim world. The Sheikh presented Quilliam with a robe of silk shot through with cloth of gold and the British Muslim leader was given a carriage by the Sultan to take him around the city and to the official receptions held in his honour. On 12th May, Quilliam was called to another audience with the Sultan and was awarded the Order of the Osmanlieh. Ahmed Quilliam was awarded Medaille des Beaux Arts, along with other prominent Liverpool Muslims. On 13th May, Abdullah Quilliam left Constantinople for Smyrna, where he was received by prominent Muslims of the city until his boat departed later that day for Greece.[45] Quilliam returned to England without Ahmed, who was enrolled in the elite Mekteb Sultaniyah College in Constantinople.[46]

The reception given to the Sheikh demonstrates the esteem that he was now held in by the highest authorities of the Ottoman court, and it is reported that long discussions took place on the prospects of Islam in England. Further details of the discussions between Quilliam and various Porte officials, either in Turkey or in Liverpool, remain obscure because the Sheikh's private diaries were destroyed in a fire at his house on the South Coast after his death. Ottoman official records previously kept at Yildiz still exist in Istanbul. At the Annual General Meeting on 15th June 1898, it was reported that the Sultan had commissioned two gold candelabras and carpets for the mosque in Liverpool and had offered a donation of £500 for the benefit of the Liverpool Muslim Institute.[47]

The relationship taken to such heights in May was further established by the most high profile Ottoman visit later in the summer. In July 1898, General Syed Mahomed Fridoun Bey, the Minister Plenipotentiary of the Sultan's court, travelled to Liverpool to meet Quilliam on the occasion of Queen Victoria's Jubilee celebrations. At Lime Street Station, he was met by the Liverpool Muslims who wore their fezzes and carried Ottoman banners. He toured the city in Quilliam's carriage and attended Zuhr prayers. Quilliam was chosen by the Mayor to introduce the Minister to local dignitaries on Sunday evening, when he attended a lecture by Quilliam entitled 'Islam: A Better Way', in which the Sheikh argued persuasively that 'Islam and science were twin sisters', unlike Christianity, which was antagonistic to new discoveries.[48] At a special meeting, the Minister declared to the assembled British Muslims that, 'the Caliph watches every detail of your progress in Liverpool with the keenest interest. He knows that the interests of Islam will be ever efficiently guarded while your president is Sheikh al-Islam of these Isles.'[49]

In 1899, Abdullah Quilliam was appointed Persian Consul for Liverpool by the Shah of Persia, while Ahmed, who had remained behind in Constantinople, was serving as an aide-de camp to the Sultan.[50] In 1900, Quilliam visited Constantinople once again, this time with his younger son Billal. They arrived on the 9th April and the following week Quilliam delivered an obituary for Ghazi Osman Pasha, a famed Turkish general.[51] *The Crescent* of the 9th May confirmed his return to Liverpool, noting that the rank of Salisse had been conferred on Ahmed Quilliam by the Sultan, that he had received his graduation diploma from the Gelata Serai (Mekteb Sultanieh) and that he had been attached to the Ottoman consulate in Liverpool.[52] At the end of May, the Sultan visited Tripoli so that the tribes of North-East Africa could offer him their allegiance. Quilliam called for such unity across the Muslim world and claimed that such pan-Islamism was the way to unite Muslims under one legitimate authority, the descendent of Abu Bakr, the first Caliph, who had been appointed to rule the Muslim community after the death of the Prophet.[53] In the same edition, it was reported that both Ahmed and Billal had left Constantinople and returned to Liverpool. The following week's edition confirmed that Ahmed would commence his diplomatic career as Chancelier at the Consulate in Liverpool and that the Sultan had awarded him a war medal for his volunteer services in the Turkish-Greco conflict, when he was attached to the Ertoghrul Imperial Lancers. All the leading newspapers of Constantinople reported his departure from the city.[54] The relationship of the Sheikh with the Ottoman court had become a family affair.

On the occasion when the Sultan's Jubilee was celebrated in Liverpool, both in the Mosque and at a gathering of all Ottoman subjects in the city organised by the Corporation, flags were flown from the mosque and all buildings with a Muslim connection. Quilliam delivered a special *khutba* (Friday sermon) praising the Sultan at *jumu'a* prayers, and it was reported that the banquets in the evening were the first in Britain to be served with only Turkish dishes.[55] The following week *The Crescent* announced that George Gholam Quilliam, the Sheikh's brother and manager of the family's watchmaking firm, Samuel Quilliam and Co., had made a Gold Hunter watch for the Sultan worth one hundred guineas, to be presented to Abdul Hamid II by the Sheikh and the Turkish Consul.[56] An interesting story appeared the following week in an article written by Henri de Léon, which pointed out media attitudes to the Sultan and their inaccuracy.[57]

Such close political, religious and personal relations with the Ottoman court during a period in which a series of major conflicts occurred in its Christian dominions was always going to involve a difficult balancing act for the Sheikh's competing loyalties. The first test of the Sheikh's allegiances occurred when the Armenian disturbances initiated a series of acts of rebellion against the Ottoman Empire. Quilliam took up an aggressive response to the position of the British media, with its reports of Muslim atrocities against brave Armenian attempts to free themselves from the imperial yoke. His strategy of resistance to the media's coverage was twofold. Firstly, he held to a position that the predominantly Christian state of Armenia was a legitimate part of the multi-religious Ottoman state and that Britain would be outraged if any one of her dominions attempted to break away because their religion was different, however just the cause. Secondly, he went out to attack Christians who were supporting the Armenian complaints against Ottoman rule by pointing out that this involved a strong element of hypocrisy if the Christians were pointing their fingers at anyone else when their own house was far from clean. As early as 1893, he wrote an editorial which commented on the trial of Armenian rebels for high treason at Marsovan and Caesarea.[58] Quilliam showed surprise that the British newspapers considered the Armenian rebels to be legitimate simply because they were Christian, and asked whether they would have accepted the right of Turkey to interfere with British Muslim subjects in India. The editorial takes up his usual political position on foreign policy and exhorts England to cultivate a friendship with Turkey for commercial concerns, also commenting on the political need to seek allies in the duel with Russia on the frontiers of India. [59]

In November 1894, Quilliam drew upon his concerns for the rights of the American 'Negro' to form a political comparison with the situation in Armenia. Reporting on a public burning of a black man in Texas, Quilliam argued that, if the Turks suggested that they would send a commission of inquiry to look into this incident, there would be public and political outrage in America. Yet Gladstone, he argued, had proclaimed that it was the duty of England to interfere in any part of the world where horrors and injustices accumulated. Quilliam demanded to know if the Royal Navy would cross the Atlantic to take action against Christian atrocities in the southern states of the USA. He described the Prime Minister as 'goody-goody Gladstone'.[60] Two weeks later in a lead article, Quilliam reported on the terrible circumstances of the mutilation of a black male in Tennessee who had been lynched for an alleged assault on a white woman. The mob had cut off his ears and fingers, hung him from a telegraph pole and sent his head to the family of the victim as a trophy. Quilliam directly compared the media view of this incident to their coverage of atrocities in Armenia and noted that the perpetrators in America were white Christian men, not the diabolical Turk; he asked, 'Is there not something rotten in the state of Christianity?'[61]

Between 1893 and 1895, the Sheikh wrote a number of articles that accused the Armenian insurgents of criminality, seeking to ferment problems for the legitimate Ottoman authorities, giving details of the robberies, rapes and murders perpetrated under the pretext of political agitation. He defended the Ottoman Government for its tolerant approach towards crimes that were almost too grim to describe in print.[62] He also took the opportunity to search the world's press and looked for Christian atrocities in the region. These were reprinted in *The Crescent*. For example, he noted a story in the British media telling of forced conversions of

Armenian Christians by Kurdish Muslim militia, and juxtaposed this with a news item that announced that fourteen Muslims of Uja Russia had their property confiscated because they refused to join the Orthodox Church; he observed that the Christian Tartars had never been shy of forcing conversion to Christianity.[63] In 1894, he created a space in the newspaper for weekly updates on the Armenian situation.

Articles were also reprinted that defended the Porte. Quilliam was always aware that the tactic of seeking someone else who represented his views, especially from non-Muslim sources, was often more effective than publishing his own writings on a subject. Thus he noted that *The Liver* had reported that Turkey, Persia and Morocco had pursued a far more tolerant attitude towards their Jewish populations than Eastern European Christian territories, and he reprinted a lecture by Scott Anderson on Islam, in which Muslims were described as being more temperate in their policies towards Jews than the Christian powers of Russia, Greece, Austria, Germany and Romania, where persecution abounded.[64]

In January 1894, the Liverpool Muslim Institute had unanimously carried a resolution protesting against the political capital that was being made out of statements by Anglo-Armenians who had left their native land. Quilliam announced that, as a native-born Briton and a loyal subject of the Queen, he protested emphatically against such agitation; using his favourite trump card, he declared that it was not in the British interest to upset fifty million loyal Muslims in the Empire.[65] But Quilliam's defence of the Ottoman Government did not go unnoticed in his native Liverpool. The mosque was vandalised during this period on several occasions, and after the resolution was passed at the Liverpool Muslim Institute and reported in both the local and national press, two thousand people met on the 20th May 1894 in the Brunswick Wesleyan Chapel in Moss Street, Liverpool, to express their support for the Armenians and to protest against Quilliam's defence of the Ottoman authorities.

Sir Edward Russell presided over this meeting, supported on the platform by around a dozen clergymen. The Chairman noted amidst applause that a distinguished bishop had commented that a Christian crusade in Armenia was worthwhile if the long-term effect was to force the Muslims out of the Hagia Sophia in Constantinople. An Armenian woman addressed the audience and argued passionately that the massacre at Sassoun was not a solitary instance, but was part of a systematic campaign of religious perse-cution by the Turks.[66] She argued that 'Mohammedanism' was the cause of all backwardness in Armenia and that Christianity was the only force that helped towards creating progressive values. A motion was proposed and seconded to create a petition that could be sent to the House of Commons urging the Government to inter-fere on behalf of the oppressed Armenians and bring to justice the perpetrators of crimes against Armenian individuals.

It was at this point that a woman identified as Mrs Keep walked onto the platform and requested that an amendment be made to the motion. In brief, the amendment requested that the meeting 'protests against the wholesale imputations of cruelty and inhumanity and the insolent abuse which have been levelled against the Sultan of Turkey and the Turkish army without any authentic evidence of the truth'. Mrs Keep was heckled and booed, but maintained her position. Trying to keep order, the Chairman asked if there was anyone in the gathering who would second the amendment. At this point, Sheikh Abdullah Quilliam sprung up onto the stage and declared that he would second it. Someone in the audience shouted, 'but you are a Mohammedan', to which Quilliam replied, 'Certainly. I am and proud of it.' The Chairman stated that he had to give Mr. Quilliam a fair amount of time and allowed him seven minutes to finish his statement, after which time the motion and the amendment would be put to the meeting. Quilliam defended the Ottoman position and argued that the individuals accused of atrocity, such as Osman Pasha and Zekki Pasha, were personal friends with whom he had enjoyed hospitality

A caricature of Abdullah Quilliam published in *The Porcupine*, a satirical
newspaper in Liverpool, during the time of the Macedonian Crisis.

at the Palace of Yildiz; he declared that he knew that they were
above reproach and honourable men. The audience erupted and
cries of 'Burn him', 'Throw him out' and 'Strangle him' were heard
from the auditorium. Such sentiments played perfectly into the
Sheikh's hands and he replied, 'I am sure that there are people here
who would love to burn me, just as you burnt the Muslims in Spain
centuries ago.' He went on to accuse the audience of being 'nice
people to demand toleration for the Christians in Armenia. You are
so intolerant as to refuse to hear one of your own countrymen, born
and bred in your own city, because he has renounced your religion
for conscience sake.' Thirteen Muslims in the audience voted
against the motion, and copies of *The Crescent* along with leaflets
explaining the tenets of Islam were handed out to the audience as

they departed from the hall.[67] Quilliam's hijacking of the meeting, called partly in reaction to his public defence of the Ottoman position, indicated that he was prepared to go on the counter-attack when challenged and that he was fearless in defending Islam. The Muslim community in Liverpool may have been a small minority of the population, but it was remarkably resilient and active under the Sheikh's leadership.

In September 1895, The Liverpool Muslim Institute passed another resolution in which they declared that, 'at this meeting of British, Asian and African Muslims we strongly protest against the mischievous agitation that is taking place in this country against the Ottoman Government, and the manner in which attempts are being made to foment a quarrel between the Christian and Muslim powers.'[68] The Press were invited to attend and listen to Quilliam's speech. There is no doubt that this meeting was organised to coincide with the arrival of Gladstone in Liverpool later in the week. Quilliam's speech, delivered in front of an international gathering of Muslims who joined with the converts, expounded upon a number of familiar themes used by the Sheikh. He first pointed out that the vituperation directed at the Sultan was personally insulting to millions of Muslims who recognised his authority as the Caliph of Islam. He also noted that the media was partisan and 'practically preaching a new crusade'. Quilliam went on suggest that the agitation was actually caused by Christians who considered that the Armenians were simply the product of Muslim intolerance towards Christianity. He accused them of being ignorant of the multi-religious constituency of the Ottoman Empire, which contained Christians of all denominations. He argued that the true reason for the Ottoman attempts to put down insurrection was because large numbers of Armenians had formed secret societies engaged in revolutionary schemes to overthrow a legitimate government by recourse to bombs and dynamite. He argued that the Turks were not engaged in a religious war, but a political struggle against insurgents. Quilliam warned that, if the Caliph continued to be insulted and if the British Government made the mistake of being lured into Christian desires for a new crusade, they risked the wrath of 240 million Muslims and the declaration of jihad. He finished his speech by declaring that the crusades of past centuries had been disastrous for the nations that participated in them.[69]

The media were outraged and accused Quilliam of holding the Government hostage by threatening jihad. The newspaper articles generally took up the cry that Quilliam was mistaken in believing that all sects were reasonably tolerated in Turkey. One reporter declared that 'the wily Sheikh' had timed his speech to cause Gladstone and other speakers to be more circumspect. The *Shipping Telegraph* urged Gladstone not to be unnerved.[70]

Quilliam continued to defend the Ottoman position on Armenia into the twentieth century, noting just before Christmas 1899 that Turkish soldiers had been required to keep Greek, Latin and Armenian Christians apart in Bethlehem's Church of the Nativity.[71] However, his continued agitation lost him powerful friends and influence in Liverpool and turned the media against him. In October 1900, when he announced his intention to campaign for a place on Liverpool's County Council, there was strong opposition and even *The Porcupine* announced, 'He is a lawyer, he is not a Christian, he is a friend of the Sultan of Turkey, he is responsible for the Armenian atrocities.'[72] The media campaign almost certainly destroyed Quilliam's chances of election.

Yet, however much Quilliam might try to defend the Ottoman position in the province of Armenia, the spark of insurrection in its Christian territories moved closer to Western Europe and European concerns. In March 1898, Quilliam delivered a speech on the topic of an attempt by Greece to land troops in Crete to take advantage of Ramadan. He declared that there was a crusade by some British newspapers to raise volunteers from Britain to protect Christian Crete. As always, the suggestion of a 'holy war' between Christians and Muslims was like a red rag to a bull for the Sheikh. He announced that Muslims had been killed on the island by Christians whose Bible forbade murder and whose leader they claimed to be the Son of God and the Prince of Peace. As to the suggestion of volunteers, Quilliam declared that two could play at that game and he threatened to issue a fatwa requesting Muslim volunteers from Britain, India, West and South Africa to serve the cause of the Sultan. Quilliam controversially stated his position, emphatically declaring that the proper position of all Greece is that of a Turkish province and that the Great Powers should stand aside and let Turkey and Greece fight it out without interference.[73] A week later, at the celebration of Eid al-Fitr at the end of Ramadan in Regents Park, London, a gathering of Muslims drank the health of the Sultan and unveiled his portrait publicly. Quilliam addressed them and spoke of the death of three thousand Muslims in Crete, voicing the hope that the Sultan would intervene. He congratulated the Emperor of Germany for his stand in supporting the Sultan and the Ottoman people and prayed that the present Turco-German relations would continue.[74] He reported that many letters had been sent to him criticising the Government policy as being too one-sided or heavy handed, and in *The Crescent* of the following week he published a letter sent to him by Thomas Edwards, Assessor for the Home office, who also opposed the Government's position.[75]

A month later, recognising that the torch of insurrection was spreading, Quilliam stated that no sooner had the Sultan succeeded in suppressing Christian outrages in one part of his dominion than they immediately broke out in another. He argued that these were caused mainly by religious hatred fomented by priests and aided by 'holy Russia' for her own devices. He defended the Turkish people as being 'noble, brave and simple-minded' and 'immeasurably superior in the scale of humanity'; he stated that they were not 'half so bloodthirsty' as the Christian nations that surrounded them. He exclaimed that the geographical position of the Turkish nation beneath Russia and adjacent to Christian Europe had caused the Turks to have an abundant experience of Christian 'cant and hypocrisy' directed towards them.[76]

In the same month, the Sultan intervened and declared war on Greece, with considerable military success. *The Crescent* followed the campaign very closely, with detailed daily reports of the battles that arrived from the front, which were sent by telegraph from various Muslim correspondents. Quilliam was overjoyed at the Muslim military success, especially as the defeated armies were not British. On the Sunday evening at the start of the conflict, he was able to read two telegrams at the Liverpool Muslim Institute that informed his audience of notable Turkish victories. The news was received with great applause and Quilliam rhetorically declared, 'the Cross recedes before the Crescent of the Prophet of God, the Giaour trembles as the foot of the triumphant Muslim treads on the land of the Nasuranee. We ask our Muslim brethren to continue calm in this hour of their elation, and thank God for the victories that he has given to His people.'[77] Ahmed Quilliam Bey wrote to Constantinople upon the declaration of war and placed his sword at the feet of the throne, offering at once to join the Ertoghrul Cavalry. The Sheikh issued a fatwa or 'proclamation' as he termed it.

> Muslims in every land! Now is the time to exhibit to the world the unity of Islam and the brotherhood of true believers. Let volunteers from every land offer their services to the Caliph of the Faithful.[78]

The British Muslims sent congratulatory telegrams to the Sultan on hearing of the Turkish military success, and the Liverpool Muslim Institute was decorated with Turkish flags. Quilliam raised the question of whether it was permissible in international law for the Greek Government to request Greek subjects in Cyprus to join the army for active service. He pointed out that Cyprus was legally part of the Ottoman Empire and that the war would present difficulties for the British Government who had occupied the island.[79]

For the next few months, *The Crescent* contained detailed coverage of the war, including full biographies of all the Turkish commanders.[80] Quilliam scoured the world's press for articles that commented favourably on the Turkish conduct of the war. For example, he reprinted a piece from *The Times* which reported that the Turks displayed great humanity towards prisoners and that no outrages had occurred in captured villages.[81]

There are a number of elements in Quilliam's reception of the news that the Turks had been victorious that are of interest. First of all, it should be noted that modern communications were able for the first time to provide current information virtually immediately on conflicts taking place around the world. Quilliam lived at the beginning of a globalised international community, in which the media was able to report to the public for the first time on the same day that events occurred so as to inform opinion. *The Crescent* was able to engage in a battle to influence and supply another point of view. Even if it was not in wide circulation amongst British readers, it had the ear of the mainstream media and of Muslims worldwide. The *Liverpool Daily Post* on the 26th April carried an item that the telegrams received by Quilliam were from a reliable source and that they had been posted on the noticeboard of the Mosque.[82]

Quilliam's view of conflicts such as that taking place in the Balkans was clear in his mind. They were not political conflicts, but were religious struggles between a dominant European militant Christianity and an oppressed Muslim world. Yet Quilliam believed, as did millions of Muslims, that the final victory must belong to Islam. The tone of Quilliam's announcement in the immediate elation of triumph demonstrated the degree to which Muslims were anticipating and longing for such success to occur and fulfil both the promise implicit in the final revelation and the Qur'an's pronouncement of 'manifest victory' to the true believers. When Quilliam declared the struggle to be between 'Cross' and 'Crescent', he provided an emotive and powerful religious narrative that drew upon concepts of 'crusade' and 'jihad' that had echoed across Europe and the Middle East for fourteen hundred years, since the rise of Islam had threatened Christian domination for the first time. Of equal significance was the official 'proclamation' of the Sheikh al-Islam of Britain to the Muslim world calling for volunteers to fight in Greece. The Sheikh called upon Muslims to fight in a jihad (although he did not use the term), and it is evident that his pan-Islamism drew upon the narratives of 'umma' that were so successfully utilised by many Muslims in the latter half of the twentieth century.

Quilliam took note of the divisions between the political parties in how they responded to the situation. He welcomed the more careful response of Lord Salisbury, who only insisted that the Sultan was bound by the treaty with the Great Powers to provide reforms to his people. The treaty demanded that the Sultan promote more liberal attitudes and human rights, but did not say anything about the Ottoman Empire conducting a war against other states or breakaway provinces. Salisbury argued that intervention by Britain was not required because the matter did not imply a breaking of the treaty's terms. Quilliam complimented Lord Salisbury on his policy towards Turkey, but condemned Gladstone's call for British mobilisation to support Greece as being 'unutterably stupid' and 'hysterically preached along with shrieking Christian brotherhood'. It should be remembered that Gladstone had spoken in Liverpool the previous autumn on the topic of the Armenian uprisings and recommended that Britain take unilateral action against the Turks. Quilliam pragmatically noted that Turkey had mobilised 500,000 men against Greece and that it would not be in Britain's interest to combat such an army, as this could not be done without leaving India or South Africa defenceless.[83]

The British media were quick to pick up on Quilliam's use of emotive religious language in defence of the Turkish forces. In Liverpool, *The Porcupine* criticised the Mosque and its leader for their support of the Ottomans. The writer of the article drew upon popular opinion, common sentiments and the national mood to declare that, 'at such a time when all England is crying shame on the "Great Assassin", this "renegade Englishman" is decorating the wretched Mosque which he runs in West Derby Road, in honour of the triumph of the Crescent over the Cross.'[84] The article clearly indicated that, although Quilliam may have felt at ease with his dual loyalty to Crown and Caliph, the British public and the media could not see the distinction between Sultan and Caliph.

The Cretan situation attracted the attention of Britain when the Royal Navy landed forces on the Island after the Government had insisted that all Ottoman forces should be withdrawn. After a British naval bombardment, their troops were fired upon from a house in the village of Candia. The British retaliated by destroying thirty-nine houses and arresting forty-three ringleaders. The Porte requested that their trial should be held by an international commission and not in a British court, and refused to withdraw Turkish troops from Crete. They blamed Britain for the disorders at Candia and protested against the bombardment.[85]

However, in spite of the British interest and involvement, Quilliam could at least feel relieved that this time he was not commenting on a direct conflict between British forces and Muslim rebels. The war provided him with the opportunity to extol the virtues of the Ottomans. He noted that Turkey had put into the 'field an army as well armed, disciplined and officered as any country in Europe could muster;[86] and that the conflict had made it more difficult for the Powers to control and regulate the Ottoman Empire and the Porte, which could no longer be regarded as decadent by the British Government, public and media because their military forces had revealed themselves to be 'alert, successful and triumphant'.[87]

Such a triumphalist note indicated how much Quilliam had imbibed the current desire of the Sunni Muslim world for success, but he was angered when the Great Powers, including Britain, began to insist that Turkey should hand back any territory gained through the military victories. In a fatwa, he argued that the Ottomans were bound by the laws of war formulated by the Prophet. In Islamic law, the spoils of war belong to the victor. The fatwa provides numerous insights into Quilliam's thinking with regard to mixed loyalties and how Muslims should behave, at least those in the British Empire, when the actions of the state conflicted with the best interests of Muslims worldwide.

> In the Name of Allah, the Compassionate!
>
> Abdullah Quilliam by the grace and permission of the One Eternal God, Sheikh of the True Believers in the British Isles, to his brother Muslims throughout the World, Greeting!
>
> May the peace of Allah rest upon us all!
>
> Know, O my brethren, that it hath pleased the Almighty to give triumph to the armies of the Faithful in Greece, whereby the name and memory of the Holy Prophet has been once more exalted, the sneers and boastings of the unbelievers brought to naught, and the Giaour driven back before the triumphant soldiers of Emir al-Mumeneen.
>
> Praise be to God, the King of the Day of Judgement.
>
> According to all the laws of Allah, the precepts of the Prophet, and even the customs of man, the spoils of war are the property of the victors, and the land conquered by the valour of arms belongs to the conqueror.
>
> Yet, because in this case the victor is a Muslim and the conquered are Nasuranee, certain Christians are endeavouring to induce the six Great European Powers to interfere between the conqueror and the conquered, and to prevent the Mussulman from reaping the reward of his valour, assisted as it has been by the blessing of God.
>
> Mussulmans, our Kitabi-Shareef, the thrice-blessed Koran, has declared that 'all Muslims are brethren'. The triumph of the Ottoman Muslim is yours, is my triumph, and an undeserved insult to one Muslim is an insult to every Muslim in the world.
>
> Interference with our Khalif in the exercise by him of his undoubted rights under the laws of God and the custom of nations by any combination of Christian powers is an insult to the whole Mussulman community.
>
> But, brethren, let not the just vials of your wrath pour themselves out in idle words or foolish deeds. Remember yet,

the command of the Eternal One: 'Bear ye the insults of the unbelievers for a time with patience'. Yet let your voices be heard loud and clear in protest against this vile and wicked attempt to prevent the Mussulman retaining the justly merited fruits of his well-earned victories.

Those of you who reside in lands under the dominion of those of an alien faith should be doubly careful in the presence of this crisis. Ye dwell among strangers: 'They worship not that which ye worship, neither de ye worship that which they worship'. Therefore, beloved brethren, be circumspect and discreet.

Yet every Mussulman who resides in any land over which the British flag cloth floats by law has the unalienable right to petition his sovereign, the Queen-Empress, and the Imperial Parliament of the British Isles.

Let me then, as your brother in the Faith Most Excellent, whose heart throbs with every pulsation of yours, fraternally suggest to you in all calmness and moderation that every Muslim society and congregation in any and every of the British dominions adopt this peaceful and lawful mode of making their feelings known upon this momentous question to the British Government.

Brethren, there are 100,000,000 Muslims living in the various portions of the British Empire. No Government will dare to refuse to listen to the unanimous voice of these law-abiding, honest and industrious people.

May Allah direct us all into the right way, the path of peace!

Salaam Aliekoum![88]

Quilliam advised Muslims who lived in a land which was not under the domain of Islam to be patient, but in particular he advised those in the British Empire to draw upon the means of legitimate protest that were available by law to citizens of the Empress and her Government. He was more circumspect when Britain was directly involved, and although there were occasions when he would use the threat of a fatwa to call for jihad, he would usually take the line of legitimate protest. Where other nations were involved in a war with Muslim powers, Quilliam did not hesitate to call for Muslims to rise up from across the world. But Quilliam also reminded Muslims that victory was always achieved by the blessing of God; when the Caliph had triumphed, the victory was to be celebrated by all in the Muslim world. An insult to the Caliph was an insult to every Muslim, and therefore all should be concerned; but diplomatically, he reminded his readers that the Qur'an calls for patience in adversity.

The next crisis to anger Quilliam occurred in Macedonia. In February 1899, Quilliam reported that there was unrest in the province from groups wanting autonomy.[89] However, it was not until the 22nd October 1903 that Quilliam raised the issue after a speech by Dr Chavasse, the Bishop of Liverpool, at a meeting in the Town Hall.[90] Quilliam was present at the meeting and famously responded. The media picked up the contents of his speech and his refutation of the Bishop, and for several weeks he was the subject of their attention. In response, the first three editions of the *The Crescent* in November carried the full transcript of the meeting. The Bishop had called for a resolution condemning Turkish forces for their attempts to quell the unrest in the Province and insisted that it was the duty of England as a Christian nation to support Macedonia and put pressure on the Turkish Government, according to the Treaty of Berlin. The motion was seconded by Reverend J.H. Atkinson, the President of the Liverpool Free Church Council. Major W.H. Edwardes supported the Resolution, stating that 'he hoped to see the day when not a solitary Christian on the face of the globe was under the rule of the Turk.'[91] But when the Lord Mayor of Liverpool rose to put the resolution to the meeting, Quilliam used his familiar tactic and stood up to suggest an amendment. The main speakers of the meeting had played into Quilliam's hands by giving the conflict a religious element.

The Sheikh had always argued that the problems in the Ottoman Empire had been fomented by Christians opposed to Islam. Consequently, Quilliam's amendment asked for the addition of Bulgaria to the Resolution, and he argued in his speech that it was Bulgarian agitation that was causing the problem. To those who argued that Turkey was backward and resisted attempts to reform, Quilliam noted that he had seen no attempts to modernise by the 'Christian' Government of Bulgaria since its independence twenty-five years previously. Quilliam also pointed out to the Christians present that he did not notice any attempt to intervene on the 'Negro' question in the United States nor on the ill-treatment of Jews in the Christian parts of the Balkans by those who claimed the cause of 'universal justice' when referring to 'atrocities' carried out on Christians by Turks. The opportunity to speak in public provided the Sheikh with the time to defend the religion of Islam since its inception, through the rule of the Caliphs, the Umayyads, the Abbasids, the Mughuls and up the time of the Ottomans. Pandemonium broke out in the hall as some very irate Nonconformist ministers attempted to drag Quilliam off the stage. The speech by Quilliam was picked up by the national press in Britain and most European countries, and was published by the Sheikh as a booklet entitled *The Trouble in the Balkans*.[92]

The speech and the booklet did not go unnoticed in Constantinople, and at the end of 1904 the Sheikh was once more invited to be a guest of the Sultan. He left England on the 10th December accompanied by Karsa Bey, the Turkish Consul in Manchester.[93] *The Crescent* reported that the invitation was in fact a summons from the Caliph and that Quilliam was to be given a special mission.[94] On arrival he was met by Ottoman high officials, including Tahin Pasha, the First Secretary of the Sultan and the Court Chamberlains.[95] Quilliam had left Liverpool in poor health after contracting Russian influenza, and on reaching Constantinople he suffered a relapse and was hospitalised in the Hamediah Hospital on the Sultan's orders. He remained there from the 26th December until 8th January 1905. On his recovery he was invited to the Yildiz, where the Sultan conferred on him the double decoration of the *Imtiaz*, in both gold and silver, bearing the inscription, 'This man has done his very best for his God, his religion, his Caliph, and for Turkey.'[96] The award of the Grand Order of the Nichan-i Chefakat, a five-pointed gold star set with diamonds, emeralds and rubies, which was usually awarded for philanthropic services to the State, was given to Hannah Quilliam, and the Nisan-es-Sanie was given to Hanifa, her youngest daughter. Ahmed was appointed Consulate-General of Turkey in Liverpool, and the Sheikh was raised to the rank of Oula-et-Eval (equivalent to a Brigadier-General), which permitted him to use the honourable appellations of 'His Excellency' before his name and 'Effendi Bey' after it. He was also appointed Consul-General of the Isle of Man, a position that he was never able to take up because of British Foreign Office objections. An imperial order commanded the Sheikh to visit Constantinople every two years. On the 19th January, Quilliam was once again called to the Sultan's presence where he was awarded the medal and grand star of the Osmanieh, an honour reserved for high officials in the Ottoman service. The award ceremony was carried out by Ibrahim Pasha, the Grand Master of Ceremonies to the Sultan.[97]

On the 20th January, after having dinner with the Sultan, Quilliam boarded the train for England. In February he was back on the warpath again, this time in defence of Turkish policy in Macedonia and Armenia, at another meeting in Liverpool that had been called by concerned citizens at the Town Hall. Once again Quilliam defended the Turks and argued that the troubles were fomented by Bulgaria and other Christian malcontents, but this time the meeting was ready for his interruption and his familiar strategy of adding an amendment to the resolution. This time he was restricted by the Chairman to only ten minutes to present his case, and this avoided the possibility of the Sheikh delivering a lecture on the topic.[98]

The special mission that summoned the Sheikh to Constantinople is not mentioned anywhere in *The Crescent*, and it must be assumed that it was confidential. It is reported that he presented to the Caliph a report on Muslim education in West Africa whilst in Constantinople.[99] But by late February, he was once again in Constantinople and was dispatched by the Sultan on an important fact-finding mission to the Balkans. This time he was accompanied by his eldest son and Major Nuruddin Ibrahim Bey, an aide de camp to the Sultan.[100] The small party had been driven with a guard of honour from the railway station in Constantinople to a train bound for Salonica. They departed in a special saloon carriage attached to the train. *The Crescent* announced that the Sultan has sent the Sheikh on a fact-finding mission to obtain an independent and reliable report of the conditions in Eastern Roumelia, but secrecy was maintained as to the exact nature of the mission, which had been revealed to Quilliam after a prolonged meeting with the Sultan on the 24th February.[101]

Whatever the true purpose of the expedition, Quilliam would provide detailed accounts of his travels that were reported in *The Crescent* throughout March until his return to Liverpool on the 24th April. From the precise travelogue it is possible to ascertain that the Sheikh's mission was to enquire about the exact nature of the insurgencies in the region and especially the degree of Bulgarian involvement. He had travelled from Salonica to Negovana, a village in the district of Monastir, where outrages by Christian insurgents had been reported, including the murder of six Wallachians. He opened the enquiry there, but suspended it for ten days whilst he travelled on to Monastir to investigate the murder of two Greeks and the rape of two Greek girls in the village of Kristofar. The accused were being held in prison after their arrest by Turkish soldiers and were questioned by Quilliam. He then went on to Ochrina, via Kopara and Resna, before returning to the small town of Florina to visit the prison there and interview prisoners. In Florina, he would re-open the investigation into the case of the Negovana murders. Quilliam noted that many of the murders of Greek Christians were being carried out by Bulgar insurgents, who then shifted the blame onto the Turks.[102] After his investigations in Monastir, he passed some time in Kosovo on the Serbian border.

It would appear that Quilliam's time in the region of Monastir was eventful. On 22nd March he reported that he had observed a skirmish between Turkish gendarmes and Bulgarian brigands at Kriveni,[103] and he must have told the Liverpool Muslims of a Christian attempt on his life. Although this is not mentioned in his accounts of the journey, when he again left for Constantinople in 1908, he reassured the Muslims who came to see him depart from Lime Street Station in Liverpool that the chances of another assassination attempt were remote because he intended to stay in Constantinople and that it was highly unlikely that his life would be in danger from a Turk.[104] It is also evident that the Sheikh took the opportunity to preach Islam in the region of Monastir. A weekly journal published in the district reports that large audiences were crowding into places of worship to hear him.[105] One unlooked for side effect of the Sheikh's activities in the region was the banning of *The Crescent* in Bulgaria.[106]

In 1908, Abdullah Quilliam took up residence in Constantinople after experiencing professional difficulties in Liverpool. He remained there with his son until 1909, but Ahmed may have remained longer. The next decade was to be one of the most difficult in his life as he witnessed the Young Turk's revolution, the siding of Turkey with Germany in World War I and the subsequent collapse of the Ottoman Empire and the loss of the Caliphate when Turkey re-emerged as a nation-state in the early 1920s. The position that he had maintained of dual loyalty to Crown and Caliph would become untenable and would leave him in many ways a bitterly-disappointed man. He would always continue to maintain that an errant foreign policy had driven Turkey into the arms of Germany.

The period of his life as Sheikh al-Islam of Britain that passed in his home city of Liverpool coincided with a particularly difficult era in the relations between Britain and the Muslim world. As in recent decades in Britain and the West, loyalty and identity issues for British Muslims would prove to be fraught with difficulties as crises occurred in various parts of the Muslim world. Quilliam's strategy of loyalty to Queen and Caliph was always going to be difficult when the Caliph was the ruler of a rival Empire that was nearing its end. Not all Muslims could accept his position of antagonism towards British foreign policy in the Middle East; many Indian Muslims had never been close to the Caliph or accepted his authority over them. They did not welcome Quilliam's calls for them to protest or disobey their British rulers out of allegiance to the Ottomans. They knew that this would only create difficulties for them in an already complex political situation. In return, Quilliam never really warmed to the Indians, except for those that formed the Indian Khilafat movement. In spite of these difficulties, Quilliam does offer contemporary British Muslims insights into the problems of negotiating conflicting loyalties.

In 1895, the Archbishop of Canterbury had commented on the power and spirit of Islam at a meeting of the Society for the Propagation of the Gospel. He stated that, 'all that has been said of the extreme difficulty of making the slightest impression upon the rock of Islamism has been verified a thousandfold. It is a rock beneath which are volcanic forces of the most terrible kind. In Mohammedanism there lies a double difficulty. There is its thorough belief in extermination and also a very high degree of cultivation. For the cultivation of its leaders is as marvellous as the fanaticism of its rank and file.'[107] The attitudes of some leading churchmen have changed little up to the present, and neither has the media coverage. Quilliam accused the media of being 'intolerant, mendacious and unfair' and tried to demonstrate that Christians were equally or even more culpable than Muslims. In 1896, he cited examples of 'Christian' atrocities such as the Philippine Rebellion against the Spanish and the Rinderpest guards in the Waterberg District, who were responsible for 'cruelty against unfortunate natives literally dying of starvation', and argued that 'Christians are far from being changed in their natures to what they were in bye-gone centuries'.[108] He argued that the tales of alleged Armenian atrocities, 'mostly originating in the perfervid imaginations of

English penny-a-lining journalists and hypocritical missionaries of the Annanias and Sapphira type', were greatly exaggerated and that Abdul Hamid II was a great reformer, intent upon removing any remaining backward elements from Ottoman life and therefore worthy of British support and sense of fair play.[109] He also pointed out that nations such as Serbia and Albania were notorious for brigandry. His final argument was that the destruction of the Ottoman Empire would knock out the keystone of European equilibrium and would plunge the world into the most costly war of modern times.[110] Sometimes in exasperation he would threaten that it was high time that the 'Mohammedans' of the whole world began to ponder the actions of England towards the Sultan and the Ottoman Empire.

However, it was unlikely that the British public could differentiate between Quilliam's various statements regarding his relations to the Sultan of Turkey. At the meetings in Liverpool that were gate-crashed by the Sheikh, he declared that he was not in the employ of Turkey. When described as the representative of Turkey by the Lord Mayor of Liverpool, he answered, 'I do not officially represent Turkey in Liverpool, but I do represent the Muslim Faith, and I am the Sheikh of Mussulmans in the British Isles. I do not receive one penny from the Turkish Government.'[111] Perhaps the best summary of Quilliam's position is contained in the following excerpt from a prayer that he wrote on behalf of Edward VII on the eve of his coronation. The Sheikh wrote:

> We believe that Thou hast appointed Edward, the son of Victoria, to be the King of these realms, even as Thou didst direct and appoint Thy servant Abdul Hamid to be the Sovereign of the Ottoman Empire and Caliph of the True Believers. We beseech Thee, O God, to bless him whom Thou hast appointed to be the ruler of these realms. Give to him, O Lord, that wise understanding that he may ever maintain his realm in peace with all Muslim peoples and their sovereign rulers.[112]

His position was difficult for most to grasp. The difficulty was complicated by two contrasting ways that Quilliam perceived the relationship between religion and state. Sometimes he would compare Christian and Muslim civilisations with each other as though such entities were synonymous with religious life. There was also a lack of consistency: he was not adverse to the typical strategy of religious rivals of comparing the ideal of the religious teachings as taught by sacred texts or founding figures with the reality that historically presented itself. At other times, he would separate religion and state; but when defending the Ottomans, the two areas were always conflated. Quilliam certainly increased the difficulty for British Muslims when their nation of birth found itself in conflict with Muslim powers or insurgents. His chosen tactic was to protest within the legitimate means provided by British democracy, and he was certainly the first to harness feelings of discontent from amongst British Muslims and draw upon international support from Muslims around the world. The tactic was as controversial then as it is now, but for Quilliam it was further complicated by his conflation of the legitimate representation of Sunni religious leadership with the Ottoman state.

CHAPTER 8

A Mysterious Twilight: Abdullah Quilliam as Henri de Léon, 1908-1932

At 1pm on the 28th April 1932, Sheikh Abdullah Quilliam, also known as Henri de Léon, was buried at Brookwood Cemetery, Woking, close to the graves of other twentieth-century Muslim luminaries such as Lord Headley and Marmaduke Pickthall and the plot reserved for the lascars, the sailors whose rights he had fought for in Liverpool so assiduously. Strangely, while the plot number is known, his last resting place cannot currently be identified. The fact that the precise location of his grave is unknown has led to rumours and speculation about his death. Yet there is little mystery in the undertaker's report. Measured at five feet and six inches in height and 18 inches across the shoulders, his total funeral costs were just short of £65, the sum paid for a grave in the Muslim plot, a hearse, two limousines and the labour of six men from the funeral company. The funeral was paid for by the last woman in his life, Edith Miriam Spray, who had been his partner since around 1915. At the time of his death, which occurred in Devonshire Place after an operation for an intestinal blockage and an enlarged prostrate, they had been living together for seventeen years, dividing their time between Bloomsbury and Mount Road, Newhaven, in Sussex, where they had both retired in 1924. The funeral was also attended

Henri de Léon with his wife Edith Miriam Léon at a reception given at the Shah Jehan Mosque, Woking, in June 1931 in honour of the two princely sons of the Nizam of Hyderabad. Front row from left to right: Prof. H. Léon (circled), Madame Léon, Mrs Quraishi, Mr H. Lovegrove, Mrs H. Buchannan-Hamilton, Lady Headley, Lord Headley, Prince Azam Jah Bahadur, Prince Moazzam Jah Bahadur, Prince Aly Khan (son of H.H. the Aga Khan), Abdul Majid (Imam of the Mosque), Mrs Salway White, and Brigadier Osam Yar ud Dawla Bahadur.

by his legal wife, Mary Lyon, and their five children, the four children of Hannah, his deceased first wife, his many grandchildren and large numbers of British Muslims from the Woking Mosque community.

Even after his death, controversy continued to follow this remarkable man. Although there were times during his life in Liverpool when Quilliam had been a wealthy man, the probate that was granted to Edith Miriam Leon and Lilian Ayesha Quilliam, one of his daughters from Mary Lyon, showed an estate worth just short of £502. It is said that Edith had expected to be left this money and may have thought that it would be a larger sum. However, she was left only his papers, and it is speculated that, in a fit of pique, she destroyed them in a fire in the house at Newhaven. Whether this was intentional or accidental, she did burn down the cottage that contained all his possessions. Whatever exactly happened, there was enough suspicion around the event for the police to investigate and for the insurance company to refuse to pay her claim.

In photographs of the London Muslims who congregated around Woking Mosque, Henri de Léon can be seen sitting, sometimes with a veiled Edith, on the fringes of the main luminaries. The ubiquitous Turkish fez remains on his head. Witnesses described him as a scruffy, unkempt man who passed many of his days in the reading room of the British Museum.

What had happened to Abdullah Quilliam, the leader of the Liverpool Muslims, the Sheikh al-Islam of the British Isles? And why had he reappeared in London as a member of the Woking Mosque community in the guise of the Edwardian polymath, Henri de Léon, who had been his companion, confidante and physician in Liverpool and who he claimed had died in his arms?

To answer these questions it is necessary to return to the summer of 1908. On the 27th July, the King's Proctor, the official charged with investigating any breaches of the law committed by solicitors, received notice from John Bateman, the solicitor to Martha May Peters, to the effect that his client did not intend to contest the overturning of her *decree nisi* that had been made by the King's Proctor on the 10th July. John Bateman stated that he was replacing William Henry Quilliam, who had originally represented Martha May Peters. It was stated that Quilliam could not be traced and was travelling in Asia Minor. As a result of suspicions raised by the King's Proctor, the Attorney General had accused Quilliam of not bringing certain material facts before the court, which had resulted in a false case being presented on behalf of the petitioner for the divorce.[1] The situation was to worsen and, in June 1909, *The Times* reported that William Henry Quilliam had been struck off the Rolls.[2]

What had happened that summer that had such a disastrous impact on both Quilliam's career as a lawyer and the future of the Muslim community in Liverpool? The answer can be traced back to 31st January 1899, when Martha May Peters married Enoch Griffiths Thompson in Liverpool. The marriage lasted for eight years and produced one child. On the 17th June 1907, she had petitioned for a divorce on the grounds of her husband's cruelty, desertion and adultery. Quilliam was asked to represent Martha May. There are suggestions that she was penniless, and she did not defend the overturning of her divorce in 1908 on the grounds that she could not afford to pursue the case any further. Quilliam was notoriously quixotic when it came to women in distress and was famous for representing the wives and mistresses of the rougher areas of Liverpool, often without financial recompense. He was also a vocal advocate for the liberalisation of Britain's strict divorce laws and may have taken the case out of principle, kindness or gallantry.

On the 16th January 1908, the *decree nisi* was awarded, undefended by the husband. The grounds for the divorce were adulteries committed in 1899, 1900, 1902 and a specific incident used to prove the case on 31st May 1907. It was stated that the husband had visited a brothel in Glasgow where he had sex with Suzie Burns after his ship had docked in the city. The act of sexual intercourse had been observed by a man named Evans, who had drunk with the accused and accompanied him to the address in Glasgow. Quilliam also testified that he had witnessed the husband visit the house on the 28th May and on several other occasions from the 24th May. It was this testimony by Quilliam that had raised the suspicions of the King's Proctor, because it was discovered that *The Praetorian* had not docked until the 28th May and that the respondent had not come ashore until the 29th May.

Further investigation revealed that Evans had formerly been employed by Quilliam as a 'clerk'. The court described him as a 'species of police-court tout' and he described himself to the investigating tribunal's President as a ship's butcher. It appeared that Evans, pretending to be an acquaintance of the husband, had visited the house of the parents, where he had obtained the name of the ship and the time of arrival. He befriended the husband and prevailed upon him to visit a brothel after plying him with drink. The King's Proctor accused the petitioner and her solicitor of procuring adultery of the respondent with Susie Burns, brought about 'by an agent of the petitioner who had been employed by and on behalf of her to watch the respondent for the purpose of obtaining evidence of his adultery upon which she might apply for a divorce'.[3] The President of the Tribunal commented that such cases were a frequent occurrence, commonly used to subvert Britain's divorce laws, but were difficult to prove. Although *The Times* treated the case factually, reporting it only in its records of the proceedings of the King's Bench Division, the Liverpool media were more sensationalist in their coverage, making much of the connection between Quilliam the lawyer and his public life as the leader of Britain's Muslims.

The fact that such practices were common amongst divorce lawyers begs the question why Quilliam, a very intelligent and successful lawyer, would leave himself open to discovery and public scandal by mixing up the dates and, even more suspiciously, how did the case come to the King's Proctor when it appeared to go through the courts without a hitch? These questions have led to a number of conspiracy theories, especially in view of Quilliam's claim that he never went to Glasgow on the dates mentioned.

There has been a lot of speculation about Abdullah Quilliam's activities after his traumatic disgrace and downfall. There are stories that he remained in Constantinople until the end of World War I, engaged in spying for Britain, and then returned to the house in Onchan on the Isle of Man in 1919, where he scandalised the local population by indulging in orgies and maintaining a harem of women.[4] Most of these tales were generated on the Isle of Man and can be attributed to family gossip, the benefits of a colourful character for the local tourist industry and the inability of a conservative rural population that was made up of predominantly low-church Protestants to deal with eccentricity of any kind at the turn of nineteenth century. To this list may be added a general Protestant fear of Islam and the public's fascination with the exotic East.

The media on the Isle of Man presented Quilliam as, 'one of the Island's most flamboyant characters', who, after a career 'as varied and exciting as a swashbuckling screen hero returned to his grassroots and set up house at The Towers in Onchan'.[5] This article in the *Isle of Man Examiner* claimed that Quilliam had travelled to Persia and Afghanistan and had lived in Turkey throughout 1914-18, where he had spied for the Allied cause. The demonisation of Quilliam was further compounded by the activities of Quilliam's descendants. His son Billal had been involved in a number of dubious financial transactions, resulting in his being struck off by the Law Society in 1938 and serving several prison sentences, including eighteen months on the Isle of Man from 1934. Billal had married the daughter of a prominent Manx family, and one of their two sons also achieved notoriety in 1967 when he was sentenced to four months imprisonment for failing to keep proper financial records for his company.

It is this grandson of Quilliam, Bill Kerruish, who over the years before his death contributed some of the wilder tales that added to the dubious reputation of Abdullah Quilliam. Outrageously, Bill Kerruish actually claimed that William Henry Quilliam never existed. He tells a tale that he attributed to a certain Gerald Hamilton, a grandson of the Duke of Abercorn, which claimed that Henri de Léon, a native of Trebich in Moravia, had taken part in an uprising against the Austro-Hungarian Empire around 1880 and had then fled Trieste on a boat bound for Liverpool. De Léon had assumed the identity of a twelve-month old child whose name he had obtained from a Liverpool cemetery. The family of the child, the parents of William Henry Quilliam, had for some unknown reason gone along with this deception. There was an apparent liaison with a French girl named Louise Ruoy, which had led to a daughter named Laetitia.[6] This 'Crowleyisation' of Quilliam makes it more difficult for the serious researcher to discover the facts in this period of Quilliam's life,[7] and this is further complicated by the fact that Quilliam himself was not sure of his public position and reception in Britain after the events of 1908 and thus deliberately maintained a separate identity as Henri de Léon.

The implications of this for Quilliam's ability to be a public and credible voice for Islam in Britain were immense, particularly with regard to the Liverpool Muslim Institute, as the converts had to deal with the fall-out from the newspaper publicity and the disappearance of their leader. Quilliam had given his son Billal power of attorney over his various properties in the city, including the Mosque at Brougham Terrace. With Ahmed accompanying the Sheikh to Constantinople and Billal having recently qualified as a solicitor under his father's tuition, he was the obvious choice to protect the family's possessions legally in Abdullah's absence. In fact, Billal ran his father's company in Liverpool as Quilliam and Son from time of his father's de-barring in June 1909 until 1922. But Quilliam's trust in his younger son was shown to be misplaced, at least as far the interests of Islam in Britain were concerned.[8] Billal quickly disposed of the property that had been used so successfully as a mosque and Islamic centre, leaving the already reeling Muslim community bereft of a base. Over the next few years, the more mobile members migrated to London where they became part of the interwoven Woking Mosque communities and Lord Headley's significant convert group, which was primarily located in London. The Liverpool Muslim Institute never recovered, despite the efforts that were made by Robert Ahmed Quilliam to revive and look after the interests of Liverpool Muslims on his return to the city. The cause of Islam was still upheld in Liverpool in 1912 through the efforts of F. Djaffer Mortimore, Prof. Stephen Hasan Arculli and Resched P. Stanley (the Late Mayor of Stalybridge),[9] and media records show that Robert Ahmed Quilliam became involved with the interests of migrant Muslims more than two decades later, when he supported the efforts of an Indian Muslim to become a city councillor.

There has been a lot of speculation concerning the years after 1908. That Quilliam departed with Ahmed to Constantinople is not in doubt, and accompanied by the young woman involved in the divorce proceedings, according to some sources.[10] When exactly he returned to England is more uncertain, but he was not foolhardy enough to remain there after war commenced between England and Turkey in 1914. In the book written by Abdullah Quilliam under the pseudonym of Henri de Léon about the life of Sheikh Haroun Abdullah, he noted that the research for the book was carried out between 1903 and 1908 whilst he was in attendance upon the Sultan and that the remainder was written after the Young Turk's revolution in 1909. The author informed his readers that, 'when I was living in retirement at Bostondjik on the Asiatic side of the Sea of Marmara'.[11] Abdullah Quilliam wrote to *The Liverpool Mercury* and *The Liverpool Post*, printed on the 7th May 1909, stating that he had not been in the city of Glasgow or anywhere near Bligh Street, a house described by the Liverpool Press as 'a house used for disreputable purposes', and was completely innocent of the allegations laid against him. He seemed to claim that he was already in Constantinople in 1908 when Martha Peter's husband was compromised with Sally Burns.

The letter was addressed from 'Eskishehr', which is most probably Eskisehir, a city in northwest Turkey located on the bank of the Porsuk River, 155 miles west of Ankara and 217 miles southeast of Istanbul. In the same letter, Quilliam mentions that he had been a close witness of the Young Turk uprising and the surrounding events in Constantinople.

Quilliam's retirement did not last a long time in Turkey. By 1910 he was definitely already back in England and living in Christian Road, Preston. His first wife Hannah died on the 18th November 1909 in Hoylake from cancer of the colon. Her death would have freed Quilliam to remarry if he so wished, and he may have returned for the funeral. He had long promised Mary Lyon in response to her pressure that he would give her a legal 'Christian' marriage and legitimise their five children. She had never been happy with her status as a 'Muslim' wife, confirmed by a mosque marriage in Liverpool. Their last child together, May Habibah, had died on the 7th April 1908 from scarlet fever and diphtheria aged eleven. Two other children from the family had been admitted to hospital and were dangerously ill. These recent events along with the death of Hannah may have made Quilliam reconsider his relationship with Mary Lyon and return to England, accepting her wish to legalise their union. On the 31st December 1910, he married Mary in the Preston Registry Office at the age of 54. She was 47 and had waited patiently for this event to happen since she was a young showgirl in Liverpool when they had first met. Edith Miriam Spray (also known as Edith de Léon) and Hannah's daughter Lilian Ayesha were the witnesses, a role that they would both repeat at his death. One has to assume that Edith Miriam was already involved in a relationship with Quilliam, possibly known to Mary.[12] Quilliam was certainly living with Edith only three years later in Mount Horton Road, Nottingham, from 1913 to the outbreak of war in 1914.[13] By this time, Abdullah Quilliam was registered at this address as Dr de Léon and gave a lecture on Geology in the city on the 29th November 1912, which was later published in *The Philomath* in 1915.

Some time after his return from Constantinople, Abdullah Quilliam took the name of Henri Mustapha (Marcel) de Léon. He would remain partially concealed by this identity until his death in 1932, although it is apparent that family and friends were aware of the alternative identity. John Deane Potter affirmed that this happened on Quilliam's return to England and suggested that he did it to avoid raising again the scandal of the divorce case in Liverpool. Potter also commented that the family fortune that the Sheikh had once possessed was gone and that he earned his living for a while writing sermons for Christian clergymen at half a guinea a time. This dual identity has led to considerable speculation after Quilliam's death. There is no doubt that Abdullah Quilliam and Henri de Léon were one and the same person, confirmed at the funeral by Edith Miriam; but there are those who believe that Quilliam masqueraded under the identity of Henri de Léon even during his Liverpool years as a means of speaking about his own achievements without appearing to be egotistical. Quilliam certainly had a number of pseudonyms during the Liverpool years, including that of 'Sam Snidger', a writer of scurrilous gossip of Liverpool life, but I do not believe that he was Henri de Léon prior to 1912, when he began to live with Edith Miriam. It is clear from the evidence presented by the Liverpool media that Henri de Léon was one of the trusted confidantes of Abdullah Quilliam and even attended to the Sheikh and his family during bouts of illness.

Quilliam always described Henri de Léon as a French Muslim convert who came to visit him on a number of occasions in Liverpool. Edith Miriam claimed that he was born in Paris of a Jewish mother, but oddly conflated the two men in her obituary valediction, which was printed in 1932 in a special combined edition of Quilliam's two magazines, *The Philomath* and *The Physiologist and Optogolist*. She may have done this to protect the elaborate narrative created by Quilliam over the years. Henri de Léon first surfaced as the writer of an article referring to Quilliam's visit to West Africa in 1894.[14] In another piece written in 1900, he attacked the French occupation of Inghar Oasis in present-day Algeria, where forces killed over two thousand tribesmen with little loss of French life.[15] In August of that year, he claimed he was present at the Sultan's Jubilee celebration at the Liverpool mosque,[16] while in September he was at the reception given by the Turkish Consulate in the Alexandra Hotel, Liverpool, presenting the watch made by the Sheikh's brother as a gift for the Sultan. He appeared on the guest list as Dr Henri Mustapha Léon (Paris) and sat on the left of the Consul, with Quilliam on the right.[17] Soon after this event he returned to Paris, apparently suddenly.[18] Whilst he was in Liverpool, Quilliam used de Léon as his unofficial biographer, providing him with access to his childhood diaries and allowing extracts to be published in *The Crescent*. De Léon was back in Liverpool from 1903 until 1908, when he attended to Quilliam's young daughter who died of diphtheria. He was present at her deathbed and movingly described Quilliam's last moments with his daughter. He would appear to be a physician and wrote MD after his name. Sensibly, this was the only qualification Quilliam did not claim when he conflated their two identities.

Since Henri de Léon does not reappear after 1908, except in the new identity adopted by Abdullah Quilliam, it is possible that the real de Léon had died in the period that the Sheikh was in Constantinople between 1908 and 1912. If he was still alive, he may have returned to continental Europe and co-operated with the deception as an act of friendship. Although only speculation, this would resolve the mystery of Edith Miriam Spray being known as Mrs de Léon and Quilliam explaining that his reason for taking the new name was the insistence of his last wife. It is possible that Edith Miriam was Henri de Léon's widow. This was confirmed by Quilliam's grandson, John Deane Potter, who stated that the Sheikh took the name of his last wife and that the families always referred to her as Madame de Léon. If the latter version of events is accurate, then de Léon's death is the most plausible explanation.

Quilliam seems to have built a new identity not only for himself but also for de Léon. The character assumed after 1912 appears to be a construction that was based upon various orientalists, including Dr Leitner, the founder of Woking Mosque, rather than the real person who had visited Liverpool. Although there will always be some uncertainty about the exact nature of the dual identity, there is no doubt that the 'new life' under the name of Henri de Léon permitted Abdullah Quilliam to rebuild his life and re-establish himself as a devout Muslim after leaving Liverpool.

The life of Abdullah Quilliam had been shattered by events, some outside his control. 1908 had begun with the death of his daughter and the disgrace in Liverpool; although he fled to Constantinople, family tragedy followed him with the death of Hannah in 1909. Politically the world was changing dramatically, with the gradual disintegration of the Ottoman Empire, the Young Turk revolution and the entry of Turkey into World War I on the side of Germany – events that threatened the Sultan, and undermined and eventually led to the final end of the Caliphate, which had been founded so many centuries ago on the death of the Prophet.

A return to Liverpool for Quilliam was out of the question, and the activities of Billal led to the end of Quilliam's law firm and any hope of maintaining the family's financial fortunes through the profession of the law. No longer could Abdullah Quilliam lay claim to be Britain's Sheikh al-Islam with any credibility. Some of his Muslim converts from Liverpool had moved to London, where a new focus of Muslim activity had concentrated around a number of high-profile Muslim converts and upper-class Indian Muslims at the Woking Mosque. It would have been an act of humility for Abdullah Quilliam to place himself under the leadership of these new Muslim converts and to participate in their activities at Woking. During his period as Sheikh al-Islam, he had never fully accepted the Mosque outside London as being entirely legitimate. This may have been because the Muslims at Woking never submitted to his authority or because he had difficulties with the early way in which the Mosque was run. However, it was in London and as part of the Woking Mosque community that Abdullah Quilliam was able to once again serve his beloved Islam under the guise of Henri de Léon, French gentleman and Victorian polymath.

Dr G.W. Leitner, a Hungarian Orientalist and ex-Registrar of the University of Punjab in Lahore, had founded the first purpose-built British mosque in 1889 at Woking. The Mosque had been constructed with significant financial assistance from Begum Shah Jahan, the female ruler of Bhopal in India. Abdullah Quilliam had corresponded with Leitner, but had objections to the conditions that Leitner imposed upon the mosque. Quilliam wrote that Leitner opposed the conversion of Englishmen to Islam, any attempts to promote the religion in Britain and any engagement in political activities by Muslim organisations; but above all, he objected to the use of a mosque to promote 'generally unhappy marriages between Mohammedans and Englishwomen'.[19] Leitner wanted the mosque to be used by Muslims of good families who desired to practise their faith whilst visiting Britain.

Quilliam was doing everything in Liverpool that Leitner forbade in Woking and would have had the sympathies of many Muslims in the country who regarded the maintenance and promotion of Islam as fundamental to the faith. Until his departure from Liverpool in 1908, Quilliam had consistently allied himself to the Anjuman-i Islamia at Regents Park, and it is likely that the many Indian students who used the premises in central London objected to Leitner's restrictions at Woking.[20] Quilliam considered the strictures to be so prohibitive that they annulled the right of Woking to be referred to as a mosque. However, by the time of Quilliam's return to England, the Mosque had fallen into disuse after Leitner's demise. Around the time that Quilliam was re-establishing himself as Henri de Léon, Khwaja Kamaluddin, an Indian barrister from Lahore, took over the site and established the Woking Muslim Mission in 1912. Kamaluddin became the focus for the Indian Muslims in England who arrived at the turn of the century and, together with other leading luminaries such as Abdullah Yusuf Ali and Syed Ameer Ali, he set about creating an environment for practising Islam in

Britain. However, these Muslims were of a very different social class to those that would arrive in Britain in the middle of the twentieth century. On the whole, they belonged to the emerging, professional upper-middle and upper-landed classes and were able to move in the elite circles of British society.

They were aware that Islam was poorly thought of in Europe and took on the challenge of acculturation, demonstrating that Islamic and Christian values were not opposed to each other. In order to achieve this, they engaged in rational debates to defend Islam and were even prepared to modify certain traditional practices in order to integrate with the wider society. Abdullah Quilliam, now submerged in his new identity as Henri de Léon, would have had no difficulty with such efforts to convince those around him that Islam was a religion of reason. Indeed, he had been engaged in similar activities for the last twenty-five years. He would have to acclimatise to their efforts to show the similarities between Islam and Christianity, since his approach had always been to show the 'corrupted' condition of institutionalised religion in the West and to argue that this proved the truth that was taught by the Qur'an concerning the earlier revelations of Judaism and Christianity. This was more difficult for the Indian Muslims, who were both guests in Britain and, regardless of their class, subordinate citizens of the Empire.

The other problem that these Muslims needed to resolve was their attitude to Turkey and the collapsing Ottoman Empire. Criticism of the Turks and their government was closely linked to British negative attitudes towards Islam. The 'backwardness' of the Ottomans was perceived by the media to be caused by the religious practices of the rulers and their subjects. Any defence of Turkey after 1914 was likely to be regarded as treachery, and yet it was equally difficult for Sunni Muslims to condemn the Caliphate. In spite of the dangers inherent in defending the Ottoman Empire, the South Asian Muslims embarked on a campaign to alter the widespread public opinion. In order to achieve their aims, they worked with a number of British peers who were prepared to listen.[21] They also created a number of pressure groups that tried to influence government policy. The Central Islamic Society and the Islamic Information Bureau organised meetings and published articles defending the Ottomans. In January 1914, Marmaduke Pickthall formed the Anglo-Ottoman Society to lobby on behalf of Turkey and to promote the values of Ottoman culture. One would expect Abdullah Quilliam, the former Sheikh al-Islam of Britain and confidante of the Sultan, to have been involved in these activities. Unsurprisingly, the name of Henri de Léon appeared as the Vice-President of the Anglo-Ottoman Society until he resigned on the declaration of hostilities in November 1914.

However, Pickthall and de Léon disagreed with regard to the Young Turks revolution in 1908. Quilliam had been in Constantinople at the time of the uprising and was never going to accept the legitimacy of an attempt to overthrow his beloved Sultan. On the other hand, Pickthall saw the rebellion as a hope for a renewal of the ailing Ottoman Empire. Quilliam in his new identity as de Léon felt that his opposition to the Young Turk movement was proved correct by the disasters of the Balkan War of 1912, when the Ottoman Empire lost almost all its remaining European territories. However, they were both concerned about the Unionist decision to side with Prussian militarism during the First World War.[22]

The two men disagreed on the Ahmadiyya or Qadiani movement, to which Kamaluddin belonged. Mirza Ghulam Ahmad, the founder of the movement, had died in 1908, and the Ahmadiyya had become divided into the Qadianis and the Lahoris. The former declared their deceased founder to be a prophet, whilst the Lahoris remained closer to the central doctrines of Sunni Islam. Both Quilliam and Pickthall declared themselves to be Sunni Muslims of the Hanafi school; but Pickthall, although prepared acknowledge the Lahoris as legitimate, was not sympathetic to the Qadianis. Henri de Léon, on the other hand, was happy to write articles for both the Lahori and Qadiani publications, a position of tolerance that perhaps reflected the pan-Islamic position of tolerance towards all Muslims that he had preached in Liverpool.

They would both have been staunch allies of the Indian Khilafat movement, but the significance of their agreements and disagreements lies in the underlying relationship of the two men and Quilliam's place amongst the Muslims in London, which had replaced Liverpool as the centre of Islamic activities in Britain. Pickthall had assumed the role of a natural leader amongst the capital's Muslim institutions in Notting Hill, as well as the Islam Society, the Muslim Literary Society and the Anglo-Mughal Mosque in Woking. When Khwaja Kamaluddin returned to India in 1919, Pickthall preached the Friday sermons in Woking. Quilliam may have chosen to relinquish his old identity as Sheikh al-Islam of the British Isles and conceal himself under the new identity of Henri de Léon, but he was not beyond disagreeing publicly and in print with the new leaders of Britain's Muslim community, whilst at the same time working closely with them.

The outbreak of war presented de Léon with the issue of dual loyalty that had created problems for him in an earlier period, when he had condemned British foreign policy in the Muslim world so vociferously as Abdullah Quilliam. His close links to the Ottoman court raised suspicions, and files were kept on him and other prominent British Muslims by the intelligence services of the Foreign Office, Home Office and the India Office. He was suspected of pro-Turkish activities by military intelligence, and this was probably also the view of other intelligence agencies.[23] Yet de Léon seemed keen to indicate that his loyalties lay firmly with the Crown. In November 1914, he wrote to the Secretary of State, Sir Edward Grey, stating: 'I am absolutely and entirely loyal to the British Crown and if I can be of any use in assisting to promote loyalty amongst the Muslims throughout the Empire I am at the service of the Government.'[24] In 1915, he wrote again to inform the Foreign Secretary that a ticket had been sent from the

Anglo-Ottoman Society inviting their former Vice-President to a meeting. De Léon pointed out that he had accepted the invitation and offered assurance that the organisation did not conflict with British interests in their desire to resolve the conflict between the two Empires harmoniously. He pointed out that his presence at the meeting could help to restrain any 'political firebrands' who might attempt to use the organisation for their own devices.[25]

It is not known whether the intelligence services ever picked up on de Léon's offer of help, but the Foreign Office memos seem to suggest that they did not. It is unlikely that they would have trusted him completely – he was suspected of being too close to the Ottomans after his various sojourns in Constantinople, Turkey, the Balkans, West Africa and Morocco. He was openly proud of his services to the Sultan and advertised his various awards and honours from the Caliph of Islam, many of which were Ottoman military medals. Even as de Léon, Abdullah Quilliam refused to dispense with these achievements in the Muslim world, which he wore as trophies of his service to Islam. The honours that were allocated to de Léon match those of Abdullah Quilliam, and it is almost certain that he was the only man to have two almost identical entries in *Who's Who?*[26] Quilliam had also been closely observed by the intelligence services in Liverpool, as two of his imams were under suspicion and observation. Barakatullah, first imam of the Liverpool Mosque, was a native of Bengal and was considered something of a 'firebrand' by the authorities. He later moved to Japan, where he promoted Islam and published a very strongly anti-colonial journal in which he condemned the British presence in India and called upon Indian Muslims to fight for independence. His successor, Maulvi Rafiuddin Ahmad, had once been Vice-President of the Anjuman-i Ishatul Islam in Bombay. He was a fervent member of the Indian Khilafat movement and was considered to be a bad influence on Queen Victoria, who had sought his counsel on Islam.

As Abdullah Quilliam considered that he could no longer openly offer his services to Islam in a leadership capacity, he sought to rebuild his life as a polymath. Even in Liverpool, he had often lectured on a wide variety of subjects including geology, Manx history and the history of Islamic civilisation. As Henri de Léon, he began to lecture and write widely, utilising organisations and journals that he created during this period. He began to publish *The Philomath* in June 1913, with Edith Miriam de Léon as a co-editor. She proved herself to be a valuable partner during this period. Neither Hannah nor Mary Lyon had been his intellectual equals and had been happy to raise his children. Hannah had been of the right class to appear with him in public functions and society occasions during the period in Liverpool. However, Edith seems to have been able enough to work with him on his various attempts to re-create himself as an Edwardian gentleman of letters. *The Philomath* remained in publication after his death in 1932, when Edith Miriam continued to edit it alone for a short period. The publication was advertised as the official organ and journal of the Proceedings of the Societé Internationale de Philologie Sciences et Beaux-Arts, with de Léon as General-Secretary and Robert Ahmed Quilliam as President. In 1917, a second publication, *The Physiologist*, appeared as the magazine of the college that had been opened by de Léon and Edith Miriam in Bloomsbury. Henri de Léon appeared as the Dean of the Faculty. One of the names that appeared as a functionary was Lord Headley, who was the Chairman. The first mention of the Societé Internationale de Philologie Sciences et Beaux-Arts, the society that was to provide Quilliam with a new identity from 1910 after his return from Turkey and his adoption of the name Henri de Léon, had been at the Annual General Meeting of the Liverpool Muslim Institute in 1902, when it was declared that the Muslim school in Liverpool would be affiliated with the International Society of Philology, Science and the Arts.[27]

The connection to Lord Headley,[28] described by Quilliam's grandson as 'a great friend of my grandfather',[29] is significant in placing the Sheikh's continued presence in the British Muslim scene. There was a small but important group of upper and middle-class converts in London who congregated under the leadership of Headley. Prominent amongst these were Marmaduke Pickthall, the translator of the Qur'an, Khalid Sheldrake, an early convert and the son of a pickle manufacturer, Sir Archibald Hamilton, Deputy Surgeon-General of the Royal Navy and a prominent Conservative, Sir Lauder Brunton, a barrister, and Lady Evelyn Cobbald, surely the first Englishwoman to perform the Hajj. This group mixed freely with the Indian students and Ottoman citizens in London who made up the Woking community, and between them they set out to establish a form of Islam that could be acceptable to British society. The Islam that both groups practised could be described as modernist and their approach to conversion was gradualist. They tended to be relaxed regarding halal food strictures, the moderate use of alcohol, dress codes and the free mixing of the sexes; as Quilliam had in Liverpool, they presented Islam as the religion of reason.

Lord Headley had formed the British Muslim Society in December 1914 as a parallel organisation to the Woking group and published *The Islamic Review* as a means of promoting their tolerant and open-minded understanding of Islam. Henri de Léon was a regular subscriber,[30] and between 1928 and 1929 he was elected to be joint Vice-President of the British Muslim Society along with Khwaja Kamaluddin. There is no doubt that the group was aware that de Léon was Abdullah Quilliam. Several members of the Liverpool Muslim Institute were actively involved in the British Muslim Society and would have known their old Sheikh. Prominent amongst these would have been Yehya-en-Nasr Parkinson, whom Khalid Sheldrake confirmed as someone converted to Islam by Quilliam. Sheldrake also knew Quilliam very well, and these and others must have known that Henri de Léon and Abdullah Quilliam were one and the same person.

One can assume that these aristocratic and respectable members of British society did not consider that the events which took place in Liverpool that had led to Quilliam's exile in Turkey

were a sufficient disgrace for them to withhold their company
or to prevent them accepting him in their midst. This is borne
out by a tribute to Quilliam written by Khalid Sheldrake in July
1912. Sheldrake mentioned that he had known Quilliam well and
confirmed that he had formed the first organised community of
Muslims in Britain. He wrote, 'Although, unfortunately, he is no
longer with us, having committed a technical offence though not
in any way a criminal one, and I who know the facts of the case
consider him morally justified in his action which only showed
very eloquently the superiority of the Islamic legal code over that
in use in England at the present day which is far from reaching
the standard laid down by our Holy Prophet 1300 years ago.'[31]
Khalid Sheldrake was a prominent convert, highly respected by the
Muslim communities in Britain, and was the first secretary of the
British Muslim Society. His view would suggest that the British
Muslims regarded Quilliam's 'disgrace' in Liverpool as a legal, but
not a moral, lapse of judgment and that his subsequent exile and
removal from the Bar was part and parcel of a personality that,
in Sheldrake's words, led to Quilliam being known as 'the Poor
Man's Solicitor' because of the scores of occasions on which he
'fought cases for men who were penniless and charged no fee'.[32] To
all intents and purposes, it would appear that Abdullah Quilliam,
under his new identity of Henri de Léon, was a respected member
of the London and Woking Muslim communities and continued
to be a prominent member of the British Muslim community until
his death. Sheldrake's statement that Quilliam was no 'longer with
us' seems to suggest that the London Muslims respected Quilliam's
desire to remain incognito.

Evidence of the esteem in which he was held can be found in
an early edition of *The Islamic Review*, where there is a report of the
first public meeting of the British Muslim Society that was held on
the 20th December 1915.[33] The report stated that the meeting was
addressed by Professor H. Mustafa Léon. The proceedings opened
with the reading of a letter from Yehya-en-Nasr Parkinson, the

Vice-President of the Society, who could not be present in person. The presidential address was given by the Right Hon. Lord Headley and this was followed by that of Professor H. Mustafa Léon. *The Islamic Review* described the address as being delivered with 'intense feeling'. The speech is of great interest because it is the only place on record where Abdullah Quilliam recounted the story of his conversion to Islam. As de Léon, he claimed to have been a Muslim for thirty-one years and to have been converted to the religion in Morocco. This would, of course, tie in with the dates of Quilliam's own accounts of his conversion as told in *The Crescent*. However, Quilliam as Henri de Léon provided far more details of the event. He stated that, while dining in Morocco, he met with a Jew and a Muslim at a table in a restaurant where, in a friendly way, they began to investigate those points in religion upon which they agreed or differed with each other. After the Jew and the Christian (Quilliam) had offered their arguments concerning the superiority of their respective religions, the Muslim said to the Christian, 'your creed is superior to that of the Jew because you have a later revelation, but Islam is superior to your creed, for we have an imperishable revelation in the Holy Qur'an given through our Blessed Prophet Muhammad (peace be ever to his soul!)'.[34] The speech in London was completed with a plea for non-Muslims who were present in the audience to accept Islam.[35] It is revealing that de Léon recounted the story as if he were the Christian. When Henri de Léon was described in *The Crescent* during the time he was visiting Liverpool, it was mentioned that he was of Eastern European Jewish origins with French residency. Quilliam, of course, had begun his religious life as a devout Christian.

In 1920, a delegation led by Mohammad Ali Jauhar (1878-1931) visited England to promote the Khilafat Movement that had been launched in India in 1919 after the defeat of the Ottoman Empire. The intention of the movement was to campaign for the survival of the Caliphate, its rule over the Arabian Peninsula and its custody of the sacred places of Islam in Makka and Medina. During their stay,

Woodland Towers, Quilliam's house in Onchan,
the Isle of Man, which he purchased in 1903.

the delegation visited Woking Mosque in March 1920. This visit
was certain to have attracted the attention of Abdullah Quilliam,
after he spent so many years as a staunch advocate of the Turkish
Caliphate and was indeed known to the Khilafat Movement because
his writings had been published in India. *The Islamic Review* reported
the occasion under the heading, 'Indian Delegation at the Mosque'.
The article contains the following statement:

> The three members of the Indian Khilafat Delegation paid a
> visit to the Woking Mosque on Sunday 21st March, 1920. They
> drew a large gathering of British and Indian Muslims and
> non-Muslim English men and women. The Mosque being
> unable to hold the congregation, the meeting was held on the
> lawn on the premises of the Mosque. It was presided over by an
> English Muslim, Prof. H.M. Léon, Ph.D., LL.D.[36]

It is not surprising that the old Sheikh al-Islam was given the opportunity to preside over the meeting. The speech by Mohammad Ali on this occasion echoed Quilliam's oft-repeated message that His Majesty's Muslim subjects, whose number was greater than those of the Christians in the Empire, were all devoted to the Caliph. The meeting was filmed by British Pathé under the title of 'The Problem of Turkey'. The opening clip shows Mohammad Ali Jauhar making his speech, and directly behind him on the platform sits Professor H.M. de Léon.[37]

The Isle of Man continued to pose a problem for Quilliam. He had purchased Woodland Towers in Onchan in 1903 and the house remained within the family until his death in 1932; at various times he took holidays there with his growing family. In 1915, Henri de Léon had published *English Manx-Gaelic Etymologies* with W. Ralph Hall Caine, an old friend of Quilliam's and the brother of the famous Victorian novelist and playwright, Hall Caine. The continuing interest in Manx history and geology brought Henri de Léon an invitation to lecture on the island to promote interest in the preservation of the Manx-Gaelic language. A deputation of the Celtic section of the Societé Internationale de Philologie Sciences et Beaux-Arts arranged to visit Ellan Vannin on the Island in the early part of July 1919. Henri de Léon was accompanied by Edith Miriam and the eccentric but respected Lord Ashbourne, described as the President of the Society.

The speakers were invited to attend the Tynewald ceremony and to speak at the World Manx Association meeting on the 5th July. They were also special guests at a church service in Manx arranged by the Manx Society and they were to visit Calf Island, as well as addressing several meetings organised by the Manx Society. Billal Quilliam, already the managing director of the Manx Fishery Association, placed a trawler at their disposal.[38] The speakers in the group throw some light on the organisation that Henri de Léon and Edith Miriam had created around them. Lord Ashbourne was a renowned Celtic scholar and a familiar figure at Celtic gatherings, where he dressed in the traditional attire of an Irish clan chieftain. He was the son of a former Lord Chancellor of Ireland and a speaker of various Celtic languages. Robert Holmes Edleston, the son of a Cambridge professor, is described as a special envoy to San Marino and an antiquarian. He had recently replaced Sir John Cockburn as overall President of the Society. The final two members of the party were Reverend Professor F.W. O'Connell, an expert in Celtic and Oriental languages, who lectured in Celtic literature at Queen's University, Belfast, and Charles Hall Betts, a Fellow of the Colonial Institute and author of several books on religion and botany. The last named was a Vice-President of the Society.

The articles that appeared in the Manx Press describe Henri de Léon as speaking nine languages with fluency and as an extensive traveller in the Middle East, Europe and Africa, who regularly lectured both nationally and internationally. He is presented as having written and translated several books, including *The Language and Literature of Bohemia*, *The Targum* (containing translations from Aramaic), *The Haggadah* (from Hebrew), *The Chelonia or Shield Reptiles from Palestine* and *Sheikh Abdullah Haroun: His Life and Works*. Edith Miriam was described as an author of several works on botany and chemistry.[39] There is no mention of any of the works that were written on Islam by Abdullah Quilliam, although the last title had been researched by him while in Constantinople.

Unfortunately, the lecture tour turned out to be a disaster. When Henri de Léon rose to address the conference in Douglas Town Hall, where the delegates had been invited to speak by the incumbent mayor of the town, T.W. Kelly, an excited buzz went around the audience. Although the lecture was reported to have been well received by the mayor and the Corporation, they were to discover within minutes of its completion that the excitement generated in the audience came from a recognition that the speaker was Abdullah Quilliam. On such a small island, which Quilliam had been visiting since the 1890s, sometimes accompanied by 'exotic' Asian princes and their English brides whom he had married in the Mosque in Liverpool and at other times by one of his wives and their children, it could be expected that he would be recognised. A number of the Islanders considered that a deception had taken place and, although the organisers tried to continue the lecture tour, the outraged public successfully petitioned for it to be cancelled. The Speaker of the House of Keys (the Government of the Island), John Robert Kerruish,[40] and Henry Percy Kelly, ironically the father of Dollin Kelly, the writer of *The New Manx Worthies* (which includes an entry on Quilliam), were delegated to inform Henri de Léon that he could not speak publicly on the island. After enough time had elapsed to allow the public to cool down, de Léon was forced to leave the island. One can only assume that this experience was both humiliating and galling after so many years as President of Liverpool Manx community.

The incident is interesting in two respects. Firstly, it provides an insight into how successfully Abdullah Quilliam had rebuilt his life as a Victorian man of letters and how he was able to attract prominent upper-class professionals and well-known members of the aristocracy, albeit eccentric individuals, to gather around him and play prominent roles in his Society. This was achieved without compromising his integrity as a devout Muslim who was able to participate actively amongst the Woking and London Muslim communities. On the other hand, the double identity was fraught with difficulties and, at least on the Isle of Man, Abdullah Quilliam was regarded with considerable suspicion. The small conservative population found his flagrant breaching of conventional sexual morality impossible to tolerate and associated it with the popular myths of Eastern perversions that were part and parcel of popular Orientalism at the time.

I came across one final note regarding this rather one-sided and frankly exaggerated perception of Abdullah Quilliam that was found on the island in a study unusually entitled, *An Historical Account of Tainted Women in the Manx Mental Health Services, 1895-1922*, which was carried out by a postgraduate student of Chester University in 2008. Case study 55 records the case of a married female in her early thirties who had been admitted to the asylum in 1903. She had lived with her son, mother and stepfather. The hospital records described her as having problems with 'gin-drinking'. Although, on the surface, this would appear to be a sad tale of a disturbed woman with no connection to the history of Islam in Britain in the nineteenth century, the hospital notes stated that she suffered from the delusion that 'her mother had turned against her since she has become a Moslem'. She claimed to be 'one of the chosen girls of Abdullah'. She was readmitted to the hospital in 1905, 1907, 1910, 1912 and finally in 1914, the last time remaining until 1924. The hospital staff described her as a sexual fantasist who claimed to be married to Sheikh Effendi Quilliam and to be of the Mohammedan faith – 'therefore she doesn't rise up when grace is said and of course doesn't go to church'. The woman apparently passed her time writing scurrilous sexually explicit letters addressed to many different people and her conversation was described as 'objectionable'. Oddly, there is no trace of her or her son in the census records or the Lawson's database of births, marriages and burials.[41] Was this woman one of Abdullah Quilliam's lost wives or does she demonstrate the degree to which the Sheikh had become a part of the sexual fantasies of mentally disturbed and delusional women on the Isle of Man? Even now, contemporary articles on the island refer to Woodland Towers as the house 'where once a harem was kept' and to Quilliam's story as the 'thousand and one nights of a Manx Muslim'.[42] It is unlikely that anything approaching a harem was ever kept in Woodland Towers, since the house is not particularly large and would have had problems accommodating Quilliam and his children. It is more likely that Quilliam was accompanied to Oncham by his wives in turns and thus inflamed local gossip.[43]

The mystery of the women in Quilliam's life will never be resolved, but this is part of the reason why I have called this chapter 'the twilight years'. Although the description could be used for Abdullah

Quilliam's latter years, it is intended to convey more than simply his age. He was 52 when he left Liverpool and 76 at his death in London. He had served Islam in some capacity for over forty years. His work for Islam and his involvement in the British Muslim community is obscured by the fact that he took less of a leadership role in the Woking group than he had in Liverpool. Although remaining in publishing with *The Philomath* and *The Philologist*, these were vehicles for the polymathic knowledge of Henri de Léon, rather than the overt attempts to promote Islam that were found in *The Crescent* and *The Islamic World*. The publication of Muslim journals and literature was left to others such as Lord Headley or Marmaduke Pickthall. However, he never stopped providing articles to these new outlets that were disseminating Islam in Britain. The real significance of 'twilight' lies in the metaphoric suggestion of a falling darkness that obscures the light and makes vision difficult. The double identity of Quilliam/de Léon may have provided the Sheikh with the means to rebuild his life after the events of 1908, but it also makes it difficult to draw conclusions on this man's life or to determine exactly what was taking place during these years. Abdullah Quilliam's life in Liverpool was lived under the intense scrutiny of the media, but even so the converts and his family members chose to protect his private life from public sight. After 1908, Quilliam deliberately chose to hide his true identity, and once again he was aided in this deception by those who knew him well. To many commentators, the double identity following upon the divorce scandal and his debarring from the law society, the multiple relationships with women and the shady financial dealings of his son and grandson point to a dubious personality, a 'con man' and an adventurer. From this view, we are encouraged to look back to the hints of financial scandal during the Liverpool period and judge that the events of 1908 were only the final act of a life lived on the edge of society, and therefore form a kind of moral 'comeuppance'.

A number of controversies surrounded the finances of the Liverpool Muslim Institute in the 1890s. In 1893, *The Crescent* had

reported that the *Ahkbar-Islam* of Agra published a long list of
subscribers to the Liverpool Mosque and Graveyard Fund, and
showed that this amounted to a large sum. The Indian newspaper
was concerned that not all the donations were reaching their
intended destination. The Liverpool Muslim Institute offered to
present all its receipts for publication.[44] There were a number of
Indian Muslims who had collected donations for the printing press
and a graveyard for Indian sailors in Liverpool. As early as 1892, Peer
Mahomad Allarakia had collected money from India to pay for
the printing works, and Quilliam had often used *The Crescent* to
admonish Indian Muslims for doing so little to support his efforts to
represent the interests of Indian lascars in Liverpool; at the Annual
General Meeting in 1896, the Committee had recommended that
greater efforts needed to be made to collect money from abroad. At
the same meeting, Quilliam referred to donations collected in India
to spread Islam in England, but not apparently received by him.
He observed that, as a result of these dishonest attempts to extract
money from honest Muslims in India, he had been accused of the
fraudulent collection of money. He reminded everyone that such
people were not authorised to collect on his behalf, and that there
had been no donations from abroad in the last year. The impression
given at the meeting is that the society that had received money had
misappropriated it.[45]

There had also been a falling out with Alexander Webb in the
USA, in spite of the mutual respect that the two men had for each
other. Webb had always acknowledged the inspiration of Quilliam
on his conversion to Islam, but relations between the two men had
deteriorated after Webb's departure to promote Islam in the USA.[46]
One reason for this can be found in Webb's publication of an
accusation made by a Russian Muslim who had stayed in Liverpool
that there were secret accounts kept under lock and key at the
Liverpool Muslim Institute. Quilliam was furious with Webb for
not checking his sources and believing in hearsay. The information
had come to Quilliam in a letter from Emin Nabokoff, who had

been on the committee of the Liverpool Muslim Institute before joining Webb in New York. Nabokoff wanted to reassure Quilliam that he was not the source and affirmed that no expense had ever been incurred without the consent of the committee during his time in Liverpool. He accused Webb of being 'the author of so many astonishing lies'.[47] Quilliam also had to defend himself against self-aggrandisement after a newspaper article declared that he tried to raise £6000 in Turkey to build a mosque in Liverpool that would contain an elaborate mausoleum for Quilliam himself. Quilliam responded that he would leave the choice of his sepulchre to his children and fellow Muslims in Britain. He defended himself, stating that his character found it hard to beg and that he had never asked anyone for anything. He declared that he did everything for Islam, at his own expense wherever possible.[48]

These various suspicions would have meant little if Quilliam had not been struck off from his legal practice in 1908 or offended the sensibilities of Victorian and Edwardian society through his multiple relationships with women. When combined with the apparent obscurantism caused by the Henri de Léon identity, there is a view of Abdullah Quilliam that is best represented on the Isle of Man and has been maintained by his descendants there, and which continues to fascinate Dollin Kelly, the writer of *New Manx Worthies*.

This negative judgement of Quilliam needs to be acknowledged, but there is an alternative assessment of his life and work. There would be little gain for a successful lawyer to convert to Islam in late nineteenth-century Liverpool. On the contrary, his conversion caused Quilliam considerable loss of income, negative publicity and a loss of social approbation. The accusations of financial impropriety are unproven and there is evidence that Quilliam spent considerable sums of his own wealth on promoting Islam and supporting the activities of the Liverpool Muslim Institute. In 1896, the treasurer of the society reported that there were no donations from abroad that year, except for £10 to purchase a cot for the Medina Home, and that the secured income had only amounted to £50 a year. Quilliam compared this to the £7 million budget of the Church of England and rhetorically asked what could be achieved by Muslims if they had such resources at their disposal.[49] At the Annual General Meeting in 1897, the total expenditure of the society amounted to £434, of which £90 had been donated. The balance of £344 had been advanced by Quilliam. The committee noted that the printing works were the most expensive drain on resources, and somehow they should become self-supportive. It was noted that it was deeply unsatisfactory for the Sheikh to pay so much out of his own pocket towards the costs of the society and that the total advances made by him now stood at £1,350. This figure had risen to well over £2,000 two years later. The auditors noted that Quilliam used his own money to supplement the activities of the organisation to the tune of £200 per year.[50]

Abdullah Quilliam's financial sacrifice on behalf of the Liverpool Muslim Institute, his work on behalf of the lascars, his Temperance activities, his representation of early attempts to organise labour in Liverpool, his efforts to repeal capital punishment and his obvious sense of the equality of all human beings regardless of colour, nationality, religion or class tell another story. It would be hard to understand why a man who spent considerable energy voicing his concern at the moral behaviour of Christian society in Europe would embrace the stricter codes of Islam. Nor is it likely that the Muslim converts of Britain, drawn from the respectable drawing rooms of Victorian society, would have accepted and highly respected a rogue in their midst. These facts beg a different explanation for Sheikh Abdullah Quilliam's apparent flagrant flouting of the moral codes and laws of his time, to the point of risking his successful livelihood.

This book has tried to examine Quilliam's relationships with women fairly. There is no doubt that he was a man who was attracted to women and such feelings were reciprocated. However, Quilliam was perfectly frank in his defence of polygamy as a superior system for satisfying human sexual needs and for organising family life. As far as he was concerned, he only obeyed the laws laid down in the Qur'an, even if non-Muslim moral codes frowned upon such behaviour. He did not consider the women in his life as mistresses, nor did he take his commitment to them lightly. He supported his ten children and they joined together as one family, playing with each other at the family residence on the Isle of Man. According to his grandchildren, they played with each other as one family on the island. There were rivalries between the women, but Quilliam always carried out Muslim marriages in the Mosque to legalise their position within the codes of Islam. He even provided Mary Lyon with the legal 'Christian' marriage that she desired to legitimate their five children after the death of Hannah Quilliam. It is clear that both Mary and Edith Miriam mourned together at his funeral.

I suspect that most of the Isle of Man tales of 'harems' were the consequences of rural imaginations and the exotic Oriental fantasies that existed during the Victorian and Edwardian periods. Quilliam's insistence on wearing the fez around the tiny village streets, the various 'wives' and their children visiting the house at Onchan and Quilliam's insistence on offering hospitality to various 'foreign' Muslim dignitaries would have been more than enough to create his dubious reputation on the island.

The divorce case in 1908 is not unconnected to Quilliam's view on polygamy. Fundamentally, Quilliam did not consider himself bound by 'Christian' law, even though he earned his living from it. Where Islamic law and Christian law clashed, to the Sheikh al-Islam it was Islamic law that superseded the Christian in the eyes of God and which, in his final judgement, counted ultimately. The lawyer may have thought differently, in that he was sworn to obey certain oaths and to uphold the law of the land, but conscience would have negotiated the two conflicting positions. Quilliam considered that Islam's religious, social, moral and political codes were able to perfect both advanced societies and the 'rudest and most barbarous people'.[51] He commented in a lecture that the social aspect of Islam improved upon Christian society in a number of ways. Amongst these benefits were polygamy and divorce, since it was consequently rare to find an unmarried adult in Muslim countries and the freedom of divorce permitted escape for those trapped in unhappy marriages. Both the Muslim and the lawyer were agreed that this was preferable to Christian England, where many were forced to remain in unhappy marriages. He also commented that there was no such thing as an unemployment problem in Muslim lands and that they prohibited gambling and drunkenness.[52] Three weeks after making these comments, Quilliam picked up on the point about divorce again in the editorial of *The Crescent*. He wrote that British divorce laws were a 'social evil that is a direct result of the polity and teachings of the Christian churches and that such evils do not exist in Islam'.[53]

In the same edition, he quoted the Marquis of Queensbury's comments that 'the attempt to realise a strictly monogamous social system has only resulted in producing a "thinly disguised polygamy and polyandry" infinitely more injurious to the moral and social welfare of the country and the people than an open, but rightly adjusted system of polygamy'. To Quilliam, both the divorce laws and the insistence upon strict monogamy were part of the intransigent sexual morality of Christianity that had been replaced by Islam's more open and tolerant understanding of human nature. In living a life with parallel sexual relationships and in flouting the divorce laws of the nation, Quilliam was asserting that he was ultimately bound by the laws of Islam and that it was a moral duty to assist those who found themselves trapped by laws that required reforming.

I will leave the last words on Abdullah Quilliam to his granddaughter, Patricia Gordon, spoken when she unveiled the plaque to commemorate her grandfather that was placed on the building that had been the Mosque in Liverpool on the 10th October 1997.

He did much for Muslims in this country in his lifetime, and in particular, Liverpool. He lived the Qur'an, and one must remember that all this happened in England, in an age when if you didn't conform, your picture was turned to the wall for all time. But the wolves after his flesh never deterred him – he was immune and a man of conviction. He believed that multiculturalism adds to the richness in our community, rather than dividing it. He was tolerant of all denominations, providing they were sincere in their beliefs. My greatest memory of him, is being compassionate at all times, a man of great courage and vision and way ahead of his time, and a credit to Islam.[54]

CHAPTER 9

Quilliam's Children: His legacy and significance for British Muslims

Muslims in Britain often enquire whether there are any descendants of the Liverpool Muslim communities who remained members of the religion. Although I heard that one such family existed in the Cheshire area, the answer to the question is no. Even amongst Quilliam's surviving family members, there are no Muslims. Nor are there any links between the present Arabic-speaking communities and Quilliam's nineteenth-century activities in the city, other than that they both developed within the context of the colonial significance of Liverpool as a port and a centre of international trade. In spite of the valiant efforts of the Abdullah Quilliam Society, which is organised by a group of leading Muslim figures in the city, the Mosque and Islamic Centre at Brougham Terrace remain a ruin after many years of service as Liverpool's Registry of Birth, Marriages and Deaths. The Society has grand plans to rediscover Quilliam's heritage and to restore the building as a mosque once again. It is in their efforts that Quilliam's legacy and significance for British Muslims can be discerned. The question has to be asked why a group of Muslims of Pakistani, Indian and Arab origins, both first and second generation, who have committed their lives to community service in Liverpool feel that they need to re-establish Quilliam's mosque in a city where the Al-Rahma Central Mosque is already a thriving centre for Liverpool's Muslims.

A recent photograph (2009) of the former Liverpool Muslim Institute
(8-12 Brougham Terrace), which the Muslim community of Liverpool
now plans to have renovated as an Islamic centre and mosque.

Liverpool's Muslims are proud of the fact that they have a
nineteenth-century predecessor and a community pre-dating their
presence, and often refer to the mosque in Brougham Terrace as
Britain's first mosque. This is probably not the case, since there
were earlier attempts to establish buildings reserved for prayer in
Manchester and Cardiff, although these were not registered as
mosques. Yet Quilliam's mosque was unique. It was certainly the
first centre of Islamic activity which brought together a community
of converts working alongside Muslim migrants and multi-
national visitors from Muslim nations. It set the precedent for a
Muslim community united by religious conviction rather than
ethnic identity, and that makes it both symbolically and politically
significant for the contemporary Muslim presence in this country.
In addition, Quilliam's active involvement in challenging British

foreign policy was the first emergence of British Muslims into the political arena. Perhaps even more symbolically important for British Muslims is the fact that Quilliam engaged actively, and successfully, in *da'wa,* the obligatory activity of a devout Muslim to promote Islam.

It is in the psychological domain that Quilliam remains so fascinating to British Muslims. As in the nineteenth century, Muslims today continue to be excited by the knowledge that Islam is able to attract 'Christian' converts in the lands of the old colonial adversaries. Whenever I have the opportunity to speak to Muslims about Quilliam's activities in Liverpool, they gather around avidly, demanding that I tell more and more incidents from his life. Both collectively and individually, these are a people that are hungry for good news. Any assessment of Quilliam's legacy, then, needs to look away from a direct heritage in terms of a continuing community or individuals who remain Muslims, and rather to explore his significance to the contemporary situation in Britain. We need to ask the question: What does Quilliam's legacy signify for British Muslims today and why has he become such a significant figure for them?

Sheikh Abdullah Quilliam is significant for a number of reasons. He is a vital part of the attempts by Muslims to reclaim their history in the West. This may not have been a priority for the first-generation migrants, who were more concerned with the practical challenges of resettlement and who brought their religion with them from their places of origin, attempting to reproduce it faithfully in the new non-Muslim environment. For second and subsequent generations born in Britain, the priorities changed and identity issues became more complex and challenging. Identities and the loyalties that accompany these identities had to be carved out creatively from the tensions that exist between British citizenship, the ethnic origins of their parents and grandparents and their commitment to Islam practised in the context of a non-Muslim nation. Abdullah Quilliam takes on an iconic aspect for young British-born Muslims. He is, first and foremost, a religious figure who cements Islam in Britain as a faith conviction, not simply as a migrant presence. Indeed, as a British Muslim who gathered around him over two hundred and fifty converts in the nineteenth century, he provides a potent symbolic presence for today's British Muslims to show that they have a history and a presence in this country that is deeper than a mere geographical relocation in the second half of the twentieth century.

The challenges of shaping a British identity have been hindered by the international situation. Perhaps the saddest aspect of Quilliam's story is that we still face the same unresolved problems in the Muslim world as he did in the late nineteenth century. The hotspots of Quilliam's time remain with us; Afghanistan, Sudan, Iraq, Iran, the North-West Frontier Province of Pakistan, Somalia and the Balkans still confront today's politicians with challenges, and they would seem to be no more competent at dealing with them without antagonising Muslim sensitivities than their nineteenth-century predecessors. The colonial inheritance has become a post-colonial nightmare, and Muslims in Britain have to resolve already fraught identity formation and degrees of religious conviction with images of wars carried out on Muslim territory, in which the invading armies are the same colonial forces as in yesteryear. Even worse, some Muslims, even British Muslims, have responded to the challenges of a post-colonial world by resorting to a violent strategy to solve their problems, which they perceive to be the consequences of a deliberate hostility towards Islam in the Western world. Abdullah Quilliam wrestled with these same conflicting loyalties, and his solution may remain as a model for present-day Muslims in Britain.

Leadership has been equally problematic for British Muslims today. Despite numerous attempts to create national umbrella organisations that can represent the communities, all of these have only had limited success. To this day, Quilliam remains the only 'Sheikh al-Islam' appointed formally to represent British Muslims. Today, in a post-Caliphate world, it is not possible to appoint such a figure and the acceptance of any such attempt to create a single leader for the diverse ethnic and religious British Muslim presence would be doomed to failure. However, there is another element beyond mere title to Sheikh Abdullah Quilliam's leadership of the Liverpool Muslim Institute. The community of converts and international Muslims was led by a British Muslim who was uniquely placed to adapt Islam to a British context without compromising the integrity of its core practices and beliefs. In the twenty-first century, as in the second half of the twentieth century, Muslims who are as British by birth and nationality as Quilliam was, even if, unlike him, their families arrived as migrants, seek to differentiate their religion from the ethnic customs of their families' places of origin. They challenge the traditional leadership of the mosques and look to imams of their own generation who are able to represent their interests more skilfully. At the same time, religious leadership has become a political issue, and British governments are scrutinising the traditional training of imams as part of a strategy to prevent extremist views and religious violence. Abdullah Quilliam has much to offer as a precedent for Muslim leadership: activist, devout, passionate, dissenting, but able to communicate the truths of Islam to a Western mindset.

For historians of modern Britain and scholars of religion, the story of Quilliam and the Liverpool Muslims provides not only evidence of the presence and scope of the Muslim community in Liverpool and Britain in the late nineteenth century; their experience also speaks to us about the impact of early globalisation and the relations of Muslims in Britain with foreign policies that impacted on the Muslim world, the rise of British multiculturalism and multi-faith pluralism and the challenges confronting nineteenth-century Christianity in Britain, thereby furthering our understanding of religious conversion.

Throughout this book, I have tried to place Quilliam in the context of the changes that were taking place in Britain during the latter half of the nineteenth century. The city of Liverpool was at the hub of the social and economic transformation and became Britain's first multi-cultural city. Even when Quilliam was a child growing up in Liverpool and enjoying his holidays in Peel on the Isle of Man, he may have observed Yemeni, Somali and Indian Muslims in the dock areas of the city. In particular, Yemeni villagers had become global seaman.

The existing literature on nineteenth-century Islam would seem to suggest a fragmented presence, consisting of various constituencies that had little contact or even knowledge of each other. In some instances, the overwhelming numerical dominance of South Asians due to economic migration in the mid-twentieth century has resulted in a view that earlier Muslim presence consisted of 'individual pioneers' with little community building around religion. Some have mentioned the significance of the portside Arab communities in Cardiff or Tyneside as being the first to organise themselves around religious centres that were led by North African Alawi Sufis between the two world wars. Rozina Visram makes us aware that the eighteenth and nineteenth century South Asian Muslim presence was much greater than previously indicated, but she does not include Arabs or Africans in her study.[1] It is only with the publication of Humayun Ansari's historical study of Muslims in Britain that the full scope of the nineteenth-century presence begins to emerge.[2] Ansari acknowledges Quilliam's efforts at community building, but it is only in the detailed study provided to scholars by the weekly publication of *The Crescent* from 1893 to 1908 that the full picture begins to emerge.

A study of the over eight hundred editions of the newspaper published in the closing years of the nineteenth century and the early years of the twentieth century reveals not only that the various constituencies that formed the Muslim presence in Britain were drawn together during this period, but also the extent to which Quilliam successfully created the means to bring together converts from across the world and assist them in the promotion of Islam globally. In addition, *The Crescent* became an international voice for pan-Islamism and took on, sometimes in heated debate, its critics.

As was pointed out by Ansari, from the nineteenth century, Britain established widespread connections with many parts of the Muslim world and was beginning to involve itself in sometimes aggressive colonial enterprises. India, Egypt and parts of West Africa were under direct rule. Further industrial expansion and competition with European empires, who also had colonial ventures in predominantly Muslim territory, not only fuelled foreign interaction with the Muslim world, but also created a demand for labour well before the successors of this European colonial expansion arrived in the twentieth century. These early arrivals shaped the way in which Muslims organised themselves religiously and maintained their religious lives in the contested space of non-Muslim European society. These early efforts to establish an Islamic presence are central to the origins of Islam *in* the West, as opposed to Islam *and* the West, despite the pre-existing presence in the Balkans. Indeed, Nathalie Clayer and Eric Germain demonstrate that the two are not unconnected and argue that the Western European Muslim populations of interwar Europe were already engaged in intense correspondence and the exchange of ideas with Albanian religious leaders, and that the emergence of a distinctly 'European' Islamic identity had already occurred during this period.[3]

Until the early decades of the twentieth century, the East European presence could draw upon the political and material resources of the Ottoman Empire to protect Islam in Europe. This would not be the case for the first relatively permanent Muslim populations established in Manchester, Cardiff, South Shields, and the ports of London and Liverpool. The decades of considerable commercial activity, when Britain clearly emerged as the major imperial and industrial power, coincided with the period in which Quilliam was most active – centred in Liverpool, but spreading his influence nationally and internationally. These communities might have been able to seek some financial and spiritual support from Muslim heartlands, but they could not protect their position by the advantages that accrued to the Muslim populations protected by the Ottomans. Although ethnicity might have played a role for the Muslims in Cardiff, South Shields, Manchester and London dockside, this was not the case in Liverpool. Quilliam and his community of converts were not interested in the ethnic dimension of Muslim identity. For them, Islam was, above all else, a religion revealed by God for the guidance of humanity and to replace the corrupted previous monotheistic revelations of Judaism and Christianity. It was, as Quilliam and others reiterated, the truth.

In preaching Islam as a religious truth-claim that was able to challenge and undermine the dominant exclusivist message of Christianity successfully throughout its history, Quilliam became one of the first international voices who not only defended Islam, but did so without resorting to apologetic discourse. He firmly believed that Islam and Islamic ethical systems – the egalitarian laws of marriage and divorce, matters of sexual morality, family life, views on alcohol consumption, doctrinal positions on the unity of God, the understanding of revelation and the modes of worship – were all superior to Christianity, a religion which he believed to be in decline, morally defunct and unable to deal with reason, as represented by the new scientific discoveries. He saw the rise of science in the nineteenth century not so much as a clash between two discourses, with religion on one side and science on the other, but as a light shone onto Christian falsehood that the religion could not bear. A true religion could not clash with the truths of creation, and therefore science provided Islam with the opportunity to promote itself as the religion of reason.

Quilliam's egalitarian spirit also found deep solutions in Islam to the iniquity of elitism and the inequalities that drove human communities apart. As a supporter of the rights of black human beings, Quilliam visited on a number of occasions the West African states that were formed from freed slaves, and was a great admirer of Dr Blyden of Sierra Leone. He shared with Blyden the view that Islam had a stronger claim than Christianity to represent non-white populations and to provide the ideal of a brotherhood of nations that Christianity's partnership with white European elitism had lost.

Quilliam's converts were not people who had lost their faith in God, nor were they the disenfranchised. They were Christian and respectable. As such, they are able to shed light on the loss of Christian faith and the search for other spiritual alternatives that began in the nineteenth century and continued apace in the latter decades of the twentieth century.

The two hundred converts to Islam in Liverpool were predominantly people who had become disillusioned with their own religion for various reasons. Their stories of conversion provide evidence of the religious doubt that was growing in the Victorian era, complicated by the unique features of Christianity in Liverpool, where sectarian divisions were deep and sometimes violent. In these narratives of conversion, we hear the growth of religious unbelief, or at least doubt, to use a word that was very current in the later Victorian period. Agnosticism became one of the generally available religious options in the last decades of the nineteenth century.

There were several factors contributing to this mood of religious uncertainty whereby many people, whether they ended up on the Christian or the agnostic side of the fence, felt that Christianity rested on less secure foundations than it had thirty or fifty years earlier. Scientific discoveries called into question the literal accuracy of some biblical passages, especially the creation myths in Genesis. Quilliam was a geologist and knew that the earth must be much older than the writers of Genesis had realised; but so did many others who listened to the voices of reason. Knowledge derived from science called into question knowledge derived from the Bible, and led to increasing uneasiness with the many accounts in the New and Old Testaments of miraculous events that conflicted with the laws of nature. More fundamental questions were later raised by Darwin.

The critical study of the New Testament, which had been pioneered in England in the eighteenth century but had mainly been the achievement of German scholars, was asking questions about the accuracy and consistency of the biblical accounts of the life and teaching of Jesus presented in the Gospels and the degree to which the various accounts in the New Testament were undermined by the polemical purposes of their authors or by the need to match events with Old Testament prophesies.

Consequently, the idea that science had replaced religion, or at least made it much harder to believe in any kind of religion, had won wider acceptance; but there was also a growing set of doubts concerning the morality of Christian doctrines and the specifically the doctrine of the Atonement. Accepting that all human beings deserved to suffer in hell for their sins, and that God's justice demanded this was one thing, but believing that God had proposed the solution that one sinless man should atone for these sins as a substitute for fallen humanity was becoming difficult. The voices of reason insisted that the whole idea of one person standing in for another was offensive to the moral sensibilities of thinking people. The idea that the human race had inherited a burden of sin from their first parents was beginning to be doubted by some members of the British middle-classes of the period.

The growing awareness of other faith systems also had an impact. Christian exclusivism was challenged by a growing pluralism which insisted that each religion should be judged on the basis of its moral fruits, and perhaps the non-Christian religions contained ethical and moral truths that were at least as good as those of Christianity, or even better. The missionary impulse of Christianity was weakened, and there were those who recognised its involvement with the colonial enterprise and many who felt that other nations had religions of their own. The relativisation of adherence to religious belief did not result in an overnight transformation, and publicly challenging religious authority in mid-Victorian England remained a courageous decision that could bring down the opprobrium of an outraged society upon the dissenter to the status quo. Christian belief and practice remained part of convention. Doubts made public brought shocked reactions, but Quilliam had his finger on the pulse of the *zeitgeist*. He had undergone this spiritual journey of doubt throughout his own life and was enough of an intellectual to express this very well both in public lectures and in the growing media of print. The solution was not in recourse to atheism or agnosticism, but in a renewed religiosity that acknowledged Islam as the religion which had the answers to all of the above questions that deeply challenged nineteenth-century Christianity.

Even so, deeply entrenched respectability and the deep distrust of Islam created a number of problems for him to deal with in Liverpool; the growing band of Liverpool converts provided both a religious alternative to the doubters and would act as a powerful reminder to Muslims that, although Islam may possess a covering of a historically created civilisation, it was more than a culture whose entry was by birth. Not that these two positions were by any means fully differentiated by Quilliam. Once a Muslim understood that they held God's truth in trust for all generations since the time of the Prophet, then it followed that the Muslim culture that had originated in the truths of the religion was the best possible way of life for human beings and had to be protected. This reminder rejuvenated and energised many ethnic Muslims in Britain and showed them that it was possible not only to live an Islamic life outside Muslim territory, but that it was even possible to re-create Islam as a missionary force in the heart of the British Empire. British converts to Islam, especially those from educated or high-status classes, stood as iconic symbols not only for Muslims in Britain but also for those who remained living in Muslim-majority nations. Muslim countries may have been dominated by Western technology and concomitant military might, but Islam as a religion could still reach the hearts and minds of the 'infidels'.

Thus the Muslim sailors, merchants, entertainers, servants, students and even princes who visited Britain were treated to the experience of an English mosque with an English Sheikh patronised by Muslim rulers. They were able to visit this mosque, which they did, and to take part in Islamic festivals and Friday communal worship where they would line up with respectable Englishmen and their families from across a wide spectrum of classes. At the same time, they would be reminded of the egalitarianism of Islam, its prioritising of social justice and charity, the glorious history, the unique spirituality of its Prophet, the harmony between religion and science, the emphasis upon human reason in the quest for truth and the injustice being perpetuated upon the Muslim world, which was so superior in morality and religious belief, by Christian aggression and greed for conquest. This would not be done by an imam imported to serve their needs, but by an English lawyer and man of letters, who was versed in the Qur'an and acknowledged as an *'alim* by the Ottoman authorities after his conferral with an honorary *'alimiya* by the Sultan of Morocco.

Whilst it has to be acknowledged that the majority of Muslims arrived in Britain due largely to economic reasons, in most cases leaving their families behind them, their religion remained significant to them. Connected as they were, in the most part, either to the British Empire and its colonies or protected territories or to the last Muslim imperial power, they were concerned about the accusations of 'superstition' and 'backwardness' which were used so successfully by Western propaganda and which undermined their confidence in the state of Islam in their period. Educated Muslims were increasingly required to demonstrate a 'modern' outlook and come to grips with the 'modern' world. Many had been genuinely impressed by the effectiveness of Western ideas and institutions. To many that came as visitors – the students who enrolled in British universities, the businessmen who came to seek opportunities, the professionals who furthered their careers, the imams who saw a chance to influence hearts and minds, the diplomats who found themselves stationed here – the possibilities of engaging with modernity in the heart of Europe were immense and far-reaching;

but they probably did not expect to be invited to participate in a community of converts to whom modernity and Islam were natural allies.

It was the ideas of Muhammad Abduh and Ahmed Sayyid Khan that impressed the Muslim converts of Liverpool, but these were combined with an empathy for the heritage of traditional Islam. Quilliam frowned upon Wahhabism, not so much for ideological reasons, but because it rebelled against the traditions, customs and political leadership of the Ottomans. He admired and respected the Sufi poets and mystics, but had little time for the wilder excesses of popular religion. Yet he had no problem with the institution of shrines as long as the behaviour exhibited there did not offend reason. He celebrated the *mawlid*, the birthday of the Prophet, every year at the mosque in Liverpool and saw no objection to decorating the mosque in the traditional mode of the Ottomans.

Thus the appearance and practices that were maintained in the mosque would also have been familiar to the increasingly wide range of visitors from the Ottoman world. Such interaction had occurred since the eighteenth century, and perhaps earlier, but by the nineteenth century there was a sophisticated relationship with Turkey, not always marked by equanimity, which had led the two countries to develop close military, political and commercials links. This had led to an increase in the number of Ottoman subjects visiting Britain.

Quilliam always appeared to be at ease with the sophisticates of the Ottoman diplomatic, military and court officials, but before and during the reign of Sultan Abdul Hamid II (r.1876-1909), who was so beloved by Quilliam, Ottoman sailors were visiting Britain's seaports more often and for longer periods of time. Inevitably some would take up permanent residence as running hostels or food outlets became more attractive than a life at sea. The sailors transported traders, and some of these also saw opportunities to remain. Thus a small Yemeni presence manifested in Liverpool serving the itinerant sailors, and the traditional aspects of the mosque would have been familiar to them as they dealt with the challenges of the unfamiliar. The mosque provided a place of refuge from racism, a centre to socialise with fellow Muslims and a focal point for legal redress against the petty irritants of migrant life. How useful it must have been to have a socially-committed lawyer at your side ready to represent your grievances.

Quilliam's Muslim community in Britain was no less diverse than its twenty-first century successor. It consisted of many nationalities drawn from the Ottoman world and beyond. Quilliam recorded the nationalities of visitors to the mosque, and there are very few Muslim nations or communities that were not represented. In addition to the Ottoman officials, businessmen and sailors, there were travellers from India, driven by the desire to experience the wider world, and from the 1840s, Indian students of the upper and middle classes who came to study law and medicine at English and Scottish universities.

Amongst this group, there were individuals who belonged to royalty or who were sons of royalty. The Empire also permitted an internationalisation of the religious experts of Islam. Mawlawis and imams moved between South Africa, West Africa and India, seeking opportunities to lead and advise spiritually on Islamic law and faith where Muslims wondered what was the correct application in non-Muslim lands. Some came to trade and others to seek adventure or even wives. They gravitated towards Britain's centres of industry, education and commerce. Many disembarked at Liverpool and some remained there. New transport systems allowed for easy travel between cities and linked these divergent groups of Muslims to each other.

Liverpool and Manchester had been brought closer together by trade and commerce, and also by the building of the railway that connected them. Manchester already had an established community of Muslims by the time Quilliam began his activities in Liverpool. As Ansari points out, Moroccan and Arab merchants had been drawn to the city's reputation as the capital of textile manufacturing since the late 1830s, and the signing of the Anglo-Ottoman Commercial Treaty at Balta Liman in 1838 allowed for an increase in the volume of textiles exported to Ottoman dominions, improving the possibilities of trade to India and China. Ansari reveals that, by the end of nineteenth century, the Sultan's dominions were taking more Manchester goods than all the combined European trade. The first Arab trading house was established in 1833, and by the middle of the 1860s there were over thirty such houses.[4] The Ottomans maintained a consulate there as they did in Liverpool, and Quilliam was a familiar figure at both, socially and officially. Quilliam knew this Manchester Arab community well; he performed their marriages and funerals and they attended special occasions at the mosque.

But there was one feature in all this Muslim ethnic, class and religious diversity that has so far not been achieved by Muslim communities in twenty-first century Britain, for all the rhetoric of unity. In Liverpool, they prayed together along with a mix of English social classes amongst the converts, even if they would then return to their ethnic and class conclaves to conduct their private and public lives.

Quilliam has other lessons for British Muslims and policymakers who can engage with them currently. I have attempted to argue that Quilliam was the nation's first multiculturalist, in the way in which people of other faiths and ethnicities have been dealt with in a uniquely British solution to the issue of integrating migrant populations since the end of World War II: a mode of living together which acknowledged difference and diversity. Liverpool was one of the first cities in Britain to engage with a changing demography through developing modes of behaviour that led to the institutions and policies that formed British multiculturalism and multi-faith pluralism in the twentieth century. The populations involved may have been tiny compared to later twentieth-century migrations: a few hundred Lebanese and Syrians, a few thousand Yemenis, perhaps a few thousand North Africans and a few hundred Palestinians, joined with Jews who had fled from Eastern Europe from the 1880s onwards. However, it should not be forgotten that the city faced considerable challenges integrating the substantial numbers of Irish Roman Catholics and Protestants, with deep historic hostilities between the two groups, who had fled the agricultural crisis of the 1840s. There were also predominantly Protestant Welsh and Scottish migrations. The intensity of Protestant and Catholic divisions often led to blood on the city's streets, which the Corporation tried to keep away from the showpiece centre and confined to the poverty-stricken ghettos adjacent to the docks. Public health, prostitution, alcohol abuse and crime were major problems in the areas where migrants settled.

By the end of World War I, the city's population contained 10% who had been born outside England. Quilliam lived in the city during the period when these demographic changes began to take place and created a mosque and Islamic centre which joined with the Jewish synagogue as the city's first non-Christian places of worship. Inside the premises he regularly performed Muslim marriages, including highly controversial mixed marriages, funerals and other rites of passage, and he established a reputation for dealing with officialdom and employers who did not play fair with the increasing numbers of Muslim sailors in the city. He also participated in civic ceremonies organized by the Corporation, always dressed officially as the Sheikh al-Islam of the British Isles. He engaged in interfaith activity, speaking at meetings organized by the Jewish community in Liverpool and Manchester and was a convinced Zionist. He was an early pioneer of the pattern that is well established in Britain today whereby local government officials, politicians and other dignitaries visit non-Christian places of worship. It was in Liverpool that the first Lord Mayor of the city, John Houghton, first officially attended the mosque at the celebration of Eid al-Fitr.

In the topical debates surrounding Islam, identity and citizenship, Quilliam provides a precedent from the past that can inform the present. Quilliam was convinced that only English Muslims could successfully establish Islam in Britain. His reasons for this were straightforward. Firstly, only Muslims born in Britain would be able to establish an Islam that did not carry cultural baggage from elsewhere in the Muslim majority world. The second point is not unconnected: in order to avoid carrying cultural baggage, a Muslim had to practise their faith from conviction rather than by birth. As he noted in 1896, 'English Muslims have adopted the faith not for personal advantage but because they believe it to be true, and the world will then know how to appreciate these courageous men and women who have boldly made a stand for truth'.[5] Such a position might not preclude all Muslims who were part of the *umma* through birth, but they would need to go through similar processes to the converts, in other words, a conscious re-examination of their commitment to Islam. The first imam of the Liverpool Muslim Institute, Barakatullah, reiterated this point in a lecture given in 1896. He stated that Muslim countries were experiencing a time of crisis and that true Islam would revive from the West. In the East, 'education of the masses was neglected and superstition prevailed all over the Islamic countries. Democracy was crushed down under the feet of despotism. It is time now for the sun of Islam to arise from the West. The Muslim Institute in Liverpool and the other one in New York promise to turn out the pioneers of civilisation in future. *Simply because the Muslims in the West are Muslims by reason, not by birth.*'[6]

In raising the issue of people who were Muslim by birth and Muslim by conviction, Quilliam and Barakatullah began a discourse that remains highly relevant amongst contemporary British Muslims. The same debate arose in the late twentieth century and was particularly creative and public during the 1990s. It was the younger generation of British-born Muslims of South Asian parentage, especially those influenced by a modified post-Islamic political radicalism, who began to examine critically the relationship between religious and ethnic identity as they grappled with three major factors in their identity formation: being British, Muslim and Pakistani/Bangladeshi/Indian. In fact, the latter category of identity went further because, within each national category, there were intense regional identities such as Punjabi, Bengali, and Mirpuri.[7] Many years ago, I represented these three markers of identity diagrammatically as follows:

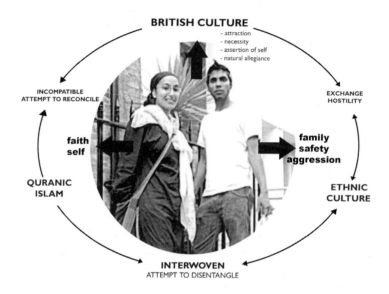

The model in the diagram claims that, in the first stages of migration, the major interactions take place between British culture and ethnicity. Islam principally plays a functional role as a marker of identity, as first generation Muslims engage in micro-politics focused on community building.[8] However, the second generation find themselves being drawn towards British identity as a natural allegiance of birth and as a result of socialisation processes. The tensions that can exist between the loyalties of parents towards ethnic identity at the place of origin and the social norms of the new culture can be very difficult to negotiate. Thus we find British-born Muslims beginning to move away from the engagement with ethnic cultures and developing a discourse based on religion as their primary identity. The term 'British Islam' was beginning to gain currency amongst the generation born and raised in Britain even back in the early 1990s and found institutional expression with the advent of the Islamic Society of Britain and a number of other Muslim organisations. In this position, Islam is paramount and moderates over and determines the content and shape of ethnic and national identity. The debates of the 1990s set religion and ethnicity at odds with each other and resulted in attempts to discover an Islamic identity that could resolve these tensions. The advantages of this approach were that Islam was perceived as a universal identity that could be allied with any national loyalty, and as a primary identity that provided a global ethic and code of behaviour that transcended locality. Today the picture is changing again. As young British Muslims have begun to negotiate Islamic identity with British identity, issues of religion and citizenship have become paramount, and the main arena of contestation now lies between negotiating Islamic identity and Britishness.

Quilliam never had to engage with these three identities in his attempts to fashion 'British Islam'. He had to draw together the various constituencies that formed the backgrounds of the users of the Liverpool mosque, but he drew upon his Ottomanism to emphasise the internationalism of Islam rather than the idea of 'British' or 'European' Islam. His personal ethnicities were only Liverpudlian and Manx. They may have contributed to his unique identity, but they were not major factors in forming his 'Muslimness'. But his efforts do parallel those of recent years, after the various crises and tensions generated by religious extremism and terrorism exposed and emphasized discourses around the issue of being Muslim and British. Ironically, there are connections between the two moments in the history of the British Muslim presence. Quilliam was English and Muslim in a period of colonial tensions between the country of his birth and the religion of his choice. Today, British Muslims find themselves inheriting the colonial relationship in a post-colonial form; yet there are some who argue that the colonial relationship between Britain and parts of the Muslim world has not ceased and that it is still too early to speak of the 'post-colonial' period.

The statement made by the Mayor of Liverpool in 1898 to the effect that he found 'Muslims to be honest, industrious and god-fearing'[9] has been echoed down the years by a number of local politicians who have represented constituencies of Muslims. But such statements that form part of the narratives of multicultural Britain have been ripped apart by the activities of those whose religious discourse is more extreme and whose enmity towards the West can result in violent action. The attacks on London in July 2005 had a traumatic impact on both British Muslim and non-Muslim communities because they were carried out by Muslim citizens of Britain. The attacks induced a sense of crisis amongst British Muslims and British policymakers concerning fundamental precepts of British democracy in the twenty-first century. A number of issues have come under the microscope, including issues of race, religion and discrimination, media depictions of Islam, the complexities of plural societies, identity formation and citizenship, cultural literacy, the quality of educational provision by both Muslim and non-Muslim providers, freedom of speech and the intellectual capacity of British Islam and the inadequacy of religious leaders to meet modern challenges. In the aftermath of this event, a new rhetoric concerning plurality has begun to emerge from government policymakers in which an overemphasis on diversity in multicultural and pluralist discourses has been perceived to be at the cost of integration.

In 2009, the left-wing journalist Seumas Milne argued that the Government preaches globalisation but refuses to face up to the multiple identities and loyalties that flow from this. Writing in *The Guardian*, he stated, 'Ministers want Muslims to accept shared values. Luckily they already do, including opposition to wars of aggression.'[10] For those of us who may have sympathies with Milne, it is depressing to realise that his sentiments could have been expressed at the time of Quilliam's efforts to create a Muslim voice in Britain in the last decades of the nineteenth century. Globalisation was about more than using steamships, trains, telegraph and wireless to lessen the impact of the geographical distance between nations, or even the increasing occurrence of migration to weaken the gulf between cultures; globalisation was also about empire and the attitudes of Muslims in Britain to British foreign policy with regard to the Muslim world. Even back then, these areas raised issues of loyalty and citizenship.

Muslims were forced to come to terms with the power of the European imperial state through which their material and human resources were joined to the needs of the European empires. Migration itself was part of this process but, more insidiously, European ideas began to shape Muslim institutions, bending existing systems in the Muslim world to Western interests. British laws and policies began to transform many societies that came under their control.[11] Quilliam was never fully at ease with the process of colonisation that went along with globalisation, nor should it be surprising that the sons of Muslim migrants who arrived from the ex-colonies would be any more acquiescent to the continuity of a foreign policy that they perceive to have historical kinship with nineteenth-century colonialism. This was expressed by the social anthropologist, Pnina Werbner:

> As long as political confrontations in the Middle East, Kashmir or Bosnia continue, and as long as anti-Muslim or immigrant sentiments and practices persist in Britain, the conjunction between Islam and social-liberal values is unlikely to be ideologically severed.[12]

However, various ministers in the Labour government have refused to acknowledge this point. When Quilliam insisted that he was 'a loyal British subject by birth and a sincere Muslim from conviction',[13] he did so in an environment in which to be Roman Catholic in Britian still raised issues of divided political loyalty. Gwilliam Beckerlegge states that a 'Muslim living according to the imperatives of Muslim law' was no less perceived to be 'answerable to authorities beyond and other than the British monarch and the British state'.[14] The difficulty was that most Protestant English people identified their religious conviction more with the struggle for civil and religious liberty than they did with theological or ritual differences, and they regarded both Islam and Roman Catholicism as being open to the acceptance of arbitrary power. The challenge for Abdullah Quilliam in Liverpool and later with the Woking community that he was involved in was to offset this view and to present Islam as the religion of reason and toleration, which was allied to the values of toleration and moderation that public opinion insisted were part of the British worldview.

Beckerlegge claims that individuals who followed those religions whose centre of authority was abroad were perceived with deep suspicion by the British public, and this was particularly true when the foreign nations that were associated with the religion were hostile or at war with Britain.[15] This suspicion could take the form of religious prejudice, but Quilliam never shied away from being forthright in his criticism of imperial policies in the Muslim world; neither did he take the line of the Woking Muslims, who were more conciliatory towards Christianity. Quilliam was openly and publicly hostile to the religion he had left when he embraced Islam and often conflated Christianity and imperialist ventures in the Muslim world.

Quilliam's fatwas show that he was not afraid to antagonise public opinion, the media and British politicians as he vociferously opposed British government colonial ventures in Sudan and Afghanistan and fully supported the rights of the insurgents. It might be argued that the presence of significant Muslim populations with recent roots in parts of the world where British troops are fighting unpopular wars is one reason why domestic and foreign policy can never be separated as was possible in colonial times; but Quilliam demonstrated that, even with a much smaller Muslim presence in Britain, it was not possible to separate the two policies even in colonial times. Both the Foreign Office and Home Office were intensely interested in his activities and maintained files on him.

In this context, a brief observation might be made concerning the Quilliam Foundation. The assumption made by the appropriation of Quilliam's name is that the members of the Foundation are a direct continuation of a moderate or liberal 'Western Islam' espoused by Abdullah Quilliam, which is an integrated part of British life. They directly link themselves with Abdullah Quilliam and state that their Foundation was created in his memory. Their brief biography describes the Liverpool Muslims as, 'Quilliam's community of nineteenth century Muslims who were our forebears in British Islam'. None of this is particularly problematic as far as it goes. However, the appropriation of Quilliam would appear to suggest a construction of loyal and moderate Muslims that oversimplifies the complex process of identity formation and the challenge of conflicting loyalties that British Muslims face.

It would appear that Quilliam is being reinvented in some circles to provide narratives of integration. This seems to be an example of 'invented tradition' that is normally used to describe a process whereby religious symbols, persons, rituals or a set of practices are given authenticity and power to mobilise through ascribing 'truths' that are set in the past, but which in reality are recent in origin.[16] If there are inaccuracies or even misrepresentations of Quilliam today, the interesting point is that this tells us more about British Muslims now than it does about Quilliam himself.

The reality is that Quilliam was deeply enmeshed in the politics of the Muslim world. The Liverpool Muslim community was in touch with a global awareness of a Muslim sense of crisis and felt that it was part of an Islamic revival that was occurring at the time. The Muslim presence in the second city of the Empire provided a sense of being part of this mobilisation of the 'true religion' both for the converts and for Muslims who lived in parts of the world where European domination was felt. Quilliam was always clear that his ultimate ambition and the goal for which he worked was the final victory of Islam. Even though he may have considered Islam the religion of reason, he did not believe in the Westernisation of the Muslim world, but rather the opposite. Quilliam struggled for the Islamisation of the West. Quilliam believed in the *umma* and as such he was aware that there could be no Islam that was purely regional and only responded to local conditions. The 'bitter politics' of the Arab world cannot be kept away from Muslims in Britain because these politics were formed in the cauldron of colonialism and belong as much to the West as 'the Arab and Muslim world'.

When it came to conflict between the West and the Islamic majority world, Abdullah Quilliam would proclaim, 'harm one Muslim and you harm us all'. He was not beyond threatening the British governments of his time with the prospect of inciting the Muslims of the Empire to rise up in the cause of injustices inflicted upon fellow Muslims. It is unlikely that his fatwa could have achieved this, but he was ready to do it. Such behaviour, if undertaken by a Muslim leader today, would be labelled extremism.

Abdullah Quilliam believed in 'active citizenship'. While he may not have used this actual term, he belonged to an age when Britain's democracy and civil society were being forged. He was a devout and committed Muslim, trade union leader, active supporter of 'negro' rights, committed advocate on behalf of the campaign to abolish capital punishment and a philanthropist in his own city. Not all of his political struggles were on behalf of Islam, but he did not differentiate between struggling for social justice and being a British Muslim. He created a strategy in which his patriotism was to the person and the institution of the monarch, but he had no faith in the respective governments who served the reigning monarchs of his day. He considered it the duty of Britain's Muslims, as an ethical and moral presence in the land, to challenge the decisions of government when necessary and to resist the implementation of these decisions when dissent was not heeded. He resisted Britain's divorce laws to the point of breaking the law and sacrificing his career as a lawyer, and was not beyond threatening ministers when he considered that they were encroaching on the rights of various Muslim populations. He engaged in a successful campaign to withdraw a play from the West End which he considered insulted the reputation of the Prophet, and was a vociferous critic of the jingoism that was prevalent as part of the propaganda of empire. I would argue that it is precisely that which makes Quilliam problematic that makes him an iconic figure for British Muslims. It is his struggle to reconcile the deep loyalties to nation and religion that make him typical of a Muslim in a Muslim-minority nation, and he was not always successful in integrating the two loyalties. Abdullah Quilliam was not against the idea of citizenship, or as he expressed it, 'being a British subject', but he did not confuse citizenship with acquiescence or an uncritical patriotism that declared 'my country right or wrong'.

It is likely that both first generation and British-born South Asian Muslims have been far more conscious of citizenship and identity issues than an equivalent proportion of white citizens. This is certainly true in the case of the first generation male elders who are involved in the processes of micro-politics and second generation Muslims carving out a space for Islam in Britain's public realm. British Muslims have had to address citizenship not only within the framework of the legal and political structures of their new home, with its emphasis on democracy, secularism, individual rights and pluralism, but also in negotiating and harmonising this in terms of *shari'a* and Islamic state discourse. They have had to discover how to be Muslim in a secular society and to develop the appropriate strategies for living as a minority in a non-Muslim country. It has been essential to reconcile faith-based identity and citizenship, individual rights and community rights, in an environment where the concept of others has dominated, and doing this without retreating into isolationism. Perhaps above all, they have needed to discover how they can participate in a society that previously had no need for Islam in its public life. Quilliam realised only too well that the society that he lived in had no such space; neither did he serve a significant Muslim population that could draw upon the laws that framed the protection of ethnic minorities in the second half of the twentieth century. He struggled with all his resources to create a public space for Islam in Britain, knowing that the colonial mentality would always resist such a venture.

As previous citizens of the subcontinent, British South Asian Muslims have inherited the colonial history of their past relations with Britain. This, combined with the racism that is endemic in their new home, creates an environment of suspicion in which British Muslims may place non-Muslim citizens outside their own communities under the scrutiny of a 'gaze' that over-simplifies and essentialises, reinforcing perspectives of the 'other'. The same 'gaze' returned often demands assimilation under impossible conditions. Assimilation of an ethnic minority is not the same issue as that concerning a religious minority. A religious minority may refuse assimilation not merely to protect their language, dress code and customs of another place, but because participants feel that they have a duty to an all-powerful Deity to protect moral and ethical codes given through revelation. In addition, the 'gaze' that is directed at Muslims has a history that has nothing to do with ethnicity. The problems experienced by the Liverpool Muslims in the nineteenth century with the attacks on property and persons did not occur because of skin colour, class, competition for jobs or unfamiliar cultural practices. This was a discrimination against Islam that was whipped up by patriotic fervour and a perception that Muslims were the enemy.

Today, new organisations have provided the means for British-born Muslims to create dialogue with local and national governments on specific and achievable agendas, whilst simultaneously demonstrating that the majority of Muslims in Britain are moderate and peace-loving, duty-bound to respect the law of the land and able to find creative solutions to Islamic issues of citizenship that are based primarily on interpretations of revelation and British democratic institutions based on human rights. New alliances were forged with the New Labour government as these organisations realised that Muslims living outside *dar al-Islam* needed to work with the institutions of Muslim-minority nations not as ethnic minorities from a geographical region, but as representatives of a religion that occupied a new space. At the same time, they created critical discourses asking if such an entity as *dar al-Islam* was even viable in the new world order where none of the traditional interpretations of *fiqh* concerning minority living were workable. When a generation of British Muslims began this process of forging a religious community out of various ethnicities, classes and sectarian loyalties, they were repeating a process initiated by Quilliam in the final decades of the nineteenth century.

Quilliam always perceived British Muslims in his own time as being a community of religious dissent that could find allegiance with others in a commonality of social injustice, inequality and issues that arose from the international world order. However, such alliances were both temporary and pragmatic. In the final analysis, Muslims stood alone because their long-term goals were different. In the recent past, the Stop the War protests against the occupation of Iraq were qualitatively different from previous protests in that the Muslims who participated found themselves alongside a range of dissenters from the wider non-Muslim population. As such, they were able to bond with 'communities of suffering' or elements of the population seeking social justice for those who had been violated. This behaviour repeats a pattern established by Quilliam in the nineteenth century. In his dual roles as Sheikh al-Islam of the British Isles and defence advocate in the British legal system, Quilliam would have agreed with the contemporary sociologist Habermas, who argued that such demonstrations mobilise broad alliances that defend the nation's civic culture.[17] Although such alliances may be temporary, as in the case of the American civil rights movement and the anti-Vietnam war protests, they can create new moral communities that transcend ethnic or religious differences.

Quilliam believed that Muslims should ally themselves with such moral causes, but should never forget that there was a longer term moral imperative to ensure that the final revelation of the God of Jews, Christians and Muslims was implemented throughout the world. Emancipatory struggles can transform society and lead to new freedoms, but religious truth is a moral imperative to change the world order. This may provide uncomfortable reading, but it is a dilemma of loyalties that was never resolved by Quilliam and which he bequeaths to British Muslims today.[18]

Quilliam was aware that social justice discourse, so much a part of Islam's original message, not only links Muslims in a global resistance to perceived injustices, bringing together disparate alliances of moderates and radicals, but also creates links with non-Muslim organisations that are concerned with similar issues of inequality, neo-colonialism, ecological concerns or other imbalances between the nations of the world. By entering into such a framework, many British-born Muslims discover that dissent is also a time-honoured method of enacting citizenship. The struggle for democracy itself was achieved step-by-step, victory-by-victory over the voices of powerful establishments that did not want to relinquish their advantages or to share their privileges with the less powerful. Quilliam was part of that struggle in Liverpool when he chose to lead a trade union or to represent legally the rights of the city's womenfolk in the docks free of charge. Those who protested for a wider franchise or the basic rights of workers were regarded as dissenters. Although they were sometimes imprisoned and deported, the nineteenth-century radicals, often using a language that combined politics with religion, were no less citizens than those they struggled against, although they were accused of anti-social or deviant behaviour.

Many Muslims in Britain are beginning to challenge or question the narrative of 'Westophobia'. This term, which is used by Islamists, refers to a perception of cultural decay and encourages young Muslims to engage in an affirmation of Islamic identity and a revival of religious values. From this view, British society is seen as woefully and perhaps fatally undermined by sexual promiscuity, alcohol abuse, psychological disorders, crime, drugs, the collapse of the family and juvenile disobedience to parental discipline. In opposition to this social sickness, Islam posits moral precepts of justice, equality, opposition to materialism, greed and egoism, and a correct appreciation of family values. The challenge is to separate the rhetoric of the Islamists from the religious conviction that accepts the moral superiority of the Qur'an and the belief that the West has much to learn from it.

Quilliam's ideas were not substantially different from this view. Although he would not have described himself as 'Westophobic', it must be remembered that he adopted an Oriental lifestyle which he saw as superior to that of Victorian society. He certainly felt that the society around him was 'sick' and required purification on an Islamic model. Quilliam's version of critical opposition to the norms of British society was not directed towards secularism, as is that of many Muslim activists today. Britain at the end of the nineteenth century could not be described as secular. Society was predominantly Christian and Quilliam blamed a corrupted and fallen Christianity for the ills that he saw around him. It was thus not a Muslim struggle against godlessness that absorbed the Sheikh, but rather a need to replace one religious revelation with another. However, his objections to the norms of 'Christian' society alert us to the inherent weakness in the Foundation that has named itself in his honour. The borders between Islam and Islamism are blurred and are far from straightforward.

Was Quilliam a devout Muslim or an 'Islamist'? His story highlights the problem with applying such blanket labels to currents of Muslim activism. Certainly his fatwas reveal a religious position that refused to separate religion from politics and that was prepared to take radical positions against the decisions of governments. However, these were made in regard to the international situation. Domestically, Quilliam was far from the kind of conservative Muslim leader who fears *bid'a* (innovation) and clings to *taqlid* (imitation) to defend an Islam under threat. Debates around gender separation, the rights of women, dress codes, food and the language in which Islam's ritual life took place all happened in the context of reproducing Islam in a new cultural space, and the nineteenth and early twentieth-century communities achieved an adventurous spirit of investigation that has yet to be matched in the twenty-first century. Arguably, the most important lesson that Abdullah Quilliam can teach to British Muslims who inherited his attempt to establish Islam in Britain is inclusiveness. I still feel the impact of my first visit to Quilliam's mosque when I saw the prayer mats on the floor for the first time since 1908. In my mind's eye, I visualised the prayer rows back then and knew that the diversity of the Liverpool Muslim community a century ago had not yet been achieved in any mosque in Britain today. I hope that, when the mosque is formally opened, the Abdullah Quilliam Society in Liverpool remembers this and invites in the same class, ethnic and gender differentiation that prayed in the mosque back then. If there was one thing that dominated Quilliam's attraction to Islam, it was equality and brotherhood of all.

References

CHAPTER I

1. *The Crescent*, hereafter referred to as *TC*, No. 499, 6th August 1902.
2. *Manchester Clarion*, 29th July 1893, reprinted in *TC*, No. 29, 5th August 1893.
3. *Sunday Telegraph*, 29th October 1896.
4. Waller, P.J. (1981) *Democracy and Sectarianism: A Political and Social History of Liverpool 1868-1939*. Liverpool: Liverpool University Press, p.xiv.
5. Belchem, J. (1992) *Popular Politics, Riot and Labour: Essays in Liverpool History 1790-1940*. Liverpool: Liverpool University Press, p.1.
6. Brooke, R. (1853) *Liverpool as it was during the last quarter of the 18th century, 1775-1800*. Liverpool. J. Mawdsley and Son
7. Power, M.J. (1992) 'The Growth of Liverpool' in *Popular Politics, Riot and Labour: Essays in Liverpool History 1790-1940*, John Belcham (ed.). Liverpool: Liverpool University Press, p.21.
8. Ibid.   9. Belcham, 1992, p.17.
10. Muir, R. (1907), *A History of Liverpool*. Liverpool: University Press of Liverpool, p.271.
11. Young, R. (1998) 'Herbert Spencer and "Inevitable" Progress' in *Victorian Values: Personalities and Perspectives in 19th Century Society*, Gordon Marsden (ed.), 2nd edn. London, New York: Longman.
12. Fraser, D. (1998) 'Joseph Chamberlain and the Municipal Ideal' in *Victorian Values: Personalities and Perspectives in 19th Century Society*, Gordon Marsden (ed.), 2nd edn. London, New York: Longman.
13. McLeod, H. (1996) *Religion and Society in England 1850-1914*. London: MacMillan Press, p.1.
14. Op. cit., p.71.   15. Op. cit., p.76.   16. Op. cit., p.78.
17. Op. cit., p.83.   18. Op. cit., p.77.   19. Op. cit., p.5.
20. Op. cit., p.170.
21. By the third century, the four Muslim schools of law, that of Hanafi, founded by Abu Hanifa (d.767), Hanbali, founded by Ahmad ibn Hanbal

(d.855), Shafi'i, founded by Muhammad ibn Idris al-Shafi'i (d.820), and Maliki, founded by Malik ibn Anas (d.796), had been established and then adopted respectively by various geographical and cultural regions. Today, the Hanafi school is predominant among the Sunnis of Central Asia, Afghanistan, Pakistan, Bangladesh, India and China, as well as in Iraq, Syria, Turkey, Albania, Bosnia, Kosovo, Macedonia in the Balkans and the Caucasus. The Hanbalis had a presence in the Middle East and their teachings were revived in the eighteenth century by the Wahhabi movement in Arabia. The Malikis are to be found in North and West Africa and Upper Egypt. And finally, the Shafi'i's are based in East Africa, the Middle East and South-East Asia (Geaves, R. (2005) *Aspects of Islam*. London: Longman, Darton and Todd).

22. In the last years of his life, Sayyid Ahmad Khan wrote against Abdul Hamid II's claim to be a legitimate caliph, in particular against a rising tide of anti-British and pro-khilafat sentiment in India (see Hardy, P. (1972) *The Muslims of British India*. Cambridge: Cambridge University Press, p.178). However, like Quilliam but unlike Abduh, Sir Sayyid Ahmad Khan was an advocate of the benefits of British imperialism (ibid, pp.111-12, 130, 133). Khan and Abduh diverged over reason and revelation; both stressed the rationality of Islam and held it to be compatible with science, but Abduh thought that part of the revealed truth is inaccessible to human reason, while Khan did not. There were other differences (see the discussion in Troll, C. (1978) *Sayyid Ahmad Khan: An Interpretation of Muslim Theology*. New Delhi: Vikas, pp.223-30), but I was unable to find any evidence of Quilliam entering into these more subtle debates and he tended to pair them together as the voices of an enlightened Islam.

23. Germain, E. (2007) 'Southern Hemisphere Diasporic Communities in the Building of International Muslim Public Opinion at the Turn of the Twentieth Century' in *Comparative Studies of South Asia, Africa and the Middle East*, 27/1, pp.131-2.

24. Beckerlegge, G. (1997) '"Followers of Mohammad, Kalee and Dadu Nanuk": The Presence of Islam and South Asian Religions in Victorian Britain' in *Religion in Victorian Britain*, John Wolffe (ed.). Manchester: Manchester University Press, p.251. The *Liverpool Review* article cited by Beckerlegge refers to the Sunday meeting of the Liverpool Muslim Institute as containing speakers of Gujarati, Urdu, Arabic, Turkish and French, in addition to English (*Liverpool Review*, 29th August 1891, p.13).

25. Robinson-Dunn, D. (2006) *The harem, slavery and British imperial culture: Anglo-Muslim relations in the late nineteenth century*. Manchester: Manchester University Press. See notes 23 and 24 for Germain, 2007 and Beckerlegge, 1997.

CHAPTER 2

1. An anonymous handwritten diary known as the *Family Annals of W.H. Quilliam*, which is in the possession of the Abdullah Quilliam Society in Liverpool, records a number of salient events in his life. It is possible that the diary was maintained by Harriet, his mother. It notes that he attended the Liverpool Institute from 1866 and was awarded the Midsummer Certificate of Merit in the Preparatory Year. He was moved to the 1st Form at Christmas 1866, where he was awarded the 2nd Prize for his year group. In 1867 and 1868 he won 1st Prize for his respective year (2nd and 3rd Form) and in 1869 won 1st Prize as top pupil for the school. In January of that year according to the Annals he won the prize for top student at the Russell Church Sunday School, described as a United Methodist Free Church. His interest in geology came outside of school and began as a result of attending a lecture by F.P. Marrett of the Liverpool Museums Scientific staff. Quilliam went on to collect fossils and stones and sought Mr. Marrett's advice from time to time (*Liverpool Mercury*, 10th December 1907).

2. *Family Annals.*

3. The details about Quilliam's qualifications as a solicitor are also from the *Family Annals.*

4. *The Manxman,* 29th January, 1898.   5. Muir, 1907, p.208.

6. Op.cit., p.235.   7. *TC*, No.383, 16th May 1900.

8. There is a considerable difference of opinion concerning the existence of Henri de Léon. Efforts to trace him in the French records of the nineteenth century have so far failed. I contend that he existed in his own right, at least whilst Quilliam remained in Liverpool until 1908. There is no doubt that, after Quilliam's return to England, he took upon himself the identity of de Léon until his own death in 1932. For my position on this controversy, see p.260-2.

9. Henri de Léon, 'Some leaves from the Life-History of a Busy Life' in *TC*, No. 383, 16th May 1900.

10. Thompson, 1988, p.311.   11. Op. cit., p.310.   12. *Family Annals.*

13. *TC*, No. 253, 17th November 1893.

14. Quilliam would appear to be a significant figure in Liverpool's early trade unionism. I have not pursued this line of inquiry, as it would distract from the main theme of the nineteenth-century Muslim presence. However, the archives of the trade unions that he was involved in would be a fruitful line of inquiry for further research.

15. Bradley, I.C. (1998) 'Titus Salt – Enlightened Entrepreneur' in *Victorian Values: Personalities and Perspectives in 19th Century Society*, Gordon Marsden (ed.), 2nd edn. London, New York: Longman, p.94.

16. Belchem, 1992, p.2.   17.Op. cit., p.3.   18. Op. cit., p.27.

19. Lane, T. (1987) *Liverpool: Gateway of Empire*. London: Lawrence and Wishart.

20. Belcham (1992), p.3.   21. Op. cit., p.25.

22. Moss, W. (1796) *The Liverpool Guide; including a sketch of the environs: with a map of the town*. Liverpool: W. Moss, p.118.

23. Waller, P.J. (1981) *Democracy and Sectarianism: A Political and Social History of Liverpool, 1868-1939*. Liverpool: Liverpool University Press, p.16.

24. Ibid.   25.*Family Annals*.   26. Waller, 1981, p.16.

27. Op. cit., p.23.

28. Wolff, J. and Arscott, C. (1998) '"Cultivated Capital": Patronage and Art in 19th Century Manchester and Leeds' in *Victorian Values: Personalities and Perspectives in 19th Century Society*, Gordon Marsden (ed.), 2nd edn. London, New York: Longman, p.37.

29. Yates, N. (1998) 'Pugin and the Medieval Dream' in *Victorian Values: Personalities and Perspectives in 19th Century Society*, Gordon Marsden (ed.), 2nd edn. London, New York: Longman, pp. 68-69.

30. Op. cit., p.70.

31. Norman, E. (1998) 'Stewart Headlam and the Christian Socialists' in *Victorian Values: Personalities and Perspectives in 19th Century Society*, Gordon Marsden (ed.), 2nd edn. London, New York: Longman, p.191.

32. Englander, D. and O'Day, R. (eds.) (1995) *Retrieved Riches: Social Investigation in Britain, 1840–1914*. Aldershot: Ashgate.

33. Op. cit., p.11.   34. McLeod, 1996.   35. Op. cit., p.179.

36. Op. cit., p.184.

37. Rowbotham, S. (1998) 'Commanding the Heart: Edward Carpenter and Friends' in *Victorian Values: Personalities and Perspectives in 19th Century Society*, Gordon Marsden (ed.), 2nd edn. London, New York: Longman, p.245.

38. McLeod (1996), p.187.   39. Brooke, R. (1853).

40. Power, M.J. (1992) 'The Growth of Liverpool' in *Popular Politics, Riot and Labour: Essay in Liverpool History 1790-1940*, John Belcham (ed.). Liverpool: Liverpool University Press, p.24.

41. Muir, 1907, pp.300-4.   42. Op. cit., p.306.   43. Op. cit., p.309.

44.Op. cit., p.324.   45.Waller, 1981, p.107.   46. Op. cit., p.106.

47. Op. cit., p.12.   48. Muir, 1907, p.325.   49.Waller, 1981, p.11.

50. Ibid.

51. Smith, J. (1986) 'Class, Skill and sectarianism in Glasgow and Liverpool before 1914' in *Class, Power and Social Structure in British 19th Century Towns*, Swift R. and Morris R.J. (eds.). Leicester: University Press, pp.158-215.

52. Waller, 1981, p.12.   53. Op. cit., p.19.   54. Op. cit., p.25.

55. Op. cit., p.15.   56. Op. cit., p.26.   57. Ibid.
58. Op. cit., p.200.   59. Ibid.   60. Op. cit., p.202.
61. Op. cit., p.13.   62. Power, 1992, p.36.   63. Muir, 1907, p.290.
64. Rowbotham, 1998, p.244.   65.Ibid.   66. Norman, 1998, p.194.
67. Op. cit., p.193.   68. Op. cit., p.197.
69. Collins, P. (1998) 'Dickens and His Readers' in *Victorian Values: Personalities and Perspectives in 19th Century Society*, Gordon Marsden (ed.), 2nd edn. London, New York: Longman, p.55.
70. Ibid.
71. Hannah is recorded of dying from carcinoma of the colon at 8 Market Street, Hoylake (Death Certificate, Entry 384, Registry Book of Deaths 18, Registration Department of the Wirral).
72. Thompson, F.M.L. (1988) *The Rise of Respectable Society: A Social History of Victorian Britain 1830-1900*, London: Fontana Press, p.109.
73. Op. cit., p.106.
74. *Daily Post*, Tuesday, 9th February 1897.
75. *Liverpool Courier* (hereafter *LC*), 11th February 1897.
76. Thompson, 1988, p.109.   77. Ibid.   78. Ibid.
79. Tosh, J. (1998) 'New Men? The Bourgeois cult of Home' in *Victorian Values: Personalities and Perspectives in 19th Century Society*, Gordon Marsden (ed.), 2nd edn. London, New York: Longman, pp.80-1.
80. Op. cit., p.82.   81. Ibid.
82. *Daily Express*, 18th May 1905. The lecturer claims that polygamy is not prohibited in either the New or Old Testament.
83. *TC*, No. 10, March 25th 1893. The Marquis of Queensbury was quoted as saying, 'the attempt to realise a strictly monogamous social system has only resulted in producing a thinly disguised polygamy and polyandry infinitely more injurious to the moral and social welfare of the country and the people than an open, but rightly adjusted system of polygamy.'
84. *TC*, No. 288, July 20th 1898.   85. *TC*, No. 327, April 19th 1899.

CHAPTER 3

1. *The Pall Mall Gazette,* 10th November 1906.
2. B.G. Orchard's, *Liverpool's legion of Honour, LPRO* (p.563) is the only source that maintains the story that Quilliam visited Algeria for 'health reasons'. Although this is also mentioned in Gwilliam Beckerlegge (1997) '"Followers of Mohammad, Kalee and Dadu Nanuk": The Presence of Islam and South Asian Religions in Victorian Britain' (in *Religion in Victorian Britain*, John Wolffe (ed.). Manchester: Manchester University Press, p.246), there is no reference to an original source.

3. Pool, J. (1892) *Studies in Mohammadanism: Historical and Doctrinal with a Chapter on Islam in England*. Westminster: Archibald Constaple, pp.xiii-xiv.

4. *Family Annals*.

5. Khan-Cheema, M.A. (1979) 'Islam and the Muslims in Liverpool', unpublished MA Dissertation, University of Liverpool, p.10.

6. *Islamic World* (hereafter referred to as *IW*), Vol. 3, July 1895, p.312.

7. *TC*, No. 410, 21st November 1900.

8. Fatima Cates wrote the story of her conversion for the *Allahabad Review*, October 1891.

9. Henri de Léon writing in *TC*, No. 410, 21st November 1900.

10. Beckerlegge, op. cit., p.261.

11. Germain, E. (2007) 'Southern Hemisphere Diasporic Communities in the Building of International Muslim Public Opinion at the Turn of the Twentieth Century' in *Comparative Studies of South Asia, Africa and the Middle East*, 27/1, pp.126-38.

12. *TC*, No. 11, 1st April 1893.   13. *TC*, No. 22, 17th June 1893.

14. *TC*, No. 43, 11th November 1893.   15. *TC*, No. 145, 23rd October 1895.

16. *TC*, No. 243, 8th September 1897.

17. *TC*, No. 246, 29th September 1897.

18. *TC*, No. 247, 6th October 1897.   19. *LC*, 17th September 1897.

20. *TC*, No. 480, 26th March 1902.   21. *TC*, No. 646, 31st May 1905.

22. *TC*, No. 264, 2nd February 1898.

23. *TC*, No. 244, 15th September 1897.   24. Germain, op. cit., p.132.

25. Tetens, K. (2008) 'The Lyceum and the Lord Chamberlain: The Case of Hall Caine's *Mahomet*' in *Henry Irving: A Re-evaluation of the Pre-eminent Victorian Actor-Manager*, Richard Faulker (ed.). Aldershot: Ashgate.

26. Ibid.   27. *TC*, No. 6, 25th February 1893.

28. An early Muslim convert who assisted Alexander Webb in the US. He was the author of *The Disintegration of Christianity* and the poem 'A Muslim Prayer'.

29. *TC*, No. 12, 8th April 1893.

30. Zerhoun (also spelled Zarhun or Zarhon) is a mountain in Morocco, north of Meknes, on whose hillside is the town 'Moulay Idris Zarhona', named after Moulay Idris I, the founder of the Moorish empire, who was buried there in 791, see Margaret Bidwell and Robin Bidwell (2005) *Morocco: The Traveller's Companion*, Tauris Parke Publishing..

31. *TC*, No. 13, 15th April 1893; No. 14, 22nd April 1893.

32. *TC*, No. 708, 7th December 1898.

33. For full details of the significant relations between West African Muslims and the Liverpool Muslim Institute see the article by Brent Singleton

(2009) 'That Ye May Know Each Other: Late Victorian Interactions between British and West African Muslims', *Journal of Muslim Minority Affairs*, 29/3, September, pp.370-85.

34. The Presidential address delivered by Sheikh Abdullah Quilliam at the AGM of the Liverpool Muslim Institute, July 1896. Minutes reported in *IW*, Vol. 4, No. 39, July 1896.

35. Op. cit., p.65.   36. Op. cit., p.75.   37. Op. cit., p.78.

38. *TC*, No. 155, 1st January 1896.

39. The Janissaries formed the standing Ottoman Turkish army.

40. *TC*, No. 209, 13th January 1897.

41. *TC*, No. 257, 15th December 1897.

42. *IW*, Vol. 4, No. 39, July 1896, pp. 72-3.

43. *TC*, No. 157, 15th January 1896.

44. 'A Sunday with the Muslims' in *Christian Monthly* reprinted in *IW*, Vol. 4, No. 39, July 1896, pp.107-8.

45. *TC*, No. 289, 27th July 1898.   46. *IW*, Vol. 4, No. 39, July 1896, p.67.

47. Muir, 1907, p.6.   48. Ibid.

49. Waller, P.J. (1981) *Democracy and Sectarianism: A Political and Social History of Liverpool, 1868-1939*. Liverpool: Liverpool University Press.

50. *TC*, No. 236, 21st July 1897.

51. Quilliam always claimed that the Empress had accepted the title. The evidence as such is anecdotal. He was certainly called upon by the British Government to hold the state funeral of a Muslim soldier who had died whilst taking part in the Coronation of Edward VII. In addition, Quilliam was very proud that Victoria had written to him to request copies of his book *Faith of Islam* for her children after reading it herself. The Empress was known for her sympathies towards Islam.

52. *TC*, No. 236, 21st July 1897.   53. *IW*, Vol. 4, No. 39, July 1897, p.103

54. Op. cit., p.106.   55. Op. cit., pp.106-7.   56. Op. cit., pp.82-3.

57. *TC*, No. 253, 17th November 1897.   58. Ibid.

59. *TC*, No. 255, 1st December 1897.

60. *TC*, No. 248, 13th October 1897.

61. *The Freethinker*, 31st October 1897. *The Freethinker* was a radical magazine that would often quote Quilliam's attacks on established Christianity. Atheist in outlook, it enjoyed the discomfort of Christians under Quilliam's scrutiny. Founded by G.W. Foote in 1881, it is still published and is the world's oldest surviving humanist freethought magazine publication (www.freethinker.co.uk).

62. *TC*, No. 255, 1st December 1897.   63. *TC*, No. 268, 2nd March 1898.

64. *Liverpool Mercury*, 20th April 1898.   65. *TC*, No. 286, 6th July 1897.

66. *TC*, No. 315, 25th January 1899.   67. *TC*, No. 329, 3rd May 1899.
68. *TC*, No. 321, 8th March 1899; No. 323, 22nd March 1899.
69. *TC*, No. 345, 23rd August 1899.   70. *TC*, No. 335, 21st June 1899.
71. *TC*, No. 362, 20th December 1899.   72. *TC*, No. 347, 6th September 1899.
73. *TC*, No. 357, 19th November 1899.

CHAPTER 4

1. *TC*, No. 678, 10th January 1906.   2. *TC*, No. 679, 17th January 1906.
3. *TC*, No. 684, 21st February 1906.   4. *TC*, No. 705, 18th July 1906.
5. *TC*, No. 684, 21st February 1906.   6. *TC*, No. 523, 21st January 1903.
7. *Lahore Observer*, 5th July 1905.
8. *The Porcupine*, 23rd September 1905.
9. *TC*, No. 653, 19th July 19th 1905.   10. Germain, 2007, p.126.
11. *TC*, No. 383, 16th May; No. 384, 23rd May 1900.
12. *TC*, No. 397, 22nd August 1900.
13. *TC*, No. 399, 5th September 1900.
14. *TC*, No 403, 8th October 1900.
15. *TC*, No. 411, 28th November 1900.
16. *TC*, No. 486, 7th May 1902
17. *TC*, No. 487, 14th May 1902.   18. *TC*, No. 595, 8th June 1904.
19. *TC*, No. 419, 30th January 1901.   20. *TC*, No. 495, 9th July 1902.
21. *TC*, No. 586, 6th April 1904.
22. John Abdul Hamid Le Mesurier was a convert to Islam and a high-ranking civil servant in Ceylon (see *TC*, No. 144, 16th October 1895; No. 157, 15th January 1895; No. 163, 26th February 1895; No. 474, 12th February 1902; No. 487, 21st May 1902).
23. *TC*, No. 586, 11th April 1904.
24. *TC*, No. 645, 24th May 1905. Edward Wilmot Blyden (1832 -1912) was a Sierra Leone creole and American-Liberian educator, writer, diplomat and politician in Liberia and Sierra Leone (see Hollis R. Lynch, *Edward Wilmot Blyden: Pan-Negro Patriot, 1832-1912* (New York: Oxford University Press, 1967), p.4.
25. *TC*, No. 394, 1st August 1900.   26. *TC*, No. 525, 4th February 1903.
27. *TC*, No. 588, 20th April 1904.   28. *TC*, No. 590, 4th May 1904.
29. *TC*, No. 678, 10th January 1906.   30. *TC*, No. 695, 9th May 1906.
31. *Daily Mirror*, 9th May 1906.   32. *TC*, No. 698, 30th May 1906.
33. *TC*, No. 709, 15th August 1906.   34. *TC*, No. 734, 6th February 1907.
35. *TC*, No. 562, 21st October 1903.   36. *TC*, No. 563, 28th October 1903.
37. *TC*, No. 520, 31st December 1902.   38. *Daily Mail*, 28th January 1903.

39. *TC*, No. 564, 6th November 1903.

40. *TC*, No. 568, 2nd December 1903.   41. *TC*, No. 574, 13th January 1904.

42. *TC*, No. 579, 17th February 1904.   43. *TC*, No. 601, 20th July 1904.

44. *TC*, No. 619, 23rd November 1904.

45. *TC*, No. 621, 7th December 1904.

46. *TC*, No. 594, 1st June 1904. In 1830, Abeokuta had been established as a city state by escaped Africans running away from slavers, which achieved independence in 1893.

47. *TC*, No. 612, 5th October 1904.

48. Quilliam wrote extensively in his volumes on Freemasonry and his activities. This aspect of his life is not the focus of this book. Freemasonry was important in the late Ottoman Empire (see Dumont, P. (2005) 'Freemasonry in Turkey: a byproduct of Western penetration' in *European Review*, 13, pp.481-493). The more liberal Scottish and Non-Conformist lodges of which Quilliam was a member were inclusive of the Ottomans. One line of enquiry worth undertaking in the future would be to ascertain whether one potential avenue that allowed Quilliam to obtain initial access to Yildiz was his Freemason credentials.

49. Germain, 2007, p.120.   50. *TC*, No. 604, 10th August 1904.

51. *TC*, No. 618, 16th November 1904.

52. One theory insists that Freemasonry evolved from a remnant of the Knights Templar who settled in Scotland following the Order's demise in 1307. This was disseminated by Scots throughout the world from 1688, and the first written Constitution of the Freemasons can be found in Scotland dated 1598. In their book, *The Knights Templar of the Middle East: The Hidden History of the Islamic Origins of Freemasonry*, the authors argue that the roots of Templarism were linked to Islam and secret esoteric brotherhoods that existed in the Fatamid empire (HRH Prince Michael of Albany and Salhab, W.A. (2006) *The Knights Templar of the Middle East: The Hidden History of the Islamic Origins of Freemasonry*. San Francisco: Weiser Books).

53. *TC*, No. 595, 8th June 1904.   54. *TC*, No. 583, 16th March 1904.

55. *TC*, No. 585, 30th March 1904.   56. *TC*, No. 602, 27th July 1904.

57. *TC*, No. 605, 17th August 1904.   58. *TC*, No. 584, 23rd March 1904.

59. *TC*, No. 594, 1st June 1904.   60. *TC*, No. 714, 26th September 1906.

61. *TC*, No. 625, 4th January 1905.   62. *TC*, No. 626, 11th January 1905.

63. *TC*, No. 610, 21st September 1904.   64. *Daily Dispatch*, 16th June 1902.

65. *TC*, No. 497, 23rd July 1902.   66. *TC*, No. 498, 30th July 1902.

67. *TC*, No. 652, 12th July 1905.   68. *TC*, No. 726, 12th December 1906.

69. *TC*, No. 662, 20th September 1905.

70. *TC*, Nos. 668-671, 1st, 8th, 15th, 21st November 1905.

71. *Daily Express*, 31st August 1904.   72. *TC*, No. 615, 26th October 1904.

73. *TC*, No. 389, 27th June 1900.   74. *TC*, No. 677, 3rd January 1906.

75. *TC*, No. 701, 22nd June 1906.

76. *TC*, No. 599, 28th February 1906. The following issue carries an article on the Indian visitors. They were en route for Northern Nigeria where they would serve as indentured labourers for three years. *The Crescent* describes them as Pathans, Punjabis, Afghans and Afridis, including six Sikhs. They were being retained by the British Government as veterinary surgeons, telegraph electrical engineers and operators, master carpenters and blacksmiths, Inland Revenue supervisors and clerks. The men carried their tools with them as well as four gramophones. Quilliam met with them personally in the evening (*TC*, No. 686, 6th March 1906).

77. *TC*, No. 690, 4th April 1906.

78. *The Truth* was the organ of J.M. Loubouchere, MP, and purported to have received information from anonymous sources in Constantinople which claimed that Quilliam had no right to the titles and awards that it was claimed he had received from the Sultan and that the Liverpool Muslim Institute was established to further the advancement of Quilliam, rather than to promote Islam. The correspondents protested at Quilliam's fund-raising requests in Muslim countries (*TC*, No. 450, 28th August 1901).

79. *Liverpool Courier*, 15th April 1901.   80. *TC*, No. 421, 6th February 1901.

81. *TC*, No. 422, 13th February 1901.   82. *TC*, No. 465, 11th December 1901.

83. *TC*, No. 570, 16th December 1903.

84. *TC*, No. 571, 23rd December 1903.

85. *Daily Dispatch*, 18th December 1903.   86. *TC*, No. 279, 18th May 1898.

87. *TC*, No. 342, 2nd August 1899.   88. *TC*, No. 362, 20th December 1899.

89. *TC*, No. 384, 23rd May 1900.   90. *TC*, No. 396, 8th August 1900

91. *TC*, No. 451, 4th September 1901. The obituaries of the first members of the LMI were always written by Henri de Léon. In this obituary, he mentions that Omar Byrne was the last surviving member of the original converts that had heard Quilliam in Mount Vernon Street. All had died between 1899 and 1901.

92. The mosque in Regents Park is not to be confused with the present location in London, built upon land bequeathed by George IV. The property used for prayer in Regents Park seems to have been under the control of Cape Town Muslims from South Africa and attracted some converts. Quilliam appeared to prefer links with this Muslim community in London during his Liverpool period. They accepted his position as Sheikh al-Islam and the South African Muslim presence in Cape Town, made up of Gujaratis and

Pathans, had already been successfully targeted by the Liverpool Muslim Institute (Germain, 2007, p.121). The story of the mosque in Regents Park needs to be researched as part of the history of Muslims in London.

93. *TC*, No. 263, 26th January 1898.

94. Quilliam had announced Edwards' funeral in Portsmouth (*TC*, No. 463, 27th November 1901). He mentioned that he had been a convert for seven years.

95. *TC*, No. 263, 26th January 1898.   96. *TC*, No. 387, 13th June 1900.

97. *TC*, No. 366, 17th January 1900.   98. *TC*, No. 588, 20th April 1904.

99. Future issues in July and August 1906 ran a series of articles explaining in English the details of the ritual practices of Islam for the benefit of British Muslims.

100. George Wise was a popular Anglican preacher in Liverpool who founded the British Protestant Union and who later entered politics (*www.orangenet. org/liverpool/GeorgeWise*).

101. *TC*, No. 596, 15th June 1904.   102. *TC*, No. 612, 5th October 1904.

103. *TC*, No. 583, 20th March 1904.   104. *TC*, No. 587, 18th April 1904.

105. *TC*, No. 718, 17th October 1906.   106. *TC*, No. 730, 2nd January 1906.

107. *TC*, No. 734, 6th February 1907. Both Barrett College and the University of Liberia were products of slavery. The University of Liberia had been established after that nation had become one of the first African nations created from the activities of those who escaped slavery. Barrett College was founded by Charles Barrett in the township of Pee Dee in Anson County, one of the poorest in the State of North Carolina and around fifty miles east of Charlotte, the state capital. A book written by an African-American minister named Latta has a chapter about Barrett, and his college. Latta states that Barrett toured Europe at the beginning of the 20th century to raise funds for his project (Latta, M.L. (1903) *History of my Life and Work*, reprinted in 2000. Chapel Hill, University of North Carolina, p.260). It is possible that Quilliam donated to what he perceived to be a good cause, considering his interest in equal rights for American blacks. The Doctor of Law may have been a reward for a donation (p.260).

108. *TC*, No. 777, 11th December 1907.   109. *TC*, No. 487, 21st May 1902.

110. *TC*, No. 781, 8th January 1908.   111. Ibid.

112. *TC*, No. 785, 5th February 1908.

113. *TC*, No. 786, 12th February 1908.   114. *TC*, No. 795, 15th April 1908.

115. *TC*, No. 791, 18th March 1908.   116. *TC*, No. 795, 15th April 1908.

117. *TC*, No. 800, 20th May 1908.   118. *TC*, No. 799, 13th May 1908.

119. *TC*, No. 801, 27th May 1908.

CHAPTER 5

1. Multiculturalism can be used simply to denote a pluralist society, or it can have a more specific meaning associated with particular policies towards minorities. This depends on how we define the term. Tariq Modood links multiculturalism to the US civil rights movement, feminism, gay rights of the 60s and 70s and, in a broader sense, to identity politics. A more restricted British and/or European political meaning is, 'the recognition of group difference within the public sphere of laws, policies, democratic discourses and the terms of shared citizenship and national identity' (see Modood, T. (2007) *Multiculturalism: A Civic Idea*. Cambridge: Polity, p.2). However, modern settler societies with longer histories of immigration, which were themselves built by immigrants, were among the first to describe themselves as 'multicultural', like Australia, the US and Canada. Sander Gilman (2005) in a fascinating book, *Multiculturalism and the Jews* (London: Routledge), describes the figure of the Jew as pivotal in shaping the idea of the multicultural, an idea developed in Europe in the late nineteenth century that flourishes in America in the twentieth century. The two models – the idea of an optimum blend of cultures and the recognition of cultural diversity – converge together to form the idea of the multicultural. Gilman develops his thesis in Chapter 3, which is somewhat similar to that described here. He argues that it is in the late nineteenth century that a religious group, the Jews, became ethnicised and defined by cultural difference, and thus the building blocks for multiculturalism were laid down.
2. *TC*, No. 571, 23rd December 1903.
3. *Liverpool Daily Post*, 27th December 1892.
4. *TC*, No. 155, 1st January 1895.   5. *TC*, No. 259, 29th December 1897.
6. *TC*, No. 266, 16th February 1898.   7. *TC*, No. 268, 2nd March 1898.
8. *TC*, No. 358, 22nd November 1899.   9. *TC*, No. 276, 27th April 1898.
10. *Jewish Chronicle*, 10th June 1898.   11. *TC*, No. 783, 22nd January 1908.
12. *TC*, No. 505, 17th September 1902.
13. *The Independent* (Sheffield), 24th February 1908.
14. *TC*, No. 507, 1st October 1902.   15. *TC*, No. 502, 2nd September 1902.
16. *Liverpool Mercury*, 11th September 1902.
17. *TC*, No. 277, 4th May 1898.   18. *TC*, No. 278, 11th May 1898.
19. Ansari, H. (2004) *The Infidel Within*. London: Hurst, p.31.
20. Since the eighth century, the title of Sheikh al-Islam was given to individuals who governed Islamic affairs in larger communities or who were judges. It became a prestigious formal position in the Ottoman Empire. Overall, the Sheikh al-Islam governed the religious affairs of the state. There were also lesser officials under his authority who functioned as local Shuyukh

al-Islam in the various provinces of the Ottoman Empire. The office was replaced by the Presidency of Religious Affairs in the new Republic of Turkey after 1920. The Presidency of Religious Affairs remains the most authoritative entity in Turkey in relation to Sunni Islam.

21. Halliday, F. (1992) *Arabs in Exile: Yemeni Migrants in Urban Britain*. London: I.B.Tauris, p.6.
22. Halliday, 1992, p.51. 23. Op. cit., p.52.
24. Foreign Office Record, RG/48/310.
25. *Sunday Chronicle*, 1st January 1894.
26. *Liverpool Mercury*, 23rd July 1898. 27. *Evening Express*, 23rd July 1898.
28. *TC*, No. 21, 10th June 1893. 29. *Liverpool Review*, 17th June 1895.
30. *TC*, No. 466, 18th December 1902. 31. Ansari, 2004, p.30.
32. *TC*, No. 1, 14th January 1893. 33. *Daily Post*, 17th January 1893.
34. *TC*, No. 3, 28th January 1893. 35. *TC*, No. 44, 19th November 1893.
36. *Liverpool Courier*, 18th November 1893. 37. Ansari, 2004, pp.30-5.
38. Op. cit., p.39. 39. Op. cit., p.38.
40. Reported in *TC*, No. 266, 16th February 1898.
41. *TC*, No. 42, 5th November 1893. 42. *TC*, No. 521, 7th January 1903.
43. *TC*, No. 146, 30th October 1894. 44. *TC*, No. 147, 6th November 1894.
45. *TC*, No. 505, 17th September 1902.
46. *Daily Dispatch*, 15th September 1902. 47. *TC*, No. 271, 23rd March 1898.

CHAPTER 6

1. Summerfield, P. (1986) 'Patriotism and Empire: Music Hall Entertainment 1870-1914' in *Imperialism and Popular Culture*, John MacKenzie (ed.). Manchester: Manchester University Press, p.19.
2. Springhall, J. (1986) 'Up Guards and at 'em! British Imperialism and Popular Art 1880-1914' in *Imperialism and Popular Culture*, John MacKenzie (ed.). Manchester: Manchester University Press, p.49.
3. Marcham, A.J. (1973) *Foreign Policy: Examining the Evidence in Nineteenth-Century England*. London: Methuen Educational, p.92.
4. Op. cit., p.107. 5. Op. cit., p.103. 6. Op. cit., p.43.
7. Op. cit., p.102. 8. Op. cit., p.104. 9. Op. cit., p.105.
10. Op. cit., p.106. 11. Ibid. 12. Op. cit., p.107.
13. Op. cit., p.108. The particular term 'Porte' was used in the context of diplomacy by the western states, as their diplomats were received at the porte (gate). The Sublime Porte was the name of the open court of the Sultan. It got its name from the gate to the headquarters of the Grand Vizier in Topkapi Palace in Istanbul, where the Sultan held the greeting

ceremony for foreign ambassadors (see 'Sublime Porte'. *Encyclopædia Britannica*. 2010. Encyclopædia Britannica Online, accessed 2nd Feb 2010, *http://www.britannica.com/EBchecked/topic/570790/Sublime-Porte*

14. Marsham, 1973, p.110.   15. *IW*, Vol 4., No. 37, May 1896, pp.86-7.

16. Op. cit., p.89.   17. Op. cit., p.87.

18. *TC*, No. 320, 1st March 1899.   19. Marcham, 1973, p.90.

20. In 1881, a Sudanese Muslim holy man named Mohammed Ahmed declared himself the Redeemer of Islam, the 'Mahdi'. On reaching adulthood, Mohammed became convinced that the Egyptians were not loyal to Islam, so he began to preach sermons about driving them out of the Sudan. Many people believed in him and he raised an army of revolt. After conquering most of the Sudan, the Mahdi attacked the capital, Khartoum. The siege of Khartoum began in March 1884. The Egyptian troops, under the command of British General C.G. Gordon, managed to fight off the Mahdi's army for ten long months. Finally, the city fell in January 1885.

21. This title, known for its use by the Muhammad Ali Dynasty of Egypt and Sudan, is recorded in English from 1867, derived via the French *khédive*; it is based on the Turkish *hıdiv*, which is itself derived from the Persian *khidiw* (prince), a derivative of *khuda*, 'master, prince' from Old Persian *khvadata* (lord) (see http://*www.thefreedictionary.com/khedive*).

22. Marcham, 1973, p.48.   23. Op. cit., p.49.

24. Springhall, 1986, p.51.   25. Op. cit., p.55.   26. Op. cit., p.57.

27. *TC*, No. 261, 12th January 1898.   28. *TC*, No. 274, 13th April 1898.

29. Springhall, 1986, pp.58-9   30. Op. cit., p.59.

31. *TC*, No. 295, 7th September 1898.

32. *TC*, No. 296, 14th September 1898.

33. *TC*, No. 297, 21st September 1898.   34. *TC*, No. 299, 5th October 1898.

35. *TC*, No. 302, 26th October 1898.   36. *TC*, No. 320, 1st March 1899.

37. *Evening Express*, 22nd March 1899.   38. *TC*, No. 24, 29th March 1899.

39. *TC*, No. 325, 5th April 1899.   40. Ibid.

41. *TC*, No. 331, 17th May 1899.   42. *TC*, No. 334, 5th June 1899.

43. *TC*, No. 359, 29th November 1899.   44. *TC*, No. 360, 13th December, 1899.

45. *TC*, No. 365, 10th January 1900.   46. *TC*, No. 366, 17th January 1900.

47. Henri Mustapha de Léon, *TC*, No. 377, 4th April 1900.

48. *TC*, No. 377, 4th April 1900.   49. *TC*, No. 416, 2nd January 1901.

50. *TC*, No. 356, 8th November 1899.   51. *TC*, No. 396, 15th August 1896.

52. *TC*, No. 372, 28th February 1900.   53. *TC*, No. 490. 4th June 1902.

54. *TC*, No. 365, 10th January 1900.   55. *TC*, No. 396, 15th August 1896.

56. The Durand Line was named after Sir Mortimer Durand, the Foreign Secretary of the British Indian government, and divided Afghanistan from

the North West Frontier Province, the Federally Administered Tribal Areas and Baluchistan, which were given to British India to administer and now form part of Pakistan.

57. Modrzejewska-Lesniewska, J. (2002) 'Another Kashmir? The Afghanistan-Pakistan Border Dispute' in *IBRU Boundary and Security Bulletin*, Winter 2001-2, p.70.

58. *TC*, No. 248, 13th October 1895.   59. Ibid.   60. Ibid.

61. *TC*, No. 243, 8th September 1895.   62. *TC*, No. 320, 1st March 1896.

63. *TC*, No. 364, 3rd January 1900.

64. Hopkirk, P. (2001) *The Great Game: On Secret Service in High Asia*. London: John Murray, p.1.

65. Corbett, R.G. (1902) *Muhammedanism and the British Empire*. London: Kegan Paul, Trench.

66. *TC*, No. 495, 9th July 1902.

67. *TC*, No. 575, 20th January 1904.

68. MacKenzie, J. (ed.) (1986) *Imperialism and Popular Culture*. Manchester: Manchester University Press, p.28.

69. Op. cit., p.29.

70. Steiner, Z. (1969) *The Foreign Office and Foreign Policy 1898-1914*. London: Ashfield Press, pp.23-8.

71. Op. cit., p.38.   72. Op. cit., p.46.   73. Op. cit., p.53.

74. Op. cit., p.58.   75. Op. cit., p.96.   76. Op. cit., p.105.

77. Op. cit., p.106.

78. Bratton, J.S. (1986) 'Of England, Home and Duty: The Image of England in Victorian and Edwardian Juvenile Fiction' in *Imperialism and Popular Culture*, John MacKenzie (ed.). Manchester: Manchester University Press, p.74.

79. Op. cit., p. 77.

CHAPTER 7

1. Perhaps the most impressive and complete view of Sayyid Ahmad Khan is contained in the article that Quilliam wrote for *The Crescent* after the death of the latter in 1898. Quilliam had heard of the death of Khan by telegram from Allahabad in April 1898. He described him as 'the most powerful political force in the Muslim world of India' (*TC*, No. 273, 6th April 1898). He later published an obituary from *The Muhammaden* that was published in India, and stated he would write a full article assessing the life of the great Muslim.

2. *TC*, No. 495, 9th July 1902.   3. Ibid.   4. Ibid.

5. *TC*, No. 623, 21st December 1904.   6. *TC*, No. 495, 9th July 1902.

7. *IW*, Vol.4, No. 39, July 1896.   8. *TC*, No. 565, 11th November 1903.

9. See the account of relations between Elizabeth I and the Ottoman Court in Kupperman, K.O. (2007) *The Jamestown Project* (Harvard: Belknap Press of Harvard University Press). Kupperman notes that Murad III described Elizabeth I as, 'the pride of women who follow Jesus, the most excellent of ladies honoured among the Messiah's people' (p.40). She notes that England alarmed Catholic Europe when it supplied the Ottomans with tin and lead, raw materials for casting cannon and manufacturing ammunition (p.41).

10. The Khilafat movement (1919-24) was a political campaign launched mainly by Muslims in South Asia to influence the British government and to protect the Ottoman Caliphate during the aftermath of World War I. In India, although it was mainly a Muslim religious initiative, the movement became a part of the wider Indian independence protests. The movement was the topic of a conference in London held in February 1920, where Quilliam met with the delegates at Woking Mosque (see *http://www.wokingmuslim.org/pers/khilafat.htm*).

11. *TC*, No. 347, 6th September 1896.   12. *TC*, No. 241, 25th August 1895.

13. *TC*, No. 322, 24th May 1899.

14. Choueiri, Y. (2005) 'Nationalisms in the Middle-East: The Case of Pan-Arabism' in *A Companion to the History of the Middle-East*, Youssef Choueiri (ed.). Oxford: Blackwell, p.293.

15. Op. cit., p.298.   16. Op. cit., p.300

17. Op. cit., p.299.   18. Op. cit., p.301

19. Grigoriadis, I. and Mansari, A. (2005) 'Turkish and Iranian Nationalisms' in *A Companion to the History of the Middle-East*, Youssef Choueiri (ed.). Oxford: Blackwell, p.316.

20. Choueiri, 2005, p.305.

21. *TC*, No. 171, 22nd April 1896, pp.681-2, original punctuation and spelling retained.

22. *TC*, No. 391, 11th July 1900.   23. *TC*, No. 368, 31st January 1900.

24. *TC*, No. 26, 15th July 1893.   25. *TC*, No. 28, 29th July 1893.

26. *The Lancaster Standard*, reprinted in *TC*, No. 331, 17th May 1899.

27. *TC*, No. 238, 4th August 1898.   28. *TC*, No. 229, 2nd June 1898.

29. *TC*, No. 295, 7th September 1898.   30. Ibid.   31. Ibid.

32. Ibid.   33. Ibid.

34. Ansari, H. (2004) *The Infidel Within*. London: Hurst, p.80

35. In 1899, Quilliam reported that the magnificent stallion given by the Sultan to Ahmed Quilliam in 1890 had died. Quilliam offered the carcass to the

Liverpool Museum to be stuffed and mounted and the offer was accepted (*TC*, No. 312, 4th January 1899).

36. *Tit-Bits*, 20th February 1897.

37. This is the first article that I could trace that is signed by Henri de Léon and would appear to mark the beginning of Quilliam's relationship with the French-Hungarian convert who would visit and stay in Liverpool on a number of occasions in the early years of the twentieth century. The article appears under his name in the *Liverpool Mercury* and is reprinted in *TC*, No. 332, 24th May 1899. Later on, Sheldrake also took on the penname of a Belguim aristocrat.

38. *TC*, No. 151, 4th December 1897.   39. *TC*, No. 135, 14th August 1897

40. Reported in *Liverpool Daily Mercury*, 12th April 1899, and reprinted in *TC*, No. 274, 13th April 1899.

41. *TC*, No. 275, 20th April 1898 and No. 276, 27th April 1898.

42. *TC*, No. 277, 4th May 1898   43. Ibid.

44. *TC*, No. 279, 18th May 1898.   45. *TC*, No. 280, 25th May 1898.

46. Quilliam had corrected an article in the *Bath Argus* (28th December 1898), which claimed that there were no universities in the Muslim world. He gave examples of the Al-Azhar, the University of Fez, the Mekteb Sultaniyah in Constantinople and countless other *madrasa*s and commented on the curriculum, suggesting that improvements should be made by the introduction of modern sciences and the translation of modern English textbooks into Arabic.

47. *TC*, No. 284, 22nd June 1898.

48. 'Many of the old Christian beliefs and orthodox ideas were now as dead as if they had been interred in the tombs of the Capulets; and either a man had to pin his faith upon some authority (real or assumed), upon a belief imparted in his breast when he knelt at his mother's knee, or to follow the path of unbelief and absolute atheism. Science and Christianity were antagonistic elements, but Islam and Science were twin sisters. It was a faith agreeable to reason, demonstrable by logic and suitable for requirements and necessities of mankind.' (*TC*, No. 288, 21st July 1898.)

49. *TC*, No. 288, 21st July 1898.   50. *The Porcupine*, 6th April 1900.

51. *TC*, No. 379, 18th April 1900.   52. *TC*, No. 382, 9th May 1900.

53. *TC*, No. 385, 30th May 1900.   54. *TC*, No. 386, 6th June 1900.

55. *TC*, No. 398, 29th August 1900.   56. *TC*, No. 399, 5th September 1900.

57. De Léon reported the loss of the Sheikh's robes and decorations on the eve of the celebration of the Jubilee. They were missed from the Brougham carriage when they were transported by Quilliam's daughter, but were found and returned within three days by a lamplighter who responded to the

adverts. The attitude of the national media is revealing. Newspaper articles declared that the Sultan had announced that Quilliam would be beheaded if he was found on Ottoman territory and that Quilliam was forbidden to function as the Sheikh al-Islam without them. They also reported that the Sheikh had been so distraught that he had torn his clothing into strips. De Léon pointed out that the media could not report on Islam or Muslims without exaggeration or even deceit (*TC*, No. 401, 19th September 1900).

58. *The New York Times* of 17th April 1893 published a report written by H.E. Newberry, Secretary of the United States Legation in Constantinople, in which he investigated the recent reports of the persecution of Christians by Mahommedans and the burning of the Marsovan College. It is interesting to read that American opinion was more in line with Quilliam and noted that incendiary and seditious notices had been placed on the door of the college by Armenian agitators, some of whom were carrying dynamite. Newberry considered that the Turkish authorities handled the matter as well as could be expected and released many of those arrested. This was very different to the reaction in the British media.

59. *TC*, No. 24, 1st July 1893.   60. *TC*, No. 147, 6th November 1895.

61. *TC*, No. 149, 20th November 1895.   62. *TC*, No. 30, 12th August 1893.

63. Ibid.   64. *TC*, No. 155, 1st January 1896.

65. *TC*, No. 108, 2nd Jan 1895.

66. A battle between Armenians and Turkish forces at Chelchuzan in the District of Mush. A total of 136 Turkish troops were killed, but many Armenians lost their lives when the Turks laid waste to Sassoun (*The New York Times*, 19th May 1904).

67. *TC*, No. 127, 24th May 1894.   68. *TC*, No. 140, 20th September 1895.

69. *TC*, No. 141, 27th September 1895.

70. *The Shipping Telegraph*, 24th September 1895.

71. *TC*, No. 360, 6th December 1899.   72. *TC*, No. 407, 31st October 1900.

73. *TC*, No. 217, 10th March 1898.   74. *TC*, No. 218, 17th March 1898.

75. *TC*, No. 219, 24th March 1898.   76. *TC*, No. 223, 24th April 1898.

77. Ibid.   78. Ibid.   79. Ibid.

80. *TC*, No. 224, 28th April 1898.   81. Ibid.

82. *Liverpool Daily Post*, 26th April 1898.   83. *TC*, No. 226, 12th May 1898.

84. *The Porcupine*, 1st May 1898, and reported in *TC*, No. 225, 5th May 1898.

85. *TC*, No. 297, 21st September 1898.   86. *TC*, No. 228, 26th May 1898.

87. *TC*, No. 229, 2nd June 1898.   88. *TC*, No. 224, 28th April 1898.

89. *TC*, No. 316, 1st February 1899.   90. *TC*, No. 563, 28th October 1903.

91. Ibid.   92. *TC*, No. 590, 4th May 1904.

93. *TC*, No. 620, 30th November 1904.

94. *TC*, No. 622, 14th December 1904.   95. *TC*, No. 623, 21st December 1904.

96. The Imtiaz Medal was the higher ranking of two medals for meritorious military service that were awarded by the Ottoman Turkish Government. It was 37mm in diameter, in silver and gold, with a trophy of arms on the obverse and an elaborate Arabic inscription on the reverse. The ribbon was half red, half green, with the red on the right.

97. Léon, H.M. (1905) 'Honours for Sheikh Abdullah Quilliam' in *TC*, No. 631, 15th February.

98. *The Liverpool Courier*, 10th February 1905.

99. *TC*, No. 631, 15th February 1905.

100. *The Journal de Salonique*, 25th February 1905.

101. *TC*, No. 634, 8th March 1905.　　102. *TC*, No. 635, 15th March 1905.

103. *TC*, No. 636, 22nd March 1905.　　104. *TC*, No. 792, 28th March 1908.

105. *Journal al-Asre*, 20th March 1905.

106. The news of the ban was reported in *The Liverpool Courier*, 7th June 1905, and in *The Daily Mail* on 8th June 1905. It was also reported in *The Hellenium*, which was published in Paris, and the *Bulletin D'Orient*, which was published in Athens.

107. Quoted by Quilliam in his annual address to the AGM of the LMI in *IW*, Vol.4, No. 36, April 1896, pp.84-5.

108. *TC*, No. 98, 26th November 1896.　　109. *TC*, No. 99, 3rd December 1896.

110. *TC*, No. 150, 27th November 1897.　　111. *TC*, No. 564, 4th November 1903.

112. *TC*, No. 421, 6th February 1901.

CHAPTER 8

1. *The Times*, Probate, Divorce and Admiralty Division, 25th November 1908.

2. *The Times*, King's Bench Division, 9th June 1909.

3. *The Times*, Probate, Divorce and Admiralty Division, 13th October 1908.

4. Such stories are maintained by the Isle of Man media and were included in *The New Manx Worthies* entry for Abdullah Quilliam by its author, Dollin Kelly. In a lecture to the Victorian Society on 24th April 2009, Dollin Kelly repeated these tales, maintaining that Quilliam had returned to the island in 1919, and repeating the allegations that he had spied for the Allies during the war. One Isle of Man newspaper asserted that he was decorated for these activities. Dollin asserts that, 'the local society in Onchan was scandalised with tales of orgies, multiple marriages and the Sheikh could hardly step outside the front of door of Woodland Towers without starting another colourful story' (Notes of the talk to the Victorian Society, 24th April 2009). Dollin Kelly, however, is quoting from John Guildford's entry in the *Oxford Dictionary of Biography*.

5. *Isle of Man Examiner*, 'Thousand and One Nights of a Manx Muslim', 16th April 1978.

6 . This story of an illegitimate daughter born to Louise Ruoy is interesting. In July 1899, a marriage took place at the mosque between the Nawab of Rampur and Emily Florence Blanche Rouy, the daughter of a French count, Emile Rouy. The Nawab and his young bride of sixteen were guests of the Quilliams on the Isle of Man, where they passed their honeymoon. The wedding received full coverage from the Liverpool media, along with the information that the dowry bestowed on the young woman was £20,000 (*TC*, No. 289, 27th July 1899). In Bill Kerruish's account, Louise had married a French count who had adopted the illegitimate child as his own. He claims without any substantiation that his father Billal had often visited 'Laetitia' in Nice, where she was married to a Scottish baronet, Sir Cyril Rose.

7. Aleister Crowley (1875-1947) was an English occultist, writer, mountaineer, poet, alleged spy and Orientalist who was involved in several occult organizations, including the Golden Dawn and Ordo Templi Orientis. Crowley also gained much notoriety in the Edwardian era for his eccentricity and lack of sympathy for the morals and sexuality of respectable society. He was branded, 'the wickedest man in the world' and a 'monster of depravity', and like Quilliam spent some time living in rural areas at the end of his career. Paul Newman ((2007) *The Tregerthen Horror*. UK: DRG Books) argues that such individuals with motley reputations attract 'rumours and hearsay' and are often claimed to be in locations where they would have been either out of place or unavailable (see *http://abrax7.stormloader.com/tregerthern.htm*). I have described this phenomenon as 'Crowleyisation'.

8. Billal was something of a disappointment to his father. In November 1934, he was sentenced to eighteen months imprisonment on the Isle of Man, and a further two years in England in 1938. On the 19th May 1938, he was also struck off as a solicitor.

9. Khalid Sheldrake, writing in the *The Review of Religions*, July 1912, pp.286-9.

10. According to John Deane Potter, the son of Miriam, his grandfather 'had an overwhelming weakness for women' and took the woman for whom he had rigged the evidence for a divorce to Turkey with him. He describes her as the wife of a Wallasey tobacconist. However, the stories recounted by the family are rather colourful. The *Times* article in 1908 suggests clearly that Martha May Peters was in England whilst Quilliam was in Asia Minor (*The Times*, 25th November 1908).

11. Found in the Forward of the book entitled, *Sheikh Haroun Abdullah: A Turkish Poet and His Poetry*, which was published in 1915. The authorship

is attributed to Henri de Léon, MA, PhD, LL.D, FSP. It is the life and translation of the poetry of an Osmanli dervish described by the author as possessing 'profound philosophy, deep religious fervor, and soul-inspiring mysticism'.

12. This is pure speculation. *The Crescent* (No. 578, 10th February 1904) briefly mentions that Quilliam visited Nottingham on professional business whilst Mrs Hannah Quilliam and her two daughters were in Cannes. By this time, Hannah was spending her winters in Cannes and her summers on the Isle of Man with her daughters on a regular basis, and it must be assumed that the relationship with her husband was strained.

13. *Wrights Directory*, 1913-64, proved by Nottinghamshire County Council in response to a letter from Richard Cain dated 4th December, 1997. Richard had converted to Islam and had become fascinated by the Quilliam story, spending many years researching his life.

14. *TC*, No. 332, 24th May 1899.   15. *TC*, No. 377, 4th April 1900.

16. *TC*, No. 398, 29th August 1900.

17. *TC*, No. 400, 12th September 1900.

18. A letter from Henri Mustapha Léon stated, 'I leave for Paris ce soir, and therefore cannot be with you.' (*TC*, No. 399, 6th September 1900.)

19. *TC*, No. 47, 9th December 1893.

20. By the beginning of the twentieth century, the number of Indian Muslim students in Britain had increased significantly. In 1903, an Indian newspaper reported that eighty-eight students from Aligarh alone were in the country (see Lahiri, S. (2000), *Indians in Britain, Anglo-Indian Encounters, Race and Identity, 1880-1930*. London: Frank Cass, p. 7).

21. Ansari mentions Lords Mowbray, Morley, Lamington, and Newton who were used as 'front men' tactically by the South Asian Woking group of Muslims (see Ansari, 2004, p.128).

22. For a short biography of Marmaduke Pickthall, see A.H. Murad, 'Marmaduke Pickthall: A Brief Biography' (n.d.), *http://www.masud.co.uk/ ISLAM/bmh/BMM-AHM-pickthall_bio.htm*.

23. Memo from the Director of Military Intelligence to the Under-Secretary of State for Foreign Affairs, Public Record Office, FO3715273 (1921).

24. Letter to the Foreign Office from the Société Internationale de Philologie, Sciences et Beaux-Arts, and signed by Henri de Léon as General-Secretary, dated 9th November 1914.

25. Letter to the Foreign Office from the Société Internationale de Philologie, Sciences et Beaux-Arts, and signed by Henri de Léon as General-Secretary, dated 23rd January 1915.

26. The entries in *Who's Who?* were not simultaneous. From 1902-8 the entry was for William Henry Abdullah Quilliam and read as follows: 'Sheikh al-Islam

of the British Isles; solicitor (England); Commissioner for Oaths (England); Special Commissioner for Canadian Oaths since 1884; b. Liverpool 10th April 1856; o.s. of Harriet and Robert Quilliam; m. 1879, Hannah, e.d. of the late Robert Johnstone. Education: Liverpool Institute; King William's College, Isle of Man; Alim of the University of Fez (Morocco); Medaillé des Beaux-Arts (Constantinople); koola-izzat and medal in gold (Afghanistan); Imperial Order of the Medjidiah (3rd Class), Turkey; Imperial Order of the Osmanieh (3rd Class), Turkey; Member of the African Society; Liverpool Geographical Society; Liverpool Geographical Association. Admitted a solicitor 1878; G.C.T. of I.O.G.T 1881; visited Morocco 1884; became Muslim 1885; instituted Liverpool Muslim Society 1887; audience with Shah of Persia, 1889; special guest of the Sultan of Turkey at the Palace of Yildiz, 1890; founded The Crescent Newspaper, 1892; visited Morocco again in 1893, and received degree at Fez, and audience with the then Sultan of Morocco; special mission to Lagos, West Africa, as a bearer of a decoration from the Sultan of Turkey to Mohammad Shitta Bey, 1894; entertained by the Shahzade of Afghanistan and received title and £2500 from the Ameer of Afghanistan, 1895; guest of the Sultan of Turkey at Constantinople, 1900; special audience with the Shah of Persia in Paris, 1900; appointed solicitor to the Lancashire Sea Fishery Board, 1892. *Publications*: Faith of Islam, 1887; Fanatics and Fanaticism, 1888; Religion of the Sword, 1889; Polly (a novel), 1891; The Wages of Sin (a novel), 1894; Moses, Christ and Muhammad, 1897; Studies in Islam, 1898; Manx Antiquities, 1898; The Balkan Question from a Turkish Standpoint, 1903; Az-Nazir-ud-deen, 1904; King Bladud of Bath, 1904. *Recreations*: fishing and horse-riding. Address: Fernbank, Fairfield Crescent, Liverpool, Woodland Towers, Onchan, Isle of Man (*Who's Who?*, 1905).The entries for Henri Marcel Leon run from 1926 to 1932 and read: 'MA, ScD, LLd, Phil.D/FSP etc. Le Secretaire-General de la Societe Internationale de Philologie, Sciences et Beaux-Arts; editor of Philomath and Physiologist; born 1855. Dean of London College of Physiology; Hon. Life President of the Edinburgh University Oriental Students' Society; Hon. Vice-President of the Ethological, Evolution, Anglo-Turkish, and Oneirological Societies; Medaille des Beaux-Artes (Constantinople); Izzat medal in gold (Afghanistan); Imperial Order of the Osmanieh (grand star), Imperial Order of the Medjidiah (2nd Class), Turkey; Grand Cross; Imperial Order of the Lion and the Sun (Persia); Commandant (Or et Argent) of the Imperial Order of the Imtiaz (Turkey); Etoile de Merite (Paris). Publications: Bache (The Garden), a collection of Turkish poems (in Turkish), 1900; Through Roumelia and Albania on Horseback (in Turkish), 1904; Kanli Katil Kanjalos (Turkish drama), 1907; Some Ancient Jewish Philologers, 1912; English-Manx-Gaelic Etymologies, 1914; Geology of the Isle of Man; 1915; Sheikh Haroun Abdullah, A Turkish Poet and his Poetry, 1916; The Haggadah, 1916; Pipe Fishes, 1917; The Chellonia, or Shield-Covered Reptiles from Palestine, 1917; Two Sussex Parishes, 1918; Memory Scientifically Considered, 1919; The Excellent Name of God, 1920; Ionization, 1921; Influenza, 1922; Asbestos and Asbestiform Minerals, 1922; The Curiosities of the Calendar, 1922; Sleep and the Psychology of Dreams, 1923; Herbal Theurapeutics, 1925; The Psychology of Oriental Peoples, 1926; Der Prophet gleich Moses, 1927; Arabian Poets, 1928; The Folklore of Herbal Theurapeutics, 1928; Medicine and Physiology among the Arabs (published in India, 1927-28); The Celtic Discovery of America, 300 years before Columbus, 1929; Pukkto, the Language of Afghanistan, 1929; Memory, 1929; A Great Arabian Astrologer, 1930; The Diffraction of Light, 1931. Address: 8 Taviton Street, WC1.

27. *TC*, No. 484, 23rd April 1902.

28. According to the biography written in *Islam – Our Choice [Impressions of Prominent Converts to Islam]* by Khwaja Kamal-ud-Din, Lord Headley al-Farooq (Rt. Hon. Sir Rowland George Allanson) was born in 1855 and was a leading British peer, statesman and author. Educated in Cambridge, he became a peer in 1877, served in the army as a captain and later on as Lieutenant-Colonel in the 4th Battalion of North Minister Fusiliers. Although an engineer by profession, he had wide literary tastes. At one time he was the editor of *The Salisbury Journal*. He was also the author of several books, the most well known being, *A Western Awakening to Islam*. Lord Headley embraced Islam on 16th November 1913 at the hand of Khwaja Kamal-ud-Din, and adopted the Muslim name of Shaikh Rahmatullah al-Farrooq. He played a prominent role in the work of the Woking Muslim Mission established at Woking, England, by the Khwaja. In the 1920s, he toured Muslim communities in many countries, including India (in 1928) in the company of the Khwaja, also performing the pilgrimage to Makkah.

29. Letter from John Deane Potter to Mohammad Akram Khan, General-Secretary of the Abdullah Quilliam Society, 5th January 1979.

30. Several articles attributed to Professor H.M. Léon appeared in early issues of *The Islamic Review*. A list of his first few articles and the issues in which they appeared is as follows: 'Acrimu-al-Hirrah!, Respect the cat. A poem', December 1914, pp.546-7; 'Islam, A Rational Faith', January 1915, pp.24-5; 'The Prophet and the Jew. A poem', February 1915, pp.73-4; 'The Second Pledge of Akaba', April 1915, pp. 182-7; 'Review of Leaves from Three Ancient Qurans', May 1915, pp.239-50; 'In praise of the Prophet. A poem', June 1915, p.286; 'Islam and Temperance', June 1915, p.310.

31. The full article can be found in *The Review of Religions*, July 1912, pp.286-9.

32. Op. cit., p.286.   33. *The Islamic Review*, January 1915, pp.4-7.

34. The story of the meeting is as follows: 'One learned brother pointed out that all consented to the belief in the One Supreme Ruler of the Universe, the Provider of everything, and consented in the revelation made to Adam for the guidance of mankind. Further, they all accepted the Divine mission of Noah. The Professor showed that when the needs of the time demanded a further revelation from Allah, He sent a guide to teach mankind His will. Then Abraham came; and Muslim, Jew and Christian still were in complete accord. Then the great Law was revealed through the Prophet Moses, and each still agreed. Thus far Muslim, Jew, and Christian were in complete harmony; but then came the point of divergence. Yet another revelation was made by Allah through the person of the Prophet Jesus; here the Jew could not travel with the others, but still the Muslim and Christian were in accord; each accepted the Injil, the Gospel of Jesus. Then the Muslim said to Prof. Leon: 'You think your creed superior to that of the Jew because you have a later revelation, but Islam is superior to your creed, for we have an imperishable revelation in the Holy Quran given through our Blessed Prophet Muhammad (peace be ever to his soul!)'

The Professor went on to point out that this is Islam; it is the same creed, the same simple guidance given by Allah to man since the commence-ment of time. He states that Islam confirms the earlier revelations, that Muhammad brought everything to perfection and that he was the "Seal of the Prophets", as the Holy Quran is the final Word of Allah. He recounted the story of when a man came to our Holy Prophet and said that he was an unlettered, an uneducated man, and he desired to know one thing about Islam which he could follow, promising to try his utmost to do so. Our Holy Prophet replied, "Do no evil". The man departed, and in a year's time returned and said to Muhammad, "It was hard, very hard, but I managed to act up to your words, I have done no evil, tell me more". Then Muham-mad replied, "Speak no evil", and again the man departed. He returned after another year had elapsed and said, "It was a harder task, but I have succeeded; I have spoken no evil, tell me more". Then Muhammad said to him, "Think no evil". and the man again left the place. He came to the Prophet at the end of another year and said, "The task was the hardest of all, but I have accomplished it; I have thought no evil, tell me more". The Holy Prophet replied with a smile, "There is no more, thou art a Muslim". The Professor asked those present if this was not a creed to be proud of, a creed that taught us to "Do no evil, speak no evil, think no evil". and was it not a creed to teach in the West?' (*Islamic Review*, January 1915, pp.4-7.)

35. He urged those present who had not accepted Islam, but who by their presence showed their sympathy with the movement, to study Islam for themselves, and to remember that Islam was the fulfilment and final completion of those other revealed religions, Judaism and Christianity, which preceded the final revelation made to man from Allah by our Holy Prophet Muhammad (*Islamic Review*, January 1915, pp.4-7).

36. *The Islamic Review*, April 1920, p.139.

37. The clip can still be found online at the British Pathé archive at *http://www.britishpathe.com/record.php?id=27701*.

38. Billal Quilliam had formed the Manx Fisheries Association after World War I with the intention of bringing fish directly from the trawler to the consumer. The business venture was substantial and involved investments from shareholders of over £2,000,000. The company was reported in many of the British national daily newspapers and over six thousand subscribers had invested, including over two thousand women. In the spring of 1922, Billal vanished. A compulsory winding up order was made against the company and it was estimated that creditors were owed over £220,000. After an eight-day trial at the Old Bailey, Billal was sentenced to two years imprisonment (*The Isle of Man Courier*, 18th August 1967).

39. *The Isle of Man Examiner*, 28th June 1919.

40. Ironically, his daughter was to marry Billal Quilliam.

41. Christian, S.L. (2008) 'The Importance of History in Public Health: An Historical Account of Tainted Women in the Manx Mental Health Services 1895-1922', BSc Public Health Dissertation, Colleish Ellan Vannin, University of Chester.

42. *Isle of Man Examiner*, 25th January 1974 and 14th April 1978.

43. For a more less sensational account of Woodland Towers, see the entry in *Historical Homes of the Isle of Man*, where it is described as being best known as the home of 'one of the most extraordinary Manxmen of modern times' (pp.119-20).

44. *TC*, No. 8, 12th March 1893.   45. *IW*, Vol.4, No. 39, July 1896, p.79.

46. Umar, A.-A. (2006) *A Muslim in Victorian America: The Life of Alexander Russell Webb*. Oxford: Oxford University Press, pp.71-5.

47. *TC*, No. 108, 2nd January 1895.   48. *TC*, No. 284, 22nd June 1897.

49. *TC*, No. 231, 16th June 1896.   50. *IW*, Vol. 4, No. 39, July 1896, p.112.

51. *TC*, No. 10, 25th March 1893.   52. *TC*, No. 7, 26th February 1893.

53. *TC*, No. 10, 25th March 1893.

54. Transcript of a speech by Patricia Gordon delivered on 10th October 1997 at Brougham Terrace to the Abdullah Quilliam Society, Liverpool.

CHAPTER 9

1. Visram, R. (2002) *Asians in Britain: 400 Years of History*. London: Pluto Press.
2. Acknowledgement should also be given to two MA dissertations completed in 1979 and 1981. They are Ally, M.M. (1981) 'History of Muslims in Britain, 1850-1980', unpublished MA dissertation, University of Birmingham; and Khan-Cheema, M.A. (1979) 'Islam and the Muslims in Liverpool', unpublished MA dissertation, University of Liverpool.
3. Clayer, N. and Germain, E. (2008) *Islam in Interwar Europe*. Columbia: Columbia University Press.
4. Ansari, 2004, p.38.   5. *IW*, Vol.4. No. 39, July 1896, p.74.
6. *TC*, No. 20, 3rd June 1896, (my italics).
7. Geaves, R. (2007) 'From 9/11 to 7/7: A Reassessment of Identity Strategies amongst British South Asian Muslims' in *From Generation to Generation: South Asians in the West*, John Hinnell (ed.). London: Palgrave Macmillan, pp.13-28.
8. Werbner, P. (2002) *Imagined Diasporas among Manchester Muslims*. Oxford: James Currey, p.49.
9. *TC*, No. 268, 2nd March 1898.
10. Milne, S. (2009) 'This counter-terror plan is in ruins. Try one that works' in *Guardian*, 26th March.
11. Ansari, 2004, p.29.   12. Werbner, 2002, p.177.
13. *IW*, Vol. 4, No. 36, April 1896, p.358.   14. Beckerlegge, 1997, p.261.
15. Op. cit., p.265.
16. Hobsbawn, E. and Ranger, T. (1992) *The Invention of Tradition*. Cambridge: Cambridge University Press, p.1.
17. Habermas, J. (1994) 'Struggles for Recognition in the Democratic Constitutional State' in *Multi-culturalism: Examining the Politics of Recognition*, Amy Gutmann (ed.). New Jersey: Princeton University Press, pp.107-48.
18. For more on the ideas expressed on Muslims and citizenship, see Geaves, R. (2004) 'Negotiating British Citizenship and Muslim Identity' in *Muslim Britain: Communities Under Pressure*, Tahir Abbas (ed.). London: Zed Books, pp.66-91.

Index